Selected Readings on Sports from English Newspapers and Magazines

体育英语报刊选读

主 编 田 慧
副主编 朱 珠

北京大学出版社
PEKING UNIVERSITY PRESS

图书在版编目(CIP)数据

体育英语报刊选读/田慧主编. —北京:北京大学出版社,2007.3
(大学美英报刊教材系列)
ISBN 978-7-301-11650-0

Ⅰ.体… Ⅱ.田… Ⅲ.体育—英语—阅读教学—高等学校—教材 Ⅳ.H319.4

中国版本图书馆CIP数据核字(2007)第022848号

书　　　　名:**体育英语报刊选读**
著作责任者:田　慧　主编
责　任　编　辑:徐万丽
标　准　书　号:ISBN 978-7-301-11650-0/H·1742
出　版　发　行:北京大学出版社
地　　　　址:北京市海淀区成府路205号　100871
网　　　　址:http://www.pup.cn　新浪微博:@北京大学出版社
电　　　　话:邮购部 010-62752015　发行部 010-62750672　编辑部 010-62759634
电　子　邮　箱:编辑部 pupwaiwen@pup.cn　总编室 zpup@pup.cn
印　　刷　者:北京虎彩文化传播有限公司
经　　销　者:新华书店
　　　　　　　787毫米×1092毫米　16开本　22.5印张　548千字
　　　　　　　2007年3月第1版　2024年1月第7次印刷
定　　　　价:49.00元

未经许可,不得以任何方式复制或抄袭本书之部分或全部内容。
版权所有,侵权必究　举报电话:010-62752024
　　　　　　　　　　　　电子邮箱:fd@pup.cn
图书如有印装质量问题,请与出版部联系,电话:010-62756370

《体育英语报刊选读》编委会

主　编：田　慧
副主编：朱　珠

编写小组成员(以姓氏笔画为序)：
　　田　慧　朱　珠　孙曙光
　　李　晶　韩　冰　韩亚辉

前　言

　　《体育英语报刊选读》是面向体育、师范院校的体育英语专业、传媒专业及体育专业高年级学生的英语阅读教材，亦适用于具有大学英语四级或相近水平的读者和体育专业人士阅读参考。

　　本书文章广泛选自英国、美国、加拿大及澳大利亚的报刊以及相应报刊名下的网站。文章编选具有以下特点：

　　一、精心选材。编者查阅了大量英文报刊，精选了当代西方一些著名报刊如 *New York Times, Times, Sports Illustrated* 等的文章。选文内容丰富，文字优美，适宜反复阅读。

　　二、编排新颖。本书所选文章分为五个部分，每一部分的十五篇文章均按由易到难的顺序排列。为了方便读者学习、理解原文，编者特为每篇文章撰写了中文导读，对文章内容或背景做了简明扼要的介绍。每篇文章均附有与选文有关的背景知识和思考题，便于读者进一步理解和掌握文章的内容，提高英语理解和表达能力。另外，文章最后列出了与选文有关的体育词汇及短语，供读者参考。

　　三、注释精当。编者对选编的文章提供了准确、详尽的词汇注释，并对文章中出现的语言、人物和文化背景进行了适当解释，对部分复杂句子还给出了译文，既省却了读者翻检词典之劳，又丰富了读者的文化知识。

　　本书共分五部分：

　　第一部分：时尚体育。介绍休闲体育、极限运动等近年来风靡一时的体育项目。

　　第二部分：聚焦体育。涉及常见体育项目和重大体育赛事的渊源和发展。

　　第三部分：赛场风云。展现重大体育赛事中的某一场精彩体育比赛。

　　第四部分：体坛明星。走近体坛精英的训练、生活、家人等诸方面。

　　第五部分：体坛多棱镜。讲述体育运动中的趣闻逸事及丑闻。

　　在本书的编撰过程中，我们参考了国外多种报刊，并注明了出处，在此谨向原作者表示衷心感谢。

　　随着北京2008年奥运会的临近，越来越多的国人渴望进一步了解奥运知识，并且对体育英语有着越来越浓厚的兴趣。本书的出版在某些方面也可满足这部分读者的需要。

　　由于时间仓促以及编者的水平和经验有限，书中疏漏及不妥之处在所难免，敬请广大读者批评指正。

编者
2006年9月

Contents

Part I　Fad Sports 时尚体育 ·· **1**

Lesson 1	Jump to It: Turn Your Way to a Better Body with This Simple but Challenging Workout— Special Section: Better Homes & Bodies—Jump Rope ··················	2
Lesson 2	Power Pilates: Tone Muscles and Reduce Body Fat with These Five Quick Moves ···	7
Lesson 3	On a Roll—the Increasing Use and Diversification of Inline Skating ················	11
Lesson 4	Bodysurfing ···	16
Lesson 5	Core Curriculum: 5 Great Yoga Moves to Strengthen Your Abs and Back ············	20
Lesson 6	Make Running Easier ··	24
Lesson 7	The Steep and Rocky Road: Steps to Successful Rock Climbing ·····················	29
Lesson 8	Paintballing Makes a Splash ···	34
Lesson 9	Ice fishing: Winter Safety ··	38
Lesson 10	Windsurfing ··	41
Lesson 11	Welcome to the Ice Age—Winter Sports (I) ··	46
Lesson 12	Welcome to the Ice Age—Winter Sports (II) ···	51
Lesson 13	Is Bowling a Sport? ··	56
Lesson 14	Even Flow: No, It's Not a Chase Scene from a'70s Cop Show. It's the French Extreme Sport Le Parkour ···	61
Lesson 15	The Rodeo Today ··	65

Part II　Sporting Kaleidoscope 聚焦体育 ·· **69**

Lesson 1	Olympic Athletes Largely Barred from Posting Online Diaries ·····················	70
Lesson 2	Cities Make Their Final Pitches as Olympic Committee Nears Vote ···················	73
Lesson 3	Beijing 2008 Olympic Journal: China's Olympic Legacy ·································	79
Lesson 4	Fresh Perspectives—A Look at Torino 2006's as Olympic Committee Nears Vote ···	83
Lesson 5	'Pastime' Reveals Story of Two Sports ··	87
Lesson 6	Seeking Acceptance, Rugby Gives It a Try ···	92
Lesson 7	IAAF Struggle to Get Athletics Back on Track ··	96
Lesson 8	U.S. Snowboarders Key to Winning: Have Fun ···	100
Lesson 9	A Life in Sport: Synchro-swimming—An Interview of Gayle Adamson ·············	104
Lesson 10	See the Ball, Hit the Ball: A Guide to Baseball ···	108
Lesson 11	Ice Hockey ···	113
Lesson 12	Pole Vaulting: Doing the 'Seemingly Impossible' ··	118

Lesson 13	Making the Connections—Ballet Classes Enhance Skating Technique in Many Ways	122
Lesson 14	LTA: Long-Term Aims or Leading Tennis Astray?	126
Lesson 15	Team Spirit, Yes, but Not Too Much	130

Part III Sporting Memories 赛场风云 — 135

Lesson 1	The Men's 200m Freestyle	136
Lesson 2	El Guerrouj Wins Double Gold	139
Lesson 3	Oxford Conquer the Waves to Win Boat Race	142
Lesson 4	United Haunted by Ghost of '79	146
Lesson 5	Italy Wins 2006 World Cup Championship	150
Lesson 6	Federer Beats Roddick to Win Wimbledon Yet Again	155
Lesson 7	Yan and Zheng Win China's First Wimbledon Title	161
Lesson 8	Yankees' Victory Is Long Time Coming	164
Lesson 9	Somerset Overseas Aides Increase Australia's Anxiety	169
Lesson 10	Uphill Racer	173
Lesson 11	Williams Impresses to Put Bath out of Reach	179
Lesson 12	Busch Leaves Pack, and the Debris, in the Dust	183
Lesson 13	Hurricane Blows Away Rivals	187
Lesson 14	Andrei Arlovski Defends Heavyweight Title at the UFC 53	191
Lesson 15	Heat of the Moment	195

Part IV Glimpses of the Superstars 体坛明星 — 201

Lesson 1	Yao Has Grown into One of NBA's Biggest Stars	202
Lesson 2	Karrie Needs Jack Target to Bowl at	207
Lesson 3	Silver Lining as British Pair's Fightback Falls Short	211
Lesson 4	Attack Is the Best Form of Defence for a Fighter in Search of Gold	216
Lesson 5	For "Table Tennis Mozart," Few High Notes	220
Lesson 6	Taste of Future as Rice Comes to Boil	225
Lesson 7	Jumping a Self-made Obstacle Course	230
Lesson 8	After Falling, She Rises and Shines	235
Lesson 9	Andre the Mastermind	240
Lesson 10	Schumacher's Race Not Over Yet as New Talent Arrives on Grid	245
Lesson 11	Armstrong Blames "Setup" for Charges	249
Lesson 12	German Boxing Legend Max Schmeling	255
Lesson 13	Accidental Hero	260
Lesson 14	Still a Perfect 10	265
Lesson 15	Flawed Best Had It All	271

Contents

Part V	**Sporting Mosaic 体坛多棱镜** ··	**277**
Lesson 1	Beijing Gets the Games ··	278
Lesson 2	U.N. Urges Members to Uphold Olympic Truce ························	283
Lesson 3	The Kelli White Follow Up ··	287
Lesson 4	Tears of Joy as Holmes Leads the Celebrations ·························	291
Lesson 5	Rooney Says Sorry to Beckham ··	295
Lesson 6	Owen Restates His Case for Doing It the Eriksson Way ·············	299
Lesson 7	Junior Hockey Players Chase Dream in America's Heartland ······	303
Lesson 8	Troubling History Bulls' Concern for Curry Based on Multiple Incidents ············	308
Lesson 9	Racing for a Cause ··	313
Lesson 10	Building an Olympic Vision ··	319
Lesson 11	Wembley Stadium, can we fix it? Er, well, sorry, no we can't, actually ... ··········	324
Lesson 12	Mansell Boys Happy to Drive Hard Bargain ·····························	329
Lesson 13	Death by Tarmac: the Sorry Fate of Hackney Marshes in Pursuit of Our Olympic Dream ···	334
Lesson 14	Illusionists Who Shade the Rest with Nothing to Declare Except Their Genius ··	340
Lesson 15	Seconds Needn't Be Sloppy ···	345

Part I

Fad Sports

时尚体育

Lesson 1

你运动的目的是什么?如果是减肥的话,那最好的方法就是通过合适的运动把多余的脂肪燃烧掉。所有的有氧运动都能帮你完成这个梦想,不过先要确定哪种运动适合你的体质。如果想要有点线条、结实一点,那么就可能要迈向无氧运动了。

有一项运动不用花你很多的金钱,却能在短时间内收到减肥与健身的双重功效,它就是——跳绳。

Jump to It: Turn Your Way to a Better Body with This Simple but Challenging Workout[1]— Special Section: Better Homes & Bodies—Jump Rope

By Bobby Aldridge
April-May 2002
Muscle & Fitness Hers[2]

Can you remember the last time you jumped rope? Whether you did it for exercise or play—probably both—most likely, the intent was fun. The good news is that jumping rope is a great way for just about anyone to get a super workout, no matter what her shape, size or fitness level[3]. Jumping rope is also an excellent way to burn lots of

1. workout /ˈwɜːkaʊt/ *n.* 锻炼,训练 to work out 锻炼,运动

2. *Muscle & Fitness Hers*《健美丽人》,是由国际健美联合会授权主办的美国健美主流刊物,以女子健美、健身、健康保健为主线,并介绍肌肉锻炼的各种方法。

3. fitness level 健康水平

calories[4]: approximately 200 per 15-minute workout[5]. Other benefits include:

* Improved cardiovascular[6] fitness;
* Great full-body workout;
* Enhanced balance and coordination[7];
* Strengthened muscles and bones;
* Increased speed and power;
* Jump ropes are easy to use, lightweight, convenient and inexpensive.

Getting started

Of course, the first thing you need to do is get a rope that's both the right size and easiest for you to use. When shopping for a rope, you'll have a few options, including length and material. As far as material goes[8], plastic, fiber and leather are available, in addition to weighted ropes. For general fitness purposes, choose a plastic segmented[9] rope, which is probably similar to the ones you used in elementary school. It's durable[10] and inexpensive, costing around $10.

To choose the right rope size for your height, follow these recommendations offered by jumpropestore.com:

Height	Rope Length
Under 5'	7-foot jump rope
5'–5'6"	8-foot jump rope
5'6"–6'	9-foot jump rope
Over 6'	10-foot jump rope

Moving right along

Now that you've chosen the right jump rope, it's time to consider a few other points of interest when preparing for the challenge of such a demanding[11] workout.

1) Choose a good pair of shoes. Aerobics shoes[12] and cross-trainers[13] are best. A supportive sports bra[14] is also a must.

2) Avoid concrete[15] surfaces. Instead, jump on wooden, rubber or carpeted (not shag[16]) floors.

3) Jump in an area clear of obstacles that could get in the way of the rope as you turn it. If you're indoors, make sure you have plenty of room above as well.

4) Keep your elbows close to your body and hands down by your sides.

4. calory /ˈkæləri/ 卡路里(热量单位)
5. 每锻炼15分钟,可消耗大约200卡路里热量
6. cardiovascular /ˌkɑːdɪəʊˈvæskjʊlə/ a. 心血管的
7. coordination /kəʊˌɔːdɪˈneɪʃən/ n. 协调
8. As far as material goes 就材料而言……
9. segmented /segˈmentɪd/ a. 节状的
10. durable /ˈdjʊərəbl/ a. 耐用的

11. demanding /dɪˈmɑːndɪŋ/ a. 要求高的,吃力的
12. aerobics shoes 健美操鞋
aerobics /eəˈrəʊbɪks/ n. 有氧运动 [指在有氧代谢状态下做长时间(大于15分钟)运动,使得心、肺得到充分的有效刺激,从而提高心肺功能,如慢跑、游泳、骑自行车等。]
anaerobics /ˌæneɪəˈrəʊbɪks/ n. 无氧运动(指肌肉在缺氧状态下高速剧烈运动,如短跑、举重、投掷、跳高等。)
13. cross-trainer /ˈkrɒsˌtreməˈ/ n. 慢步鞋
14. sport bra 运动胸衣
15. concrete /ˈkɒnkriːt/ n. 水泥
16. shag /ʃæg/ n. 厚粗绒地毯

5) Keep your jumps low to the ground and turn the rope by flipping your wrists, limiting your upper-arm involvement.

6) Warm up[17] for 5-10 minutes by walking or doing light "practice hopping" without the rope. Stretch your calves[18] and thighs before and after jumping. (Always warm up before stretching.)

The basic jump

Although you'll be jumping the same way whether you're a beginner, intermediate or advanced trainee, the length of time you spend doing it will vary. Instructions for the basic jump are as follows:

* Stand with your feet together and knees slightly bent.
* Allow your arms to relax by your sides while holding the grips[19] lightly in each hand.
* Keep your hops small and close to the ground.
* Flick[20] your wrists in a circular motion while keeping your elbows close to your sides.
* Jump once for each rope rotation[21].

Keep it in your range[22]

How can you tell if you're "in the zone" during aerobic exercise?[23] You can monitor your heart rate or you can go by "feel." If you don't want to mess around[24] with numbers, you can fairly accurately judge your level of intensity based on how hard you feel you're working. If you feel like you're at a 7 on a scale of 1–10[25]—with 10 being most intense—you're probably working out at about 70% of your maximum heart rate (generally 220 minus your age). If you'd rather go by the numbers, then follow the directions below to estimate your target heart-rate[26] (THR) zone.

First, determine your resting heart-rate[27]. The most accurate measure of this can be taken upon rising in the morning. Simply count your heartbeats[28] while lying quietly for 60 seconds. Jot[29] that number down as your resting heart rate. This formula is called the Karvonen method[30] of heart-rate calculation, also known as the heart-rate reserve method[31]. This method of calculating your target heart rate considers individual differences in fitness levels.

Next, plug[32] the appropriate numbers into the following target heart-rate formula:

[220 − _____ (age) − _____ (resting hr)] × _____ (desired %) + _____ (resting hr) = THR[33]

17. to warm up 热身,做热身活动
    warm-up n. 热身运动
18. calf /kɑːf/ n. 小腿,腓

19. grip /grɪp/ n. 把手

20. flick /flɪk/ v. 轻快地移动
21. rotation /rəʊˈteɪʃən/ n. 旋转
22. in one's range 在某人能力范围之内
23. 在进行有氧锻炼时,如何能判断自己锻炼得当呢?
24. to mess around 浪费时间
25. ...you're at a 7 on a scale of 1-10 ……在一至十这十个等级中,你位于七
26. target heart-rate 靶心率(是指在进行身体锻炼时要达到并保持的心率范围)
27. resting heart-rate 静息心率
28. heartbeat /ˈhɑːtbiːt/ n. 心跳
29. jot /dʒɒt/ v. 记下
30. Karvonen method 心跳保留法（由 Karvonen 首先提出）
31. heart-rate reserve method 心跳保留法（用于运动者随时掌控自我的运动强度）
32. plug /plʌg/ v. 插入
33. (220−年龄−静息心率)×运动强度范围+静息心率=靶心率

Beginners should work at 60%–70% of their maximum[34] heart rate, while intermediate level exercisers can work at 70%–80% of their max. If you're advanced, you can safely work at 75%–85% of your maximum heart rate. For example, if you're 30 years old, your resting heart rate is 60 and you want to work out at 75% of your maximum heart rate, your numbers would look like this:

220 − 30 = 190
190 − 60 = 130
130 × 75% = 97.5
97.5 + 60 = 157.5

Thus, your target heart rate is around 158 beats per minute. You can use this same method to determine both the high and low ends of your target range.

Of course, jumping rope is inherently[35] a high-intensity activity compared to many of the more common aerobic activities you may do. Because of this, you may find that your heart rate is higher than usual. This is fine, as long as you treat the session like you would any other interval session.[36] Raise your heart rate for a limited amount of time and then bring it down during a recovery phase[37]. If you'd rather keep your heart rate steady and within your target range, start jumping without the rope first, and monitor[38] your heart rate from there. If your heart rate needs to be higher, then add the rope back in.[39] (Of course, you should check with your physician before beginning any strenuous[40] exercise program.)

34. maximum /ˈmæksɪməm/ a. 最大的,最高的(常缩写为 max)
35. inherently /ɪnˈherəntlɪ/ ad. 本质地,固有的
36. ...as long as you treat the session like you would any other interval session. 只要你像对待休息时间那样对待运动时间就可以了。
37. recovery phase 恢复期
38. monitor /ˈmɒnɪtə/ v. 监控
39. 如果你想增加心率,可以加上绳子再跳。
40. strenuous /ˈstrenjuəs/ a. 费力的

Comprehension Questions

1. What are the benefits of rope jumping?
2. What are the factors you should consider while choosing the right rope?
3. Are there any requirements on the practicing field for rope jumping? If yes, what are they?
4. What's THR?
5. According to the target heart-rate formula given in the passage, what is your THR?

Background Reading

Rubber-Band Jumping (跳橡皮筋)

Rubber-band jumping was popular in my primary school which was only for girls. This game can help you to practice your jumping skills, develop coordination, and also meet lots of friends.

Rubber-band jumping is a low cost game. You only need some rubber bands. We looped (使……成环) rubber bands together tightly until we had a larger one (You can select the length you like). When we got three persons together, we could start our game.

Here's how we played this special jump rope game:
- Two persons stood opposite each other and extended the rubber band.
- One player jumped and stood on one side of the rubber band, carrying the two sides together.
- Then she jumped again and made the two sides separate.
- Then she jumped again into the middle of the rubber band and after that she jumped outside it.
- If we finished these steps without any mistakes, we started the next level.

As the game continued, the level of jumping got higher and higher. There were four jumping levels: ankle high, knee high, waist high, and under the shoulder. More and more girls tried to jump and we competed as teams. The game was fun, and I think it taught us competition and cooperation.

Relevant Words

rocker	前后钟摆跳	single bounce	单重跳
split hop	芭蕾舞跳	straddle split	分腿跳
toe to toe	脚尖跳		

Lesson 2

> 曾经有人这么描述普拉提运动:融合了西方人的"刚"——注重身体肌肉和机能的训练,与东方人的"柔"——强调练习时的身心统一,每个姿势都要和呼吸协调,达到身心灵整体和谐。无论你年龄大小,无论你是否参加过体育锻炼,无论你的性别,只要你愿意,任何时候,你都可以进行普拉提训练。普拉提使你的身体和意念达到和谐统一,让你的身体得到锻炼而不受到伤害。无需大量的练习,你就可以拥有平滑、柔软、匀称的身体,苗条的双腿和健美的腹部。普拉提,帮助你使身体达到最佳状态!

Power Pilates[1]: Tone Muscles and Reduce Body Fat with These Five Quick Moves

By Hope Wright
November 2005
Essence[2]

Through controlled, muscle-firming[3] movements and deep, calming breaths, Pilates burns fat even after you've put away the mat. Pilates has a slow pace, so it allows you to take in more oxygen than you would during high-energy cardio exercise.[4] "Your muscle cells need oxygen to burn fat," explains Jeanette Jenkins, a Pilates instructor and the president of The Hollywood Trainer in Los Angeles. "After the workout, your body uses the remaining fat as fuel to recharge the muscles you've worked[5]." Here Jenkins demonstrates the Pilates routine she created exclusively[6] for Essence. Do it three times a week for a trim physique[7].

The Hundred[8]—flattening the belly

Lie down. Keeping upper back stationary[9], raise your head and shoulders. With legs together, bend and lift knees so calves are parallel to the floor.

Step 1: Quickly pump[10] arms downward five times. With each pump, draw in a quick breath.

Step 2: For another count of five, pump arms and push air out (imagine that you're blowing out a candle). Do nine more sets for a

---

1. power pilates 强力普拉提
2. *Essence*《本质》,一本美国时尚杂志,创刊于 1970 年,是美国 100 强杂志之一。如今该杂志发行量达 110 万,读者遍布全球各地。
3. muscle-firming 肌肉紧绷的
4. 普拉提的节奏较慢,因此与给心脏带来高负荷的练习相比,你能吸入更多的氧气。cardio /ˈkɑːdɪəʊ/ a. 心脏的
5. …recharge the muscles you've worked 给你锻炼过的肌肉充电
6. exclusively /ɪkˈskluːsɪvlɪ/ ad. 专门地
7. trim physique 苗条的体形
8. the hundred 一百次(普拉提的基本动作之一)
9. stationary /ˈsteɪʃənərɪ/ a. 固定的
10. pump /pʌmp/ v. 上下拍动

total of a hundred pumps.

Obliques[11]—good for sides of torso[12]

Lie on your back, with head and shoulders off the floor, knees bent and calves parallel to the floor. With elbows bent, rest hands on the back of your head.

Step 2a: As you inhale[13], twist torso to the right, bring left elbow and right knee together, and straighten left leg. Switch sides and repeat.

Step 2b: For next rep[14], exhale[15]. Alternate inhales and exhales for two sets of 24.

Double-leg Stretch—strengthening ABS[16]

Lie on your back, with arms at sides and head resting on floor.

Step 3a: Lift head and shoulders up, pull knees into chest, and reach forward so fingertips touch ankles.

Step 3b: Exhale, touch shoulders with fingertips; straighten arms as you straighten and extend legs. As you inhale, sweep arms behind you in a circular motion and return them to starting position.[17] Do six reps.

Scissors[18]—working thigh muscles and strengthening ABS

Lie on your back, with shoulders and head off the floor. Lift right leg from the floor; grasp left leg with both hands.

Step 4a: As you exhale, pull left leg toward chest for two pulses.

Step 4b: Inhale and switch sides, grasping right leg and straightening left leg. To complete this move, exhale while reaching for the right leg for two pulses. Do two sets of eight.[19]

Leg Lift—sculpting[20] shoulders, arms, thighs and stomach

With palms and heels planted[21] on floor, legs together and toes pointed, raise hips and butt[22].

Step 5a: Inhale and lift right leg 12 inches off the floor. Exhale, and as you flex[23] right foot, return right leg to starting position.

Step 5b: To complete rep, repeat move with left leg. Do two sets of eight reps.

---

11. oblique /əˈbliːk/ n. 倾斜
12. torso /ˈtɔːsəʊ/ n. 躯干

13. inhale /ɪnˈheɪl/ v. 吸气

14. rep (repetition) 重复
15. exhale /eksˈheɪl/ v. 呼气

16. ABS (abdominals) 腹肌

17. 吸气时,手臂在体后做圆周运动后恢复至起始位置。

18. scissors /ˈsɪzəz/ n. 剪刀式,普拉提动作

19. 做两组,每组八次。

20. sculpt /skʌlpt/ v. 塑造,塑形
21. plant /plɑːnt/ v. 固定
22. hips and butt 髋和臀

23. flex /fleks/ v. 弯曲,折曲

Comprehension Questions

1. What's the principle of Pilates' burning of fat?
2. What can people benefit from practicing Pilates?
3. If you have the love handle (腰间赘肉), which move(s) can be effective to remove it?
4. Why is the fourth move named "scissors"?
5. Among the five moves, which one do you think is the most difficult one?

Background Reading

An Exercise in Balance: The Pilates Phenomenon

Well, maybe not the whole world, but certainly much of this country, parts of Canada, Europe, and Pan-Asia are experiencing the explosion in demand for Pilates, a method of exercise and physical movement designed to stretch, strengthen, and balance the body. With systematic (系统的) practice of specific exercises coupled with (加上) focused breathing patterns, Pilates has proven itself invaluable not only as a fitness endeavor itself, but also as an important adjunct (助手) to professional sports training and physical rehabilitation (复原) of all kinds. Widely embraced among dancers (舞者) for years, the exercises—"elephant", "swan", the language—"pull navel (脐) to spine (脊骨), and breeaaaathe", and the look—bright-eyed (热情的), refreshed, buoyant-without-necessarily-sweating, is popping up (突然出现) in fitness classes, physical therapy offices, corporate retreats (静思, 静修), luxury spas and wellness centers across the country. Another fad (时尚)? A cult (狂热) for the over-privileged? Think again. With the aging of our population and the increasing trend toward mindful, moderate health practices, Pilates is more likely to find itself with a wait list at the YMCA (基督教青年会), and in your local public schools —shaping the fitness ideals of our next generation.

Practiced faithfully, Pilates yields numerous benefits. Increased lung capacity and circulation through deep, healthy breathing is a primary focus. Strength and flexibility, particularly of the abdomen and back muscles, and coordination—both muscular and mental—are key components in an effective Pilates program. Posture, balance, and core strength are all heartily (彻底地) increased. Bone density (骨密度) and joint health improve, and many experience positive body awareness for the first time. Pilates teaches balance and control of the body, and that capacity spills over (溢出) into other areas of one's life.

Relevant Words

普拉提的 15 个基本动作

double leg stretch　双腿屈伸	rolling back　后滚动
scissors　剪刀式	shoulder bridge　桥式(肩)
spine twist　上体拧转	swimming　泳式
the hundred　一百次	the leg pull (prone)　俯式支撑
the one leg circle　单腿划圈	the one leg stretch　单腿屈伸
the push up　俯卧撑	the roll up　上滚动
the side bend　侧撑屈伸	the side kick　侧卧侧踢
the swan dive　天鹅饮水	

Lesson 3

> 我们常会在街头巷尾看到这样的景象,护盔、护肘、护膝一应俱全的少男少女们踏着轮滑鞋在空地上悠然地滑来滑去,玩得好的更能做跳跃、空中转身等动作,这就是我们最熟悉的极限运动——轮滑。
>
> 轮滑就是大家俗称的"旱冰"。它是一项融健身、竞技、娱乐、趣味、技巧、休闲于一体的全身运动。一般来说,轮滑运动可以分为速度轮滑、花样轮滑、轮滑球、轮滑舞蹈、"U"形槽轮滑、障碍轮滑等。
>
> 轮滑不仅能增强臂、腿、腰、腹肌肉的力量和各关节的灵活性,对提高平衡能力也有特殊效果。少年们参与其中,更会从摔倒爬起中得到启发和磨练。

On a Roll—the Increasing Use and Diversification of Inline Skating[1]

By Christina Dendy
September, 1999
Park & Recreation[2]

Inline skating is no longer a new phenomenon. Most people today can say that they have at least one friend who packs a pair of skates, or have seen a skater whizzing by[3] on the street or at the park, if they themselves have not already. Many have read reports or watched news

1. inline skating 轮滑运动

2. *Park & Recreation*《公园与休闲》,美国国家休闲与公园协会会刊之一。该刊的发行,旨在提高公民对公园休闲娱乐价值的认识,并为公园从业者提供公园管理的信息。

3. to whizz by 掠过

clips[4] on aggressive[5] or stunt skaters, the evolving inline hockey[6] league, or speed skating. Whatever the source of exposure, inline skating has penetrated[7] the recreation, fitness, and athletic industry with a momentum[8] largely unsurpassed[9] in the last decade. And it's still growing.

From the modest beginnings of Rollerblade Inc., in 1984, the inline skating industry has grown to encompass more than 30 million participants (as of 1997) and several hundred companies. According to the International Inline Skating Association[10], inline skating participation has increased 850 percent since 1989 and was the fastest growing sport in the United States in 1996.

Although this rate declined slightly in 1997, the sport itself continues to spread and diversify. Manufacturers offer an increasing range of specialized skates including inline hockey, speed, aggressive, and skates designed specifically for women and fitness skaters. Likewise, attention has turned toward the development of an off-road[11] skate for the more daring enthusiast.

Inline skating's break onto the fitness and recreation scene can be seen most effectively in its demographics[12]. Participation between men and women is split almost down the middle, with male skaters accounting for 54 percent of the skating population. And while inline skating has long been regarded predominantly[13] as a youth sport, IISA cited[14] 25-to 34-year-olds as the fastest-growing segment[15] of skaters in 1995, and predicted a dramatic increase in participants over the age of 45 by the turn of the century.

What could possibly appeal to such a broad spectrum[16] of people? How could one activity, within the course of a decade, reach so many individuals?

The answer is simple: Inline skating is not merely one activity; it encompasses a wide range of recreational, fitness, and competitive opportunities. Originating as an off-season[17] training method for ice-hockey players, inline skating now comprises inline hockey and basketball leagues, speed skating and racing, aggressive or stunt skating, inline dancing, inline soccer, and individual or social recreation and fitness skating.

"People use the words fitness and freedom a lot when it comes to skating,[18]" says IISA Executive Director Kalinda Mathis. "It's fun. It doesn't feel like a workout. It doesn't feel like a job. It's good for the body and mind."

4. clip /klɪp/ n. (录像或视频) 片断
5. aggressive /əˈgresɪv/ a. 大胆的
6. inline hockey 单排轮滑球
7. penetrate /ˈpenətreɪt/ v. 渗透
8. momentum /məʊˈmentəm/ n. 势头
9. unsurpassed /ˌʌnsəˈpɑːst/ a. 未被超越的
10. International Inline Skating Association 国际轮滑协会

11. off-road /ˌɒfˈrəʊd/ a. 道路之外的；越野的
12. demographics /ˌdeməˈgræfɪks/ n. 人口统计（这里指参与人数统计）
13. predominantly /prɪˈdɒmɪnəntlɪ/ ad. 最主要地
14. cite /saɪt/ v. 说到；提及
15. segment /ˈsegmənt/ n. 部分
16. spectrum /ˈspektrəm/ n. 范围

17. off-season /ˌɒfˈsiːzən/ a. 淡季的

18. 谈到轮滑时，人们大多会用到健康和自由这样的词。

Inline skating allows the individual to choose and gravitate[19] among several activities depending upon personal interest or goals. Inline skating gets people outside, alone or with family and friends. It is accessible, requiring no special facilities, and relatively inexpensive, requiring no membership fees or dues. Compared to many other sports such as bicycling, roller skating[20], and most contact sports[21], inline skating has a low injury rate. Most injuries could be prevented with proper safety gear, particularly helmets and wrist guards.

The selling points of inline skating are many, but perhaps the most salient[22] benefit—and the one that goes hand in hand with[23] all the others—is that inline skating is healthy. Young or old, male or female, skating provides an excellent cardiovascular workout, targets key muscle groups throughout the body, and is low-impact[24].

Because skating requires a certain amount of strength in the knees for balance, anyone with prior injuries should consult a doctor before rolling out the door. But overall, skating is easier on the joints than jogging and many other aerobic exercises[25]. Yet, as Mathis states, it does not feel like a workout.

A study conducted by Dr. Carl Foster, an associate professor[26] of medicine at the University of Wisconsin and coordinator[27] of sports medicine and sports science for the U.S. Speed Skating team, examined and compared the effects of four different workouts upon 11 volunteers. Foster tested the oxygen uptake[28] and heart and blood rates of the participants while they jogged, cycled, skated steadily for 30 minutes, and skated incrementally[29].

The results show that skating at a steady pace for 30 minutes burned 285 calories and induced[30] a heart rate of 148 beats per minute, while interval skating[31] burned 450 calories. In interval skating, the skater alternates between one minute skating in a tuck[32] position and one minute skating upright. Running and cycling each induced a heart rate of 148 beats per minute, but cycling burned 360 calories, edging out[33] running's 350.

The study also reached several conclusions regarding the aerobic benefits of each activity. Foster's team determined that inline skating constituted a more effective aerobic workout than cycling (since cyclists tend to glide), while running worked the heart and lungs better than skating. However, skaters can increase the aerobic benefits of their outings by skating harder or on hilly terrain[34].

Anaerobic[35] tests, which measure body strength and muscle

---

19. gravitate /ˈgrævɪteɪt/ v. 移动
20. roller skating 滑旱冰
21. contact sport 身体接触项目(足球,摔跤等)
22. salient /ˈseɪlɪənt/ a. 突出的
23. go hand in hand with 与……结合在一起
24. low-impact /ˌləʊˈɪmpækt/ a. 低损伤的
25. aerobic exercise 有氧运动
26. associate professor 副教授
27. coordinator /kəʊˈɔːdɪneɪtə/ n. 协调者
28. uptake /ˈʌpteɪk/ n. 吸收
29. incrementally /ˌɪŋkrɪˈmentlɪ/ ad. 递增地
30. induce /ɪnˈdjuːs/ v. 引起
31. interval skating 间隔轮滑(指轮滑者滑一段时间,休息一段时间。)
32. tuck /tʌk/ n. 折叠式姿势
33. to edge out 稍稍胜过
34. terrain /ˈterəɪn/ n. 地势
35. anaerobic /ˌæˌneɪəˈrəʊbɪk/ a. 厌氧的

development, deemed inline skating more beneficial than running and cycling. Inline skating naturally builds hip and thigh muscles, which running and cycling do not. Skating especially targets the hamstring[36] muscles, neglected by cycling, and works muscles in the upper arms and shoulders.

"Skating builds the hip and thigh muscles, buttocks[37], and upper legs. It works the abductor[38] and adductor[39] muscles, or inner and outer thighs, which can be a particular trouble spot for women," Mathis says. "Skating at a lower stance[40] works the legs and hips even more, and the more you use your arms, the better aerobic workout you get. Either way, you get both strength and cardio[41]. These adjustments just increase one or the other."

In addition to physical fitness benefits, inline skating, and aerobic exercise in general, tends to induce more positive energy overall. According to Liz Miller's guide for inline skaters, *Get Rolling: The Beginner's Guide to In-Line Skating*, during aerobic exercise the body releases certain chemicals called endorphins[42]. Miller dubs[43] the endorphin high "one of the best all-natural stress-reduction therapies around."

Inline skating can be part of an enjoyable and efficient workout routine. While all inline skating activities promote physical benefit and recreational diversion[44], 25 to 30 minutes of incremental skating and skating on hilly paths burns calories and really works the body[45]. Moreover, the IISA recommends supplementing[46] such inline exercise with further muscle training—the abdomen, lower back[47], buttocks, thighs, calves, and upper body—for total body fitness.

"I started out as a competitive ice skater, so inline skating was a natural transition for me. But I've stuck with[48] it for the fitness," Mathis states. "I would recommend inline skating to anyone, especially to adults between 30 and 50 who are looking for some sort of exercise they can do outside or with family and friends. It feels good, it's easy, and there's no need to join a gym[49]. Also, it's low-impact—easier on the knees and ankles than something like jogging[50]—for older participants or people with a previous injury."

Mathis and IISA strongly encourage potential skaters to seek a lesson.[51] Not only does instruction guarantee a safer skating experience, it may also enhance a skater's performance. And the safer and stronger an individual skates, the more benefits—recreational and fitness—he or she enjoys.

36. hamstring /ˈhæmˌstrɪŋ/ *n.* 腘窝
37. buttock /ˈbʌtək/ *n.* 臀部
38. abductor /əbˈdʌktə/ *n.* 外展肌
39. adductor /əˈdʌktə/ *n.* 内收肌
40. stance /stɑːns/ *n.* 姿势
41. cardio /ˈkɑːdɪəʊ/ *n.* 心脏功能
42. endorphin /enˈdɔːfɪn/ *n.* 脑内啡（身体释放出的一种化学物质，主要存在于大脑中，可缓解痛感并影响情绪）
43. dub /dʌb/ *v.* 授与……以称号
44. diversion /daɪˈvɜːʃən/ *n.* 消遣
45. to work the body 锻炼身体
46. supplement /ˈsʌplɪmənt/ *v.* 补充
47. lower back 后腰
48. to stick with 坚持做
49. gym /dʒɪm/ *n.* (gymnasium)体育馆
50. jogging /ˈdʒɒɡɪŋ/ *n.* 慢跑运动
    jog /dʒɒɡ/ *v.* 慢跑
51. Mathis 和 IISA 十分鼓励想要加入这项运动的人学习相关的课程。

Comprehension Questions

1. How many different kinds of skates are mentioned in the passage? What are they?
2. How could inline skating reach so many individuals?
3. What is the most salient benefit of inline skating?
4. Is there any special benefit of inline skating for women? What is it?
5. Is inline skating popular in you city? If yes, what are the reasons, in you opinion?

Background Reading

Inline Skating Safety Tips

Since unintentional (无心的) injuries can occur to even the most experienced inline skaters, the National Safety Council (安全委员会) recommends these skating safety tips:

Always wear protective equipment: elbow and knee pads, light gloves, helmets, and wrist guards.

Before your first time out, take an inline skating course to learn the basics.

Choose durable (耐用的) skates that match your needs, whether you exercise infrequently or race. Your plans will determine the type of skate you should buy.

For proper ankle support, feel the plastic of the boot: if you can squeeze it, the material is not strong enough to give you reliable support.

When buying skates, take socks to the store with you to ensure a proper fit, or buy the socks there.

Begin skating with a five-minute, slow skate to warm up; you will be less likely to tear muscles.

Start skating gradually on level ground. Practice moving forward, and ease into skating.

While skating, keep knees slightly bent, which will lower your center of gravity (重心) and keep your body balanced on the balls of your feet.

Practice stopping by bringing the foot with the heel stop forward until the heel stop is next to the toe of the other foot. Gently bend your front knee while lifting your toes up. This motion will bring you to a stop. This is known as the "heel stop." There are other stopping methods, such as T-stop and power stop, as well as several ways to slow down, for example, snowplowing (犁式制动) and running on the grass.

Relevant Words

ASA = the Aggressive Skaters Association	直排轮滑者协会
back flip 后空翻	misty flip 540 度侧空翻
Pornstar 星点特技	soul grind 丁字平衡

Lesson 4

提起冲浪，人们很自然会想到冲浪者站在冲浪板上，凭借海浪前进的动力，以及浪板踩在浪上的浮力穿梭水上。可是你是否想过，你的身体，也可以被视为一块浪板？以身体作为浪板的人体冲浪，就是利用身体的自然曲线来御浪前进，在没有浪板随身的情况下享受冲浪之乐。也许你还没有体验过这种运动，那么就让我们先饱一下"眼福"吧。

Bodysurfing

By Kevin Foley
July 1998
Men's Fitness[1]

The beach sucks, nothing but rocks and sharp shells, and the break isn't much better—the waist-high waves pop up[2] for a second, then collapse[3] like the French army during World War II. There's nothing to ride, no place to lounge[4], and my buddies[5] have set up a campfire and a case of Pacifico up on the ridgeline[6]. I can hear them laughing.

The sky is darkening and we've just completed a 200-mile drive from Los Angeles to the Baja coast at Punto San Tomas, including a 20-mile bump[7] across a dirt road intent on separating my Honda[8] from its muffler[9]. I'm tired, tense, cold; it's a stupid time to jump in the water. But I can't stop staring into the sea. Maybe it's not so bad out there. How will I know if I don't try?

I put on my suit and grab my fins[10]. I wade[11] into the water, braced against[12] the cold. I crouch[13] and slip on my fins with numb fingers. A few strokes and I'm out where the waves are breaking. They're still falling almost too quickly to ride, but they look better here than they did on shore. A wave rushes in and the chase begins. Two huge kicks[14] and I'm on it, trying to cut across the face. Friction[15] disappears. I disappear. The wave is everything now, the entire world is nothing but momentum[16] and purposeful water.

I'm gliding on top, trying to cut a sharper angle so I can outrun[17] the wave's collapse[18] for a few more delicious[19] seconds, but it

1. *Men's Fitness*《男性健康》，美国男性健康健身杂志，以提供健康和生活资讯为主，包括营养、运动和新产品等，并针对不同需求者设计个人化的健身训练。
2. to pop up 突然出现
3. collapse /kə'læps/ v. 倒塌；瓦解
4. lounge /laʊndʒ/ v. 闲逛；漫步
5. buddy /'bʌdɪ/ n. [口语] 伙伴
6. a case of Pacifico up on the ridgeline 山上传来 Pacifico 般的歌声。Pacifico 意大利著名歌手
   ridgeline /'rɪdʒlam/ n. 山脊
7. bump /bʌmp/ n. 颠簸
8. Honda（日本）本田汽车
9. muffler /'mʌflə/ n. 消声器
10. fin /fɪn/ n. 橡皮脚掌
11. wade /weɪd/ v. 涉水
12. to brace against 抵御
13. crouch /kraʊtʃ/ v. 蜷缩
14. kick /kɪk/ n. 踩水（人体冲浪的一个技术动作）
15. friction /'frɪkʃən/ n. 摩擦力
16. momentum /məʊ'mentəm/ n. 冲力
17. outrun /aʊt'rʌn/ v. 超过
18. collapse /kə'læps/ n. 崩溃（这里指海浪退去）
19. delicious /dɪ'lɪʃəs/ a. 美妙的；极有趣的

shatters[20] in a straight line and sends me skittering[21] into the foam. Before the wave breaks, though, there's a freeze-frame[22] moment, a weird[23] instant of athletic clarity. It's a flash of blue and shore, the feeling of being encased[24] in a cocoon[25] of liquid speed, a compelling[26] sense of being in the right place at the right time. It almost doesn't register because I'm bouncing into the rough, riding the whitewater, trying to stop before my belly plows[27] into the rocks.

This isn't my favorite kind of bodysurfing. Small, sharp waves lack elegance; their quick rush and crash stunts[28] the style that attracts me to the sport. Yes, style. Bodysurfing is the art of finding the right wave, then the right combination of angle and force to ride it the way it's meant to be ridden. A degree of arc[29], a kick, a second earlier or later on your takeoff mean everything. There are no intermediaries[30]; it's just your skill, your skin and the ocean.

It's this immediacy[31] that explains why the freeze-frame instants keep coming on this lousy[32] day, in these lousy conditions. I chase them until I can barely swim. Then I stagger[33] shivering onto the beach, picking my way up the ridge. I wrap myself in a huge towel and stand over the fire. Someone hands me a beer. Someone else starts talking mess[34].

"What's with the whooping[35]?" he says. "Every wave you caught, you were bellowing[36] like a sick whale."

I don't believe him at first. Out there, bodysurfing, I didn't realize I was making a sound.

Starting

1. Bodysurfing is a soul sport[37]: The only equipment you absolutely need is a bathing suit. You'll have a better time, though, if you pick up a good pair of fins. I prefer longer swim-type fins over shorter bodyboarding[38] styles.

2. Before you go out and hit a break, spend a few minutes assessing the conditions. You're looking for safety—beware[39] rocks and rip tides—and also to see if the waves are breaking at an angle. If they are, you can work with it to lengthen your rides.

3. Figuring out when to start your take-off on a wave is all instinct. If the swell[40] isn't cresting[41], you can kick until your knee-joints pop without catching it. Start too late, just before the wave breaks, and you'll get pinned[42] under 10,000 gallons of saline[43] solution[44].

20. shatter /ˈʃætə/ v. 粉碎
21. skitter /ˈskɪtə/ v. 滑行；掠过
22. freeze-frame /ˈfriːzˌfreɪm/ a. 静止的
23. weird /wɪəd/ a. 不可思议的
24. encase /ɪnˈkeɪs/ v. 包围
25. cocoon /kəˈkuːn/ n. 茧
26. compelling /kəmˈpelɪŋ/ a. 强烈的
27. plow /plaʊ/ v. （用犁）挖，这里指撞
28. stunt /stʌnt/ v. 阻碍发展
29. arc /ɑːk/ n. 弧
30. intermediary /ˌɪntəˈmiːdɪərɪ/ n. 中间物；器材
31. immediacy /ɪˈmiːdɪəsɪ/ n. 直接（性）
32. lousy /ˈlaʊzɪ/ a. 糟糕的
33. stagger /ˈstæɡə/ v. 蹒跚

34. to talk mess 闲聊
35. whoop /wuːp/ v. 大叫，呐喊
36. bellow /ˈbeləʊ/ v. 咆哮

37. 人体冲浪是一项关乎精神的运动
38. bodyboarding /ˈbɒdɪˌbɔːdɪŋ/ n. 冲浪（身体趴在板子上）
39. beware /bɪˈweə/ v. 小心

40. swell /swel/ n. 巨浪
41. crest /krest/ v. 到达最高点
42. pin /pɪn/ v. 固定；困住
43. saline /ˈseɪlaɪn/ a. 盐的
44. solution /səˈluːʃən/ n. 溶液

Comprehension Questions

1. What are the author's friends doing when he is bodysurfing?
2. What's the definition of bodysurfing according to the author?
3. What doesn't the author realize but his friends do?
4. What equipments does bodysurfing need?
5. After reading this passage, will you try bodysurfing? Why or why not?

Background Reading

Bodysurfing: 5 Tips to Make It a Blast

Bodysurfing, as you probably know, is the sport of catching waves with your body and riding them as far as they'll take you.

It can be a blast (游戏), and it's much faster to learn than board riding, and of course the only equipment you really need is yourself.

So, here are five tips for having more fun when you're doing it:

(1) Don't be a wave snob (自命不凡者). Small swells that break close to shore can be powerful and give you great, albeit (虽然) shorter, rides, so don't turn your nose up at them. Plus small to average surf is what you'll see most of, so if you pass on them, you'll be taking yourself out of the action a lot.

(2) Positioning (定位) is crucial to effective body surfing. Literally, you have to go where the waves are breaking. Most people screw this up (没有做到) by staying in the shallows or just missing the bigger breaks. Study the sets as they break and make a mental calculation as to where you'd need to be as the next wave curls to its peak. Then, maneuver (移动) to that place in the water before the next set comes in. That's the spot to get your rides.

(3) Timing is also very important. If you have to swim more than a stroke or two to catch your waves, you're too early in the break formation, and as you look toward the shore you'll see they're breaking several feet in front of you. This is an avoidable frustration. Most of my rides don't require me to swim at all. I look like I'm falling forward and catching them at the last possible second.

(4) If you can, bodysurf with a buddy, or have a lookout (看守) posted on the beach, or do it in front of a lifeguard tower. Surf can pound you and you can swallow water fast and need help, so you want it to be available. Rest before you're fatigued (筋疲力尽). Go sit on the sand for ten or fifteen minutes, at least, and then head back out for a shorter period. If waves are so big that they scare you, heed (注意) that fear, and stay away from them.

(5) Watch people who are good at it, that are catching half or more of the waves that they're trying for. Where are they positioned? How is their timing? Which waves are they selecting? Learn from them; they're out there!

Today, I followed these tips and I had a great time, and I have the memories to prove it!

Part I Fad Sports

Relevant Words

世界四大冲浪胜地

California　加利福尼亚州　　　Hawaii　夏威夷
Golden Coast　昆士兰黄金海岸(位于澳大利亚)
Tahiti　大溪地(位于南太平洋)

Lesson 5

> 拥有柔软的身躯,美丽纤细的腰身,是每个女性的梦想。其实不一定非要到健身馆去大蹦小跳,传统而又古老神秘的瑜珈,能让你有意外的收获。
>
> 瑜珈其实并不复杂。一般的体育锻炼,往往注重的是外在的美丽,而内在的东西却很少顾及。瑜珈则不同了,它在雕塑你外在形象的同时,还给你一种源自内心的力量。经过一段由内而外、由外而内的锻炼后,你会惊奇地发现心态已经变了个样子,你会因为快乐而美丽,因为美丽而快乐。

Core Curriculum[1]: 5 Great Yoga[2] Moves to Strengthen Your Abs[3] and Back

By Ayana D. Byrd and Bevin Cummings
May 2005
Essence

1. core curriculum 基础课程
2. yoga /'jəʊgə/ *n.* 瑜珈
3. ab (abdominal) 腹肌

Yoga's not only good for achieving balance, fostering calm, and making you flexible enough to put your leg behind your head, but "it can also build core strength[4]," says Teresa Kennedy, hatha[5] yoga instructor and founder of Harlem's Ta Yoga House. "And targeting those abdominal and back muscles can ease lower-back pain." Do this series of asanas[6] (the Sanskrit[7] word for yoga postures), modeled by Kennedy, three times a week. In as many months you should have a tighter stomach and a more limber[8] back.

4. core strength 核心力量,人身体主干区的力量
5. hatha /'hɑːtə/ *n.* 瑜珈气功
6. asana /ɑːˈsənə/ *n.* 瑜珈的任何一种姿势
7. Sanskrit /'sænskrɪt/ *a.* 梵语的
8. limber /'lɪmbə/ *a.* 柔软的

The Cobra[9]—Relieving minor backache and toning[10] abs

Step 1: Lie on your stomach with legs and feet together. Plant palms on the floor beneath shoulders with fingers facing forward.

Step 2: Raise upper body by slowly lifting the head and chest, making sure to keep shoulders down. (Pelvis[11] and thighs shouldn't leave the yoga mat.)

Step 3: Hold pose for 20 to 30 seconds as you take even breaths through your nose.[12] Return to your starting position and repeat once.

9. cobra /'kəʊbrə/ *n.* 眼镜蛇式
10. tone /təʊn/ *v.* 强化
11. pelvis /'pelvɪs/ *n.* 骨盆
12. 保持姿势不变20到30秒,用鼻子进行平缓的呼吸。

Chair Pose[13]—Strengthening abs

Step 1: Stand with legs hip width apart[14], holding arms straight ahead with palms facing downward.

Step 2: Bend knees and squat[15] as if you're about to sit in a chair. Be sure to center weight in your heels, and don't bring hips lower than the knees.

Step 3: Reach forward, and focus eyes straight ahead while inhaling and exhaling through the nose. Hold for 20 seconds. Slowly return to standing position, then release arms.

Wind-Relieving Pose[16]—Stretching spine[17] and aiding digestion (which explains the embarrassing name)

Step 1: Lie on your back. As you inhale[18], pull right knee to your chest. Keep left leg straight and on the floor.

Step 2: Press shoulders and the back of neck into the floor while tightly holding knee. Breathe for ten seconds.

Step 3: Switch sides, holding left knee to chest for ten seconds. Complete set by hugging both knees to chest and holding for ten seconds. Repeat set.

Upward Boat Pose[19]—Strengthening abs, improving balance, and aiding digestion

Step 1: Sit on the floor. Bend knees and plant feet on the floor.

Step 2: Inhale, lean back and lift heels off the floor, straightening your legs as much as possible.[20] Extend arms with palms facing down. If this is too difficult at first, you can place your hands under your knees for support.

Step 3: As you hold the pose for 30 seconds, keep your back straight, and make sure your abs are doing the work.

Bow Pose[21]—Strengthening spine and increasing lung capacity[22]

Step 1: Lie facedown with forehead on the floor. Part[23] legs, bend knees, then take hold of ankles.

Step 2: Lift upper body and thighs by raising your head toward the ceiling and pressing ankles back against your hands.

Step 3: Balance on your stomach; the goal is to hold the pose without rocking. After 20 seconds, ease into starting position[24].

---

13. chair pose 凳子式
14. Stand with legs hip width apart 双腿与胯同宽站立
15. squat /skwɒt/ v. 蹲
16. Wind-Relieving Pose 释放肠气式（放屁式）wind /wɪnd/ n. 肠气；胃气；(委婉语)屁
17. spine /spaɪn/ n. 脊骨
18. inhale /ɪnˈheɪl/ v. 吸气
19. Upward Boat Pose 上船式
20. 吸气,身体向后倾斜,脚后跟离地同时尽可能地伸直双腿。
21. Bow Pose 弓式
22. lung capacity 肺活量
23. part /pɑːt/ v. 分开
24. ease into starting position 放松至起始体位

Mind Control: Simple Ways to Get More Out of Meditation[25]

When you're used to ripping and running, quiet reflection can be a tall order[26]. Use these mind-be-still tips, courtesy of Maya Breuer, a Kripalu yoga[27] instructor in Providence, Rhode Island, who hosts retreats[28] for women of color[29].

Find an open space. Clutter[30] creates distractions. Help prevent the mind from wandering by sitting in a serene[31] area.

Set a timer. A clear ending time makes meditation less daunting[32]. Start at five minutes and gradually work your way up to 20.

Sit comfortably. "You may think meditation has to be done cross-legged, but for many the position is difficult," says Breuer. Feel free to sit with your back against a wall and your legs in front of you. The key is to keep your spine erect.

Feel the rhythm. Focus on the rhythm of your breathing as you inhale through your nostrils[33] and exhale through your mouth. The steady beat promotes relaxation.

Use a mantra[34]. Silently repeating a sacred[35] word such as amen[36] or om[37] can help you tune out[38] racing thoughts. A short phrase such as "I am breathing in; I am breathing out" also works.

Watch your thoughts. Rather than trying to suppress what's on your mind, imagine that it's a silent movie you're passively watching. This allows you to acknowledge your thoughts without losing yourself in them.

---

25. meditation /ˌmedɪˈteɪʃən/ n. 沉思;冥想
26. tall order 离谱的要求;苛求
27. Kripalu yoga 瑜伽的一种,注重瑜伽姿势带给人在感情以及心理上的感受。
28. retreat /rɪˈtriːt/ n. 静思;静修
29. woman of color (有色人种的)女性
30. clutter /ˈklʌtə/ n. 混乱
31. serene /sɪˈriːn/ a. 平静的
32. daunting /ˈdɔːntɪŋ/ a. 令人畏缩的
33. nostril /ˈnɒstrɪl/ n. 鼻孔
34. mantra /ˈmæntrə/ n. 颂歌
35. sacred /ˈseɪkrɪd/ a. 神圣的
36. amen /ɑːˈmen/ int. 阿门(用在祈祷或陈述的结尾表示承认、赞成)
37. om /ɒm/ int. 唵(祷文,用于进行郑重断言和祝福的时候)
38. to tune out 关掉(这里指停止)

Comprehension Questions

1. According to the passage, what can we benefit from practicing yoga?
2. What are the benefits of the cobra?
3. What are the functions of bow pose?
4. What are the key points for meditation?
5. Among the five poses, which one do you think is the most difficult one? Why?

Background Reading

Types of Yoga

The science of yoga has developed a vast amount of techniques which all lead to the same point of unification (统一,一致) of the mind-body-spirit.

Karma Yoga (卡玛瑜珈): the way of right action, serving without the motivation of obtaining the results of labor.

Bhakti Yoga (虔信瑜珈): the way of devotion, devotion to a supreme being absorbing the emotions and self in pure love.

Jnana Yoga (智者瑜珈): the way of knowledge, studying god and learning to discriminate (区别) between illusion (幻想) and the reality that all is god.

Hatha Yoga (哈达瑜珈): the physical path, using the body through asana and pranayama (调气) to control the mind and senses.

Tantric Yoga (密宗瑜珈): the feminine path, worshiping the goddess energy and seeing the body as the temple of the divine.

Kundalini Yoga (灵量瑜珈): the path of energy, arousing the energy stored in the chakras (气轮) through breathing and movement.

Raja Yoga (胜王瑜珈): the path of meditation, controlling the mind from wandering and obtaining mastery over thought.

Relevant Words

balance posture	平衡姿势	prone posture	俯姿
seated posture	坐姿	standing posture	站姿
supine posture	卧姿	twisting posture	扭转姿势

Lesson 6

> 国际著名的德国医学专家赫尔曼教授指出:"慢跑是保持健康的最好手段,关键是运动中它能有效提高供氧,慢跑时的供氧能力比静坐时多 8 至 12 倍。"近几年的科学研究已证明,跑步能够增加血液流动,提高血液对氧气的输送能力;跑步可使肺功能增强,从而提高肺活量和吸入氧气的能力;跑步可以改善心脏功能,防止心脏病的发生,使心肌变得强壮有力,改善心肌血液供应;跑步可以增加骨密度,防止骨质疏松。
>
> 那么,怎样跑步才是最科学的?

Make Running Easier

By Roy M. Wallack
September 2003
Men's Fitness

Lots of us have a love-hate relationship[1] with running. We love the pure fitness, the endorphin high, the feeling of accomplishment, the peerless[2] love-handle-zapping[3] power. Yet we hate the aching knees, ankles and Achilles tendons[4], the elaborate[5] warm-up and warm-down times, the endless stretching. In fact, we often hate running simply because it seems too much like work—hard work.

Wouldn't we enjoy running more and do it more often (and thus keep up the calorie burn and fat loss) if there was some way to make it a little, uh, easier?

"Da![6]" says Nicholas Romanov, Ph.D., a Miami-based[7] Russian sports scientist who has devoted his adult life to that seemingly impossible dream. A trainer of world-class athletes such as Svetlana Zakharova, who won the Boston Marathon earlier this year, Romanov says he not only can make running easier, but he will make you faster and reduce your injuries, too—all in the span of[8] a couple of hours. All you need to do is something you probably never thought of before: Learn how to run.[9]

"You learn how to shoot a basketball and how to play golf," says Romanov. "But you don't learn how to run—you just do it, and suffer the consequences. People tell you how to train, to run four miles on

---

1. love-hate relationship 爱恨交织的关系
2. peerless /ˈpɪələs/ a. 出类拔萃的;无可匹敌的
3. love-handle-zapping 去除腰部赘肉的
4. Achilles tendon 跟腱
5. elaborate /ɪˈlæbərət/ a. 费事的
6. Da! 是!(俄语)
7. Miami-based /maɪˈæmɪbeɪst/ a. 以迈阿密为基地的;长驻迈阿密的
8. in the span of 在……范围内
9. 你所需要做的可能是你之前从未想过的事情——学习如何跑步。

Monday, then six on Wednesday and so on. But no one teaches running as a skill. Well, efficient, safe, fast running involves real skill. Unless you're a natural[10], you must learn it."

After discovering that great runners have certain technique similarities, Romanov institutionalized[11] an ideal running body position, or pose, he teaches as the "pose technique", which he says will make you more efficient, require less effort, lessen impact, and greatly reduce strains[12] to muscles and connective tissues[13]. It's been effective enough to be adopted by top coaches of the official sanctioning[14] body of American triathlons[15], not to mention high-profile[16] fitness enthusiast, radio-show host and King of All Media Howard Stern. Whether you love or hate running, Romanov's pose technique could help you get much more out of it.

Controlled Falling

Explained biomechanically[17], Romanov says the pose technique is "controlled falling".

"Think of a pendulum[18]," he says. "It uses gravity to swing forward—not mechanical or muscular power." Leaning over just to a point where he will nearly fall over, a good runner actually is letting gravity swing his lifted leg forward. That simplifies[19] the process of forward motion quite a bit. "Theoretically, legs should not play a major role in propulsion[20]," says Romanov. "They are just carriers, like wheels."

The hardest part of the pose technique may be learning to flick the heel up toward the butt the second the forefoot touches the ground rather than pushing off with the toes.[21] To help you master this movement, imagine you're running barefoot on broken glass, or that you're stepping on something very hot. Or visualize[22] yourself as a bouncing ball, a rock skipping across a lake, or a perpetual-motion[23] machine.

Breaking A Habit

The pose technique is simple, but the hard part is practice, practice, practice—undoing[24] years of running the wrong way. Among the most egregious[25] of the ingrained[26] running inefficiencies is landing on the heel.

"That is the worst possible thing you can do," says Romanov. "Not only does it transmit a tremendous amount of ground shock to knee and hip, but it applies a blunt braking force to your forward motion." Instead of slamming into[27] the pavement, he explains, you

10. natural /ˈnætʃərəl/ *n.* 在某方面有天生才能的人
11. institutionalize /ˌɪnstɪˈtjuːʃənəlaɪz/ *v.* 使……制度化
12. strain /streɪn/ *n.* 张力
13. connective tissue 结缔组织
14. sanction /ˈsæŋkʃən/ *v.* 批准，认可
15. triathlon /traɪˈæθlən/ *n.* 三项全能
16. high-profile /ˌhaɪ ˈprəʊfaɪl/ *a.* 著名的
17. biomechanically /ˌbaɪəʊmɪˈkænɪklɪ/ *ad.* 生物力学地
18. pendulum /ˈpendjʊləm/ *n.* 钟摆
19. simplify /ˈsɪmplɪfaɪ/ *v.* 简单化
20. propulsion /prəˈpʌlʃən/ *n.* 推进
21. 这种姿势技巧中最困难的部分可能在于学习如何在前脚触地的瞬间将脚后跟向臀部方向轻弹起来，而不是用脚趾将脚推离地面。flick /flɪk/ *v.* 轻弹
22. visualize /ˈvɪʒʊəlaɪz/ *v.* 想象
23. perpetual-motion /pəˈpetʃʊəlˈməʊʃən/ *a.* 永恒运动的
24. undo /ʌnˈduː/ *v.* 清除
25. egregious /ɪˈɡriːdʒəs/ *a.* 惊人的
26. ingrained /ɪnˈɡreɪnd/ *a.* 根深蒂固的
27. slam into 猛烈撞击

want to feel more like you're springing along. Romanov says his method transmits 30% less shock than normal running.

Getting Results

"For me, the benefits of the pose technique readily became apparent. On a treadmill[28] at 8 mph, I saw my heart rate drop and my labored[29] breathing disappear when I switched in midrun[30] from my normal long-striding[31] style to the pose method. Now I definitely can run longer at the same speed. Other graduates of Nicholas Romanov's nationwide weekend clinics I've met are ecstatic[32]. Of the dozens of 'posers' I've met, none has said the technique did not produce benefits. Once it's been explained to them, I've yet to hear any non-posers criticize it."—Roy M. Wallack

The Basics

* Lean machine[33]: At all times, angle your body forward to the point where you feel you're about to fall. Do not bend at the waist. To go faster, lean more.

* S-shaped body form[34]: Run with your back straight and your knees slightly bent at all times, including at impact. You should run at a height two or three inches shorter than your normal standing height.

* Short stride[35]: Your foot should land under your body, not ahead of it. Remember that "distal[36]" (far from body) equals weak, poor leverage[37], while close to core equals strength and good balance.

* Land on forefoot, not heel: Initially contact the ground only on the ball of the foot. Landing on the heel transmits maximum shock and has a momentum-killing "braking" effect[38].

* Fast cadence[39]: Minimum leg turnover should be 180 to 190 strides per minute. Increase as you get fitter and want to go faster. Remember: The longer the foot's on the ground, the more momentum you lose.

* Pull, not push: This is the hardest-to-master part of the pose technique. After the foot strike, pull the heel straight up in the direction of the butt by contracting the hamstring. It should go up like a rubber band. Fight the urge to push off from the toes as you normally do, instead using the quads[40] and calves.

* Flick it: Don't yank[41] the foot up; flick it up just enough to get it off the ground an inch or so. It will continue upward on its own; the faster you're running, the higher it goes.

28. treadmill /ˈtredˌmɪl/ *n.* 单调的工作
29. labored /ˈleɪbəd/ *a.* 费力的
30. midrun /ˈmɪdrʌn/ *n.* （跑步的）中途
31. long-striding /ˈlɒŋ ˈstraɪdɪŋ/ *a.* 大迈步的
32. ecstatic /ɪkˈstætɪk/ *a.* 狂喜的
33. lean machine 倾斜身体
34. S-shaped body form S形体姿
35. short stride 小步幅
36. distal /ˈdɪstəl/ *a.* 末梢的
37. leverage /ˈliːvərɪdʒ/ *n.* 杠杆作用
38. 脚跟落地会传导最大冲击并有减小动力的刹车效应。
39. cadence /ˈkeɪdəns/ *n.* 步调
40. quads (quadriceps) /ˈkwɒdrɪseps/ *n.* 四头肌
41. yank /jæŋk/ *v.* 猛拉

* Free fall: Once airborne⁴², don't reach with your stride. You're in flight, carried along by your center of mass. The foot will travel in a natural arc⁴³, then drop like a plumb line⁴⁴ without any muscle activity.

42. airborne /ˈeəbɔːn/ *a.* 在空中的
43. arc /ɑːk/ *n.* 弧
44. plumb line 铅垂线

Comprehension Questions

1. What attitude does the author think many people hold to running?
2. According to the passage, do we need to learn to run? Why?
3. According to the author, is Romanov's technique easy to learn?
4. What are the basics of Romanov's technique?
5. After reading the passage, can you state some key words or phrases about the new running techniques?

Background Reading

Health Benefits for Runners

Running is one of the best activities most people can do to improve their health. Running regularly can help with weight loss, fighting aging and disease, and with generally staying healthy.

Many people start running in order to win the battle of the bulge (发胖). Whether they are obese (肥胖的) or just want to lose that last five pounds, or even if they just want to stay at the weight they are at, approximately 60% of runners start running to manage their weight. Running is one of the top activities for burning fat. In fact, with the exception of cross country skiing, running burns more calories per minute than any other form of cardiovascular (心血管的) exercise.

Running regularly also has been proven to help fight the aging process. It prevents muscle and bone loss that often occur with age. Our bones are made to accommodate the demands placed upon them. By sitting at a computer all day many of us allow our bones to grow weaker, but by running regularly our skeleton (骨骼) gets the demand it needs to stay healthy. In addition to keep our insides from aging quickly, regular, high-intensity exercise, like running, has also been proven to promote the human growth hormone (荷尔蒙), which celebrities have taken injections (注射) of for years to keep them looking young.

Amazingly running also helps to fight disease. Running reduces the risk of stroke (中风) and breast cancer. Regular running has become a treatment option for doctors to prescribe (指示，开处方) to patients who are at a high risk, or early stages, of osteoporosis (骨质疏松症), diabetes (糖尿病), and hypertension (高血压). It reduces the risk of heart attacks, by strengthening the heart and lowering blood pressure. Running lowers blood pressure and maintains the elasticity (弹性) of arteries incredibly well because as you run your arteries expand and contract nearly three times as much as usual.

Running also helps maintain and improve general health. It raises HDL (高密度脂蛋白) (or "good") cholesterol (胆固醇), reduces the risk of blood clots (血栓), and encourages use of the 50% of your lungs that usually go unused. Running also boost the immune (免疫的) system by creating a higher concentration of lymphocytes (淋巴细胞) namely white blood cells that attack disease.

Relevant Words

> Fartlek   法特莱克训练法(一种加速跑与慢跑交替进行的中长跑训练方法)
> hill training   山坡跑训练   MaxHR (Maximum heart rate)   最大心率
> PB (personal best)   个人最佳

Lesson 7

> 只身入云端,举步蹑太虚——攀岩
>
> 在极限运动中,攀岩运动以其独有的凭空凌虚的刺激感,登临高处的征服感,挑战自我与自然的成就感,给予了众多渴望成功、希望证明自己的勇士们以独特的吸引力。
>
> 攀岩运动的起源可以上溯到 18 世纪的欧洲,其目的在于克服登山过程中的一些终年积雪的冰岩地形。它真正成为一项独立的运动项目是始于本世纪中叶的欧洲,那时一般以自然的岩壁为主。直到本世纪 80 年代,攀岩运动才完成其萌芽到发展的过程。此后,攀岩运动以势不可挡的态势席卷整个欧洲大陆,掀起了一股改善生活方式,提高生活质量,远离喧嚣城市,融入自然的清风。

The Steep and Rocky Road: Steps to Successful Rock Climbing[1]

By Chuck Roberts
July, 2004
Airman[2]

After hang gliding above the earth and diving through the depths of the ocean, Don Vincent was searching for something different.

He hadn't hit a brick wall[3] yet, but he was soon climbing something similar after visiting the outdoor recreation office at Nellis Air Force Base, Nev[4]. He signed up for the beginner climbing clinic and soon found himself harnessed[5] to a rope propelling[6] himself up a rocky edifice[7] inside a local climbing center.

The retired captain described the experience as exciting, challenging and physically exerting[8]. He hopes to lure[9] his wife, Lt. Col[10]. Angela Vincent, into the sport so they can begin exploring numerous climbing possibilities at nearby Red Rock Canyon located about 30 miles from Nellis.

Those are the emotions everyone should experience after their first time on the rocks, said Fred Frazzetta, an instructor at the Power House Rock Climbing Center in Las Vegas where Mr. Vincent and other Air Force people took that first step[11] into rock climbing.

That feeling never left Mr. Frazzetta after his first climb 13 years

---

1. rock climbing 攀岩
2. *Airman*《空军》,美国空军官刊,每月发行,每年另发行年鉴。它是美国空军的全军性指标刊物,为美国以及其他国家的空军人员提供信息,有极高的参考价值。
3. to hit a brick wall 碰壁;遭遇困难、阻力等
4. Nev (Nevada) 内华达(美国州名)
5. harness /ˈhɑːnɪs/ v. 系住
6. propel /prəˈpel/ v. 推动,推进
7. edifice /ˈedɪfɪs/ n. 大建筑物
8. exerting /ɪgˈzɜːtɪŋ/ a. 费劲的
9. lure /ljʊə/ v. 吸引
10. Lt. Col (Lieutenant Colonel) 陆军中校
11. to take the first step 开一个头

ago at Red Rock. Neither will the memory of his introduction to the sport. As a novice[12], he scrambled[13] onto the rocks without rope, harness or safety helmet. Nearby, a father and son had finished their day's climb and were putting away[14] their gear[15] when the son pointed out to his dad how the young Mr. Frazzetta climbed without the use of gear. He overheard[16] the father's reply: "It's a … like him who get themselves killed."

However, the father followed his remark with an offer to Mr. Frazzetta to try the sport with the proper gear.[17] The ropes, harness and metal clips[18] looked convoluted[19] to Mr. Frazzetta, but everything fit perfectly.

"It was an experience I'll never forget," he said. "That was 13 years ago, and I still enjoy it as much today as that first time."

He also enjoys teaching beginners who come in all shapes and sizes and from different backgrounds. They take up[20] the sport for various reasons, he said, to include natural curiosity, seeking an alternative workout or attempting to overcome the fear of heights. Reasons vary as widely as the ages of his students, which have ranged from 4 to 81.

Regardless of[21] age or background, rock climbing offers the same benefits to all while also demanding attention to detail.

"Climbing keeps you in the moment. You're not thinking about anything else," Mr. Frazzetta said. "It's also cleansing[22] and soothing[23] for the soul, and places you in touch with your body."

Fellow rock climber Jon Spindler agrees. As the recreation[24] specialist at the Cadet[25] Outdoor Recreation Center at the Air Force Academy in Colorado Springs, Colo.[26], he routinely accompanies the beginning rock climbing class to Glen Cove at nearby Pikes Peak. He observes the same reaction in young cadets, Airmen and family members that he experienced when he took up the sport 12 years ago.

"You get a great sense of accomplishment when you make it[27] to the top of a climb," he said. "It's a little hit of a thrill,[28] too." But not necessarily dangerous, even though rock climbing is a sport that can take participants hundreds of feet above the playing field.

"The most important aspect is safety," Mr. Frazzetta said. "That technique has to be flawless[29] or someone could get hurt."

Safety is addressed in a beginner's class where basic skills are taught such as tying figure-eight knots[30], tying oneself to the harness and belaying[31]—securing the safety of your fellow climber through

12. novice /ˈnɒvɪs/ n. 新手,初学者
13. scramble /ˈskræmbl/ v. 攀登
14. to put away 放好
15. gear /ɡɪə/ n. 装备
16. overhear /ˌəʊvəˈhɪə/ v. 无意中听到
17. 然而,那位父亲在做出评价之后,向 Frazzetta 先生提出应使用适当的装备来做这项运动。
18. metal clip 金属夹
19. convoluted /ˈkɒnvəluːtɪd/ a. 复杂的
20. to take up 开始从事
21. regardless of 不管,不顾
22. cleansing /ˈklenzɪŋ/ a. 净化的
23. soothing /ˈsuːðɪŋ/ a. 安慰的
24. recreation /ˌrekrɪˈeɪʃən/ n. 休闲活动,休闲运动
25. cadet /kəˈdet/ n. 军校学员
26. Colo (Colorado) 科罗拉多(美国州名)
27. to make it [口]达到
28. 有一些激动
29. flawless /ˈflɔːləs/ a. 无缺点的
30. figure-eight knot 8字结
31. belay /bɪˈleɪ/ v. 把绳索拴在系绳栓上

rope control.

The first level of rock climbing is sport climbing. The climber wears a harness with a rope extending from the harness, up the route of ascent[32] and back down again to where his climbing partner acts as the belayer[33]. As the climber ascends, the belayer takes in[34] the slack[35]. If the climber were to slip and fall, the belayer can tighten the rope with a moderate pull and instantly stop the climber's fall.

After taking a class, Mr. Frazzetta recommends continuing work on climbing techniques such as traversing[36] and bouldering[37]. Mr. Spindler recommends taking a few classes and joining a local climbing club to provide opportunities to meet fellow climbers and join trips. Many clubs also offer classes. In Colorado, that could include ice climbing, using pick axes[38] and wearing crampons[39] on your feet to dig into the ice frozen on rock formations[40].

The second level is traditional climbing, in which a lead climber will ascend and secure the rope onto preset anchors. The second climber below is attached to the lead climber, and it's his or her job to belay the lead climber in case of a fall. The two climbers can alternate taking the lead. Progressing to this level can range from a few months to a year,[41] and it's the level where most climbers remain, Mr. Frazzetta said.

The next level is aid climbing, which involves setting anchors into the side of the mountain and climbing at times where you're only using the rope. In extreme cases, climbers may spend the night in a special tent suspended[42] in midair from a rope.

Regardless of the proficiency[43] level you're seeking, it's important to get off to a fun start[44]. "Be open, don't be afraid and be comfortable with an instructor. It should be fun," Mr. Frazzetta stressed.

That was Mr. Vincent's experience. Getting off to a good start[45] with good instruction made him realize the sport was physically and technically easier than he had expected.

"It was a challenge, and I gained satisfaction from accomplishing the task," he said. "I would like to do it more."

32. ascent /əˈsent/ n. 上升
33. belayer /bɪˈleɪə/ n. 保护者
34. to take in 收回
35. slack /slæk/ n. 绳子松散的部分
36. traverse /ˈtrævɜːs/ v. 横跨
37. boulder /ˈbəʊldə/ v. 攀登
38. pick axe /ˈpɪkæks/ n. 镐
39. crampon /ˈkrɒmpən/ n. 鞋底尖钉
40. formation /fɔːˈmeɪʃən/ n. 构成物
41. 向这个级别发展需要几个月到一年的时间
42. suspend /səˈspend/ v. 悬浮
43. proficiency /prəˈfɪʃənsɪ/ n. 熟练,精通
44. to get off to a fun start 有个有趣的开始
45. to get off to a good start 有个好开端

Comprehension Questions

1. What equipments does a novice usually need for safety?
2. What is the most important factor in safe rock climbing?

3. How many levels does rock climbing include? What are they?
4. How can a beginner have a fun start?
5. After reading the passage, do you think rock climbing is an interesting activity? If yes, what do you think you can get from it?

Background Reading

Learning the Ropes

While climbing doesn't require the cardiovascular (心血管的) strength of marathon running or the power of competitive weightlifting (举重), focused training—on muscular endurance, balance and flexibility—can help you avoid the, um, inconveniences I experienced during my first foray(冒险) into the vertical (垂直的) world. And training at an indoor climbing gym can boost (推进) your skills and confidence. With more than 500 indoor climbing gyms throughout the country and even more climbing walls tucked away (隐藏) at universities, YMCAs (基督教青年会), sporting-goods stores and even cruise ships, climbing indoors is accessible and never subject to Mother Nature's whims (大自然的任性,这里指自然形成的峭壁).

The first and most important thing to do in a gym is to familiarize (熟悉) yourself with the equipment. Rock climbing can be dangerous. The best way to be safe is to understand the tools of the trade (行当). After getting your knots and harness in order and learning how to belay, or secure your climbing partner with a rope so she won't fall, you're ready to go up. As with most sports, the key here is to start slow. Climbing gyms usually have designated (指定的) routes, often marked with various colors of tape and graded on a scale from 5.0 to 5.14, the latter being the most difficult.

As you're racing for the top, remember your legs. "It's natural for people to climb with their arms and forget their legs," says Robyn Erbesfield-Raboutou, a four-time World Cup climbing champion and current climbing coach. "But legs are so much stronger than arms. You want to push with them instead of pulling with your arms." Erbesfield-Raboutou recommends that beginners try a footwork exercise she calls "crushing ants." On every foothold (立足处), make a motion like you're putting out a cigarette—twisting your foot back and forth on the hold. "It makes you pay attention to detail, and eventually you'll start to develop a feeling of where to best place your foot on a hold," she says.

Good technique—getting your footwork down, learning how to place your body—is the part of indoor climbing that translates (转变) the best to outside, Erbesfield-Raboutou says. But don't expect it all to translate. "I've seen indoor climbers quit the sport after trying it outside," says Mattie Sheafor, founder of the Women That Rock climbing clinic and a guide with Jackson Hole, Wyoming-based Exum Mountain Guides. "They're used to climbing 5.10 or higher inside and expect to do the same outside but find they can't right away. Initially, holds aren't as obvious and might not be as optimally (最佳地,最理想地) placed as in the gym. Just have some patience and be willing to adapt."

Part I Fad Sports

Relevant Words

攀岩比赛种类
bouldering match   抱石赛   difficulty match   难度赛
difficulty-duel match   难度淘汰赛   speed match   速度赛

Lesson 8

PAINT 的英文原意是指"油漆、颜色、涂料"。BALL 的意思是"球"。这两个字连在一起在狭义上是指"一种含有不同颜色染料的球",广义上则指以特定的击发器作"枪",以特定的彩球作为"枪弹"的一种对抗射击式的体育娱乐项目。

Paintballing Makes a Splash[1]

By Matt Ryno
January 7, 2002
The Milwaukee Journal Sentinel[2]

Your heart races, and the wind rushes against you as you desperately dive[3] behind a barrel[4], narrowly escaping the enemy fire. The shots ricochet[5] off the ground, inches from your feet. Outnumbered 3-to-1[6], you are the sole survivor on your side. Your hands shake from the adrenaline[7] rush as you slowly, nervously raise your gun up over the top of the barrel and take what may be your last shot.

Welcome to the world of paintballing, a sport that taps[8] the real-life action, suspense[9] and strategy of warfare and molds it into[10] a relatively safe, fun game everyone can enjoy in their own backyards.

According to Tina Mouser, an employee for Paintball Dave's in Milwaukee, paintballing has been popular for at least the last decade. And teens[11] are beginning to show an increased interest in the sport.

Some economists relate the rise in teen paintballers to the fact that many teens are working at a much earlier age, and putting more money in their wallets. Three hours of paintballing starts at about $30 for most teens at Paintball Dave's, and costs can rise depending on how much ammunition[12] you use, and whether you paintball with a private party.

But some teens think paintballing is popular simply because it's plain fun.

According to Derek Wolf, 17, a student at Kettle Moraine High School, paintballing has become a common pastime for teens in general.

Daniel Drashick, 17, of Racine, agrees.

1. to make a splash 引人注意

2. *The Milwaukee Journal Sentinel* 《密尔沃基新闻卫报》是一份大版印刷的晨报,每日发行,总部在美国威斯康星州密尔沃基市。该报创刊于 1995 年,由《密尔沃基新闻》和《密尔沃基卫报》合并而成,是密尔沃基市的主要报纸,威斯康星州最大的报纸,全州发行。发行量平日版达 25 万份,星期日版则高达 40 多万份。

3. dive /daɪv/ v. 冲去

4. barrel /ˈbærəl/ n. 桶

5. ricochet /ˈrɪkəʃeɪ/ v. 弹跳

6. outnumbered 3-to-1 三比一,指人数上的差别

7. adrenaline /əˈdrenəlɪn/ n. 肾上腺素

8. tap /tæp/ v. 运用

9. suspense /səˈspens/ n. 悬而未决的状态

10. to mold into 塑造成……

11. teens /tiːnz/ n. 十几岁的少年

12. ammunition /ˌæmjʊˈnɪʃən/ n. 弹药

"Paintballing is an exciting thing to do with a group of friends," he said. "It gives teens a different thing to do, rather than the same thing over and over."

According to Zach Thomas, 13, of Muskego, paintball is a very popular sport at his school, St. Jacobi Lutheran. Friends at school eventually got Thomas interested in paintballing last July. Since then he has bought his own gun, and he said he is still very involved in the sport.[13]

For some, paintballing is an outlet[14] for aggression. Michael Miller, 15, of Fredonia, likened[15] paintball to a modern-day psychologist[16] for teens. It's a great sport, he said, to let one's aggressions out on somebody and then leave it all on the paintball field.[17]

"Paintballing is about the closest you can get to shooting someone without actually hurting him," he said.

Some parents, however, are much more skeptical[18].

"I think any sport that encourages shooting someone to win is promoting violence," said Nancy Jacobson, a Grafton mother of two. "Maybe that is the reason kids walk into schools and decide to shoot at classmates. I think it's one way kids get desensitized[19] to what's around them."

Tina Kolmoltz, of Milwaukee, simply worries about the safety of her children. She thinks paint balls are dangerous and can cause welts[20], as well as potential blindness.

"That is why I don't let my son participate," Kolmoltz said. "I just do not believe the sport is that safe, especially at age 13."

Mouser at Paintball Dave's said the business deals with concerned parents quite often. She said she doesn't recall any major accidents at Paintball Dave's during her time working there.

"Overall, the parents are very understanding," Mouser said. "They just want their kids to have a fun, safe time, and that is exactly what we give them."

What is paintball?

—Paintball is a combination of the childhood games "tag[21]" and "hide & seek[22]," but is much more challenging and sophisticated[23]. Although there are many different game formats[24], typically a group of players will divide into two teams to play "capture the flag."

The object of the game is to go out and capture the other team's flag while protecting your own. While you are trying to capture a flag,

13. ... he is still very involved in the sport. 他仍然很热衷于这项运动。
14. outlet /ˈaʊtlet/ n. 发泄途径
15. liken /ˈlaɪkən/ v. 把……比做
16. psychologist /saɪˈkɒlədʒɪst/ n. 心理学家
17. 他说，这是一项很好的运动。人们把攻击性发泄在别人身上，留在彩弹场上。
18. skeptical /ˈskeptɪkəl/ a. 怀疑的
19. desensitized /diːˈsensɪtaɪzd/ a. 麻木的
20. welt /welt/ n. 伤痕

21. tag /tæg/ n. 贴签游戏
22. hide & seek 捉迷藏
23. sophisticated /səˈfɪstɪkeɪtɪd/ a. 复杂的
24. format /ˈfɔːmæt/ n. 版式, 类型

you also try to eliminate[25] opposing players by tagging them with a paintball expelled[26] from a special air gun called a "paintgun."

—A paintball is a round, thin-skinned gelatin[27] capsule[28] with colored liquid inside it. Paintballs are similar to large round vitamin capsules or bath oil beads. The liquid inside paintballs is non-toxic[29], non-caustic[30], water-soluble[31] and biodegradable[32]. It rinses[33] out of clothing and off skin with mild soap and water.

—Paintguns, also called "markers", come in a variety of shapes and styles. They may be powered by carbon dioxide[34], nitrogen[35] or compressed[36] air. Many have power systems that use large refillable cylinders[37] called "tanks" or "bottles" that give hundreds of shots before needing to be refilled. Some use small 12-gram carbon-dioxide powerlets[38] as their power source, each powerlet being good for 15 to 30 shots.

25. eliminate /ɪˈlɪmɪneɪt/ v. 消除
26. expel /ɪkˈspel/ v. 发射
27. gelatin /ˈdʒelətɪn/ n. 凝胶
28. capsule /ˈkæpsjuːl/ n. 容器
29. non-toxic /ˈnɒnˈtɒksɪk/ a. 无毒的
30. non-caustic /ˈnɒnˈkɔːstɪk/ a. 非腐蚀性的
31. water-soluble /ˈwɔːtəˈsɒljubəl/ a. 可溶于水的
32. biodegradable /ˌbaɪəʊdɪˈɡreɪdəbəl/ a. 可生物降解的
33. rinse /rɪns/ v. 冲洗掉
34. carbon dioxide /ˈkɑːbən daɪˈɒksaɪd/ n. 二氧化碳
35. nitrogen /ˈnaɪtrədʒən/ n. 氮气
36. compressed /kəmˈprest/ a. 压缩的
37. cylinder /ˈsɪlɪndə/ n. 圆筒
38. powerlet /ˈpaʊəlɪt/ n.（较弱的）火力。-let名词后缀，表示"小"。

Comprehension Questions

1. Why is paintballing becoming popular?
2. Why do some parents worry about the game?
3. What's the object of the game?
4. What can people get from the game?
5. Having the chance, would you let your child play this game? Why or why not?

Background Reading

History of Paintball

The evolution of paintball into the modern sport that it is today took place fairly quickly in comparison to most other sports. The history of the paintball gun begins in the early 1970s, when it was used as a tool for marking trees and livestock (家畜). In 1981, twelve friends played the first recreational paintball game using these industrial paintball guns on a field measuring over 100 acres.

One of the first names given to the sport that we now call paintball was "The National Survival Game." This name reflects the nature of paintball as it was first played—a small group of friends getting together in the woods to play total elimination games. Sometimes the friends broke into teams to play each other, but most games were "every man for himself."

Over the years, recreational paintball has become more sophisticated.

Because more people were playing, using teams became the standards. Different playing variations (变化) began to form, the most popular being "capture the flag", but offensive/defensive scenarios (游戏的"情节") also were popular. Also, as the number of people interested in paintball grew, so did the development of the commercial paintball industry.

The first outdoor commercial paintball field started in 1982. The first indoor paintball field followed in 1984. The fields allowed large groups of people to meet in one place to play, and the business owners were pushed to develop new and exciting ways to keep these paintballers entertained. This drove the development of new scenarios and styles of playing.

The biggest style of play change to come about because of commercial fields was the "bunker (碉堡; 掩体)-style" game. Smaller fields let players start the action quicker, instead of having to stalk (寻找) through the woods for 15 minutes before seeing anyone. Also, players purchased more paintballs when they were in a constant firefight, which made the commercial fields more money.

Today, commercial paintball fields are everywhere, but there are still a large number of people that prefer playing paintball out in the woods. While outlaw (不合法的) paintball is generally much cheaper, it is also more problematic (有问题的) than paying to play at a commercial field.

The first professional tournament was held in 1983. Even then, the prizes were worth $14,000. Today, major tournaments have hundreds of thousands of dollars worth of prizes. One of the major forces in tournament games, the NPPL (National Professional Paintball League), was founded in 1992–93.

Relevant Words

annihilation	歼灭战	batman	通讯员
flag-capture	夺旗战	monitor	班长
reencounter	决斗	scout	侦察员
sharp-shooter	狙击手		

Lesson 9

冬季冰钓有很大的吸引力,垂钓乐趣不在其他季节之下。因为水面冰封,其他季节够不着的地方,钓友们都可以去,比起其他季节自由多了。另外,浮漂就在眼前,浮漂的细微变化都能看得清清楚楚。施钓得法,收获颇丰。这些都吸引着冰钓爱好者。

但是,在冰上垂钓,首先是安全问题。在这个问题上,一定要引起足够的重视。那么就让我们通过下面的文章了解一下冰钓的安全因素。

Ice fishing: Winter Safety

By Ben Bloker
Feburary 2004
Combat Edge[1]

Picture this: A misty white view of frozen Canandaigua Lake[2] accompanied by the cold chill of a winter morning. The snow-covered ice makes an eerie[3] crunch[4] noise beneath each step. A seasoned[5] ice fisherman leads a novice[6] out on the ice to experience this winter activity firsthand[7].

For those looking for the peaceful solace[8] of this incredible sport, there are some safety precautions[9] to think about before walking out on the ice. Regardless of the amount of experience someone has, safety is always a priority on the ice.

The number one concern is the ice's condition. Many factors affect the ice's thickness, and more importantly, its weight bearing capacity[10]. Some of these factors are temperature, air bubbles or pockets[11], and water conditions under the surface. Knowing what the air temperatures were the preceding 2 or 3 days before you fish are just as important as the temperature the day you fish.[12] If the temperature is above freezing for 24 hours prior to your trip out on the ice, it may not be safe. Additionally, large drops in temperature are equally problematic[13] because it makes the ice brittle[14].

For example, ice that appears blue or clear is stronger than milky looking ice[15]. The milky look is caused by tiny air bubbles which significantly weakens the ice.

---

1. *Combat Edge*《战斗前沿》,隶属于美国空军,是一本美国空中战斗司令部的事故预防杂志,为指挥人员提供与飞行、武器和地面安全有关的信息。
2. Canandaigua Lake 肯地哥瓦湖,位于纽约。
3. eerie /ˈɪərɪ/ *a.* 奇异的
4. crunch /krʌntʃ/ *n.* 嘎吱声
5. seasoned /ˈsiːzənd/ *a.* 经验丰富的;老练的
6. novice /ˈnɒvɪs/ *n.* 新手,初学者
7. firsthand /ˈfɜːstˈhænd/ *ad.* 直接地;第一手地
8. solace /ˈsɒlɪs/ *n.* 安慰
9. precaution /prɪˈkɔːʃən/ *n.* 预防措施
10. weight bearing capacity 承重能力
11. pocket /ˈpɒkɪt/ *n.* 气穴
12. 了解钓鱼前两三天的气温与知道钓鱼当天的气温同样重要。
    preceding /prɪˈsiːdɪŋ/ *a.* 先前的
13. problematic /ˌprɒbləˈmætɪk/ *a.* 有问题的
14. brittle /ˈbrɪtl/ *a.* 易碎的
15. milky looking ice 不透明冰;乳浊冰

Large snowfalls are also a concern because they make the ice bow under the snow's weight and this causes slush[16] to form on top. If you see slush, you should never go out on the ice until it completely refreezes.

Finally, running water under the ice's surface weakens it as well. If you're not sure how thick the ice should be to support your weight, there are several web sites with helpful charts like the one run by the New York Department of Environmental Conservation. It has a wealth of[17] information about ice fishing including an "Ice Thickness Table."

For example, one person can walk on ice that is 2 inches thick if it's clear, blue, hard, and on a lake versus[18] a stream. In contrast, a 2-ton car can safely drive on 7 inches of ice with the same conditions. So how do you find out how thick the ice is where you want to fish? One of the best sources is your local bait shop. Many post ice thickness conditions. You also can check it yourself using an auger[19] or pick[20]. Make sure you check about every 150 feet or so since conditions can change quickly.

Besides ice thickness and condition, you also must consider the weather's effect on your body. It's paramount[21] that you dress warm and wear waterproof clothing if possible. You must also consider what type of clothing will keep you afloat[22] should the worst happen, and you fall through the ice. Waders and hip boots are a no-no,[23] and you should always wear a personal flotation device. Clothing is not the only thing you can use to protect yourself from the weather. Many use portable "ice shanty" huts[24] that keep you shielded[25] from the elements[26].

Ice fishing tends to be a place of refuge[27] for most of its faithful participants—a much needed break from our hectic[28] day-to-day work pace. Observing[29] just a few safety precautions and making some preparations, ice fishing can be a great way for you to get out and enjoy the winter weather.

16. slush /slʌʃ/ n. 雪泥,半融雪
17. a wealth of 很多的
18. versus /ˈvɜːsəs/ prep. 而不是
19. auger /ˈɔːɡə/ n. 螺丝钻
20. pick /pɪk/ n. 镐
21. paramount /ˈpærəmaʊnt/ a. 极为重要的
22. afloat /əˈfləʊt/ a. 飘浮的
23. 防水长靴和连裤靴是冰钓的禁忌。wader /ˈweɪdə/ n.(钓鱼用的)防水长靴 no-no /ˈnəʊnəʊ/ n. 禁忌
24. "ice shanty" hut 冰钓时用来御寒的小屋棚
25. shielded /ˈʃiːldɪd/ a. 隔离的
26. the elements 恶劣天气
27. refuge /ˈrefjuːdʒ/ n. 庇护(所)
28. hectic /ˈhektɪk/ a. 忙乱的
29. observe /əbˈzɜːv/ v. 遵守

Comprehension Questions

1. According to the passage, what is the most important during ice-fishing?
2. What kind of ice is safe according to the appearance?
3. What factors should we consider as to the ice safety?
4. Where can people get the "Ice Thickness Table" according to the passage?
5. Have you ever gone ice fishing? If yes, please describe your experience.

Background Reading

Everything You Need to Know About Ice Fishing

No need to stay inside during the long winter months waiting for the sun to come out dreaming about open water and summer fun. Be adventurous (喜欢冒险的), bundle up (穿暖和), get outside and try fishing in a whole new way—through the ice! Ice fishing action can be fast and furious (激烈的) when winter seals the lakes under ice. Best of all, there are no mosquitoes or flies to "bug" you.

Imagine this. You bundle up and walk out onto a frozen lake on a clear and crisp (晴朗的) winter day with your sled (雪橇) full of fishing gear and the fishing license in your pocket. Once you find the perfect fishing spot, you drill a large hole completely through the ice until you can see open water. Then, you get out the ice chisel (凿子) to widen your hole. Now, you unpack your sled and find your special lures (诱饵), jigging rods (铁板钓竿) or tip-ups (利用杠杆原理制成的钓具) to catch the fish. You will probably want to get out your portable seat to sit on so that you can look down the hole to see what's happening. Then, you grab the skimmer (撇去浮物的器具) to keep the hole clear of the ice and slush (雪泥) that forms during the day. Once your line is set, you'll need to keep a close eye on it or watch for the flag on the tip-up to see if you've caught a fish. When your hands get cold, you grab for the thermos (热水瓶) of hot chocolate you brought along, mmmm, just what you need to warm up. You end up eating fish for lunch out on the ice, cooked on the small stove you brought along. What a great day of fishing!

Believe it or not, winter fishing makes up nearly 1/4 the annual catch in Wisconsin (威斯康星州). People enjoy it for the solitude (单独) of being out on a frozen lake and the challenge of the sport. Others like the friendship and good times found in an ice shanty (木屋) town atmosphere with friends and family. Why not try ice fishing and open your senses to an exciting winter event.

You must carry your license with you when you're fishing, summer or winter. Be sure to get a copy of the current Wisconsin Fishing Regulations to find out about restrictions, special regulations, new changes and general statewide (遍及全州的) regulations. It is your best guide to staying within the law and having the most fun out on the ice!

Relevant Words

bobber 浮子	ice scoop 冰铲
jig 钓钩	needle nose pliers 针头钳
reel 线轴	

Lesson 10

> 帆板运动是介于帆船和冲浪之间的新兴水上运动项目，运动员利用吹到帆上的自然风力，站在板上，通过帆杆操纵帆使帆板产生运动速度在水面上行驶，靠改变帆的受风中心和板体的重心位置进行转向。
>
> 帆板器材结构简单，造价便宜，一叶"扁舟"高速行驶在碧海蓝天之中，玩法多端，引人入胜，使人有回归大自然的感觉，是一项让人永不厌倦的运动。
>
> 参加帆板运动，运动员始终在搏击风浪，可以磨练意志，使人的体力、耐力、平衡力与灵敏等方面得以全面发展。

Windsurfing[1]

By Tom James
June/July 1999
Sports Afield[2]

THE BASICS

Windsurfing is really a catchall[3] term for a bunch of different sports. Think of snow skiing: There's downhill skiing, cross-country skiing, even ski jumping—all completely different sports with different names, but when skiing was relatively new, anything you did with two boards strapped[4] to your feet was called skiing.

It's the same with windsurfing: If you're standing up on a board

1. windsurfing /ˈwɪndˌsɜːfɪŋ/ *n.* 帆板运动

2. *Sports Afield*《体育竞技场》，美国历史最为悠久的狩猎爱好者杂志，每月发行。主要介绍猎手狩猎探险的亲身经历。1888年出版第一期杂志。

3. catchall /ˈkætʃɔːl/ *a.* 包罗万象的

4. strap /stræp/ *v.* 系住

holding a sail, technically you are windsurfing.[5] But there are really two distinct types of windsurfing. There's the windsurfing you see on television—as visually exciting as anything in the sporting world. This type of windsurfer[6] is capable of reaching speeds of more than 40 mph or riding the biggest waves in the world. And true to the name[7], this is essentially riding a surfboard[8] with a sail propelling[9] you through the waves.

But the windsurfing most people do—the type that takes place on lakes and bays and protected waters[10] all over the world; the kind that has been in the Olympics since 1984, and certainly what all beginners do—is much more like sailing than surfing. Sure, you're standing on a board holding a sail, but this board is a lot larger and the speeds are much slower. This less extreme aspect of the sport is no less fun, but it's a lot easier to learn and more accessible[11] to the average person.

You need serious wind[12] and a lot of time on the water to windsurf in the waves, but with a gentle breeze and no experience you can be windsurfing on flatwater on your first day.

FIRST TIME OUT

Windsurfing is easier than it used to be, mainly due to advances in equipment for novices. It's still going to be a struggle[13] if you try to jump on your friend's board to "give it a go" without a little instruction or advice. But on the right gear and with a few fundamentals[14] in mind, you can quickly experience the feeling that hooks[15] all windsurfers—just you, the wind and the water.

Start in a gentle breeze—morning is usually when the wind is the lightest. In fact, if you think it's windy, it's probably too windy to learn. You don't attack the gnarliest[16] trail the first day on a mountain bike, and you don't want to start windsurfing on the wild, windy days. A light, next-to-nothing[17] breeze keeps the water calm and allows you to concentrate on the sail rather than dealing with your balance on the board and the stress of negotiating[18] chop[19] and rollers[20]. Make sure you are starting in a place with the wind blowing slightly onshore[21]. You'll want to walk the board out to about waist-deep water where you can put the centerboard[22] down. The centerboard keeps the board stable and helps you get back upwind[23] once you are under way. Initially, when you get the sail out of the water the board will feel very unstable. Think "head up; knees bent," and most of all resist the immediate urge to pull the sail in toward you. Once you feel balanced, then you can

5. 如果你脚踏帆板,手握帆杆,那么从技术上讲你就是在做帆板运动。
6. windsurfer /ˈwɪndˌsɜːfə/ n. 帆板运动员,做帆板运动的人
7. and true to the name 正如其名字的含义
8. surfboard /ˈsɜːfbɔːd/ n. 帆板
9. propel /prəˈpel/ v. 推进
10. protected waters 保护水域

11. accessible /əkˈsesɪbəl/ a. 可达到的
12. serious wind 大风

13. struggle /ˈstrʌgəl/ n. 费劲的事
14. fundamental /ˌfʌndəˈmentl/ n. 基本原理
15. hook /hʊk/ v. 吸引

16. gnarly /ˈnɑːlɪ/ a. 扭曲的,粗糙的
17. next-to-nothing 差不多没有
18. negotiate /nɪˈgəʊʃɪeɪt/ v. 应付
19. chop /tʃɒp/ n. 碎浪
20. roller /ˈrəʊlə/ n. 卷浪
21. onshore /ˌɒnˈʃɔː/ ad. 向着海岸地
22. centerboard /ˈsentəˌbɔːd/ n. 稳向板
23. upwind /ʌpˈwɪnd/ ad. 逆风地

start thinking about grabbing the boom[24] and filling the sail with wind.

To start sailing, pick a spot on the horizon[25] that is perpendicular[26] to the wind direction and try to head toward that spot. With your focus forward toward the nose of the board, put your hands on the side of the boom toward the back of the board and "sheet in" (pull the sail) slightly by rotating[27] your shoulders. This will instantly put you in motion[28]. Now you're windsurfing! You'll be surprised at how quickly you start to move. Resist the urge to look at your feet or at the sail—keep looking toward that spot on the horizon. At this point you'll feel like you're either going to be pulled forward onto the sail or fall backward, pulling the sail on top of you. The key is to grip[29] the boom lightly. If it feels like the sail is going to overpower you, let it go.

You'll notice that the nose of the board will tend to round[30] up into the wind. This is common and is caused by grabbing the boom too close to the mast[31]. The proper way to combat this problem is to grip the boom farther back. But an easier solution is to concentrate on "pushing" the nose downwind[32] with your front foot and "pulling" the tail[33] of the board into the wind with your foot. While this may sound overly[34] simple, it works.

SKILLS AND TECHNIQUE

One of greatest myths about windsurfing is that the sailor has to be really strong. And when you do it wrong, trying to power the sail into submission[35], windsurfing does take incredible[36] strength; you can fight the wind all you want and you'll never win. But this is a finesse sport—balance and technique enable the 100-pound woman to sail as easily and as well as, if not better than, the 250-pound football player.[37]

When pulling the sail out of the water, known as uphauling[38], keep your back straight and knees bent. Lean back and let your body weight, not strength, raise the sail out of the water. Stand there for a minute while holding the mast to get your balance, and then reach for the boom and sheet in.

When you aren't moving, try to stand in the center of the board. Picture a line going from the center of the nose of the board to the center of the tail.[39] This is the centerline, and it's your best friend. A board is a lot like a bike in that it's easy to stand on while moving, but it's difficult to stay up when standing still. Most people have trouble starting out because they try to stand on the edge of the board before the board gets going, which is like sitting on the rail[40] of a canoe[41].

24. boom /buːm/ *n.* 帆下桁
25. horizon /həˈraɪzən/ *n.* 地平线
26. perpendicular /ˌpɜːpənˈdɪkjʊlə/ *a.* 垂直的
27. rotate /rəʊˈteɪt/ *v.* 旋转
28. to put sb./sth. in motion 使……运动
29. grip /ɡrɪp/ *v.* 抓住
30. round /raʊnd/ *v.* 转向
31. mast /mɑːst/ *n.* 桅
32. downwind /ˌdaʊnˈwɪnd/ *ad.* 顺风地
33. tail /teɪl/ *n.* 尾部
34. overly /ˈəʊvəlɪ/ *ad.* 过度地
35. submission /səbˈmɪʃən/ *n.* 屈服，降服
36. incredible /ɪnˈkredəbl/ *a.* 巨大的
37. 这是一项技巧性很强的运动——只要掌握了平衡和技术，一名100磅的女帆板运动员可以和一名250磅的足球运动员滑地一样轻松自由，甚至可能滑得更好。
38. uphauling /ˈʌpˈhɔːlɪŋ/ *n.* 升索，起帆
39. 在脑子里想像一条连接帆板前端中心和尾部中心的线。
40. rail /reɪl/ *n.* 围栏
41. canoe /kəˈnuː/ *n.* 独木舟

Keep your feet on the centerline and you'll have accomplished one of the fundamental skills.

Another trick is to know when to say when. Often, you'll feel like you are going to get pulled into the sail and down to the water. When you start to feel this, just let go with your back hand, maintaining a light grip with your front hand. This will release the pressure on the sail and let you regain your composure[42] without having to drop the sail and haul[43] it back up.

The secret to windsurfing is knowing when the sail has enough power to hold you up—in which case you lean back against the pull of the wind and accelerate like a bat out of hell—and knowing when the wind is too light to support you, in which case you support the sail. Beginners will seem to be in a constant state of either falling backward into the wind (expecting the sail to hold them up) or getting pulled forward onto the sail (being overpowered[44] by the wind). Once you learn to gauge[45] the power of the wind, you can concentrate on more advanced moves.

42. composure /kəmˈpəʊʒə/ n. 沉着
43. haul /hɔːl/ v. 拖拉
44. overpower /ˌəʊvəˈpaʊə/ v. 压制
45. gauge /ɡeɪdʒ/ v. 测量

Comprehension Questions

1. According to the author, what's the definition of "windsurfing"?
2. In what way is a board like a bike?
3. How many tricks of windsurfing does the author mention in the passage? What are they?
4. According to the author, what is the secret to windsurfing?
5. Imagine you were a windsurfing coach, what would you tell the beginners about this sport?

Background Reading

Safety and Fitness

Windsurfing is not a dangerous sport. True, being out in the middle of a body of water on a foam wafer (薄片) doesn't seem like a big confidence-builder, but with some simple ground rules in mind, windsurfing is one of the safest sports out there. Windsurfing doesn't even appear on the National Sporting Goods Association list of dangerous sports. Of course, you're utterly exposed to the elements on a windsurfer. You'll fall in and you'll need to be able to swim back to your board. If it makes you feel more comfortable, wear a personal flotation (漂浮) device, but they are not mandatory (强制的) on most waterways.

Part I Fad Sports

The most important rule when it comes to windsurfing safety is: Never leave your board. Never. If you're on a $200 board and your $1000 sail rig (装备) somehow separates from it and starts to blow away, you still don't leave your board. It floats and will support you. You can paddle (用桨划) it to safety.

It is also imperative (必要的) to study the wind and weather conditions. Start from a beach where the wind blows slightly toward the shore. That way, you won't be blown out to sea as you would in an offshore (向海面吹的) wind. I don't know a single regular windsurfer who doesn't use a weather radio. Windsurfers, like mariners, must be tuned in to the weather and know, within reason (合理地), what to expect.

The only problem beginners can run into is that they get so caught up in the exhilaration (愉快) of their experience, they sometimes lose track of (忘记) time and underestimate (低估) the strength it may take to get back to the starting point.

Physically, the sport can be demanding (苛求的). You're constantly fighting the wind in a tropical sun, you'll get exhausted quickly. Know your limits, and always keep an eye on how far away the shore is.

Windsurfing gives you a good, whole-body workout (锻炼). However, a beginner may feel soreness in the lower back, forearms and shoulders. The best pre-windsurfing exercises are the ones that increase overall flexibility and strengthen the forearms. Many windsurfers use a weight tied to a bar that they roll and unroll to develop that "Popeye (大力水手,一个动画片人物形象)" appearance we so covet (渴望).

Relevant Words

bow 船首	CLR (Center of lateral resistance) 侧向阻力中心
COB (center of balance) 平衡中心	downhaul 收帆索
eye of the wind 风眼	rake 向船尾倾斜

Lesson 11

> 随着经济的发展,冬季体育运动已经成为很多人喜欢的时尚、健康、富有朝气的运动。那么在名目繁多的冬季体育运动中你又知道多少呢? 相信通过阅读下面的文章,你会对冬季体育运动有一个更好的了解。

Welcome to the Ice Age—Winter Sports (I)

By Randy B. Swedburg and Lisa Ostiguy

January 1994

Parks & Recreation

North America's early settlers were forced to adapt to the cold climate to survive. Intense cold and frozen lakes and rivers made travelling any distance a difficult task, and pioneers faced challenges searching for food and finding warm clothing. Today most of our basic needs are more easily satisfied, thanks to these early pioneers. Americans in northern cities no longer have to "hibernate[1]" during the winter; the traditional winter survival activities are now leisure activities. Technology has made participating in winter sports much easier; new materials such as insulate[2] and waterproof liners let people endure the elements much longer. Travel to rural destinations in the winter was difficult at the turn of the century. Today, travel in the winter poses[3] few problems.

1. hibernate /ˈhaɪbəneɪt/ v. 冬眠

2. insulate /ˈɪnsjʊleɪt/ n. 绝缘

3. pose /pəʊz/ v. 引起,造成

The traditional winter sports—cross-country skiing[4], curling[5], downhill skiing[6], figure skating[7], hunting and trapping[8], ice fishing, ice hockey[9], ski jumping[10], snowshoeing[11], speed skating[12], and tobogganing[13]—used to be left to just a handful the hale and hearty[14]. Today, more and more people are winter sports enthusiasts. We have become more mobile[15] and affluent[16], and more interested in rural activities. Some researchers report negative attitudes to winter; some even refer to conditions associated with the cold climate as a "seasonal affective disorder[17]". Many people from the north used to flock[18] south for the winter to avoid the cold conditions. Today more people are deciding to stay and enjoy the winter.

In the 1960s and 70s there was a trend toward moving outdoor winter sports indoors. We built indoor curling rinks[19], indoor arenas and acrylic[20] ice surfaces. In the 1990s activities which are not formally organized and can only be experienced outdoors are gaining in popularity[21]. Urban winter outdoor recreational activities are declining in popularity. The interest has shifted to rural-based[22] leisure activities. Many small rural communities which previously had only one tourist season are growing by offering year-round opportunities. Golf courses are converted[23] to cross-country ski trails and snowshoeing areas. Waterfront[24] resorts are now clearing the ice for skating, hockey, ice fishing and curling. Many summer activities such as golf, softball[25] and ultimate Frisbee[26] are being adapted for the winter.

In addition to traditional winter sports, a plethora of[27] new and exciting sports have sprung up[28] over the past few decades:

SNOWMOBILING[29]

Although transportation vehicles for use in snow have been in existence for more than 50 years, the snowmobile's perfection to the point where it was mobile, reliable and inexpensive enough to be enjoyed as a recreational vehicle did not occur until the 1960s. Since then this winter sport has grown rapidly. The snowmobile has opened new vistas[30] for winter camping, fishing, hunting and trapping and has become an integral[31] part of excursions[32] into the wilderness. In recent years unused railroad beds[33] have been designated[34] for winter usage by snowmobilers.

In addition, snowmobiling is today a sport unto[35] itself, with cross-country touring or racing, time trials[36] (snowmobile drag racing)

4. cross-country skiing 越野滑雪
5. curling /ˈkɜːlɪŋ/ n. 冰壶运动（也称冰上溜石）
6. downhill skiing 高山滑雪（在修整的滑降跑道上进行速度滑雪的冬季运动）
7. figure skating 花样滑冰
8. hunting and trapping 狩猎
9. ice hockey 冰球
10. ski jumping 跳台滑雪
11. snowshoeing /ˈsnəʊʃuːɪŋ/ n. 雪鞋运动
12. speed skating 速滑
13. tobogganing /təˈbɒɡənɪŋ/ n. 平底雪橇滑雪
14. hale and hearty 健壮
    the hale and hearty 健壮的人
15. mobile /ˈməʊbaɪl/ a. 流动的
16. affluent /ˈæfluənt/ a. 富裕的
17. seasonal affective disorder 季节性心情紊乱
18. flock /flɒk/ v. 成群地迁移
19. rink /rɪŋk/ n. 冰场
20. acrylic /əˈkrɪlɪk/ a. 丙烯酸的
21. popularity /ˌpɒpjuˈlærəti/ n. 流行；普及
22. year-round 整年的
23. convert /kənˈvɜːt/ v. 转换
24. waterfront /ˈwɔːtəfrʌnt/ n. 水边
25. softball /ˈsɒftbɔːl/ n. 垒球
26. ultimate Frisbee 终极飞盘
27. a plethora of 过多的
28. to spring up 大量地出现
29. snowmobile /ˈsnəʊməbiːl/ n. 雪上汽车
30. vista /ˈvɪstə/ n. 远景, 展望
31. integral /ˈɪntɪɡrəl/ a. 不可或缺的；必须的
32. excursion /ɪkˈskɜːʃən/ n. 远足
33. railroad bed 铁路路基
34. designate /ˈdezɪɡneɪt/ v. 指定
35. unto = to
36. time trial 计时赛

and circuit racing[37]. There are even events known as "snowdoeos" where a variety of activities and competitions are staged[38] to delight spectators and participants alike. Thousands of snowmobile clubs now exist in North America, with a total membership of close to a million.

The equipment needed to participate, in addition to the snowmobile itself, includes specially designed boots, mitts[39] and snowsuits. All these are important for warmth, wind protection and impermeability[40]. A real challenge is to find a helmet that offers warmth and protection against the dangers of 50 mph plus speeds. Overall the clothing will cost from $350 to $800, depending on the quality selected. The snowmobile itself is a more costly investment, with more than 25 models produced by the four leading manufacturers. The range of prices is from $4,000 to well over $10,000. The average touring snowmobile costs between $5,500 to $6,500.

FREESTYLE SKIING

This sport is the youngest member of the snow skiing family. Included under this one title are the separate activities of aerial[41], ballet[42] and mogul skiing[43]. In the early 1970s when it was known as "hot-dog skiing" there were some skiers practicing all three of the sports. However, freestyle skiing did not become common, nor was it recognized as an internationally competitive event until the mid 1980s. The 1988 Olympic Games in Calgary[44], Canada, included freestyle skiing as a demonstration sport[45] and it proved to be very popular with the spectators. In the 1992 Olympics in Albertville[46], France, freestyle skiers competed in mogul skiing with full medal status.[47] The 1994 Olympics, to be held in Lillehammer[48], Norway, will include aerial skiing and ballet skiing will likely have achieved medal status by 1998.

Aerial Skiing

This sport can be best described as a combination of downhill skiing, gymnastics and ski jumping. Skiers build speed on an in-run[49], leading to a ramp[50], which allows them to propel[51] themselves up to 20 meters in the air. After "take off" the skier performs a series of inverted[52] twists and somersaults[53], landing on a hill which has a slope of 37 to 39 degrees and a length of 30 meters. The challenge is to gain as much height as possible, travel the greatest distance, perform with form and precision while in the air and land with stability. In competition two series are judged.

---

37. circuit racing 赛道赛
38. stage /steɪdʒ/ v. 制作,导演
39. mitt /mɪt/ n. 露指手套
40. impermeability /ɪmˌpɜːmɪəˈbɪlɪtɪ/ n. 不渗透性
41. aerial /ˈeərɪəl/ a. 空中的(在这里指 "aerial skiing",空中技巧)
42. ballet /ˈbæleɪ/ n. 雪上芭蕾
43. mogul skiing 雪上技巧 mogul /ˈməʊɡʌl/ n. 雪坡
44. Calgary /ˈkælɡərɪ/ 卡尔加里(加拿大西南部城市)
45. demonstration sport 表演项目
46. Albertville 阿尔贝维尔(法国城市,1992 年第 16 届冬季奥林匹克运动会开幕式和闭幕式的举办地)
47. 在 1992 法国阿尔贝维尔冬季奥运会上,自由式滑雪运动员们参加了当时已经成为竞赛项目的蒙古式滑雪比赛。
48. Lillehammer 利勒哈默尔(挪威城市)
49. in-run /ˈɪnrʌn/ n. 斜台
50. ramp /ræmp/ n. 斜坡
51. propel /prəˈpel/ v. 推进
52. inverted /ɪnˈvɜːtɪd/ a. 反向的
53. somersault /ˈsʌməsɔːlt/ n. 翻筋斗

Ballet Skiing

In this case the performance is on a gentle slope (12 to 15 degrees) with a length of 220 to 250 meters. The participants traverse[54] the length of the slope performing a variety of spins, dance steps, multiple rotations, jumps, and flips[55]. All this is choreographed[56] to music very similar to that used in figure skating. In competition the routines are limited to two minutes.

Mogul Skiing

Every skier has experienced the odd[57] bump[58] or dip[59] (moguls) in the face of a run. With mogul skiing, a steep hill (23 to 32 degrees) is dotted with these moguls. The challenge in this sport is to negotiate[60] the face of the hill, leaping into the air from time to time, without losing control. In competition a course is set from top to bottom on the hill, which can be from 200 to 270 meters long. The sport is judged using time, technique and form as the criteria.[61]

Until recently the number of ski hills that could accommodate freestyle skiers were very few, but more and more ski areas are adding freestyle hills. The equipment used would appear to be very similar to that for downhill skiing to the uninformed[62] observer. However the skis, boots, bindings[63] and poles are modified to meet the specific conditions found in each of the three subsets[64] of freestyle skiing.

54. traverse /træˈvɜːs/ v. 横越
55. flip /flɪp/ n. 筋斗
56. choreograph /ˈkɒrɪəɡrɑːf/ v. 设计
57. odd /ɒd/ a. 不固定的
58. bump /bʌmp/ n. 凸起物, 不平物
59. dip /dɪp/ n. 陷落
60. negotiate /nɪˈɡəʊʃɪeɪt/ v. 越过
61. 评判这项运动的标准是时间、技巧以及形式。
62. uninformed /ˌʌnɪnˈfɔːmd/ a. 不了解情况的
63. binding /ˈbaɪndɪŋ/ n. 装配
64. subset /ˈsʌbset/ n. 子集, 亚类

Comprehension Questions

1. Why are there more and more winter sports enthusiasts today?
2. How many different kinds of traditional winter sports are mentioned in the passage? What are they?
3. How many new winter sports are mentioned in the passage? What are they?
4. What features does mogul skiing have?
5. As a spectator, which sport do you like most? Aerial, ballet, or mogul? Why?

Background Reading

Winter Sports Safety (I)

Heading for the ice, snow, or slopes? Bundle up with (了解) this safety advice and have a great time!

Before you sled, ski, or skate

Dress for safety. Dress everyone in several layers of tops and pants under warm jackets and add hats, gloves or mittens, and waterproof boots. Check for hanging drawstrings (拉带, 细绳) that can catch on sleds, ski lifts, and other equipment. Stuck drawstrings can cause serious injury, so remove them from hoods (头巾) and necks, and shorten those that hang from jacket bottoms. Use short, not long scarves and tuck (塞进) them into jackets.

Respect the cold: "When the temperature is below freezing, beware of (小心) frostbite and hypothermia (体温降低)," says Dr. Greensher, medical director of Winthrop-University Hospital in Mineola, N.Y. and former chairperson of the American Academy of Pediatrics (小儿科) Injury Prevention Committee. Check on kids often to make sure they don't get too cold. Beware that cold air increases the risk of exercise-induced asthma (运动引起的哮喘).

Give babies special care: Keep infants inside, if possible, when it is under 40 degrees (Fahrenheit). Make sure babies' faces remain dry and protected, as cold injury can result from wind whipping their saliva (唾液) and drool (口水). If clothing is wet, either from snow or diapers (尿布), it no longer acts as an insulator.

Provide lessons: Before starting any sport, provide lessons from a qualified instructor. Consider taking a first-aid course yourself. Make sure children are always properly supervised (监督).

Relevant Words

gate	路径(位于两竖直的杆之间的一通道, 滑雪运动员在障碍滑雪赛中必须通过)
piste 滑雪道	snowplow 雪犁

Lesson 12

通过阅读上一篇文章(Welcome to the Ice Age—Winter Sports I),相信你已经对冬季体育运动产生了浓厚的兴趣。那么,让我们在下面的文章中继续了解一下其他的冬季运动。

Welcome to the Ice Age—Winter Sports (II)

By Randy B. Swedburg and Lisa Ostiguy

January 1994

Parks & Recreation

SNOWBOARDING[1]

One of the newest snow sports is snowboarding, which uses a combination of surfing and skateboarding techniques. Two separate developments began in the late 1970s. In France the sport, known as "monoskiing", developed using waterskiing as the model. The equipment used was a wide ski with parallel bindings[2]. In North America the sport became known as skiboarding and later snowboarding. The North American version was modeled after surfing, with the bindings offset[3].

Two types of snowboards are used today. The freestyle board is curved at both the tip and tail and is shorter than the slalom board[4], used almost exclusively[5] for competition. The slalom board is less flexible and gives the boarder less mobility[6]. Both hard and soft boots have been developed for use with the snowboard, with each type having its proponents[7]. Specially padded[8] gloves and pants are also available. A board can range from $275 to $800 and boots, gloves and pants will add an additional $100 to $300.

Snowboarders[9] use the same facilities as downhill skiers. During the 1993 ski season, some ski hill operators have reported that on certain days up to 40 percent of the traffic is from snowboard enthusiasts! A survey of randomly[10] selected sporting good stores throughout Ontario[11] and Quebec[12] reported that sales of snowboards increased 60 percent over the last two years, making it difficult to keep many types of boards in stock[13].

1. snowboard /ˈsnəʊbɔːd/ n. 雪地滑板
2. binding /ˈbaɪndɪŋ/ n. 鞋套
3. offset /ˈɒfset/ v. (位置等)偏移
4. slalom board 障碍滑雪板
5. exclusively /ɪkˈskluːsɪvlɪ/ ad. 专门地
6. mobility /məʊˈbɪlɪtɪ/ n. 灵活性
7. proponent /prəˈpəʊnənt/ n. 支持者
8. padded /ˈpædɪd/ a. 加护垫的,加填充物的
9. snowboarder /ˈsnəʊbɔːdə/ n. 雪地滑板运动员
10. randomly /ˈrændəmlɪ/ ad. 随机地
11. Ontario /ɒnˈteərɪəʊ/ n. 安大略(加拿大中东部的一个省)
12. Quebec /kwɪˈbek/ n. 魁北克(加拿大东部的一个省)
13. in stock 有库存的

RINGUETTE[14]

Although the game was first played as an alternative to ice hockey for girls in Ontario in 1963 the popularity of ringuette did not spread to today's international status until the 1980s. In 1993 there are thousands of girls and women who are active in this vigorous ice sport. For the uninitiated[15], it is easier to describe ringuette by its similarity to ice hockey. It is played on ice wearing skates, using a stick and a ring[16]. The object is to shoot the ring into the opposing team's goal.

The equipment used is one of the major differences between ringuette and hockey. The stick is nothing like a standard hockey stick since it has no blade.[17] It is a straight handle from three to five feet long (depending on the height of the player), with a tapered[18] end. The ring is made of soft rubber and has an outside diameter of 6.25 inches and an inside diameter of 4.25 inches. This allows the player to place the stick in the center of the ring and thereby achieve greater control while stick handling. Major rules that greatly change the complexion[19] of the game in comparison with ice hockey are: there is no physical contact allowed; the ring must be passed across both the offensive and defensive bluelines[20] and no players, with the exception of the goalie[21], are allowed in the goal area.

The cost to outfit[22] one player including skates, stick, helmet, special gloves and padding is in the neighborhood of [23] $200 to $300. Additional expenses are incurred[24] when the game is played indoors, since ice rental can be as high as $150 per hour in some areas of the country. However, in most cases the subsidized[25] ice rental fee will be under $50 an hour.

ICE BOATING[26]/ICE SURFING[27]

As with many of the ice/snow activities growing popular in recent years, ice boating has been around for 50 years[28], but the motivation to participate for large numbers of people and the availability of equipment did not exist until the 1970s. Now modern technology has created boats that are durable, easy to transport, easy to rig[29], safe and reasonably priced. You can buy a good used ice boat for less than $1,000 and inexpensive kits are available starting at $1,600. The price for a finished[30] boat begins at about $3,200. The sport of ice surfing is so new that there is not yet an officially acceptable term. The sport began only five to six years ago and much of the early equipment was homemade. Both these sports can be linked to their summer

---

14. ringuette /'rɪŋweɪ/ *n.* 冰球的一种

15. uninitiated /ˌʌnɪ'nɪʃɪeɪtɪd/ *a.* 未入门的

16. ring /rɪŋ/ *n.* 环状物（这里指"球"）

17. 由于没有击球板，球棍与曲棍球棍并不相像。

18. tapered /'teɪpəd/ *a.* 锥形的

19. complexion /kəm'plekʃən/ *n.* 局面，情况

20. blueline /'bluːlaɪn/ *n.* 蓝线（将冰球场划分成3个均等区域）

21. goalie /'gəʊlɪ/ *n.* 守门员

22. outfit /'aʊtfɪt/ *v.* 配备，装备

23. in the neighborhood of 大约

24. incur /ɪn'kɜː/ *v.* 招致；产生

25. subsidize /'sʌbsɪdaɪz/ *v.* 资助

26. ice boating 冰帆运动

27. ice surfing 冰帆运动（另一种说法）

28. 冰帆运动已经存在了50年

29. rig /rɪg/ *v.* 配备

30. finished /'fɪnɪʃt/ *a.* 精巧的

counterparts[31] for a better understanding. Ice boating is similar to sailing a small one-person sailboat. In the winter version the hull[32] is very flat and it rides on outrigger[33] skates that skim[34] across the ice. Ice surfing can be best understood by comparing it to windsurfing. Once again the equipment is essentially the same except that the ice surfer[35] rides on blades while standing aloft[36] on the surfboard; by grasping the wishbone[37], the ice surfer can direct the craft across the frozen ice surface.

One of the things ice boaters/ice surfers claim is that their sport is not a cold sport. To the contrary, most have tried both summer and winter sailing and claim the summer version can be much colder when one takes the plunge[38] into the waters of a summer lake and then re-emerges to the windy conditions of sailing. Proper attire[39] and protection are necessary for all ice boaters/surfers. Although the water of summer may sometimes be colder to the participant, when one spills[40], the impact of the water is never harder than the ice of winter.

SNOW TUBING[41]

The sport of tubing has gone beyond being a summer sport and is now enjoyed during the winter.[42] Snow tubing has begun to grow in popularity with those who love high speed and being almost out of control. Tubing began informally with people using old innertubes[43] by testing them on the snow. Given an innertube, a slope and the right snow conditions, you are off. In tubing you start at the bottom and work your way up. Some carry their tubes and others attach a rope or cord to drag it up the slope. The most common tubes used are over-inflated[44] truck or automobile innertubes. Many downhill ski resorts and golf courses are starting to design snow tubing runs which are clear of trees and offer a lift to the top of the hill.

In 1974 the National Snow Tube championships were held in Minneapolis[45]. Since then innertube snow racing has become popular. Tubing events are often held in conjunction with[46] other events such as skiing races or special events days on the slopes. Tubing can be a dangerous winter sport. The tubes should be small enough to be controlled by the rider and there should only be one person per tube. Snow tubing should only be done in open areas where there are no trees or rocks, or on commercial slopes designed for tubing.

Winter, ice and snow are now being seen as an opportunity for many who previously dreaded[47] the cold weather. As we approach the

31. counterpart /ˈkaʊntəpɑːt/ n. 极相似的物
32. hull /hʌl/ n. 船体
33. outrigger /ˈaʊtˌrɪɡə/ n. 叉架
34. skim /skɪm/ v. 滑过
35. surfer /ˈsɜːfə/ n. 冲浪运动员
36. aloft /əˈlɒft/ ad. 在高处
37. wishbone /ˈwɪʃbəʊn/ n. 叉骨

38. plunge /plʌndʒ/ n. 跳进,投入
39. attire /əˈtaɪə/ n. 服装

40. spill /spɪl/ v. 摔下
41. snow tubing 滑雪轮
42. 滑轮运动已经不专属于夏季了。现在,人们在冬季也可以进行这项运动。
43. innertube /ˈɪnətjuːb/ n. 内胎

44. over-inflated /ˌəʊvəɪnˈfleɪtɪd/ a. 过于膨胀的

45. Minneapolis /ˌmɪniˈæpəlɪs/ n. 明尼阿波利斯(美国明尼苏达州东南部城市)
46. in conjunction with 连同

47. dread /dred/ v. 畏惧

21st century the "ice age" is becoming a greater part of every North American's life. Positive attitudes are leading to an increase in activities available to everyone.[48]

The increased interest in winter activities is resulting in[49] fewer people travelling long distances to a warmer climate. Communities are slowly beginning to realize the revenue-generating opportunities[50] of offering recreational programs year-round. Traditionally, facilities are forced to reduce staff at the end of the summer due to low demand for programming in the winter. Professionals in the field of leisure service delivery must be at the forefront of planning winter activities on blade, runner and ski.[51] Leisure service professionals should continue to increase programming to keep up with the trends[52].

48. 积极的态度使人们可以参加的活动越来越多。
49. result in 导致
50. revenue-generating opportunity 创造收入的机会
51. 休闲运动领域的专业人士应当站在最前线，设计借助冰刀和雪橇的冬季运动项目。
forefront /ˈfɔːfrʌnt/ n. 最前线
52. keep up with the trends 跟上趋势，赶上潮流

Comprehension Questions

1. Where is the name "snowboarding" from?
2. What are the two types of snowboards? What are the differences between them?
3. What's the biggest difference between ringuette and hockey?
4. When did snow tubing begin to be popular?
5. In your opinion, which sport mentioned in the passage is the most interesting one? Why?

Background Reading

Winter Sports Safety (II)

Ice skating

Children three and up can skate. Although ponds are scenic, rinks offer safer conditions for everyone. Another good option is to ask your community to flood a grassy area. Rent or buy good fitting skates and lace them tightly. Teach kids to fall on their behinds, not on their hands. Always carry skates to and from the rink—never wear them.

Some guidelines for skating on ponds: Ice is thinner and less stable at the start and end of winter, so mid-winter is the best time to try pond skating. If possible, skate over shallow water, no deeper than two to three feet. This way, if the ice breaks, you'll only get wet. Since ice is thinner at the center of a pond, skate around the edges. Never skate over water that is moving, like rivers or streams.

Sledding (雪橇)

Guidelines for safe sledding include using a sturdy (坚固的) sled with good steering (舵) and no sharp edges. Have children sled in supervised areas reserved for sledding only. Help your community organize a good sledding area if you don't already have one. Choose a spot with no holes, rocks, stumps

(树桩), trees, ice, cars, or streets. Avoid very steep hills. Try to get your children to wear their bike helmets for protection. Tell them to sit up, not lay down.

Skiing

The entire family can enjoy skiing together. Children three and up can ski, as long as you provide skiing lessons, constantly supervise children, and supply properly fitting equipment. Children should be closely supervised on lifts. Keep children away from hills that are icy or too steep.

Snowboarding

This popular winter sport is like skiing, but you don't use poles. Instead of skis, you use a single hard board like a skateboard and stand sideways (侧面地), like surfing. Parents should check everyone's bindings to make sure they will release easily during falls. As with skiing, boots that stay attached to skis during a fall are what cause most ankle injuries. Look for a resort that has separate areas for snowboarding.

Hockey

"Ice hockey is extremely safe for children under the age of ten. Older children do sustain injuries, but the incidence (发生频率) is less than other contact sports like football," says Dr. Alan Ashare, staff physician at St. Elizabeth's Medical Center in Boston and a director of USA Hockey. He recommends protective equipment such as a helmet and a full facemask; shin (护胫) guards; protective padding for the pants, shoulders, and elbows; as well as gloves and a mouthguard (护齿套). Players should cushion (减缓……的后果) collisions with body parts other than the head. If a collision is unavoidable, then "Heads Up, Don't Duck (弯下头)" helps prevent neck injuries.

Older children can stay safe by wearing the protective equipment mentioned and by following the heads-up rule. Parents should make sure the coach has had formal training in this sport. Older children should also cushion collisions with body parts other than the head

Relevant Words

downhill race 速降滑雪赛	pursuit competition 追逐赛
roller skiing 滚轮滑雪	schuss 高速直线滑雪
ski jumping competition 跳高滑雪比赛	slalom 障碍滑雪

Lesson 13

> 保龄球是一种轻松、有趣,而且有益于健康的活动。当你手抓着如大理石般的球,用灸热的眼神面对球道另一端好似和你有着深仇大恨的球瓶,恨不得能一次将所有的球瓶击倒。成功的人,往往带着微笑,和好友来个 Give me "TEN";而失败的人,更不自觉燃起一股复仇的欲望,反正君子报仇下一球也不迟嘛! 保龄球的乐趣,就体现在这一成功与失败交替的过程中,令人不忍释手。然而"静大于动"的保龄球是否真正属于体育运动呢?让我们看一看专家的分析吧。

Is Bowling a Sport?

By Lydia Rypcinski

August 2002

Bowling Digest[1]

It's an eternal question, kind of like. "Which came first—the chicken or the egg?"

Is bowling a sport? That question begets another: Are bowlers athletes?

Too often, bowling and bowlers' claims to legitimacy[2] have been pooh-poohed[3] with a dismissive[4], "It can't be a sport because ... " (choose any or all):

"You don't sweat."

"You drink and smoke while performing."

"You sit more than you move."

"You can be out of shape and still get high scores."

It's been hard to refute[5] those arguments. People with serious spare tires[6] around their middle[7] do win bowling tournaments. Not many scientific studies deal specifically with bowling and fitness. What's more, people in bowling—like people everywhere—assume that "real" sports require huffing and puffing[8], which bowling admittedly[9] does not.

However, a small but growing core of sports science professionals inside and outside of the sport has become convinced that bowling and bowlers do indeed fall within the realm[10] of sport and athletics.

1. *Bowling Digest*《保龄球文摘》,双月刊,创刊于1983年。该杂志是南美唯一一本保龄球教学杂志,主要介绍保龄球明星并提供该项目的技术指导。
2. legitimacy /lɪˈdʒɪtɪməsɪ/ *n.* 合法(性)
3. pooh-pooh /ˌpuːˈpuː/ *v.* 藐视
4. dismissive /dɪˈsmɪsɪv/ *n.* 表示轻视的话语
5. refute /rɪˈfjuːt/ *v.* 驳倒,反驳
6. spare tire 预备轮胎(这里指人体腰腹部周围的多余脂肪组织)
7. middle /ˈmɪdl/ *n.* 腰部
8. huffing and puffing 意指气喘吁吁
9. admittedly /ədˈmɪtɪdlɪ/ *ad.* 无可否认地
10. realm /relm/ *n.* 领域

"Sport is academically defined as a well-organized physical activity, with sub-factions[11] and sub-disciplines[12], that is regulated through rules. Bowling fits that definition, given all its membership groups rules and levels of involvement," points out Dr. Jeff Briggs, a lifelong bowler with a Ph.D. in administration and science and the founder of Briggs Consulting, which offers consultative[13] services to the bowling industry.

"Of course bowling is a sport, and it takes an athlete to perform it well," says David Grisaffi, a corrective exercise kinesiologist[14] in Washington State who trains boxers. Grisaffi worked with Hall-of-Famer[15] Jeanne Naccarato when she was touring regularly. "An athlete combines a God-given genetic talent with sport-specific skills that are developed to a high level. Bowling simply differs in the bio-motor[16] abilities it requires."

"Competitive bowlers who take a holistic[17] approach to their sport —that is, have a coach, train and practice—are certainly athletes," states Dr. Rob Wood, a sports scientist at the Northern Territory Institute of Sport (NTIS) in Darwin[18], NT[19], Australia. Wood specialized in long-jumping and sprinting in his younger days, and now works with elite-level Australian bowlers at the NTIS.

Bowling's bad rap[20], it seems, comes partly from the fact that it's an anaerobic sport. "'Anaerobic' means you're relying on adenosine triphosphate[21], which is stored in the muscle's fibers, for immediate energy," Grisaffi says, explaining that performance in bowling comes in short bursts of energy that stress the musculo-skeletal[22] system [muscles, joints, and bones] rather than the cardiovascular [heart and lungs]. That's why the sweating and "windedness[23]" seen in a continuous-activity sport such as soccer or long-distance running aren't present.

Bowling, Grisaffi says, is more akin[24] to weightlifting, golf, and even platform diving. "You get up, perform the activity, and then go back and wait for your next turn."

"Cardiovascular endurance plays a minor role in bowling performance," adds Wood. "Some cardiovascular fitness is important because it helps the bowler stay fresh for longer periods of play, maintain fine motor control and execute[25] properly. However, there seems to be a threshold aerobic level for bowlers, beyond which further increases have limited contribution to improving performance.[26]"

Grisaffi suggests comparing a bowler to a sprinter on a scale of

11. sub-faction /sʌbˈfækʃən/ n. 小类别
12. sub-discipline /sʌbˈdɪsɪplɪn/ n. 小分枝
13. consultative /kənˈsʌltətɪv/ a. 咨询的
14. kinesiologist /kaɪˌniːsɪˈɒlədʒɪst/ n. 人体运动学家
15. Hall-of-Famer 大师
16. bio-motor /ˈbaɪəʊ ˈməʊtə/ n. 生物动力
17. holistic /həʊˈlɪstɪk/ a. 整体的
18. Darwin /ˈdɑːwɪn/ 达尔文（澳大利亚北部城市）
19. NT (Northern Territory) （澳大利亚）北部地区
20. rap /ræp/ n. 缺点
21. adenosine triphosphate 三磷酸腺苷（一种有机化合物）
22. musculo-skeletal 肌骨骼的
23. windedness /ˈwɪndɪdnɪs/ n. 喘气
24. akin /əˈkɪn/ a. 相似的
25. execute /ˈeksɪkjuːt/ v. 完成
26. 然而，对于保龄球手来说，似乎存在着一个有氧训练量的临界点，超过了这一临界点的更大训练量并不能显著地提高竞赛水平。

one to ten in various bio-motor abilities. "Bowlers would rank very low on speed, compared to sprinters. However, a bowler's power needs would be up there with the sprinter, if you look at the full spectrum of bio-motor abilities. You'll find that bowlers actually score high on several of them—power, balance, coordination, and flexibility."

These needs blend[27] into what Briggs calls "functional fitness[28]."

"Physical fitness concerns itself more with aesthetics[29] and appearance," he says. "Functional fitness refers to how someone performs. A basketball player trains to jump higher. A bowler works to acquire and then sustain a low finishing position."

As bowling legend Carmen Salvino cautions[30], "Developing the wrong muscles—or the right muscles the wrong way—could even hurt your performance. Too many pushups[31], for instance, can overdevelop the chest muscles and force your swing off-line[32]. You want muscles that are strong but lean[33]." Salvino, a fitness butt[34] who still uses a 16-pound ball at age 68, is competing again in selected PBA national stops.

"Let's face it: You've got only so many hours in a day to eat, sleep, work, and train," Grisaffi says. "You have to allocate your training time to where it will do the most good."[35]

The principles of kinesiology (the study of the body in motion) will determine the most effective exercise program for a bowler. "Bowling is really the combination of a lunge[36], a twist, and flexion[37] and extension of the shoulder, or extending the arm straight out in front of the face after extending it behind the body," Grisaffi says.

Briggs notes that today's power game generates so much torque[38], or twisting, on the body that bowlers who generate a lot of revolutions[39] "create a 'whiplash[40]' effect on the shoulder, elbow, and wrist joints. Enormous stress is placed on the body when the ball is thrown. This is one of the biggest reasons bowlers develop 'bowler's tendinitis[41]' and many other cumulative-trauma disorders[42]."

In addition, the lunging motion of the final step stresses not only the torso[43] and upper body when the ball comes down from the peak of the backswing, but also the supporting leg and knee. "You're asking your supporting leg to bear 90% of the body weight, plus the ball, plus the centrifugal[44] forces in motion around the body as the ball swings forward. These forces are multiplied severalfold[45] when we throw the ball," Briggs says.

Bowler-specific training, then, should enhance flexibility, strength,

27. blend /blend/ v. 混合
28. functional fitness 功能性训练
29. aesthetics /iːsˈθetɪks/ n. 美学
30. caution /ˈkɔːʃən/ v. 提醒
31. pushup /ˈpʊʃʌp/ n. 俯卧撑
32. off-line /ˌɒfˈlaɪn/ a. 不在控制下的
33. lean /liːn/ a. 无脂肪的
34. butt /bʌt/ n. [口语] 人

35. 你必须给训练分配一个能达到最佳效果的时间。

36. lunge /lʌndʒ/ n. 向前的动作
37. flexion /ˈflekʃən/ n. 弯曲
38. torque /tɔːk/ n. 扭转力
39. revolution /ˌrevəˈluːʃən/ n. 旋转
40. whiplash /ˈwɪplæʃ/ n. 鞭打
41. tendinitis /ˌtendɪˈnaɪtɪs/ n. 腱炎
42. cumulative-trauma disorder 累积创伤失调 trauma /ˈtrɔːmə/ n. 外伤
43. torso /ˈtɔːsəʊ/ n. 躯干

44. centrifugal /ˌsentrɪˈfjuːgəl/ a. 离心的
45. severalfold /ˈsevərəlfəʊld/ ad. 几倍地

power, stability, balance, endurance, and general conditioning. As might be expected, programs will vary according to the trainer and athlete's priorities[46] and philosophies[47].

"Very high levels of fitness are probably not beneficial to bowling," Wood offers. "For example, you need adequate strength to hold a 16-pound ball and carry it for many games. Improving your strength beyond this level may have limited benefit. However, if a bowler's fitness level is below threshold level in key areas, bowling performance may be adversely[48] affected, especially in the later stages of tournaments."

Wood emphasizes aerobic endurance, balance, core stability (abdominal[49] strength), and flexibility in his training programs, which incorporate principles of exercise physiology, experience gained from coaching athletes in other sports, and an understanding of the physiological demands of bowling.

"I'll assess flexibility first, because if, say, the hip flexors[50] are tight, the full range of motion for the shoulder and/or the pelvis[51] can be affected," Grisaffi says. "To compensate for that rigidity[52], another part of the body—say, the back—is asked to take more of the workload, over time, which adversely affects the lower spine[53]. My feeling is that it'll stretch the short and tight muscles before you begin and make them more flexible at the beginning, you can avoid bigger problems down the road."

Grisaffi says to think of the back as the body core.[54] If the muscle "girdle"[55] supporting the lower back is weak—or if a "pot belly" hangs off that girdle—the core is more likely to crack under the strains caused by bowling's twisting action. Doing some simple exercises that focus on the transverse[56] abdominus[57]—the innermost muscle in the body's core—will help reduce the likelihood of back pain.

"Lunging is a huge exercise to strengthen this area as well as the legs," Grisaffi says. "Strengthening the core helps build endurance; your body becomes less likely to break down over the long haul[58]."

Other areas to strengthen and support are the shoulder joint, upper arm, forearm, and wrist. Grisaffi's training also addresses what he calls unbalance. "The side a bowler uses to throw the ball will always be stronger and thicker than the other side, so it's important to work the underused side, too." Grisaffi's preferred training apparatus[59] includes swiss balls[60], body blades[61], free weights[62] and cable machines with weight stacks[63].

---

46. priority /praɪˈɒrɪti/ n. 需优先考虑的事情

47. philosophy /fɪˈlɒsəfi/ n. 看待事物的方法；哲学

48. adversely /ˈædvɜːslɪ/ ad. 不利地，有害地

49. abdominal /æbˈdɒmɪnəl/ a. 腹部的

50. flexor /ˈfleksə/ n. 屈肌
51. pelvis /ˈpelvɪs/ n. 骨盆
52. rigidity /rɪˈdʒɪdɪti/ n. 僵化

53. spine /spaɪn/ n. 脊椎骨

54. Grisaffi 让人们把后背当做是身体的核心。
55. girdle /ˈɡɜːdl/ n. 带状物
56. transverse /trænzˈvɜːs/ a. 横向的
57. abdominus /æbˈdɒmɪnəs/ n. 腹肌
58. haul /hɔːl/ n. 拖拉
59. apparatus /ˌæpəˈreɪtəs/ n. 器械；设备
60. swiss ball 平衡球（用来训练平衡感）
61. body blade 健身片
62. free weight 重量训练器材
63. cable machine with weight stacks 一种健身器材，利用牵引锻炼力量。

Comprehension Questions

1. Why do some people hesitate to regard bowling as a sport activity?
2. What is the definition of sport according to the passage?
3. What are the functions of kinesiology in bowling training?
4. Which type of sport does bowling belong to according to the passage?
5. Do you think bowling is a kind of sport? Why or why not?

Background Reading

History of Bowling

Bowling has a long and rich history, and today is one of the most popular sports in the world. A British anthropologist (人类学家), Sir Flinders Petrie, discovered in the 1930's a collection of objects in a child's grave in Egypt that appeared to him to be used for a crude (原始的) form of bowling. If he was correct, then bowling traces its ancestry (祖先) to 3200 BC.

A German historian, William Pehle, asserted (声称) that bowling began in his country about 300 AD. There is substantial (丰富的) evidence that a form of bowling was in vogue (流行的) in England in 1366, when King Edward III outlawed (禁止) it to keep his troops focused on archery practice. And it is almost certain that bowling was popular during the reign of Henry VIII.

By this time, too, there were many variations of "pin" games, and also of games where a ball was thrown at objects other than pins. This would seem to imply that the games had developed over time, from an earlier period.

Today, the sport of bowling is enjoyed by 95 million people in more than ninety countries worldwide. Under the auspices (支持) of the Federation Nationale des Quilleurs (FIQ) (国际保龄球联盟) bowling's top athletes regularly compete in Olympic Zone and worldwide competitions.

Relevant Words

alley bed 球道	approach 投球区
ball rack 球架	delivery 投球
double 连续 2 次得到全中	gutter 边沟
FIQ = Federation Internationale Des Quilleurs 国际保龄球联合会	

Lesson 14

> Parkour 是一项街头疾走极限运动,有点 Free-running 的意思,再配合猿猴一样的灵活攀越。"Parkour"一词来自法文的"parcour",有"超越障碍训练场"的意思。Parkour 运动把整个城市当做一个大训练场,一切围墙、屋顶都成为可以攀爬、穿越的对象,特别是废弃的房屋,更适合飞檐走壁似的速降、跳升和飞跃……
>
> Parkour 的动作追求的是出其不意的效果,往往超出了常人的想象。法国电影 Banlieue 13(暴力街区)展示的即是 PARKOUR 街头文化,主角 David Belle 是 Le Parkour 运动的创始人之一。

Even Flow[1]: No, It's Not a Chase Scene[2] from a '70s Cop Show[3]. It's the French Extreme Sport Le Parkour

Andrew J. I. Vontz
January 2005
Men's Fitness

Throughout history, the French have given us great food, fine art, and annoying attitude. Now they've bestowed[4] upon us an extreme sport: Le Parkour. True, the name is tres[5] lame, but the concept—think skateboarding without, well, a skateboard—is the sport du jour[6] for aggressive urban athletes.

You may have seen Le Parkour (or PK, in Parkour talk) in some hip[7] commercials for Nike, Mitsubishi, and Toyota. In those TV spots, we first see traceurs (as PKers are known) running innocuously[8]. But then suddenly, they break into dangerous jumps—sometimes down staircases, sometimes off building ledges—which usually end in a ninja[9]-roll that flows beautifully back into a carefree run.

Traceurs place a premium on[10] the ability to flow[11] from one move to the next, and rolling[12] keeps things smooth. Whether they're swinging acrobatically[13] around lampposts, doing back flips off a railing, or posing for effect[14] with both feet on a wall—Spider-Man-style—traceurs have captured the imagination of youth around the planet, especially among city kids who can't afford the often-

1. even flow 流畅行进(该短语描述了这一运动的特点,即连贯地做各种动作,勇往直前。)
2. chase scene 追逐场面
3. '70s cop show 70 年代的警匪片
4. bestow /bɪˈstəʊ/ v. 给予
5. tres [法语]太……
6. sport du jour 每日运动[法语]
7. hip /hɪp/ a. 时髦的;流行的
8. innocuously /ɪˈnɒkjuəslɪ/ ad. 乏味地
9. ninja /ˈnɪndʒə/ n. 忍者
10. to place a premium on 诱发;鼓励
11. flow /fləʊ/ v. 转换
12. rolling /ˈrəʊlɪŋ/ n. 旋转
13. acrobatically /ˌækrəˈbætɪklɪ/ ad. 杂技地
14. for effect 做样子;装门面

61

expensive equipment necessary for other hobbies.

Then again, the sport's also caught on[15] with stockbrokers[16], like New Jersey's Mark Toorock. The 34-year-old caught a whiff of[17] PK action on the Web, at urbanfreeflow.com, where the sickest[18] moves can be seen in action videos and photographs. "In some sense, it's like martial arts," says Toorock, who joined a traceur "clan[19]" known as the UF (Urban Freeflow) Krew. "You don't even think about what you're going to do when you come to an obstacle. You just go over it, under it, around it, through it, flip[20] it—whatever. The idea is to move with fluidity through your environment.[21]"

Created by Frenchmen David Belle and Sebastien Foucan, PK scenes have popped up in San Francisco, Atlanta, New York, and Chicago, and there are now about 450 traceurs[22] in the States. Among them is L.A.'s Ham of the Jump Monkeys clan. Ham—and other colorfully named traceurs such as Toothy, MonkJay, Chibi, and Ambulance—hits the roofs, streets, stairs, and walls of the city where skateboarders and in-line skaters are forbidden to shred[23]. Ham, in particular, is a fearless roof-gap-leaping maniac[24] who flips from ledges[25] and vaults[26] staircases in a single bound. "You can do what you want to," explains Ham. "It's your style of flow."

And while the sport can seem almost ridiculously easy, top traceurs must possess gymnastic prowess[27], explosiveness[28], and, above all, nerve[29]. How else do you explain the leaping from ledge to ledge and hanging on to the sides of buildings with nothing but fingertips?

15. to catch on 流行
16. stockbroker /ˈstɒkˌbrəʊkə/ n. 经纪人
17. a whiff of 一点……的迹象
18. sick /sɪk/ a. 让人捏把汗的；让人不舒服的
19. clan /klæn/ n. 队
20. flip /flɪp/ v. 轻跳，弹过
21. 关键是在周围的环境中自由地移动。fluidity /fluːˈɪdɪti/ n. 流动性
22. traceur [法语]街头疾走练习者
23. shred /ʃred/ v. 破坏
24. maniac /ˈmeɪniæk/ n. 癖好者
25. ledge /ledʒ/ n.（自墙壁突出的）壁架
26. vault /vɔːlt/ v. 跳跃
27. prowess /ˈpraʊɪs/ n. 保留高超的技艺
28. explosiveness /ɪkˈspləʊsɪvnɪs/ n. 爆发性
29. nerve /nɜːv/ n. 勇气

Comprehension Questions

1. Why do you think Le Parkour appears in some commercials?
2. After reading the passage, can you give a definition for "Le Parkour" in your own words?
3. What qualities are needed for Le Parkour?
4. Who created Le Parkour?
5. In your opinion, what are the similarities between Le Parkour and martial arts?

Part I Fad Sports

Background Reading

The Latest Extreme Sport: "Free Running" Hits Britain

Forget bungee jumping. The latest craze (狂热) for any self-respecting daredevil (蛮勇的人) is "free running" or, as the French, who invented it, say, "le parkour".

Sebastien Foucan, 29, a stuntman (特级表演者) who came up with the idea, has been in London with two colleagues to introduce "free running" to Britain.

The extreme sport involves using famous buildings as obstacle courses, even if it necessitates (使成为必要) teetering (蹒跚地走) precariously (不稳地) on ledges, performing mid-air (半空中) flips and dangling from rooftop railings.

While being filmed for a Channel 4 programme, the trio (三人组) have conquered the Royal Albert Hall, Somerset House, the Royal National Theatre, Shakespeare's Globe Theatre, the Saatchi Gallery and the Tate Modern. In one instance, M. Foucan performed a 20ft jump across two storeys from HMS Belfast's bridge to its gun turret (炮塔). In another, his colleague Johann Vigroux bounded from one level of the National Theatre to another while M. Foucan did a handstand (手倒立) from the outer balcony.

The extreme sport came to the attention of the British public last year, when a BBC advert featured David Belle, a childhood friend of M. Foucan's and co-founder of Le Parkour, leaping from rooftop to rooftop across London and performing handstands 120ft above the traffic.

The team liken (把……比做) the sport to the stunts in films including *The Matrix* and *Star Wars*. It evolved in the quiet suburban town of Lisses, near Paris, where M. Foucan and M. Belle spent their childhood.

M. Foucan, who has gone on to star in television adverts for Nike and Toyota, said: "Lisses was a beautiful town but for us growing up there, there was nothing to do. We were running and jumping and going to the top of the school to play at being ninjas and it became our game."

The Mayor of Lisses, Thierry Lalon, remembered his concern as the risky sport overtook the town. "Everyone could see young people going up and down the walls like cats in the town," he said.

But M. Foucan said that the game transformed (转变) into a discipline, with a distinct philosophy. "It is not just a game, it is a discipline because it is a way of facing our fears and demons and you can apply this to the rest of your life," he said. The group's co-ordinator, Jason White, who has worked on films including the Bond movie The Living Daylights, said he was dubious (怀疑的) of the group's skills until he saw them in action. Fans of le parkour are said to include the Arsenal footballer and French international Robert Pires.

Relevant Words

Le Parkour 的技术动作

cat leap 猫跳 equilibre 平衡
wall run 走壁 monkey vault 猴跳

Lesson 15

有一首描述牛仔的英文歌叫"A Cowboy's Hard Times",里面有这样一段:
I once was a cowboy, and I used to run wild.
And I rodeoed, wrangled, and rambled in .
But I'm too old for horses, too old for the show,
And I'm too young for Heaven; now where shall I go?
rodeo 来自西班牙语 rodear,表示"四处转悠,走来走去"(go around)。它的本义是形容圈牛的圆形场地或者畜栏,牛群被"圈"(rounded up)在一个地方接受清点或检查。大约于 1834 年,rodeo 出现在美语里,表示"围场,把已拢的牛群围在一起的圈地"。直到 1914 年,才有了现代意义"牧人马术表演",即一种展示骑马或套牛等技巧的公开表演赛。

The Rodeo Today

By Vicki Hambleton
February 17, 2003
Footsteps[1]

Rodeo has changed over the years. Today, professional cowboys and cowgirls compete in seven different events.

Calf Roping[2]: Calf roping is one of the oldest events in rodeo. A cowboy and his highly skilled horse must race against the clock[3] to see how quickly they can rope a calf. The pair ropes the calf, and then the cowboy must jump off his horse, turn the calf on its side, and tie down its legs. World champion Fred Whitfield set a record of 6.9 seconds from start to finish.

Steer Wrestling[4]: Steer wrestling, or bulldogging[5], was never practiced in real life and has always been done as an entertainment event at rodeos. No cowboy would ever consider jumping off his horse and onto the back of a 600-pound steer that was traveling at 35 miles per hour. In the rodeo arena, a steer is let loose, and then the steer wrestler and his assistant, both on horses, overtake the steer. The cowboy must jump onto the bull, grab it by the horns, and wrestle it to the ground.

Bull Riding[6]: Bull riding is probably the most dangerous event in

1. *Footsteps*《脚步》,是一本以美籍非洲黑人为主题的儿童刊物,在美国曾被评选为"最受父母推崇的儿童杂志"。主要介绍黑人种族文化、历史上的杰出黑人、黑人艺术家与作品、黑人故事与诗歌等。
2. calf roping 套小牛(用绳将小牛套住,拉倒并绑住小牛的腿)
   rope /rəʊp/ v. 用绳捆绑
3. against the clock 分秒必争地
4. steer wrestling 骑马徒手摔牛
   steer /stɪə/ n. 公牛
5. bulldog /ˈbʊldɒg/ v. 摔牛
6. bull riding 骑公牛

the rodeo. Bulls are considered harder to ride than bucking[7] horses, because their jumps and twists in the air are so unpredictable. The bull rider can hold on with only one hand and must try to stay on for eight seconds. There is always a rodeo clown[8] in the arena. His job is to get the bull's attention after the cowboy is thrown off. Many bulls try to gore[9] or trample[10] the cowboy after he falls off.

Bareback Bronc Riding[11]: Like bull riding, the cowboy in bareback riding wants to try and stay on the bucking horse's back for eight seconds. It is not an easy job, considering that the horse has no bridle[12] or saddle[13]. The cowboy holds onto a single leather strap that goes around the horse's middle, just behind the shoulders.

Saddle Bronc Riding[14]: Unlike bareback riding, cowboys use a saddle on the wild horse for this event. The cowboy is judged on his style. The winner is the rider who can coordinate[15] his movements with those of the horse. The cowboy tries to keep his legs as far forward as possible on the horse' shoulders, sweeping them back when the horse bucks in the air.

Barrel Racing[16]: Barrel racing is the only professional rodeo event in which women participate. The object in this event is to race as fast as possible on horseback around three barrels placed in a triangle. Contestants must race around the barrels in a particular order and make a cloverleaf[17] pattern. A contestant who knocks down a barrel receives a time penalty[18]. The horse and rider with the fastest time wins.

Team Roping[19]: This is the only event where two cowboys compete together and share the prize money. Like calf roping, team roping closely resembles a job cowboys on the open range performed more than a hundred years ago and still perform today. On the open range it takes two cowboys to bring down a steer so that it can be branded[20]. In the rodeo arena, one of the cowboys must rope the steer's horns while his partner ropes the steer's hind legs.

7. buck /bʌk/ v. 跳跃
8. clown /klaʊn/ n. 小丑
9. gore /gɔː/ v. 顶，刺伤
10. trample /ˈtræmpəl/ v. 踩踏
11. bareback bronc riding 无鞍野马骑术　bareback /ˈbeəbæk/ a. 无鞍的　bronc /brɒŋk/ n. 北美西部产的野马
12. bridle /ˈbraɪdl/ n. 马勒
13. saddle /ˈsædl/ n. 鞍
14. saddle bronc riding 有鞍野马骑术
15. coordinate /kəʊˈɔːdmeɪt/ v. 调整
16. barrel racing 速度赛马
17. cloverleaf /ˈkləʊvəliːf/ a. 形状似苜蓿叶的
18. time penalty 比赛中的一种判罚，具体为根据情况以罚时间的方式降低参赛者的成绩。
19. team roping 分组套牛
20. brand /brænd/ v. 打烙印

Comprehension Questions

1. What's the meaning of "steer" in the passage?
2. Which event can girls participate?
3. What's the standard of winning in bull riding?
4. What's the difference between bareback bronc riding and saddle bronc riding?
5. Among the seven events, which one do you like most? Why?

Part I Fad Sports

Background Reading

Rodeo is a sport that grew out of the cattle industry in the American West. Its roots reach back to the sixteenth century. The Spanish conquistadors (征服者) and Spanish-Mexican settlers played a key role in the origin of rodeo with the introduction and propagation (繁殖) of horses and cattle in the Southwest. After the Civil War, with the abundance of wild cattle in the Southwest and a market in the East, the era of the cattle drives, large ranches (大农场), and range cowboys began. Skills of the range cowboy led to competitive contests that eventually resulted in standard events for rodeo. With its roots deep in Southwest history, rodeo continued to evolve (发展) until it has become a professional sport for men and women that is being perpetuated (使……继续) by youth rodeo organizations.

Rodeo spans American history from the Spanish era through the cattle drives and big ranch era to take its place in the twentieth century as a professional sport and a full-time business. With its multicultural heritage, rodeo characterizes the unique traits (特征) of the place of its birth: the American Southwest.

Relevant Words

broke 被驯服的	lasso 套索
outlaw 野马,未驯服或难驯服的马	quirt 皮鞭
tenderfoot 新手	

Part II

Sporting Kaleidoscope

聚焦体育

Lesson 1

> 2004年雅典奥运会期间国际奥委会禁止运动员、教练员和其他一切参与赛事的人员在网上发布有关比赛的日记、照片等,以维护获得奥委会授权媒体的报道权益。这篇文章详细报道了奥委会的禁令,同时采访了有关网站,阐述了他们对于这一禁令的看法和态度。全文篇幅短小,语言流畅,其中一些用词和习惯表达方式颇值得学习应用。

Olympic Athletes Largely Barred from Posting Online Diaries

By Anick Jesdanun
August 20 2004
USA Today[1]

Athletes may be the center of attention at the Olympic Games, but don't expect to hear directly from them online—or see snapshots[2] or video they've taken.

The International Olympic Committee is barring competitors, as well as coaches, support personnel and other officials, from writing firsthand accounts for news and other Web sites.

An exception is if an athlete has a personal Web site that they did not set up specifically for the Games.

The IOC's rationale for the restrictions is that athletes and their coaches should not serve as journalists—and that the interests of broadcast rights-holders and accredited media come first.[3]

Participants in the games may respond to written questions from reporters or participate in online chat sessions—akin to a face-to-face or telephone interview—but they may not post journals or online diaries, blogs[4] in Internet parlance[5], until the Games end on Aug. 29.

To protect lucrative[6] broadcast contracts, athletes and other participants are also prohibited from posting any video, audio or still photos[7] they take themselves, even after the games, unless they get permission ahead of time. (Photos taken by accredited journalists are allowed on the personal sites.)

The editor of a Web site that had arranged athlete diaries called the restrictions shortsighted.

---

1. *USA Today*《今日美国》,于1982年创刊,是美国唯一的彩色版全国性综合日报,每周出版五期,有国内版和国际版,发行量约为140万份。该报主要有四大特点:一是专门开辟"美国各地"和"世界新闻摘要"栏目,便于读者了解美国及世界重大新闻;二是仿效电视气象预报形式,用整版篇幅的彩色气象图表报道全国各州及主要城市3天天气趋势;三是创造性使用生动的图片和图表来配合新闻报道;四是注重使用简洁明快的报道文体,尽可能多地登载信息。
2. snapshot /ˈsnæpʃɒt/ *n.* 快相,快照
3. 国际奥委会对此禁令的解释是:应当让获得报道权的及公认的媒体对赛事进行报道,运动员、教练员、竞赛服务人员和其他各类官员都不应充当记者的角色。rationale /ˌræʃəˈnɑːl/ *n.* 基本理由 accredited /əˈkredɪtɪd/ *a.* 公认的,可接受的
4. blog /blɒɡ/ *n.* 博客,网络日志
5. parlance /ˈpɑːləns/ *n.* 说法;笔调;用语
6. lucrative /ˈluːkrətɪv/ *a.* 有利的;赚钱的
7. still photo 照片 still /stɪl/ *a.* 静止的

"This is unfathomable[8] to me," said Robert Bliwise, editor of *Duke Magazine*, Duke University's alumni publication. "I don't understand what the International Olympic Committee might be concerned about. It's a way to engage a wide audience with reporting from the field and therefore generate excitement and interest in the games."

His site had made arrangements with two graduates, pole vaulter[9] Jillian Schwartz and race walker[10] Curt Clausen, to provide firsthand accounts for the university's alumni.

"This is a means to personalize the Olympics, to excite a constituency[11] with the thrill that comes with the knowledge that a couple of their own are participants in the competition," Bliwise said.

One entry, from Schwartz, remained posted Thursday; Bliwise said he had yet to be[12] formally informed of any violations[13].

But an IOC official, speaking on condition of anonymity[14], said third-party sites like Duke's are covered by the restrictions.

The Olympic guidelines threaten to yank credentials[15] from athletes who are in violation as well as to impose other sanctions[16] or take legal action for any monetary damages.

But the official said the IOC has yet to take any action against an athlete.

The IOC distributed the policies to each country's Olympic committee in February.

8. unfathomable /ʌnˈfæðəməbl/ a. 难以理解的
9. pole vaulter 撑杆跳高运动员
10. race walker 竞走运动员
11. constituency /kənˈstɪtʃuənsɪ/ n. 支持者;赞助者
12. to have yet to do 还没来得及做某事
13. violation /ˌvaɪəˈleɪʃən/ n. 违反规定;违法
14. anonymity /ˌænəˈnɪmɪtɪ/ n. 匿名
15. ...yank credentials 取消资格
    yank /jæŋk/ v. 猛拉;拽
    credentials /krɪˈdenʃəlz/ n. 资格
16. sanction /ˈsæŋkʃən/ n. 制裁

Comprehension Questions

1. Why cannot people expect to hear directly from the athletes online any more?
2. What is IOC's reason for this ban?
3. Besides online diaries, what else are forbidden to be posted online?
4. What does Robert Bliwise think of the ban made by the IOC?
5. Do you think the ban is reasonable? Why or why not?

Background Reading

A Brief Introduction to the IOC

The International Olympic Committee was founded on 23 June 1894 by the French educator Baron Pierre de Coubertin who was inspired to revive (复兴;复活) the Olympic Games of Greek antiquity (古代遗物).

The IOC is an international non-governmental non-profit organisation and the creator of the Olympic Movement. The IOC exists to serve as an umbrella organisation (伞形组织) of the Olympic Movement. It owns all rights to the Olympic symbols, flag, motto, anthem (奥林匹克圣歌) and Olympic Games. Its primary responsibility is to supervise the organisation of the summer and winter Olympic Games.

The IOC President is elected by the IOC members by secret ballot (投票) for an initial term of eight years, renewable (可续的) once for four additional years. The President presides over all activities of the IOC, acting as its permanent representative. The current President, since 16 July 2001, is Jacques Rogge, of Belgium.

The Executive Board, founded in 1921, consists of the IOC President, four Vice-Presidents and ten other members. All the members of the Executive Board are elected by the Session, by secret ballot, by a majority of votes cast, for a four-year term.

The members of the IOC are individuals who act as the IOC's representatives in their respective countries, not as delegates of their country within the IOC. The members meet once a year at the IOC Session. They retire at the end of the calendar year of which they turn 70 years, unless they were elected before the opening of the 110th Session (11 December 1999). In that case, they must retire when they reach the age of 80. The term of office for all members is eight years, renewable every eight years. The IOC chooses and elects its members from among such persons as its nominations (提名) committee considers qualified. All Olympic Movement members have the right to submit nominations.

The IOC administration is at the service of the needs of the Olympic Movement. It prepares, implements and follows-up on a day-to-day basis the decisions taken by the main organisations of the Olympic Movement.

Relevant Words

IOC Executive Board   国际奥委会执行委员会
Olympic Congress   奥林匹克代表大会
Olympic Session   国际奥委会全会
television and radio rights holder   广播电视转播权所有者
television rights   电视转播权
the Olympic Partner (TOP) Program   奥林匹克合作伙伴计划(又称"TOP 计划")

Lesson 2

《奥林匹克宪章》规定,只有国际奥委会拥有奥运会主办城市的确定权。参与申办奥运会的城市首先要经过国际奥委会的一系列评估,由国际奥委会执行委员会进行筛选,确定三至五个候选城市。最后,候选城市要在国际奥委会全会上做陈述报告并回答委员们的提问,陈述报告和提问结束后全体委员通过投票表决的方式决定奥运会主办城市。2005 年 7 月 5 日,在新加坡举行的国际奥委会第 117 次全会上,纽约、伦敦、莫斯科、巴黎、马德里五个候选城市分别做了陈述报告,这是各城市在主办城市确定前的最后一搏,他们的报告各有特色,体现了各自的民族特点和精神。

Cities Make Their Final Pitches[1] as Olympic Committee Nears Vote

By Lynn Zinser
July 6, 2005
The New York Times[2]

SINGAPORE, July 6—Opening with a video celebrating ethnic diversity and closing with a moving portrait of a torch being run through the city, New York Olympic bid organizers unveiled[3] their vision of the 2012 Games today. They stressed the city's international flavor, its organizers' enthusiasm, the economic boost these Games would give the Olympics and also made a small emotional reference to Sept. 11, 2001.[4]

The bid founder, Deputy Mayor[5] Daniel L. Doctoroff, began by nervously telling the International Olympic Committee the story of his Olympic dream, which began at a World Cup soccer match in the Meadowlands 11 years ago when he was overwhelmed by the Italian and Bulgarian[6] fans who filled Giants Stadium with so much spirit.

"We are a city that wraps its arms around you," Doctoroff said. "When you score a perfect 10, the crowd will rise and cheer, no matter where you are from."

This was New York's last pitch before the 116-member I.O.C. chooses the 2012 Olympic city from among New York, Paris, London, Madrid and Moscow. The voting will begin today at 5:45 a.m. Eastern

---

1. pitch /pɪtʃ/ n. 投掷(这里指各申办城市在做最后的努力)
2. *The New York Times*《纽约时报》原名为《纽约每日时报》(*The New York Daily Times*),创刊于 1851 年 9 月 18 日,1857 年 9 月 14 日改用现名。现由苏兹贝格(Sulzberger)家族所有,是美国三大报纸之一,在美国最负盛名,有"档案记录报"的美称。它是一张比较严肃的报纸,能比较充分和详尽地报道国内国际大事,特别是对重大事件的报道有其独到之处。为此,它在美国报纸中得到普利策奖(Pulitzer Prize)的次数最多。
3. unveil /ʌnˈveɪl/ v. 揭幕
4. ...and also made a small emotional reference to Sept. 11, 2001. 并略有伤感地提及了 2001 年 9 月 11 日发生的恐怖袭击事件。
5. Deputy Mayor 副市长
6. Bulgarian /bʌlˈɡeərɪən/ n. 保加利亚人

time, and the winner will be announced at 7:45.

New York followed Paris in the presentations, an order that was decided by a random drawing[7]. The French presentation had an artistic flair[8], with an aerial tour of the city and Olympic rings floating around its landmarks. French President Jacques Chirac and Paris Mayor Bertrand Delanoe made emotional pleas to bring the Games to their city on its third modern bid.

In New York's sales pitch, Olympians Janet Evans[9] and Bob Beamon[10] took the stage to describe the Olympic sites and the plan for each Olympic sport. New York also had videos with testimony[11] from dozens of athletes, from the tennis star Serena Williams[12] and the boxer Sugar Ray Leonard[13] to the basketball legend Magic Johnson[14] and the cycling champion Lance Armstrong[15], in describing the plans for the Olympic sites.

Former President Bill Clinton appeared via video, as did President George W. Bush. Mayor Michael R. Bloomberg emphasized that the new Olympic stadium plan has been approved.

"Let me be clear, we are going ahead and building this stadium," Bloomberg said. "It is going ahead because New Yorkers never give up. Not now, not ever."

He also strongly emphasized that New York was not here as a setup for a bid in 2016, a charge the other cities have been using against the bid.[16] As Bloomberg introduced Senator Hillary Rodham Clinton of New York, she echoed that theme.

"2012 is the right time for New York," she said. "And it's the right time for the world to experience New York."

Bloomberg veered[17] briefly from the New York strategy of avoiding mention of the terrorist attacks of Sept. 11. Late in his remarks, he highlighted New York's rebound[18] from the tragedy, and the final video, which followed a torch runner through the city, showed a tiny clip of a child's drawing of the Twin Towers[19] with the words, written in crayon[20], "The sky was so blue."

As the final video faded to black, the NYC2012 logo appeared on

7. drawing /ˈdrɔːɪŋ/ n. 抽签
8. flair /fleə/ n. 特别的风格
9. Janet Evans 珍妮特·埃文斯(美国著名游泳运动员,1988年汉城奥运会女子400米自由泳金牌得主)
10. Bob Beamon 鲍勃·比蒙(美国著名跳远运动员,1968年在墨西哥城奥运会跳远比赛中,以8.90米的成绩创造了"神话般的世界纪录")
11. testimony /ˈtestɪmənɪ/ n. 陈述
12. Serena Williams 塞雷娜·威廉姆斯(一般称"小威廉姆斯",美国职业网球女运动员)
13. Sugar Ray Leonard 雷欧纳德(美国拳击手)
14. Magic Johnson 魔术师约翰逊(美国篮球运动员,曾经效力于洛杉矶湖人队)
15. Lance Armstrong 兰斯·阿姆斯特朗(美国公路自行车赛职业车手)
16. 他还强调,纽约并不是像其他城市指责的那样,今天来这里申办2012年奥运会只是为2016年申办热身。(意思是这次申办,纽约志在必得。)
17. veer /vɪə/ v. 转向
18. rebound /rɪˈbaʊnd/ n. 振作,从失望或衰败中迅速恢复或迅速作出的反应
19. Twin Towers 双塔(即在9·11事件中被炸毁的世贸大厦)
20. crayon /ˈkreɪən/ n. 蜡笔;有色粉笔

the screen with the words, "Thank you."

Organizers were thrilled with how the presentation went, the only stumble being Muhammad Ali[21] faltering[22] as he stood to acknowledge the I.O.C.

"What we tried to say was, this is New York," Bloomberg said afterward. "We've never tried to be anything other than what we are." The question-and-answer portion had a tense moment when an I.O.C. member from Syria, Samih Moudallal, pointedly[23] asked Mr. Doctoroff, "Would the athletes and the officials of these countries on the terrorist list, will they be allowed to enter the United States of America?" He went on to reference what he said were problems Syria had obtaining a visa for one of its Paralympic[24] athletes during the 1996 Games in Atlanta.

Dr. Jacques Rogge, the president of the International Olympic Committee, rebuked[25] Mr. Moudallal, telling him, "You should not come back to issues of the past for which New York is not responsible."

Still, Mr. Doctoroff chose to answer, saying there was "absolutely no question" all nations would be welcomed. He told of the Iranian wrestling team's visit to the wrestling world championships when they were held in New York City in 2003. "I will never forget the Iranian team competing in New York in front of packed crowds of Iranian fans," Mr. Doctoroff said.

New York was followed by Moscow, which came nowhere near the professional quality of New York, but did place a heavy emphasis on the Russian love of sports and its Olympic success. Organizers played a video from Russian President Vladimir Putin, in which he spoke in faltering English. Moscow officials said it was a Russian leader's first-ever public address in English.

Paris had begun its presentation with a note of humility[26], a nod to the criticism that its past two bids were too arrogant[27] and turned off an organization that prefers to be wooed[28].

"Each defeat has served to increase our determination," Delanoe said, in French. Then, in another nod to previous criticisms about their reluctance to speak English, he spoke a few sentences in English: "I want to thank you for setting the bar so high and pushing us further toward excellence.[29]"

President Chirac, who did not attend the presentation for the last Paris bid, in 2001, made the most emotional appeal. He emphasized his long relationship with many I.O.C. members and talked about the

---

21. Muhammad Ali 穆罕默德·阿里(美国拳击手,被称为是"最伟大的拳王")
22. falter /ˈfɔːltə/ v. 蹒跚；踉跄
23. pointedly /ˈpɔɪntɪdlɪ/ ad. 尖锐地
24. Paralympic /ˌpærəˈlɪmpɪk/ a. 残疾人奥运会的
25. rebuke /rɪˈbjuːk/ v. 斥责,指责
26. humility /hjuːˈmɪlɪtɪ/ n. 谦卑
27. arrogant /ˈærəɡənt/ a. 傲慢的
28. woo /wuː/ v. 恳求
29. 我要感谢你们把(申办的)要求设置得如此之高,激励我们在通向完美的道路上一步一步坚实前进。

French people's desire to host the Games. "I shall vouch[30] for this," he said in French. "You can put your trust in France. You can trust the French. You can trust us."

But at heart, the presentation was built around Paris pouring its heart into its third and presumably final bid. "Paris wants the Games," Delanoe said in closing. "Paris needs the Games. Paris has the love of the Games."

In the question-and-answer session afterward, I.O.C. members asked about the anti-doping[31] plans, guarantees for building the Olympic village and, bizarrely enough, the quality of French air conditioning.

London's presentation centered on the theme of inspiring young people. Bid leader Sebastian Coe told the story of how he was moved to begin running when he watched the 1968 Mexico City Olympics on a tiny, black and white television. His career culminated[32] in two Olympic gold medals.

"Thirty-five years later, I stand before you still inspired by the Olympic movement," he said.

London's film promoted the diversity of its people and the iconic[33] backdrop of its venues. It also stressed the uniqueness of its plan to put the Olympic village within the confines[34] of its Olympic park.

But the presentation kept coming back to children, including the 30 that organizers brought along from East London, the area planned for massive regeneration[35] if the Games are awarded to the British capital.

"More than six million young people visit our city every year, and more of them choose our city for their education than any other," said London Mayor Ken Livingstone. "If you wish to mobilize the youth of the world, start in London."

Madrid's presentation was the least professional, relying on still photos with type superimposed[36] for most of its visuals, as opposed to higher-quality video used by the other bids. Madrid saved its sports plans for last, with a few athletes involved in the presentation. It was the only bid to feature a Paralympian[37], Gema Hassen-Bey.

Prime Minister Jose Luis Rodriguez Zapatero of Spain made a presentation, as did Madrid Mayor Alberto Ruiz-Gallardon, who ventured[38] to speak some English. They emphasized that Madrid is the largest European capital yet to host a Games and that the public support numbers have been higher than any other city's.

"Madrid will be a fiesta[39]," Ruiz-Gallardon said. "We have been

30. vouch /vaʊtʃ/ v. 保证,担保

31. anti-doping 反兴奋剂

32. culminate /ˈkʌlmɪneɪt/ v. 达到高峰,达到顶点

33. iconic /aɪˈkɒnɪk/ a. 图标的
34. confines /ˈkɒnfaɪnz/ n. 疆界;范围

35. regeneration /rɪˌdʒenəˈreɪʃn/ n. 再生;重建

36. superimpose /ˌsjuːpərɪmˈpəʊz/ v. 置于……之上

37. Paralympian 残疾人奥运会运动员

38. venture /ˈventʃə/ v. 冒险

39. fiesta /fiˈestə/ n. (西班牙语)节日

celebrating the Olympic spirit for 50 years now."

Queen Sofia finished the presentation, stressing her family's commitment to sports.

The presentation order was decided by random drawing, with each city given 45 minutes for a presentation and 15 minutes to answer questions from I.O.C. members. Paris went first, followed by New York, Moscow, London and Madrid.

The voting will proceed by rounds, with the city receiving the least number of votes dropping out after every round. The rounds will proceed until one city has a majority of the votes.

Comprehension Questions

1. What are the factors that the New York organizers stressed in the opening video? Explain in details of the factors in your own words.
2. What is the most important reason for Paris's failure during the last two bids?
3. What is the focus of London's presentation?
4. How is the city chosen with the voting?
5. In your opinion, which city should be the host of the 2012 Olympics? Why?

Background Reading

Denise Lewis' Singapore Presentation—6 July 2005

Mr President, Members of the IOC,

I'm Denise Lewis, Olympic Heptathlon (七项全能) champion from the Sydney Games.

I have the pleasure of speaking on behalf of the London Athletes Commission.

I was eight when I was inspired by the Moscow Games.

I dreamt of emulating (仿效) the athletes I watched. And my dreams came true when I competed in Atlanta, in Sydney and in Athens.

Like every Olympian, I have unforgettable Olympic memories.

And we in London are determined every athlete will leave our city with friendships and memories which last forever.

Our Athletes Commission had to answer one fundamental question: how do you give athletes the best possible Olympic experience?

We said: give us the best Village in the most convenient location. Everything else follows.

Our Village is within walking distance of nine venues. In London, athletes will compete, not commute.

The Village is inside the Park to guarantee the athletes a special experience. Take it from me, it makes all the difference to be as close to the action as possible.

In fact, the whole London plan was conceived (构思) with our input. Everything athletes need was designed in from day one. Training venues. Security. And, of course, the needs of Paralympians.

These are the things athletes want.

When a fraction of a second, or a fraction of a centimetre, can be the difference between winning and losing and can change your life you appreciate that the small details have been worked out years before.

That's why we athletes are proud the Evaluation Commission praised our contribution.

In London your athletes will compete in venues packed with passionate fans, renowned for their sense of fair play.

Thanks to the city's diversity, there will be supporters from every Olympic nation. Every athlete will have a home crowd (本土球迷).

And every Paralympian will enjoy a fantastic atmosphere too, from British crowds famous for their love of Paralympic sport.

You, and every athlete in 2012, will never forget the magic of London.

Relevant Words

Beijing 2008 Olympic Games Bidding Committee (BOBICO)　北京奥申委
Beijing Organizing Committee for the Games of the XXIX Olympiad (BOCOG)　北京奥组委
bid for 2008 Olympics　申办2008年奥运会
bid for the Olympic Games　申办奥运会
Green Olympics, People's Olympics and Hi-tech Olympics　绿色奥运, 人文奥运, 科技奥运
host the 2008 Olympic Games　主办2008年奥运会
New Beijing, Great Olympics　新北京, 新奥运
the bidding cities　申办城市
the candidate cities　候选城市
the International Olympic Committee (IOC)　国际奥委会
the International Olympic Day　世界奥林匹克日
the Olympic ideals; the Olympic spirit　奥林匹克精神
the Universiade　世界大学生运动会

Lesson 3

> 今日的中国是奥运竞技场上的金牌大户,世人瞩目的体育大国,然而中国的奥运之路并不平坦。本文作者简要地回忆了中国加入奥委会大家庭、恢复奥运席位、驰骋诸届奥运赛场的历史,惊叹于中国运动员的出色发挥。文章最后指出,为了迎接2008年北京奥运会,中国政府正在积极行动,杜绝兴奋剂和腐败现象,运动员们也摩拳擦掌,准备在自己祖国主办的奥运会上有一番作为。

Beijing 2008 Olympic Journal: China's Olympic Legacy[1]

By Mary Nicole Nazzaro
October 2005
American Track & Field[2]

We saw two great moments in Chinese sports last month. First, 110-meter hurdler[3] Liu Xiang won both the inaugural[4] Shanghai Golden Grand Prix[5] and the Seiko Super Track and Field Meet[6] in Japan. And women's tennis star Sun Tiantian beat Serena Williams at the China Open[7] in Beijing, after which she spoke openly of her goal to win a Grand Slam title[8]. Both Liu and Sun are 2004 Olympic gold medallists, and both have dreams of more gold to come in 2008. They have quite an illustrious[9] past to look to among their fellow Chinese athletes to inspire them.

Today China is a medal-making machine, especially in the summer Olympics, where the nation has won 286 medals, including 112 golds. Even more astonishing, that medal haul[10] has come in just the last six Olympic Games. The political wheelings and dealings[11] of the past sixty years have affected China's Olympic history greatly, putting into even greater perspective the importance that China attaches to the 2008 Olympics.

China's first Olympic athlete was a sprinter[12], Liu Changchun, who ran in the 1932 Olympic Games in Los Angeles. China participated in the 1936 Summer Games in Berlin before the entire Olympic movement was halted[13] by World War II.

1. legacy /'legəsi/ *n.* 遗产;成就
2. *American Track & Field*《美国田径》,美国田径协会的官方媒体,双月刊,在世锦赛和奥运会年发行增刊,为专业运动员和教练员提供田径训练方面的信息,其内容涵盖个人项目训练、运动营养和运动心理等诸多领域。
3. hurdler /'hɜːdlə/ *n.* 跨栏比赛选手
4. inaugural /ɪ'nɔːgjʊrəl/ *a.* 首次的
5. Shanghai Golden Grand Prix 上海国际田径黄金大奖赛
6. Seiko Super Track and Field Meet 日本横滨田径全明星赛
7. China Open 中国网球公开赛
8. Grand Slam title 网球大满贯头衔
9. illustrious /ɪ'lʌstrɪəs/ *a.* 辉煌的,杰出的
10. medal haul 奖牌总数;奖牌大丰收
11. wheelings and dealings 手段
12. sprinter /'sprɪntə/ *n.* 短跑选手
13. halt /hɔːlt/ *v.* 停止

China's athletes wouldn't appear at the Olympic doorstep again until the Lake Placid winter games of 1980[14]. Joining the American-led boycott[15] of the Moscow summer Olympics that year ensured that the world would wait another four years before witnessing the return of the People's Republic to the summer Olympic stage.

It was worth the wait. The medal haul in Los Angeles began when Xu Haifeng (pronounced "shoo high-fung") won the PRC's first gold medal in shooting's free pistol[16] event. Then, men's gymnastics[17] star Li Ning won six medals, including three golds, earning him a legacy in China that continues to this day as China's "Prince of Gymnastics." His gold haul continues to this day, as Li has become a successful business owner and founder of the Beijing Li-Ning Sporting Goods Company, which aims to rival[18] Nike for China's sports market share[19]. Xu Haifeng has stayed in the sporting world as well, as the head coach for China's national shooting team. Overall, Chinese athletes won 32 medals in Los Angeles, including 15 golds, placing fourth in the medal count[20] among all nations competing. Even with the Soviet boycott, it was an impressive showing.

The Seoul haul in 1988 was a commendable[21] 28 medals, for eleventh overall in the medal count. But ever since Barcelona in 1992, the Chinese have been on fire[22]. They've won 50 or more medals in the four summer Olympics since then, and in 2004, their 63 medals brought them to second overall in the medal count behind the United States. Needless to say, the Chinese sports leadership has made no secret of[23] its hopes to take that final step to the top of the medal count in Beijing.

China's participation in the summer Olympics hasn't been without its share of controversies.[24] Doping allegations[25] concerning both the women's long-distance running squad[26] and the women's swim team dogged[27] the country through much of the 1990's. This month China is putting on its own version[28] of the Olympics, the quadrennial National Games[29], considered to be the second most important sports meeting in China next to the Olympics. The English-language press in China has reported that officials are doing everything they can to stamp out[30] doping and corruption[31] among officials. Human growth hormone[32] is being tested for at these games, according to China Daily, and 26 athletes who failed doping tests were barred[33] from even showing up in Nanjing in China's Jiangsu province to compete.

No doubt Liu Xiang and Sun Tiantian relish[34] the chance at the

14. 中国运动员直到 1980 年的宁静湖冬奥会才重返奥运赛场。Lake Placid 宁静湖（位于美国纽约州，曾于 1932 年和 1980 年承办冬季奥运会）doorstep /ˈdɔːstep/ n. 门阶；门前台阶
15. boycott /ˈbɔɪkɒt/ n. 联合抵制
16. free pistol 自由手枪
17. gymnastics /dʒɪmˈnæstɪks/ n. 体操
18. rival /ˈraɪvəl/ v. 竞争
19. market share 市场份额
20. medal count 奖牌榜
21. commendable /kəˈmendəbəl/ a. 值得赞扬的
22. to be on fire 着火（这里指在奥运会上成绩一直非常好）
23. to make no secret of 毫不掩饰……
24. 中国参加夏季奥运会的时候总是惹来争议。controversy /ˈkɒntrəvɜːsi/ n. 争论
25. doping allegations 怀疑服用兴奋剂   dope /dəʊp/ v. 服用兴奋剂   allegation /ˌælɪˈɡeɪʃən/ n. 指称；断言
26. women's long-distance running squad 女子长跑队
27. dog /dɒɡ/ v. (灾难等) 缠住
28. version /ˈvɜːʃən/ n. 版本
29. the quadrennial National Games 每四年一次的全国运动会 quadrennial /kwɒˈdrenjəl/ a. 每四年一次的
30. to stamp out 杜绝
31. corruption /kəˈrʌpʃən/ n. 腐败
32. human growth hormone 人类生长激素
33. bar /bɑː/ v. 阻止
34. relish /ˈrelɪʃ/ v. 享用

National Games to enhance their legacies as two of China's brightest hopes for 2008. As of this writing, Sun's Henan province women's tennis team had advanced to the semifinals of the team event[35]. For his part, Liu Xiang was waiting for his chance to compete once again in front of a home crowd. (Shanghai, his hometown, is just a few hours down the road from National Games host city Nanjing.)

As the buildup[36] to 2008 continues to grow, so will the expectations of success by Chinese athletes. And if the Chinese themselves have anything to say about it, so will their medal counts at all the important events leading up to the most important one of all: the 2008 Summer Olympics in Beijing.

35. team event 团体比赛

36. buildup/ˈbɪldʌp/ *n.* 舆论, 宣传

Comprehension Questions

1. What are the two great moments that the journalist refers to as happening last month?
2. Why was there an absence of Chinese competitors at the Olympics in 1980?
3. Who is known as China's "Prince of Gymnastics" and what did he do to earn this accolade?
4. What are the "controversies" referred to by the journalist and what are Chinese officials doing to stamp these out?
5. Given China's track record in the summer Olympics over the last 20-30 years, what are your expectations of their performance in 2008?

Background Reading

Bid for 2008

July 13, 2001 saw a jubilant (喜气洋洋的) and sleepless night in Beijing, capital of the People's Republic of China and winner of the bid for the Games of the XXIV Olympiad in 2008.

At the 112th IOC Session held in Moscow, the Chinese delegation's bid presentation left a lasting impression on the IOC members present. Vice-Premier Li Lanqing reaffirmed that the Chinese Government stands firmly behind Beijing in its bid for the 2008 Olympic Games and will do whatever it can to ensure a successful and excellent Games in Beijing. When IOC President Juan Antonio Samaranch declared Beijing as the host for the 2008 Olympic Games, all the Chinese watching the live telecast (电视直播) of the voting burst into thunderous cheers and applause. Beijing won in a landslide (压倒性优势) victory in the second round secret ballot with an overwhelming majority of 56 votes for from 105 voting IOC members, ahead of its rivals Toronto with 22, Paris 18 and Istanbul (伊斯坦布尔) 9. Osaka (大阪), which received six votes, bowed out after the first round.

It was not only a glory for Beijing but also a significant achievement for the entire nation, as being the host to the Olympic Games would undoubtedly bring new business and opportunities within Beijing and throughout China.

The Olympic Games are celebrated around the world as a big sports gala (节日) with great significance of maintaining peace, enhancing friendship and promoting civilization. As one of the most influential countries in the world today, China is willing to do its best to promote the Olympic Movement. It is the aspiration of both Beijing residents and the Chinese people to share the Olympic spirit, take part in Olympic affairs and host the Olympic Games. Over the past two decades, China has achieved social stability and economic prosperity through reform, opening up to the outside world and modernization, and its national strength has increased greatly.

According to the results of a public poll conducted by Gallup (盖洛普民意测验) Organization in Beijing in November 2000, 94.9% percent of the residents in Beijing strongly supported the city's bid to host the 2008 Olympics. With regard to whether Beijing would be successful in winning the bid, 62.4% were fairly confident that Beijing would win.

Beijing's renewed efforts to bid for the Olympic Games and its final success in the bid not only have the significance for sharing the Olympic spirit, celebrating humanity and expanding exchanges between the East and the West, but also help provide a good opportunity of showing the current state of economic, cultural, social and political development in China in a comprehensive way. While showing to the world a new, vigorous image of an open, modernized, civilized and well-developed metropolis in the lead-up to the 2008 Olympics, Beijing is ready to become a truly international city and make every effort to deliver a "Green Olympics," a "Hi-Tech Olympics," a "People's Olympics" and, to top it all, an unprecedented (空前的) Olympics that would leave, as an IOC Evaluation Commission report believes, a unique legacy for both China and sport as a whole.

Relevant Words

Slam 最初是桥牌用语,指 the winning of all the tricks during the play of one hand in bridge (在桥牌中全胜),现常用于体育赛事。Grand Slam 就是网球界常常提到的"大满贯赛事",包括：

> the Wimbledon Tournament （英国温布尔登网球锦标赛）
> the US Open （美国网球公开赛）
> the Australian Open （澳大利亚网球公开赛）
> the French Open （法国网球公开赛）

Lesson 4

意大利是文艺复兴的发源地,有着悠久的文化历史和传统,同时,意大利拥有丰富的广场建筑文化。2006 年在意大利都灵举行的第 20 届冬季奥运会上,意大利人在奥运的海报、宣传画上尽情展示了他们的文化和历史。他们用极富民族特色的广场文化元素和多姿的色彩巧妙地将奥运理想与民族特色融为一体,用他们特有的方式欢迎来自世界各地的宾朋。

Fresh Perspectives—A Look at Torino 2006's as Olympic Committee Nears Vote

By Glyn Wilmshurst

January, February, March 2005

Olympic Review[1]

  Back in the 1400s, Italian Renaissance[2] artist Masaccio[3] portrayed[4] an original form of perspective[5], which was then perfected by Italian masters from Michelangelo[6] to De Chirico[7], renowned the world over for their magnificent artistry. So it is fitting that Torino 2006's "Look at the Games" will mark its own place in the history books by building on these artistic traditions and the nation's modern reputation for ground-breaking[8] design, to use perspective to bring a "third dimension[9]" to Olympic visual identity for the first time.

  Perspective helps "draw in" spectators to a picture, just as Turin will welcome visitors and television viewers to the city next February.

1. *Olympic Review*《奥林匹克综览》,1894 年创刊,系国际奥委会官方出版物,主要介绍奥林匹克文化、奥运会申办、比赛以及奥运会比赛项目等。1973 年以英语、法语、西班牙语三种文字同时出版,并于 2003 年由双月刊改为季刊。
2. Renaissance /rɪˈneɪsəns/ 文艺复兴(古典艺术、建筑、文学和学识的人文主义复兴,起源于 14 世纪的意大利,后来蔓延到整个欧洲。大约从 14 世纪到 16 世纪的复兴时期,标志着从中世纪到现代时期的过渡。)
3. Masaccio 马萨乔(意大利佛罗伦萨画派画家)
4. portray /pɔːˈtreɪ/ v. 描绘
5. perspective /pəˈspektɪv/ n. 透视图
6. Michelangelo 米开朗基罗(1475—1564,意大利文艺复兴时期成就卓著的科学家、艺术家)
7. De Chirico 基里柯(Giorgio de Chirico,意大利画家)
8. ground-breaking /ˈgraʊnd ˈbreɪkɪŋ/ a. 首创的,破天荒的
9. third dimension 第三维,立体感

And while those visitors may not be aware of all the symbolism[10] in TOROC's[11] designs, there is no doubt that the vivid colours and integrated[12] designs across the city and inside and outside of the venues, from posters[13] to banners[14] and boards by the field of play, will make a huge contribution to their Olympic experience.

Turin's Look[15] first took shape in 2001 with the creation of its logo, explains Andrea Varnier, Director of Image & Communications. The next step was to define a theme—TOROC chose "passion", part of the "added value" it intends to bring to the Games. TOROC also wanted to embrace one of the key Olympic values in their Look, and selected "participation".

"We tried to make a sum of[16] the two concepts, Italian passion and Olympic participation," says Varnier. "The way we chose to do this was through the concept of the 'piazza'."

"The piazza is a very Italian concept. It is where people meet, talk, eat and drink, shop and where they celebrate."

If the Piazza Castello[17] will be at the heart of the celebrations next February, TOROC has plans that a "Virtual[18] Piazza"—a place for the athletes to meet, participate and celebrate—will be present in the designs surrounding every Olympic venue.

The arches of the piazza will be part of the perimeter[19] board by the venues. There are even plans to be submitted[20] to the International Federations that the starting gates in the ski races will have an "arched" design—rather than their usual rectangular[21] shape.

The "core graphic" of Turin's Look began with a palette[22] of colours. Alongside the red passion, each colour is intended to represent an aspect of Italian excellence: yellow (art & culture); blue (sport, the national team colour); green (environment); black (style); purple (the wine grape, representing tastes); and silver-grey (innovation).

For visual reasons, there needs to be a dominant splash of blue next to the field of play so that television pictures come through clearly.

"You can't do everything red because television would not allow it," says Varnier. "You have to create a palette that gives you a lot of opportunities outside the venues. But in the venues you need the right amount of blue."

The core graphic is full of contrasts. First there is the contrast between day and night. Then there is the contrast of the city, with its

10. symbolism /ˈsɪmbəlɪzəm/ n. 象征主义
11. TOROC = Torino Organising Committee for the XX Olympic Winter Games 第二十届奥林匹克冬季奥运会组织委员会(都灵冬奥会组委会)
12. integrated /ˈɪntɪɡreɪtɪd/ a. 综合的
13. poster /ˈpəʊstə/ n. 海报,张贴画
14. banner /ˈbænə/ n. 旗帜;标语
15. look /lʊk/ n. 形象

16. to make a sum of 把……综合起来

17. Piazza Castello 卡斯泰洛广场(都灵的政治和宗教中心) piazza /piˈætsə/ n. 广场
18. virtual /ˈvɜːtʃʊəl/ a. 虚拟的

19. perimeter /pəˈrɪmɪtə/ n. 周边;边缘
20. submit /səbˈmɪt/ v. 提交
21. rectangular /rekˈtæŋɡjʊlə/ a. 矩形的,长方形的
22. palette /ˈpælɪt/ n. 调色板;颜料

hard, architectural edges, to the soft, natural lines of the mountains. Finally there is the contrast between ice and snow—the ice venues in the city and the snow venues in the mountains.

The pictograms[23] designed for each Olympic sport are an integral part of the concept, with their dynamic[24] outlines expected to be portrayed on the banners outside the venues.

On a visit to Turin where he was presented with designs for the Turin Look, Jean-Claude Killy, Chairman of the IOC's Coordination Commission[25], said: "The new graphic elements are the fruits of the best Italian style. All of these projects, particularly in the Look, are a marvelous reflection of Italian genius."

Underpinning[26] the concepts of passion, participation and piazza, nowhere is this better reflected than in the use of perspective. With echoes going back to the Renaissance, Turin's Look of the Games will have a depth of imagery[27] that truly connects the past to the present.

23. pictogram /ˈpɪktəɡræm/ n. = pictograph 象形图
24. dynamic /daɪˈnæmɪk/ a. 动态的；动感的
25. IOC's Coordination Commission 国际奥委会协调委员会
26. underpin /ˌʌndəˈpɪn/ v. 巩固；加强
27. imagery /ˈɪmɪdʒərɪ/ n. 肖像

Comprehension Questions

1. What factors were taken into consideration when Turin's Look was designed?
2. When did Turin's Look first take shape? What is the definition of the logo?
3. How are the two concepts of Italian passion and Olympic participation combined in Turin's Look?
4. What were the starting gates in the ski races like during the previous winter Olympics? Will there be any changes on the gates in the Turin winter Olympics?
5. What are the prominent features of Turin's Look?

Background Reading

A Brief History of Winter Olympic Games

Olympic Games, international sports competition, held every four years at a different site, in which athletes from different nations compete against each other in a variety of sports. There are two types of Olympics, the Summer Olympics and the Winter Olympics. Through 1992 they were held in the same year, but beginning in 1994 they were rescheduled so that they are held in alternate (交替的) even-numbered (偶数的) years. For example, the Winter Olympics were held in 1994 and the Summer Olympics in 1996. The Winter Olympics were next held in 1998, and the Summer Olympics next occurred in 2000.

The Winter Olympic Games were first held as a separate competition in 1924 at Chamonix-Mont-

Blanc (查默尼克斯,全名为查默尼克斯勃朗峰,法国小镇,滑雪胜地), France. From that time until 1992, they took place the same year as the Summer Games. However, beginning with the 1994 Winter Olympics in Lillehammer (利勒哈默尔, 挪威奥普兰郡首府), Norway, the Winter Games were rescheduled to occur in the middle of the Olympic cycle, alternating on even-numbered years with the Summer Games. The 1924 Winter Games included 14 events in five different sports. By comparison, the program for the 2002 Winter Games, held in Salt Lake City, Utah, included more than 75 events in 15 different sports.

Relevant Words

biathlon   冬季两项
luge   无舵雪橇
Nordic combined   北欧两项(越野滑雪和跳台滑雪)
short track speed skating   短道速滑
skeleton   冰橇

Lesson 5

足球和棒球都起源于 18 世纪的英国,最初都属于贵族运动。几百年过去了,它们的发展却呈现出不同特色。棒球在财务计划方面做得很出色,却在联赛内部管理等方面缺乏活力,联盟内部的球队没有优胜劣汰的机制,使得该项运动得不到大面积推广和普及,最终被排除在 2012 年奥运会大门之外;而足球却借助了球队升降级制度使得运动本身更加精彩,风靡全世界,但同时这种制度在财务方面却有一些不安全因素。两项运动可以在财务计划、赛事组织等方面相互学习,共同发展。

'Pastime[1]' Reveals Story of Two Sports

By John Haydon
September 24, 2005
The Washington Times[2]

Those of us who remain in the press box[3] long after the last ball has been kicked at a D.C. United[4] game see RFK Stadium[5] slowly transformed from a soccer venue into a baseball park. By the time we've packed away[6] our laptops[7], the goal posts[8] are long gone and the pitcher's[9] mound[10] is taking shape[11]. It's a somewhat surreal[12] sight. Here we have baseball and soccer co-existing so closely together but culturally worlds apart.

While baseball is known as America's pastime, soccer has been called the world's pastime. Soccer has been accepted by much of the world, but baseball's influence around the globe has been limited. The impact of these sports and their strengths and weaknesses, are

1. pastime /ˈpɑːstaɪm/ *n.* 消遣,娱乐
2. *The Washington Times*《华盛顿时报》,由统一教团(Unification Church)创始人、韩国人文鲜明(Sun Myung Moon)于 1982 年在美国华盛顿创刊,是一份保守、右倾的日报。该报一直以来都努力要把自己塑造成《华盛顿邮报》的主要对手,然而其发行量仅为 12 万份左右,为《华盛顿邮报》的七分之一。该报尽管受到美国保守派的推崇,但大多数新闻记者对其评价并不高,认为其受到统一教团的宗教价值观影响,观点有失公允。
3. press box 新闻记者席
4. D.C. United 华盛顿 DC 联队(美国棒球大联盟队伍之一)
5. RFK Stadium 罗伯特·F·肯尼迪纪念体育场(一般称肯尼迪体育场,位于华盛顿)
6. to pack away 收拾,整理
7. laptop /ˈlæptɒp/ *n.* 笔记本电脑
8. goal post 球门柱
9. pitcher /ˈpɪtʃə/ *n.* (棒球)投手
10. mound /maʊnd/ *n.* 小土墩
11. to take shape 成形
12. surreal /səˈrɪəl/ *a.* 离奇的;超现实主义的

examined in a fascinating new book called: "National Pastime: How Americans Play Baseball and The Rest of the World Plays Soccer" by Stefan Szymanski and Andrew Zimbalist (Brookings Institution Press, D.C., 263 pages).

Szymanski, who teaches economics at the Imperial College in London, offers the soccer perspective, while Zimbalist, a professor of economics at Smith College in Massachusetts, gives baseball's side[13].

Baseball and soccer began at about the same time in the 1850s, as upper-middle class leisure sports, which soon spread to the lower classes. And both sports modeled their rules on cricket, which had developed its rules a century before.

The authors analyze what they term[14] the "open" system of soccer and the "closed" system of baseball, and how these systems affected the sport's influence around the world.

In the "closed leagues" of baseball, owners control the number of franchises[15] and locations of teams, and mediocre[16] clubs are offered security. In contrast, Europe's big soccer leagues are "open leagues", where poor teams are relegated and replaced by promoted clubs[17]. New teams also have the chance to advance up the ladder of the divisions in the league. As soccer teams move up and down, baseball teams stay put[18].

For example, Wigan Athletic, a small team from the provinces that entered the four-division English League in 1978, is making its first appearance in the lucrative[19] Premier League[20] this season, while Nottingham Forest[21], once the champion of Europe, has slipped down to the third division.

However, while the system of promotion and relegation expands competition and prevents long-term monopolies[22], it can also produce dire[23] economic consequences and uncertainty.

Wigan had to spend heavily on players in hopes of staying in the Premier League, while Forest had to sell all its stars to survive financially. It may be a long time before the famous club returns to the top flight[24].

There is also no territorial exclusivity in soccer.[25] Giant English clubs Liverpool[26] and Everton[27] are divided only by a mile of parkland. But the Baltimore Orioles[28] think the Washington Nationals[29], 44 miles down the parkway, are much too close.

Some have even questioned the wisdom of relegation and promotion in an age when enormous fortunes are invested into soccer

13. …gives baseball's side …… 阐述棒球的情况

14. term /tɜːm/ v. 命名,称作

15. franchise /ˈfræntʃaɪz/ n. 职业运动队

16. mediocre /ˌmiːdɪˈəʊkə/ a. 平庸的

17. …where poor teams are relegated and replaced by promoted clubs 弱队被降级,空缺出的位子被升级的俱乐部队取代。relegate /ˈrelɪɡeɪt/ v. 降级

18. put /pʊt/ a. 固定不动的

19. lucrative /ˈluːkrətɪv/ a. 有利的

20. Premier League 英格兰足球超级联赛(英格兰本土球队组成的最高级别的联赛)

21. Nottingham Forest 诺丁汉森林队(英格兰成立时间最早的球队之一)

22. monopoly /məˈnɒpəlɪ/ n. 垄断

23. dire /ˈdaɪə/ a. 可怕的

24. top flight 第一流球队

25. 足球也没有地域上的排他性。exclusivity /ˌeksklu:ˈsɪvɪtɪ/ n. 排他性

26. Liverpool 利物浦足球队

27. Everton 埃弗顿足球队

28. Baltimore Orioles 巴尔的摩金莺队(美国职业棒球大联盟的劲旅)

29. Washington Nationals 华盛顿国民队(美国职业棒球大联盟球队)

clubs. Imagine the financial consequences if Manchester United was relegated from the Premier League after Malcolm Glazer[30] has invested more than $1.2 billion in the club. It's highly unlikely, but it could happen. United was relegated in 1974 but won promotion the following year.

It should be noted that the MLS is a "closed league" with no relegation.

Baseball's "monopolistic[31] industry" has maintained tight control over profits and avoided the financial insecurity that has plagued[32] soccer, a sport that has been slow to organize the business side of the game. For many years, soccer stadiums were shabby[33] places, while baseball stadiums were state of the art. Even today, many clubs in England are flirting with bankruptcy and many critics believe the Premier League is built on sand.[34]

Still, soccer's popularity dwarfs[35] baseball internationally. Following a number of unsuccessful overseas tours in the late 1880s, baseball largely gave up on its attempt to convert the world. Baseball looked inward, as soccer spread outward, largely through the work of British expatriates[36].

Today, FIFA, soccer's governing body, boasts 207 members, four more than the Olympic Movement and 15 more than the United Nations. The International Baseball Association has 112 members. Baseball recently was voted out of the 2012 Olympics.[37]

In their conclusion, the authors believe both sports can learn from each other. Soccer could certainly study baseball's financial plan, while baseball could take a page from[38] soccer, if it wants to expand its influence around the globe.

30. Malcolm Glazer 美国富豪格雷泽,曾经在 2005 年收购曼彻斯特联合足球俱乐部,拥有逾 75%股份。

31. monopolistic /mə,nɒpə'lɪstɪk/ a. 垄断的
32. plague /pleɪg/ v. 折磨,使苦恼
33. shabby /'ʃæbɪ/ a. 破旧的

34. 直到今天,许多英国的俱乐部仍然饱受破产的困扰,许多批评家认为英格兰足球超级联赛的经济基础是不牢固的。flirt /flɜːt/ v. 飘摇 to build on sand 建立在不牢固的基础上

35. dwarf /dwɔːf/ v. 使变矮小;使相形见绌
36. expatriate /eks'pætrɪət/ n. 侨民,移居国外的人
37. 最近经过表决,2012 年奥运会将取消棒球项目。
38. to take a page from 学习,借鉴

Comprehension Questions

1. What is the book entitled *National Pastime*: *How Americans Play Baseball and the Rest of the World Plays Soccer* about?
2. What is the origin of the rules for baseball?
3. Why is the system of soccer considered to be "open" while that of baseball "closed"?
4. What is the positive side of the "open league" soccer system? What is the negative side?
5. Why was baseball voted out of the 2012 Olympics?

Background Reading

Baseball As America Exhibition

I think there are only three things that America will be known for 2,000 years from now when they study this civilization: the Constitution, jazz music and baseball. They're the three most beautifully designed things this culture has ever produced.

—Gerald Early, Scholar

Baseball As America is a national celebration of America's romance with baseball. This unprecedented (空前的) four-year program, organized by the National Baseball Hall of Fame and Museum in association with 10 of the nation's leading museums, is a once-in-a-lifetime venture (一生只有一次的冒险) that only the Hall of Fame is capable of creating.

Baseball As America, a blockbuster (一鸣惊人) exhibition, marks the first time the treasures of the Hall of Fame (名人堂) will leave their legendary (传奇的) home in Cooperstown (库珀斯敦, 位于美国纽约州中东部, 全国棒球名人堂所在地) to tour the country. This ground-breaking (破天荒的) exhibition opened at the American Museum of Natural History, New York, on March 16, 2002, and will travel to nine other cities across the United States.

Baseball As America represents the richness of baseball as the American pastime and celebrates enduring American values: freedom, patriotism, opportunity and ingenuity (独创性). It appeals to a broad spectrum (范围) of the public—from children just learning to throw a ball to the life-long fan— and, like the game itself, draws people of all ages and across all cultural heritages (遗产, 传统). It provides a revealing (有启迪作用的), inspiring, humorous and dramatic perspective on America's Game and, in so doing, fosters a new appreciation not only of baseball, but of our national character.

Baseball and America have grown up together. In exploring immigration, industrialization, integration and technology, the exhibition reveals how baseball has served as both a public reflection of, and catalyst (催化剂) for, the evolution of American culture and society. *Baseball As America* also examines how the American landscape, our language, literature, movies, and summertime living all bear the mark of (刻上了印记) a 19th-century game that continues to be identified with our nation's values and aspirations.

Part II Sporting Kaleidoscope

Relevant Words

CFA (= Chinese Football Association)　中国足球协会
FIFA (= Federation Internationale de Football Association)　国际足球联合会
FIFA World Cup Competition　世界杯足球赛
hooligan　足球流氓
IBF (= International Baseball Federation)　国际棒球联合会
MLB (= Major League Baseball)　美国职业棒球大联盟
Women's World Cup　世界女子足球锦标赛

Lesson 6

为了使橄榄球运动在2012年进入奥运会，很多人做出了一系列努力。现任国际奥委会主席罗格曾是比利时国家橄榄球队队员，橄榄球界人士期望这一历史对橄榄球运动进入奥运会能有些许帮助。全文重点描述了橄榄球运动的普及以及这项运动给社会带来的好处。文章最后也指出了橄榄球运动在美国发展的问题：职业化程度不高，运动员和教练员大多是兼职或业余的。美国国家队教练期望利用橄榄球进入奥运会的契机推动这项运动的发展。

Seeking Acceptance, Rugby Gives It a Try

By Helene Elliott
February 9, 2005
Los Angeles Times[1]

It can't hurt rugby's chances of being added to the Summer Olympics that Jacques Rogge, president of the International Olympic Committee, played for the Belgian national rugby team in his youth.

"We'd like to think it might help," said Greg Thomas, communications manager for the International Rugby Board, "but we know we need to rely on more than that."

And so rugby sevens[2], a variation of the 15-player game, will press its case[3] Saturday and Sunday at the Home Depot Center in the USA Sevens tournament.

Featuring 44 games of fast, physical play, the USA Sevens is the third stop of an eight-event tour. IOC officials are expected to attend and acquaint themselves with[4] the sport and its logistics[5] before the IOC decides in July whether to replace any of the 28 summer sports.

The 15-player version of rugby was on the Olympic program in 1900, 1908, 1920 and 1924, and the U.S. won the last two gold medals. The seven-man game is on a short list for consideration with golf, squash[6], roller[7] sports and karate[8]. For every sport adopted an equal number would be dropped;[9] softball, baseball, taekwondo[10] and modern pentathlon[11] may be in jeopardy[12]. The soonest a sport could become part of the Games is 2012.

1. *Los Angeles Times*《洛杉矶时报》，美国西部最大的对开版日报，其影响与地位仅次于《纽约时报》和《华盛顿邮报》，被称为美国的第三大报。它于1881年12月4日在洛杉矶创刊。
2. rugby sevens 7人制橄榄球
3. to press one's case 陈述
4. acquaint... with... 使……熟知……
5. logistics /lə'dʒɪstɪks/ *n.* 后勤
6. squash /skwɒʃ/ *n.* 壁球
7. roller /'rəʊlə/ *n.* 轮滑
8. karate /kə'rɑːtɪ/ *n.* 空手道
9. 每有一个项目进入（奥运会）就会有一个项目退出。
10. taekwondo /taɪ'kwɒndəʊ/ *n.* 跆拳道
11. modern pentathlon 现代五项
12. jeopardy /'dʒepədɪ/ *n.* 危险

The IRB[13] has 110 members on five continents. The U.S., with about 22,500 male and 8,000 female players, is one of rugby's last frontiers[14], as are Russia and China.

Last year's USA Sevens tournament drew about 11,000 people to the Home Depot Center, and organizers hope to double that by emphasizing the game's speed and action—and its social aspects. Each game consists of two seven-minute halves, with a two-minute intermission[15]. The teams are divided into four pools of four teams each, with the best teams advancing to bracket play Sunday.[16]

"Short, sharp entertainment," Thomas said from the IRB's Dublin, Ireland, headquarters. "You can come, watch a game, go and get something to eat and come back and see another."

"The rugby World Cup is the third-largest international event, behind Olympics and soccer World Cup. We have no pretensions[17] that we're going to be bigger than soccer in the Olympics, but there's a growing popularity of the sport and it has an ethos[18] of friendship and comradeship[19]."

Doug Arnot, chief executive of USA Rugby, ran the venues at the Atlanta Olympics and consulted with venue managers at Sydney, so he's aware that the Summer Olympics already are massive. However, he sees rugby as a good fit.[20]

"I would agree with anyone who says the Summer Games are too big and are a behemoth[21] to manage. But there are some events within sports that don't have a lot of nations competing," he said. "I would contend[22] rugby is more widespread."

"From an organizing committee perspective, I would say I'm much more interested in a sport that would fill stadiums, satisfy sponsors and use fields that exist. You could use soccer fields after soccer preliminaries[23] end. There are all kinds of reasons to say yes, but you never know."

Arnot said he believes acceptance into the Olympics would weaken the resistance rugby faces in the U.S.[24] He said people often dismiss it as a "foreign" sport, much as they do soccer, but don't realize American football evolved from rugby.

"There's a little xenophobia[25], people looking at this as somebody else's sport. But this is the way everyone else plays," Arnot said. "With the growing number of people playing and the growing number of people that have come to the U.S. from rugby-friendly countries, we see a base-building parallel to soccer.[26]"

13. IRB=International Rugby Board 国际橄榄球总会（总部设在爱尔兰）
14. frontier /ˈfrʌntɪə/ n. 边境
15. intermission /ˌɪntəˈmɪʃən/ n. 暂停，间歇
16. 16支队伍分成4个小组进行循环赛，每个小组4个队。每组第一的球队在周日进行比赛。pool /puːl/ n. 循环赛分组 bracket play 小组赛
17. pretension /prɪˈtenʃən/ n. 要求；主张
18. ethos /ˈiːθɒs/ n. 气质；风气
19. comradeship /ˈkɒmrɪdʃɪp/ n. 友谊
20. 但是，他仍然认为橄榄球进入奥运会是合适的。fit /fɪt/ n. 适合
21. behemoth /bɪˈhiːmɒθ/ n. 巨兽；庞然大物
22. contend /kənˈtend/ v. 主张，声称
23. preliminary /prɪˈlɪmɪnərɪ/ n. 预赛
24. 阿诺德说他相信橄榄球进入奥运会将大大削弱橄榄球在美国遭遇的阻力。
25. xenophobia /ˌzenəˈfəʊbɪə/ n. 对外国人（或陌生人、域外事物等）的恐惧（或憎恨），恐外症
26. 越来越多的人参与橄榄球运动，越来越多的人从支持橄榄球运动的国家来到美国，这都让我们看到橄榄球也会与足球一样构筑良好的基础。

Thomas said the U.S. has a deep player resource[27] among college football players who don't go to the NFL[28]—and Tom Billups, coach of the U.S. national team, is a prime[29] example.

A native of Burlington, Iowa, Billups played football at tiny Augustana College in Rock Island, Ill., "but knew I'd never play on Sunday." He turned to rugby, playing for the U.S. and in Europe before he became coach of the U.S. team—known as the Eagles—in 2001.

Billups said he's one of only four full-time rugby coaches in this country. His players squeeze games between their jobs as mortgage brokers[30], teachers and medical professionals and rarely practice together. Getting rugby into the Olympics could change that.

"It would be one of the fastest ways to add athletic credibility[31] in America, and add financial resources," Billups said. "We have only limited access to[32] Olympic training facilities now. As opposed to[33] being on the 'B' list, we'd move to the 'A' list."

The sport's Olympic chances, he said, "are as good as they've been in recent times. Our IOC president is a rugby man.... Rugby is the world's contact sport. American football is America's contact sport."

27. a deep player resource 广泛的运动员来源
28. NFL = National Football League 美国职业橄榄球联赛
29. prime /praɪm/ *a.* 最好的

30. mortgage broker 贷款经纪人
31. credibility /ˌkredɪˈbɪlɪtɪ/ *n.* 可信性

32. access to 通往……的途径
33. opposed to 与……相反

Comprehension Questions

1. According to the author, what events may be excluded from the Olympics in the future?
2. How long does it take to complete a rugby sevens match?
3. According to Doug Arnot, chief executive of USA Rugby, why should rugby be an event of the Olympic Games?
4. Do you agree that "rugby is the world's contact sport"?
5. Do you think rugby will be an Olympic event in 2012?

Background Reading

An Introduction to Rugby

Rugby is a popular game played by men and women of every race and creed （信念，信条）, from under age five to well over fifty, in over 100 countries of the world. In a few of those countries it is the national sport—some say religion.

The basic game involves 15 players though seven-a-side tournaments are also popular.

Part II Sporting Kaleidoscope

The object of the game is to score as many points as possible by carrying, passing, kicking and grounding (放在地上) an oval (椭圆形的) ball in the scoring zone at the far end of the field—called the in-goal area (得分区). Grounding the ball, which must be done with downward pressure, results in a try (达阵得分,在对方极阵内首先压球触地) (worth 5 points). After a try a conversion (追加转换射门) may be attempted by place kick (定位踢) or drop kick (踢落地球). If the ball passes over the bar and between the goal posts the conversion is successful and results in a further 2 points. Points may also be scored from a drop kick in general play (worth 3 points) and a penalty kick (worth 3 points).

The ball may not be passed forward (though it may be kicked forward) and players may not receive the ball in an offside (越位的) position, nor may they wait in such a position. Players may not be tackled (处理) without the ball. Play only stops when a try is scored, or the ball goes out of play, or an infringement (违例) occurs. When the ball goes out it is thrown back in at a line-out (争边球) where the opposing "forwards" line up and jump for the ball. Infringements result in a penalty, or free kick, or scrum (对阵争球). In a scrum the opposing forwards bind (搂抱) together in a unit and push against the other forwards, trying to win the ball with their feet. Substitutions are only allowed in case of injury and there is no separate offensive and defensive unit.

Relevant Words

13-a-side 联盟橄榄球(13人制)	15-a-side 协会橄榄球(15人制)
7-a-side 7人制橄榄球	neutral zone 中区
padded equipment 护衣	quarter 节
rugby 7s 7人制橄榄球	Rugby League 联盟橄榄球(13人制)
Rugby Union 协会橄榄球(15人制)	scrum cap 对阵争球头盔
Super Bowl 超级碗(美国职业橄榄球联赛一年一度的总决赛)	

Lesson 7

> 国际田径联合会理事会召开前夕，国际田联前主席助手 Luciano Barra 尖锐地指出了国际田联在赛事安排、比赛管理、市场化等方面的问题。该篇文章主要探讨了如何使田径运动和赛事更加大众化，让越来越多的普通民众喜爱田径运动。

IAAF Struggle to Get Athletics Back on Track

By Mihir Bose
November 3, 2005
Telegraph[1]

The problems besetting[2] world athletics will be at the top of the agenda[3] during a meeting of the sport's ruling body in Moscow.

There is growing unrest within the ranks of the International Association of Athletics Federations about the way things are being organised and the association's failure to market the sport in the United States.[4] The issues will be central to the IAAF council's meeting over the weekend of Nov 12 and 13.

Luciano Barra, the chief operating officer of next year's Turin Winter Olympics who for many years was the right-hand man[5] of Primo Nebiolo, the former IAAF president, said: "Nebiolo made the sport and nobody has been able to pick up his mantle[6]."

Barra accepts that the IAAF World Championships are highly successful, but at Helsinki[7], despite a wonderful showing by the United States, the event hardly registered[8] on American television screens. Barra said that however good the World Championships were, they represented only a small percentage of activity in the sport. "It is like drinking a glass of good wine only five days a year and thinking you are a wine expert," he said.

Last year, in a 16-page paper on the problems of athletics submitted to the IAAF, Barra concluded: "With the exception of the World Championships the format of athletics competition is not understandable to the large part of the public."

"Most sports have a simple formula, or at least the separate

---

1. *Telegraph*《每日电讯报》，1855年创刊于伦敦，与《泰晤士报》、《卫报》和《金融时报》并称为英国四大全国性报纸，发行量居四大报纸之首。该报主要刊登国内外消息，并辟有体育、艺术、妇女、旅游、家政等栏目。
2. beset /bɪˈset/ v. 困扰
3. agenda /əˈdʒendə/ n. 议程
4. 组织不力，田径运动在美国市场化的失败，国际田径联合会官员们深感不安。unrest /ʌnˈrest/ n. 不安 the ranks 各级官员
5. right-hand man 得力助手
6. to pick up one's mantle 抢得某人的风光；盖过某人的功绩 mantle /ˈmæntl/ n. 披风，斗篷
7. Helsinki /ˈhelsɪŋkɪ/ 赫尔辛基（芬兰首都）
8. register /ˈredʒɪstə/ v. (常用于否定句) 留下印象；被记住（这里指电视转播）

elements which make up a sport such as tennis seem to be able to lay out[9] their different events. The World Cup and the World Athletics Final make no sense. It is crazy to have a World Athletics Final [for individual athletes] only a few weeks after the World Championships. The two are not compatible[10] and confuse the public."

Barra added: "The Golden League[11], as a concept, means nothing. Zurich[12] and Brussels[13] have value on their own. The public is bored. This needs a radical change with a new format." The situation is such that in Germany, biathlon[14] attracts bigger audiences than athletics.

Barra said this week: "Our major problem is the one-day international meetings. There could be 25 athletes running in a race and 10 of them are Kenyans[15]. Can you recognise 10 Kenyans in one competition? Then there is the whole business of pacemaking[16]. People are trying to break records. I would stop pacemaking at the one-day events. Make it more human. Apart from Britain, where one-day events are well organised and they know their athletics spectators, public interest in one-day meetings is non-existent[17]."

There are also concerns that most of the IAAF sponsors are Japanese, and may not continue their backing[18] after the 2007 World Athletics Championships in Osaka[19].

Highly-placed[20] IAAF sources[21] say that all this is putting pressure on the president, Lamine Diack, who succeeded[22] Nebiolo. Diack may face a challenge from the wealthy Greek, Minos Xen Kyriakou, who is on the IAAF council, when he seeks re-election in 2007.

The IAAF council will also be considering in Moscow how to do deal with African athletes who are turning up at events with Qatari[23] passports. This not only threatens to devalue the events, but also risks alienating limited public support.[24]

9. to lay out 安排，布置
10. compatible /kəmˈpætəbl/ a. 协调的，一致的
11. Golden League 黄金联赛
12. Zurich /ˈzʊərɪk/ 苏黎士（瑞士最大城市）
13. Brussels /ˈbrʌslz/ 布鲁塞尔（比利时首都）
14. biathlon /baɪˈæθlən, -lɑn/ n. 现代冬季两项运动
15. Kenyan /ˈkenjən/ n. 肯尼亚人
16. pacemaking n.（为其他队员）定速度
17. non-existent /ˌnɒnɪɡˈzɪstənt/ a. 不存在的
18. backing /ˈbækɪŋ/ n. 支持；援助
19. Osaka /əʊˈsɑːkə/ 大阪（日本本洲岛城市）
20. highly-placed /ˈhaɪli pleɪst/ a. 排名很靠前的；重要的
21. source /sɔːs/ n. 消息来源
22. succeed /səkˈsiːd/ v. 继任
23. Qatari /ˈkɑːtəri/ a. 卡塔尔的
24. 这不仅威胁到这项赛事的价值，还将会对有限的公众支持构成威胁。devalue /diːˈvæljuː/ v. 贬值 alienate /ˈeɪliəneɪt/ v. 疏远

Comprehension Questions

1. What problems are the world athletics facing?
2. What IAAF events are mentioned in this passage?
3. What does Barra mean by saying "It is like drinking a glass of good wine only five days a year and thinking you are a wine expert"?
4. What are Barra's concerns with one-day international meetings?
5. If you are the president of IAAF, how could you solve the problems?

Background Reading

Liu Breaks 110-meter Hurdles World Record;
Marion Jones Wins 100

LAUSANNE (洛桑,瑞士小城,国际奥委会总部所在地), Switzerland—Liu Xiang of China set a world record in the 110-meter hurdles on Tuesday, breaking the record he shared with Britain's Colin Jackson.

Liu's time of 12.88 seconds at the Athletissima Grand Prix meeting (2006年瑞士洛桑田径超级大奖赛) was 0.03 better than the record he matched in winning gold at the 2004 Athens Olympics. Jackson ran 12.91 in Stuttgart, Germany, in August 1993.

Marion Jones won again in the women's 100, her sixth victory in eight meets this season, leading a U.S. sweep (席卷) of the top four places in that event. In the men's 200, American Xavier Carter ran the second-fastest race in history.

Dominique Arnold of the United States was second in the hurdles in 12.90, also faster than the previous record.

"I'm very happy," Liu said, covering his face with the Chinese flag. "I'm very tired."

Liu, who also holds the world junior record of 13.12 set in July 2002 in Lausanne, ran a victory lap—shirtless and waving to the crowd—before sitting on the track clock that showed his record time.

"It is my place of good luck and joy," Liu said. "It is where I won four years ago with such a good time. I always feel so good here."

Liu's record performance came three days after he struggled to a fourth-place finish at the Gaz de France (国际田联黄金联赛巴黎站) meet outside Paris.

"I can't believe it, I can't express it," Liu said through a translator.

"I had a good start, and after the first five hurdles it was a perfect race," he said. "I wanted to break the record last year, but it wasn't working. I think I can still run even faster."

American Terrence Trammell, who had held the season's best time of 13.06, was third in 13.02.

In the women's 100, Jones won in 10.94. Me'Lisa Barber was second in 11.03, Torri Edwards was third in 11.07 and Lauryn Williams fourth in 11.13.

Jamaica's (牙买加) Sherone Simpson, the only woman who has run faster than Jones this year, withdrew (退出) hours before the race because of injury. Organizers said she did not give details about the injury.

In the men's 200, Carter ran a stunning 19.63. Only Michael Johnson's time of 19.32, set while winning gold at the 1996 Atlanta Olympics, is faster.

Countryman Tyson Gay was runner-up with a personal best of 19.70, while Usain Bolt of Jamaica, the junior record holder, was third in 19.88, also a personal best.

In other races, Kenya's Janeth Jepkosgei posted (向世人展示) a season best in the women's 800 meters, clocking 1 minute, 56.66 seconds; Leonard Scott of the United States led from start to finish to win the men's 100 meters in a modest 10.05; American Michelle Perry posted a season-best time of 12.43 in the women's 100-meter hurdles, and Shadrack Korir of Kenya won the men's 1,500 in 3:31.97.

Relevant Words

athletics 田径运动	clear the hurdle 过栏
field event 田赛项目	hurdle step 跨栏步
hurdles (race) 跨栏跑	take the hurdle 上栏

Lesson 8

在 2006 年都灵冬奥会上，美国队在滑板项目上获得了好成绩，美国选手肖恩·怀特 (Shaun White) 夺得了单板滑雪男子 U 型管技巧赛的冠军。在怀特夺冠后,《今日美国》记者通过采访运动员、教练和有关赞助商，总结了美国滑板运动取得成功的经验。其中营造轻松的训练、比赛环境，保持运动员良好的心态，以娱乐的心情训练、比赛，特别应该值得推崇和提倡。

U.S. Snowboarders Key to Winning: Have Fun

By Sal Ruibal
February 26, 2006
USA Today

TORINO—After his gold-medal performance in snowboard-cross[1], American Seth Wescott declared "snowboarding is becoming the heart and soul of the Olympics."

It certainly has become the medal mother lode[2] for the USA. This Olympiad, the American riders won three gold medals, three silvers and a bronze in six events. Seven of the team's 16 athletes won medals.

In the 2002 Winter Games, the team brought home two golds, a silver and two bronzes in four events—including a podium sweep in men's halfpipe[3].

What's the magic formula?

"We kept it fun," says Jeremy Forster, U.S. Snowboarding program director. "We kept it about snowboarding. We made sure it wasn't too much fun, but not too serious, either."

That was evident in men's halfpipe, when gold-medal favorite Shaun White failed to get a guaranteed spot in the finals and faced a do-or-die second run.[4]

To calm White's shattered nerves[5], U.S. snowboard freestyle head coach Bud Keene took his nervous rider to the nearby slopes of the Melezet ski resort and casually carved[6] snowboard tracks in the hardpacked snow[7] in the downtime[8].

1. snowboardcross /'snəʊbɔːd'krɒs/ *n.* 越野滑板滑雪
2. mother lode 丰富的源泉　lode /ləʊd/ *n.* 矿脉
3. a podium sweep in men's halfpipe 在男子 U 形管滑雪赛中大获全胜
4. 这明显地体现在男子 U 型管比赛中。有望夺金的肖恩·怀特 (Shaun White) 在决赛中没有得到绝对优势的位置，这意味着他在第二轮中必须破釜沉舟。evident /'evɪdənt/ *a.* 明显的　favourite /'feɪvərɪt/ *n.* 最有希望获胜的选手　do-or-die /'duːə'daɪ/ *a.* 决一死战的
5. to calm one's nerves 使某人平静　shattered /'ʃætəd/ *a.* 心烦的
6. carve /kɑːv/ *v.* 开拓
7. hardpacked snow 坚实的雪
8. downtime /'daʊntaɪm/ *n.* 中间休息时间

A serene[9] and confident White returned to the halfpipe and threw down a performance that could not be touched[10]. He won the gold.

In women's halfpipe, Hannah Teter and Gretchen Bleiler snuck out between rounds for some out-of-bounds runs in the powder-snow filled woods above the Bardonecchia venue.[11]

They laughed through some spills[12] and came back to compete: Teter took the gold and Bleiler the silver.

Jake Burton Carpenter, one of the pioneers of the sport and the founder of Burton Snowboards, agrees the key to this year's success was the relaxed atmosphere.

"The problem with many Olympic sports is that an athlete may feel that their entire career comes down to one moment," he says. "These snowboarders have more going on than the Olympics. It's the biggest event in snowboarding, but it shouldn't be like having to make one putt[13] to win the Masters."

The snowboard team, and in particular the world-dominating halfpipe riders, have flourished under a relaxed system that allows them to compete most of the time as independent riders or full members of the team.

"It's market-driven," says Burton Carpenter, whose company sponsors White and Teter. "They have a choice on how they want to approach the sport."

Riders of proven abilities or ample[14] potential can get contracts with sponsors' loose-knit[15] "teams" that more than cover competition costs. Burton, for example, had 18 riders from nine nations at the Olympics.

Athletes who sign with the U.S. team are more restricted in their marketing rights, but get U.S Ski and Snowboard Association funds for travel, competition and coaching.[16]

"Take Shaun White," says USSA's Forster. "A rider of his stature[17] has so many opportunities on and off the board that a team sport would not be the best for him. But we can take the pieces that work to his benefit and everybody wins."

Even when a rider has too much fun, as when SBX[18] rider Lindsey Jacobellis let her gold medal slip away when some premature victory hot-dogging[19] went awry[20], the team is willing to forgive in the name of fun.

"So what if she tweaked[21] it?" said U.S. Snowboarding head

9. serene /sɪˈriːn/ a. 沉着的
10. touch /tʌtʃ/ v. （主要用于否定意义的句中）匹敌；比得上
11. 女子运动员 Hannah Teter 和 Gretchen Bleiler 也在比赛间隙跑出去，在巴多尼奇亚赛场上边粉状雪覆盖的丛林里尽情做着一连串高难度动作。to sneak out 偷偷跑出去 out-of-bounds /ˈaʊtəvˈbaʊndz/ a. 不可超越的 run /rʌn/ n. 连串难度动作 Bardonecchia 巴多尼奇亚（雪上滑板场地，位于距离都灵约 90 公里）
12. to laugh through some spills 虽然多次摔倒，但仍然一直充满欢笑 spill /spɪl/ n. 摔倒
13. putt /pʌt/ n. 轻轻一击

14. ample /ˈæmpəl/ a. 充足的；丰富的
15. loose-knit /ˈluːs nɪt/ a. 松散结合的

16. 与美国国家队签约的运动员在商业权利方面受到更多的限制，但是他们可以得到美国滑雪滑板联合会的资助，以支付旅行、比赛以及教练的费用。
17. stature /ˈstætʃə/ n. 成就；才干
18. SBX = snowboarding 单板滑雪
19. hot-dogging /ˈhɒtˈdɒɡɪŋ/ n. 卖弄
20. awry /əˈraɪ/ a. 错误的；偏差的
21. tweak /twiːk/ v. 以……为乐

coach Peter Foley. "That's cool, too. If she got caught up in the moment, oh well. If people don't understand that, they're missing the point of snowboarding."

Comprehension Questions

1. What results did the American athletes obtain in the 2006 Olympic Games?
2. What was the key factor that made American athletes' success in snowboarding events?
3. How are the American riders funded competition and relevant costs?
4. What are Forster's comments on Shaun White's stature?
5. What do you think is the most important factor for success in sports competition?

Background Reading

Snowboarder and Skater Shaun White: To Air Is Divine (神圣的)

Just after he turned 7, Shaun White appeared for the first time in snowboarding and skateboarding magazines. He became a professional snowboarder at 13—and a pro (职业的) skater at 16—and started winning contests shortly thereafter.

Even though White started his career before most kids start the third grade, he firmly believes it is never too late to begin skateboarding.

"The main thing you need is a board, and then you can just go do it," said White, now 19 and the winner of a gold medal in snowboarding halfpipe at the Olympics in February.

White won the silver medal for skateboarding in the Summer X Games last year, and he hopes to take gold this summer.

In between training sessions last month, he offered five important tips for beginning skateboarders.

Keep your parents involved. White's parents drove him to the skate park (滑冰场) in Carlsbad, Calif., almost every day during the summer, and they even excused him from school for occasional trips and contests. "It was so rad (好极了) how they did all that," White said. "I never could have gotten this good without them."

Start slowly. Even though his older brother, Jesse, sometimes teased (取笑) him, White started skateboarding by sitting with his knees on the board and pushing slowly through his house. Only when he finally became comfortable on the board did he start to skate standing up.

Practice, a lot. During his free time when he was a kid, White would go to the local skate park and spend six or seven hours there, and he would do that for 10 days in a row. Shaun sometimes messed up his tricks (把小技术动作做得很糟糕) and went home disappointed. "The only way to get better is to go back and try it again," he said.

Don't be scared. White learned quickly that fear is a skater's worst enemy. "If you're scared, you'll never go with 100 percent," he said. White begins each trick with complete confidence that he will land it. He sometimes pictures landing a trick in his mind before he tries it. "Then I go in feeling stoked (激励的)," he said.

　　Listen to your body. It hurts to fall and hit concrete, White said, even if you're wearing a helmet (头盔), knee pads and elbow pads. White has been injured often in his career, and he tries not to skate until his body has healed. Last month, he hurt his collarbone (锁骨) trying a new trick and spent a couple of days resting before he went back to the ramp (斜面,斜坡) and tried it again.

Relevant Words

> alpine skiing　高山滑雪
> alpine combined　高山全能;阿尔卑斯山两项(速降和回转)
> classical technique　传统式技术(无侧蹬动作的交替滑行)
> downhill　速降滑雪
> free-style technique　自由式技术(滑冰式滑行)
> snow ballet　雪上芭蕾
> tobogganing　雪橇运动

Lesson 9

> 花样游泳由游泳、技巧、舞蹈和音乐编排而成,又称"水上芭蕾"。当我们观看和欣赏这一高雅运动的时候可能很难会想到运动员在训练和比赛中所面临的挑战和困难。就让我们跟随记者的采访走进一名花样游泳运动员的训练和比赛生活,体验一下在优美的舞姿和动人微笑背后的艰辛。

A Life in Sport: Synchro-swimming[1]
—An Interview of Gayle Adamson[2]

By Charles Randall
October 26, 2005
Daily Telegraph[3]

People tend to sneer[4] at 'synchro' and ask why we have to have a fixed smile, but when they understand what is involved, they generally think it's quite good. It all seems so easy because our aim is to make it look easy. That's the frustrating thing for us and for the sport's image. Synchro is in fact incredibly difficult.

The three minutes in an individual routine[5] is very, very tiring. You spend probably half of that, if not more, under the water. It's like running and holding your breath at the same time. The more difficult the routine the harder your muscles have to work, and you run out of breath quickly.

Then when you come to the surface to do an arm section, you're working your legs to keep your body upright and as high as you can out of the water. It's high intensity and you finish the routine feeling physically sick. When I was 17, after competing at St Moritz[6], I started getting out of breath quickly. A couple of months later I felt a crushing pain in my shoulder and found that one of my lungs had collapsed[7]. The high altitude in Switzerland had caused a tiny hole to develop. It was serious.

The whole reason why swimmers smile is that the judges are not allowed to see any fatigue[8], even though the legs are aching and the lungs are burning. Leading up to competition, you practise the

---

1. synchro-swimming /ˈsɪŋkrəʊ ˈswɪmɪŋ/ 花样游泳
2. Gayle Adamson 盖尔·亚当森(英国花样游泳运动员)
3. *Daily Telegraph* 《每日电讯报》,于1855年在英国伦敦创刊,是仅存的两份传统大版面的英国报纸之一。该报以"时效性"著称,是当今英国发行量最大的大报。
4. sneer /snɪə/ v. 嘲笑,讥笑
5. routine /ruːˈtiːn/ n. 一套固定的动作
6. St Moritz /sent ˈmɒrɪz/ 圣莫里兹(位于瑞士东南部)
7. collapse /kəˈlæps/ v. 衰竭
8. fatigue /fəˈtiːg/ n. 疲劳,疲乏

facial expressions you are going to have to do to reflect the mood of the music. You have to smile to be successful.

You're marked on technical merit[9] and artistic impression[10]. There are speakers under the water. Every single beat of the music is choreographed[11]. In duets[12], which last 3½ minutes, both swimmers do exactly the same for every single second of their routine. The swimmers train on that for hours, perhaps spending five hours working on a single eight-count of music, but we do have fun spending time trying to choreograph new things.

Swimmers are becoming stronger and more flexible. In a team event when you have eight people swimming together for four minutes, you have what is called a lift: seven people will throw one person up out of the water, usually the highlight of the routine. The aim is to get the one swimmer as high as they can so that she can do back flips[13] or somersaults[14]. The higher she goes the more she can do. The girl who is thrown will have done intensive diving training for this one highlight.

What might appear funny, though not for the swimmers, are the nose pegs[15]. If you are swimming in a team with seven other people, you often get kicked and lose your peg. You always carry a spare and have only about half a second to put it on. Without a nose peg on under water, the pain can become too intense.

I was introduced to synchro—basically gymnastics in water—when I was seven. When I was 14 my coach decided to retire from coaching and my mum Vera took over. She was coach when I won my Commonwealth[16] medals, and she's still coaching at our club. A lot of coaches tend to be parents of swimmers.

My training regime became 25 hours a week at my peak in various pools. As the best swimmers were predominantly[17] in the south, I had to fly down for training at Aldershot[18] nearly every weekend to join my duet partner Katie Hooper, combining that with my degree course at Northumbria University[19]. Training included speed swimming to maintain stamina[20] and fitness, flexibility work as a gymnast, weights for muscular endurance and tone, dance training on land and long distance running.

People can judge synchro for themselves soon, because the British Championships are being held at Leicester[21] on Nov. 5-6. The favourites are Jenna Randall, the champion from Surrey, and Hannah Massey, from Bristol[22].

9. technical merit 技术价值(包括执行、协调和难度三部分)
10. artistic impression 艺术表现(指对动作组合的整体感觉)
11. choreograph /ˈkɒrɪəɡrɑːf/ v. 安排,精心编制(舞蹈动作等)
12. duet /djuːˈet/ n. 双人项目

13. back flip 后空翻
14. somersault /ˈsʌməsɒlt/ n. 空翻
15. nose peg 花样游泳运动员戴在鼻子上的护套

16. Commonwealth 英联邦国家运动会
17. predominantly /prɪˈdɒmɪnəntlɪ/ ad. 主要地
18. Aldershot /ˈæːldəʃɒt/ 奥尔德肖特(英国中南部城市,位于伦敦西南)
19. Northumbria University 诺森比亚大学[坐落在纽卡斯尔(Newcastle upon Tyne)]
20. stamina /ˈstæmɪnə/ n. 毅力;持久力
21. Leicester /ˈlestə/ 莱斯特(英国英格兰中部一城市,位于伯明翰东北偏东)
22. Bristol /ˈbrɪstl/ 布里斯托尔(英格兰西南部一港口城市,位于伦敦西部)

Comprehension Questions

1. Why should the swimmers smile all the time during the competition?
2. What criteria do the judges consider when they mark the swimmers' performance?
3. What's the function of the nose peg?
4. Why did Gayle Adamson have to fly to Aldershot for training?
5. Write a brief description of synchro-swimming with the help of the information provided in this passage.

Background Reading

Synchro-swimming—An Introduction

ABOUT

It looks like perhaps the most effortless event in the Olympic Games, but there is more to synchronised swimming than what appears on the surface. Besides demanding strength, endurance, flexibility, grace (优雅) and artistry (艺术性), it requires exceptional (异常的) breath control.

Unusual, but vital, equipment helps the women maintain the illusion (幻想) of effortlessness, no simple task considering they perform strenuous (艰辛的) movements upside down and underwater while holding their breath. A nose clip prevents water from entering the nose, allowing the swimmers to remain underwater for long periods. Gelatine (发胶) keeps the hair in place. Make-up brings out the features.

Most importantly, an underwater speaker lets the swimmers hear the music clearly while underwater, helping them achieve the split-second timing (毫秒不差) critical to synchronised swimming.

Originally known as water ballet, synchronised swimming began in Canada in the 1920s. It spread to the United States in the early '30s, where a display at the 1934 Chicago World's Fair drew rave reviews (获得好评,大受赞扬). Its popularity soared further when Esther Williams performed in a string of MGM "aqua musicals" (水上音乐剧) in the 1940s and '50s.

COMPETITION

Synchronised swimming emerged as an exhibition sport at the Olympic Games from 1948 to 1968, then debuted (初次登场) as a full medal sport in Los Angeles in 1984. It is open only to women, with medals offered in two events: duet and team.

Competition for both events consists of a technical routine and a free routine, each performed to music within a time limit. In the technical routine, swimmers perform specific moves in a set order, including boosts (推进), rockets (上升), thrusts (下沉) and twirls (转身). In the free routine there are no restrictions on music or choreography. Judges of each routine look for a high degree of difficulty and risk, flawless (无瑕疵的) execution (动作完成), innovative choreography and seemingly effortless performance.

Part II   Sporting Kaleidoscope

The judging for synchronised swimming resembles the judging for figure skating. Two panels of five judges assess a performance, one panel scoring technical merit and the other assessing artistic impression. In both cases, each judge awards a mark out of a possible 10.

Relevant Words

arched position 弓形姿势	artistic impression 艺术印象分
deck movement 岸上动作	figures 规定动作
free routine 自由自选	knight position 骑士姿势
swimming strokes 游泳动作	technical routine 技术自选

Lesson 10

> 棒球运动是美国最风靡的运动项目之一。该篇文章详细介绍了棒球的比赛规则,并通过钻石型球场中击球手、接球手的各个动作详细归纳了棒球的一般打法。文章后来还介绍了棒球发展演变的历史,提到了球拍的变化以及棒球运动与板球运动的区别。作者最后强调了棒球运动在美国的巨大影响力,可以说了解棒球运动有助于更准确地了解美国社会与文化。

See the Ball, Hit the Ball: A Guide to Baseball

By Bill Center
May 26, 2005
Times Online[1]

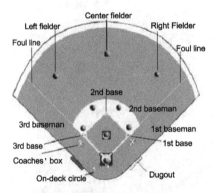

Baseball is the perfect American sport: simple in theory, complex in execution. See the ball, hit the ball. However, once the ball is hit, the possibilities are endless.

Unlike cricket, the batter[2] fails most of the time (or 70 to 75 per cent to be more specific). Either he swings and misses and strikes out or he pops it up so that a fielder[3] can catch it. Or he hits it along the ground (a grounder[4]) to a fielder who then throws to first base[5] ahead of the batter. Do either of these and he's out.

Should the batter get the ball to fall between the fielders and then get himself to first base before the ball, he is credited with a "hit". But he still hasn't succeeded yet. One hit doesn't always get the job done in baseball. To score a run—which is how baseball games are

---

1. Times Online《泰晤士报》和《星期日泰晤士报》的网络版,对英国国内外的政治、经济、体育、科技等方面进行实时报道。

2. batter /ˈbætə/ n. 击球手
3. fielder /ˈfiːldə/ n. 接球者
4. grounder /ˈɡraʊndə/ n.(棒球)滚地球,沿地面跳滚的球
5. first base 一垒

scored—the batter must travel around the four bases laid out in a diamond formation.

Incidentally, that diamond designates[6] the field of play. Again unlike cricket, where the batsman can hit the ball in any direction, only a quarter of the circle is "fair" territory in baseball.

The batter begins by straddling[7] the scoring base, called home plate. The pitcher[8] is the equivalent of cricket's bowler[9]. Only the baseball pitcher does not run up to throw. He "pitches" from a mound[10] that is in the middle of the diamond, exactly 60 feet and six inches (18.44 metres) from home plate.

The pitcher throws by pushing off a piece of hard rubber. The hardest-throwing American pitchers can deliver the ball to the plate at speeds approaching 95mph (153kmh), although the best can also get pitches to drop, sink and spin sideways by adjusting their fingers around and across the seam[11] of the baseball.

He has to be accurate, though. If the pitcher fails to throw the ball across the plate four times—he must also deliver it between the batter's knees and chest—the batter draws a "walk[12]" and reaches first base. A walk is as good as most hits. So is getting hit by a pitch, although that is far more painful.

If the pitcher induces the batter to swing and miss, or throws a ball in the strike zone—again, over the plate and between the knees and chest—three times before he throws four balls and before the batter hits the ball in fair territory, he has a strikeout[13]. The home plate umpire[14] stands behind the catcher and decides which pitches are strikes[15] and balls[16].

Once on first, the batter must advance to second base and third base before reaching home to score a run. And there are many ways to score a run.

The quickest way is the home run[17] where a ball is hit beyond the walls or fences that form the outer limits of a baseball field. In youth baseball, those fences might be as close as 180 feet (55 metres) from home plate. In the major leagues—the National and American leagues—the minimum distance down the right and left field foul[18] lines is around 325 feet (100 metres). The longest distance to straight away centre field is usually around 410 feet (125 metres).

The home run is one of the most exciting plays in baseball. The ball must be struck with power and America's top home-run hitters become legends. Babe Ruth hit homers[19]. So does Barry Bonds.

6. designate /ˈdezɪgneɪt/ v. 指明；标出
7. straddle /ˈstrædl/ v. 跨立
8. pitcher /ˈpɪtʃə/ n. (棒球)投手
9. bowler /ˈbəʊlə/ n. (板球)投手
10. mound /maʊnd/ n. (棒球的内场中央高出地面的)投球区土墩
11. seam /siːm/ n. 接线处，缝合处
12. walk /wɔːk/ n. 四坏球上垒
13. strikeout /ˈstraɪkaʊt/ n. 三击未中出局
14. umpire /ˈʌmpaɪə/ n. 裁判员
15. strike /straɪk/ n. 好球
16. ball /bɔːl/ n. 坏球
17. home run 本垒打
18. foul /faʊl/ n. 犯规
19. homer /ˈhəʊmə/ n. 本垒打

Had he played baseball, Sir Gary Sobers would have been a home-run hitter.

In between the single (one base) and home run (four bases with that one swing) are doubles[20] and triples[21]—balls hit into distant corners of the ballpark, allowing the batter to run to second or third before the fielder retrieves[22] the ball.

Once on base, the batter advances when subsequent[23] hitters get hits—unless the defense (the pitcher's team) can get three outs before a run is scored. Three outs complete an inning[24]. Nine innings make up a game. That seems like plenty of time to score runs. But five runs over the course of nine innings is usually enough to win most games. The pitching and defenses are that good in Major League Baseball.

Most hitters are right-handed and as a result the best defensive players are positioned on the left side of the infield[25], roughly the area of the diamond, created by the four bases that are separated by 90 feet (27.4 metres).

The catcher is the key to the defense. He not only catches balls thrown by the pitcher, he also controls the positioning of the other seven "position" players. Four play in the infield and three in the outfield[26].

See the ball. Hit the ball.

Run to first, run to second, run to third. Run home and score a run. Unless of course you have the ability to hit the ball out of the park for a home run when your progress around the bases is a leisurely trot[27] as opposed to the desperate sprint[28] that characterises the progress of lesser hitters around the bases.

During more than 150 years, the rules of baseball have been fine-tuned[29] but rarely changed on a large scale. One exception came before the 1895 season and represented the final split with any comparisons to cricket.

The flat bat was deemed[30] un-American and the round wooden bat became law. And everything changed. Some pitches were popped up[31]. Some were pounded[32] into the ground. The number of runs scored decreased measurably and the games grew much shorter in duration[33]. A single run in 1895 became more valuable than five or ten the previous year.

Baseball has both an ebb-and-flow tempo[34] and a focused drama that is perfectly suited to a midsummer night's recreation.

20. double /'dʌbəl/ n. 二垒打
21. triple /'trɪpəl/ n. 三垒打
22. retrieve /rɪ'triːv/ v. 重新得到
23. subsequent /'sʌbsɪkwənt/ a. 后来的
24. inning /'ɪnɪŋ/ n. 一局
25. infield /'ɪnfiːld/ n. 内场
26. outfield /'aʊtfiːld/ n. 外场
27. trot /trɒt/ n. 小跑,疾走
28. sprint /sprɪnt/ n. 冲刺跑
29. fine-tuned 有规则的
30. deem /diːm/ v. 认为;相信
31. to pop up 突然出现
32. pound /paʊnd/ v. 连续重击
33. duration /djʊə'reɪʃən/ n. 持续时间
34. Baseball has both an ebb-and-flow tempo 棒球可以像音乐一样有高低不同的节拍（指比赛节奏有快有慢） ebb-and-flow（潮水）涨落（这里指节拍的高低强弱） tempo /'tempəʊ/ n. (音乐的)节奏

Baseball is our soccer. And the better you understand baseball, the better you understand America... well, at least the sporting public of America, which makes up about 95 per cent of Americans.

Comprehension Questions

1. What are the differences between baseball and cricket mentioned in the passage?
2. How is a baseball game scored?
3. Where does the home plate umpire stand? What is his responsibility?
4. Why are the best defensive players usually positioned on the left side of the infield?
5. What are the responsibilities for a catcher?
6. Why do you think baseball is so popular in the US?

Background Reading

An Interview: Expert's View—Torii Hunter

Torii Hunter is an All-Star center fielder and American League MVP (most valuable player, 最有价值球员) candidate who helped the Minnesota Twins (明尼苏达双城队, 隶属于美国棒球联盟) win the AL (American League, 美国职业棒球俱乐部联盟) Central in 2002. He has hit 29 and 27 home runs the last two seasons.

Q: What is the hardest thing about hitting a baseball?

A: "It's a matter of precision, adjustment and accuracy, and there's not much room for error. Miss by a half-inch, and you can top the ball or hit it into the ground. You have to have hand-eye coordination (手眼协调能力) to adjust to the ball's speed, and you have to see the rotation of the ball."

"You have to hit the ball square, even though there are all kinds of mistakes that can be made. That's why three of 10 is good in baseball, but it might not be in another business."

Q: What is the most important thing about hitting a baseball?

A: "I can't even answer. I don't know where to begin.... It's seeing the ball, the hand-eye coordination. You have to put all your attention on the ball. You have to go up there concentrating on the ball. You can't be thinking about other things, such as, 'Is my stride too long?' or 'Do I have to get my hands back?' If so, you are not going to hit the ball. All your focus has to be on the baseball. The ball is coming in a blink of an eye."

Q: What secrets have you learned about hitting over the years?

A: "You have to have patience, you have to accept failure, you have to make adjustments and you have to have fun. If you are not having fun, you will not like the game and you will not be able to hit the ball. You have to understand that if you make an out in your first at-bat (上场击球), you still have three more at-bats to go. And always be ready to make adjustments."

Relevant Words

bag	垒垫,垒包	base line	垒间线
base	垒	bat	球棒
batter's box	击球员区	catcher's box	接手区
chest protector	护胸	fair territory	界内地区
foul territory	界外地区	helmet	护帽
home plate	本垒板	leg protector	护腿
mask	护面	pitcher's circle	投手圈
pitcher's mound	投手土墩	pitcher's plate	投手板
supporter	护裆		

Lesson 11

现代冰球运动起源于加拿大,距今已有两百多年历史,它最初是从欧洲众多传统体育项目中演变发展而来。该篇文章从起源、发展到最近的国际赛事情况等方面介绍了冰球运动。全文大致可以分为两个部分,前一部分通过详细描述第一次冰球比赛介绍了冰球比赛的规则;第二部分重点介绍了在冰球运动发展过程中各冰球大国在各次国际大赛中的情况。

Ice Hockey

By Andrew Podnieks
April, May, June 2005
Olympic Review

The sport of ice hockey developed from an amalgam[1] of closely related European sports variously called shinty[2], bandy[3], racket(s)[4], hurley[5], hurling[6], wicket[7] and lacrosse[8]. However, it is indisputable that the first game of hockey that truly is the forebear[9] to the modern game was played at the Victoria Skating Rink in Montreal[10] on 3 March 1875[11].

There are several factors that distinguish this game from aforementioned[12] group of anecdotal[13] and historical references. First, the Montreal game was played indoors. Second, this was the first known game to be played with a puck[14]-like object. The day after the match, the Montreal Gazette[15] reported: "Hockey is played usually with a ball, but last night, in order that no accident should happen, a flat block of wood was used so that it should slide along the ice without rising and thus going among the spectators to their discomfort." Third, an announcement in the Gazette the previous day altered "spectators" of the event, and they, in turn, made a special trip to watch this game. Fourth, only 18 men participated in the game at the Victoria Rink and these men formed two distinct "teams". Flags were put on the top of poles that were stuck in the ice to make formal "goals" and these teams kept score. Most importantly, because this game took place indoors, it was played within a restricted space (as opposed to a frozen river or lake with much greater expanse[16]). That space happened to

1. amalgam /əˈmælgəm/ *n.* 混合物
2. shinty /ˈʃɪntɪ/ *n.* (儿童玩的)简式曲棍球运动
3. bandy /ˈbændɪ/ *n.* 早期曲棍球运动;俄罗斯式冰球
4. racket /ˈrækɪt/ *n.* 网拍式墙球
5. hurley /ˈhɜːlɪ/ *n.* 爱尔兰式棒球戏
6. hurling /ˈhɜːlɪŋ/ *n.* 爱尔兰式曲棍球
7. wicket /ˈwɪkɪt/ *n.* 三柱门(这里代指槌球运动)
8. lacrosse /ləˈkrɒs/ *n.* 网棒球
9. forebear /ˈfɔːbeə/ *n.* 祖先
10. Montreal /ˌmɒntrɪˈɔːl/ 蒙特利尔(加拿大魁北克省南部的一个城市)
11. 在欧洲,日期的写法不同于美国,一般写成日—月—年。
12. aforementioned /əˈfɔːmenʃənd/ *a.* 上述的
13. anecdotal /ˌænɪkˈdəʊtl/ *a.* 轶话的,轶事的
14. puck /pʌk/ *n.* 冰球(指球)
15. Montreal Gazette 蒙特利尔报 gazette /gəˈzet/ *n.* 报纸,政府公报
16. expanse /ɪkˈspæns/ *n.* 宽阔的区域

measure 85 feet by 200 feet, the standard professional playing surface to this day.

Ice hockey appeared at the Olympic Games in 1920 when a small number of winter sports were played as part of the Summer Games in Antwerp[17], Belgium. The winter component took place over seven days (23-29 April 1920) while the summer sports were not contested until September. In truth, ice hockey was a full sport that year, but in theory, it was a demonstration sport because the term "Olympic Winter Games" did not appear until four years later when snow sports had their own host city and a full itinerary[18] independent of[19] the Summer Olympic Games.

From the first tournament in 1920 until the Soviet Union entered the international ice hockey community in 1954, Canada was the undisputed[20] world leader in the sport. The USA was a distant second, and the European nations well behind in the developing of skills, knowledge of the game, and practice of its finer points. Canada won every international gold medal from 1920 to 1952 for which it competed, with two exceptions: the 1936 Games, when Great Britain won; and in 1933 when the USA shocked the Canadians at the World Championship in Czechoslovakia[21].

The Toronto Granites team that represented Canada at the 1924 Olympic Games is perhaps the greatest ice hockey team to have competed internationally. They won four preliminary games — en route[22] to a gold medal showdown[23] with USA, with scores of 30-0 over the Czechs, 22-0 over Sweden, 33-0 over Switzerland and 19-2 over Great Britain. In the final, they beat their southerly neighbours[24], 6-1. Harry Watson, the greatest amateur the game has ever known, scored 36 goals in those five games including an unprecedented 13 goals against the Swiss. Canada's domination ended in 1956 in Cortina d'Ampezzo when it lost games to the Soviet Union and the United States and had to settle for a bronze medal. A stunning gold by the USA in 1960, spearheaded[25] by the goaltending[26] of Jack McCartan, then gave way to the Soviet machine that won four successive[27] Olympic golds (1964—1976) and 15 of the next 18 World Championships (between 1963 and 1983).

The "Miracle on Ice" victory by the USA in 1980 again gave way to Soviet wins in 1984 and 1988, but as the political landscape in Europe changed in the early 1990s, so too did the champions and a "Unified Team" of former Soviet players won in 1992.

17. Antwerp /ˈæntwɜːp/ 安特卫普（比利时北部港口城市，曾承办 1920 年第 7 届夏季奥运会）
18. itinerary /aɪˈtɪnərəri/ n. 路线；安排
19. independent of 独立于
20. undisputed /ˌʌndɪˈspjuːtɪd/ a. 无可争辩的
21. Czechoslovakia /ˌtʃekəʊsləˈvækɪə/ 捷克斯洛伐克
22. en route /ɒnˈruːt/ ad. 在途中
23. showdown /ˈʃəʊdaʊn/ n. 摊牌，最后决一雌雄
24. southerly neighbours 住在南边的邻居（指美国队）
25. spearhead /ˈspɪəhed/ v. 充当先锋
26. goaltending /ˈɡəʊlˌtendɪŋ/ n. 守门技术
27. successive /səkˈsesɪv/ a. 连续的

Part II Sporting Kaleidoscope

Leading to Turin in 2006, three of the great ice hockey nations have had their moment[28] of Olympic glory since Albertville 1992. Sweden won in 1994, the Czech Republic in 1998, and Canada in 2002, the last victory perhaps the most impressive because it signaled a resurgence[29] of the mother nation[30] which from 2002 to 2005 has gone unchecked[31].

The Turino 2006 Olympic Winter Games will be played as always under international rules, but the tournament format will be significantly different from that in Salt Lake City in 2002. In Turin, there will be two groups of six teams each (rather than four groups of four) playing a round robin[32] within each group (five games each in this qualifying round). The top four in each group then play a crossover[33] quarter-final (A1 vs. B4, A2 vs. B3, etc.) to start the elimination round of games, continuing with semi-finals and finally a gold medal game. The women's tournament will be much the same except the two groups will have four teams and the playoffs[34] will start with semi-finals (A1 vs. B2, B1 vs. A2).

International rules differ from National Hockey League rules in several pertinent[35] ways. Two-line passes[36] are permitted, and icings[37] are automatically called when the puck crosses the end red line. Fighting results in an automatic game misconduct[38], and there is one referee, not two. In the round robin, tie[39] games go on record as such, but in the knockout[40] round teams will play a 20-minute overtime period followed by a shootout[41], if necessary.

There was tremendous anticipation leading up to the men's and women's ice hockey tournaments in Salt Lake City in 2002. On the women's side, it was assumed that Canada would play the USA for gold. Canada had won every World Championship gold ever contested, but the Americans stunned Canada in the gold-medal game in Nagano[42] four years earlier in the first women's ice hockey tournament played at the Olympic Games. In the round robin, both teams overwhelmed their opposition, Canada's three wins coming with an aggregate[43] score of 25-0, and the USA's wins with a combined 27-1 score. Both teams easily won their semi-finals games and headed for the gold-medal showdown. Canada led 1-0 after the first period, but the turning point came late in the second with the Canadians ahead 2-1. Jayna Hefford broke through with just one second to give Canada an insurmountable[44] 3-1 lead. Team USA pulled one goal back in the third, but Canada held on for a 3-2 victory and the gold medal.

28. to have one's moment 走红；得意
29. resurgence /rɪ'sɜːdʒəns/ n. 苏醒；复兴
30. mother nation 指加拿大
31. to go unchecked 一直未受制止（指加拿大从2002年到2005年连续获胜，复兴的势头未停息过）
32. round robin 循环赛
33. crossover /'krɒs,əʊvə/ n. 交叉
34. playoff, 也写作 play-off, 指（平局后的）延长赛
35. pertinent /'pɜːtɪnənt/ a. 有关的，相干的
36. two-line pass 从防守区传到介于中场红线到攻击区前的蓝线之间的传球
37. icing /'aɪsɪŋ/ n. 死球（冰球运动中故意将球打出防守方区外的行为）
38. misconduct /mɪs'kɒndʌkt/ n. 不正当行为
39. tie /taɪ/ n. 平局
40. knockout /'nɒk-aʊt/ a. 淘汰的
41. shootout /'ʃuːtaʊt/ n. 罚球
42. Nagano /nə'ɡɑːnəʊ/ 长野（位于日本本州中部）
43. aggregate /'æɡrɪɡeɪt/ n. 总分；累积分
44. insurmountable /ˌɪnsə'maʊntəbəl/ a. 不可超越的

The men's tournament was more wide open. Canada had assembled a spectacular team featuring captain Mario Lemieux, but USA was on home ice and had won gold in 1980, 1960, and 1932, the only other times it had hosted the Olympic Winter Games. The Czechs[45] had won three World Championships in a row[46], and the Russians, as always, had plenty of talent representing their country.

The most shocking result from an otherwise unsurprising quarter-final round came when Belarus[47] beat Sweden 4-3. Thus, the one semi-final (Canada vs. Belarus) was anticlimactic[48] (a 7-1 Canadian victory) while the other, USA-Russia, offered one of the most exciting games of recent Olympic history. The Americans won, 3-2, but not before the Russians did everything but tie the game in a wild third period played mostly in the USA end.

The all North-American finale[49] produced a riveting[50] game, won 5-2 by Canada, which won its first Olympic gold in half a century, and which was watched by more than 10 million people in Canada. In Turin competition promises to be stiff with[51] any of the "big seven" (Canada, USA, Russia, Sweden, Finland, the Czech Republic and Slovakia[52]) capable of winning a medal.

45. Czech /tʃek/ *n.* 捷克人
46. in a row 连续地
47. Belarus /belə'ruːs/ *n.* 白俄罗斯
48. anticlimactic /ˌæntɪklaɪ'mæktɪk/ *a.* 令人失望的
49. finale /fɪ'nɑːlɪ/ *n.* 决赛
50. riveting /'rɪvɪtɪŋ/ *a.* 吸引人的
51. to be stiff with 肯定的
52. Slovakia /sləʊ'vækɪə/ *n.* 斯洛伐克

Comprehension Questions

1. When and where was the first game of ice hockey held?
2. When did Soviet Union join the international hockey community?
3. In which year was the first winter Olympic Games held?
4. Why is Canada called the "mother nation" of ice hockey?
5. Summarize the history of ice hockey with the information provided in this passage.

Background Reading

Ice Hockey—An Olympic Sport Since 1920

ABOUT

The word "hockey" comes from the old French word "hocquet", meaning "stick". The origins of ice hockey are unclear, but it is widely accepted that the British are responsible for bringing hockey to North America. Soldiers stationed in Nova Scotia (新斯科舍省,加拿大大西洋四省之一), Canada, played the earliest games. In 1879, a group of college students at McGill University (麦吉尔大学) in Montreal (蒙特利尔), organised competitions and developed the first known set of hockey rules. The sport migrated south to the United States during the 1890s. The first known hockey games took place between Johns Hopkins (美国约翰·斯霍普金斯大学) and Yale Universities in 1895. The first Olympic Games to include ice hockey for men were the Antwerp Games in 1920. However, the first Olympic Winter Games took place in 1924 in Chamonix (夏慕尼,法国著名滑雪胜地).

COMPETITION

At the Olympic Winter Games, women compete in an eight-team tournament (women's hockey was added to the Olympic Winter Games programme in Nagano in 1998), whereas men compete in a 12-team tournament. A team must not have more than six players on the ice while play is in progress. Typically, these players are one goalkeeper, two defenders, two wings (边锋) and one centre (中锋). Fewer players can be on the ice as a result of penalties: a goalkeeper can be replaced by a skater during a delayed penalty, or at any other time of the game, at the team's risk. A regular game consists of three 20-minute periods, with a 15-minute intermission after the first and second periods. Teams change ends for each period. If a tie occurs in a medal-round game in which a winner must be determined, a five-minute sudden-victory overtime period is played. In the gold medal game, a 20-minute sudden-victory period is played subsequent to another 15-minute intermission. In the case of a tie after any sudden-victory period, a game-winning penalty shoot competition takes place to determine the winner.

Relevant Words

blueliner 后卫	box formation 方形阵式
centre forward 中锋	defender 后卫
defenseman 后卫	face-off alignment 争球阵式
face-off line 争球圈	forward 前锋
period 局	puck 冰球
winger 边锋	wingman 边锋
NHL = National Hockey League 北美冰球联赛	

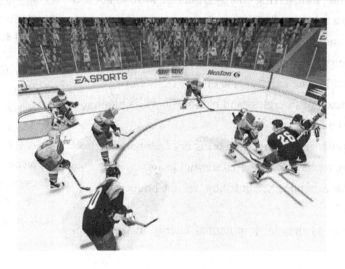

Lesson 12

撑杆跳高是田径运动中一个重要项目,它的难度大,特别对起跳前的技术要求高。那么研究撑杆跳高运动的科学家、撑杆跳高奥运会冠军和撑杆跳高的青年运动员是如何认识这一运动的?撑杆、跃杆的诀窍是什么呢?撑杆跳高是不是"不可完成的任务"?

Pole Vaulting[1]: Doing the 'Seemingly Impossible'

By Gary Mihoces
February 27, 2003
USA Today

The men's world record in the pole vault is 6.14 meters, set by Sergei Bubka[2] of the Ukraine[3] in 1994. The women's record is 4.81 meters, set by the USA's Stacy Dragila[4] in 2001.

That's 20 feet, 1 3/4 inches for Bubka and 15 feet, 9 1/4 inches for Dragila.

"The average person just wouldn't even know where to begin. The idea of going up almost 20 feet on a stick is astonishing. How could you pull that off[5]?" says Louis Bloomfield, professor of physics at the University of Virginia[6].

But Bloomfield, who teaches a course called "How Things Work" and wrote a book with the same title, knows how it's done. It's all about energy conversion[7], transferring energy from one form to another like a baton[8] passed in a relay race[9].

Standing at the end of the runway[10], the vaulter is ready with chemical potential energy[11] in his muscles. As he runs down the track, his energy converts into kinetic energy[12], the energy of motion[13].

When the pole, made of fiberglass and carbon fibers, is planted, a pivotal exchange takes place.[14]

"They bend the pole, and the bending transfers energy to the pole in the form of elastic potential energy[15]," Bloomfield says.

"In fact, it's like a bounce[16]… but they're not bouncing back. They're bouncing up."

The bounce comes as the elastic potential energy in the pole is

1. pole vaulting 撑杆跳高
2. Sergei Bubka 谢尔盖·布勃卡(乌克兰男子撑竿跳高运动员,汉城奥运会冠军,10次世界锦标赛冠军,35次创造世界纪录,现任乌克兰奥委会主席)
3. Ukraine /juːˈkreɪn/ n. 乌克兰
4. Stacy Dragila 史黛西·德拉吉拉(美国女子撑杆跳高运动员,曾获得2000年悉尼奥运会女子撑杆跳高金牌)
5. to pull off 努力实现;赢得
6. Virginia /vəːˈdʒɪmjə/ 弗吉尼亚州(美国东部的一个州)
7. conversion /kənˈvɜːʃən/ n. 转化
8. baton /ˈbætɒn/ n. 接力棒
9. relay race 接力赛跑
10. runway /ˈrʌnweɪ/ n. 助跑道
11. potential energy 势能
12. kinetic energy 动能
13. energy of motion 动能
14. 玻璃纤维或碳素纤维制成的撑杆落地撑起时,重要的能量转换便发生了。
    fiberglass /ˈfaɪbəɡlɑːs/ n. 玻璃纤维 carbon fiber 碳素纤维 carbon /ˈkɑːbən/ n. 碳 plant /plɑːnt/ v. 植入;插入(这里指撑杆落地撑起)
    pivotal /ˈpɪvətəl/ a. 关键的
15. elastic potential energy 弹性势能 elastic /ɪˈlæstɪk/ a. 弹性的
16. bounce /baʊns/ n. 跳起;弹回

transferred into gravitational[17] potential energy in the vaulter. At the top, the vaulter bends his body as he passes over the bar.

"It's a great maneuver[18], which takes enormous skill," Bloomfield says.

"But people who have really good control of their shape can do seemingly impossible things."

Expert's view—Stacy Dragila

The USA's Stacy Dragila is the 2000 Olympic women's pole vault champion and the outdoor world recordholder[19] at 15-9 1/4.

Q: In the world of sports, how hard is pole vaulting?

A: "It was terrifying at first, as a junior[20] in college, and I'm sure the bar was only 6 feet. I thought, 'How am I going to get turned up[21] and get my butt[22] over this bar?'"

"A lot of kids are overwhelmed[23] with that initial fear of going up and committing to[24] bending the pole. There's a sense of risk-taking, and you have to develop trust with your coach. There's always that fear the pole is going to snap[25]. It takes a lot of time to figure out. You have to have a lot of patience."

Q: What's the most important thing about pole vaulting?

A: "The most common mistake by beginning vaulters results from a last-second panic attack as they prepare to plant the pole. Instead of pressing the pole up ahead of them, like swinging on a high bar, they pull the pole into themselves."

Q: What secrets have you learned about pole vaulting?

A: "The pole vault is the one event where I have to have a coach with me. You have to have a trust with that person that you might not have with anyone else."

"Gymnastics training is a key to developing the agility[26] the event demands. It doesn't mean you have to join a class. There's stuff you can do on the grass, tucking[27] and rolling[28], handstands[29]. Or just finding a high bar at a local park or at a school and trying to turn over."

Average Joe's view—Tom Weir

My high school track coach, Bill "Stubby[30]" Thompson, was a great guy, except for his sadistic[31] streak[32].

Every spring he made the entire team go through all 10 events of the decathlon[33], just to make sure we didn't have some undiscovered talent performing in the wrong event.

As a sophomore 2-miler[34], it seemed a little ridiculous to have me

17. gravitational /ˌgrævɪˈteɪʃənəl/ a. 重力的
18. maneuver /məˈnuːvə/ n. 策略；行动
19. world recordholder 世界纪录保持者
20. junior /ˈdʒuːnjə/ n. 大学三年级学生
21. to turn up 翻身
22. butt /bʌt/ n. (美国口语)屁股
23. overwhelm /ˌəʊvəˈwelm/ v. 淹没；覆盖
24. to commit to doing sth. 一定要做某事
25. snap /snæp/ v. 突然折断

26. agility /əˈdʒɪlɪtɪ/ n. 敏捷性
27. tucking /ˈtʌkɪŋ/ n. 团身
28. rolling /ˈrəʊlɪŋ/ n. 滚翻
29. handstand /ˈhændstænd/ n. 手倒立
30. stubby /ˈstʌbɪ/ a. (人的体形等)短而粗的
31. sadistic /səˈdɪstɪk/ a. 虐待狂的
32. streak /striːk/ n. 性格中的某种特征(倾向)
33. decathlon /dɪˈkæθlɒn/ n. (田径)十项全能运动
34. 2-miler 2英里跑运动员

try to heave[35] the shot[36] or discus[37]. But the really imposing[38] event was the pole vault.

Everybody who has held a fly rod says, "Gee[39], fiberglass is really light."

Believe me, when it's shaped into even just a 10-foot pole, it's heavy, cumbersome[40] and not the ideal shape to be carrying on a sprint[41] down the runway.

But you see those Olympians bend it like a piece of just-boiled spaghetti[42] so it must be really flexible, right?

The only way to make a pole bend is with total body commitment. You have to fling[43] yourself into the air, and then you're at the mercy of[44] the pole.

Mine put me in the dirt twice.[45] On the last try, I considered it a moral victory when I at least somersaulted[46] into the pit[47], well under the bar. And that bar was set at the minimal height of 8 feet.

Coach Thompson loved the pole vault because he knew a good vaulter could be plugged into just about any other event on short notice.[48]

I remember him preaching[49] that "pole vaulters are almost always the best athletes on a track team."

And I remember responding, "Well, coach, that ain't me."

35. heave /hiːv/ v. 举起
36. shot /ʃɒt/ n. 铅球
37. discus /ˈdɪskəs/ n. 铁饼
38. imposing /ɪmˈpəʊzɪŋ/ a. 令人难忘的
39. gee /dʒiː/ int. 感叹词,用于惊讶
40. cumbersome /ˈkʌmbəsəm/ a. 笨重的
41. sprint /sprɪnt/ n. 疾跑
42. spaghetti /spəˈɡetɪ/ n. 意大利面条
43. fling /flɪŋ/ v. 投;掷
44. at the mercy of 受到……的支配
45. 我自己在训练撑杆跳高时曾摔下两次。
46. somersault /ˈsʌməsɔːlt/ v. 翻筋斗
47. pit /pɪt/ n. 深坑
48. 汤姆森教练最喜欢撑杆跳高这一项目,他认为优秀的撑杆跳高运动员能在短期内练好其他任何一个项目。
49. preach /priːtʃ/ v. 鼓吹

Comprehension Questions

1. What is an average person's reaction to pole vaulting, according to Professor Louis Bloomfield?
2. What are the difficulties for the beginners of pole vaulting, according to Stacy Dragila?
3. What training is needed to develop the agility that pole vaulting demands?
4. What is Bill Thompson's comment on pole vaulting?
5. Can you summarize the ways to improve the performance of a beginning vaulter mentioned in the passage?

Background Reading

The Physics of Pole Vaulting

Pole vaulting is a wonderful illustration of how one type of energy is converted to another type. Through the proper use of the pole vault, the energy of motion associated with the sprint is converted into the energy needed to overcome gravity and reach a certain height. The energy of motion is called "kinetic energy," while the energy associated with working against gravity is called "gravitational potential energy (重力位能)." The faster you can sprint toward the bar, the higher you can vault over the bar, again assuming a proper technique.

Pole vaulting is also a great example of the central principle in physics: the conservation of energy (能量守恒定律).

The conservation of energy says that energy can never be created or destroyed; it can only be converted from one form to another. When you pole vault, what you ideally want is to convert all of your kinetic energy into gravitational potential energy. In the real world, you can never get a 100 percent conversion because some of the kinetic energy gets converted into other kinds of energy, such as heat, friction (摩擦), sound, and vibrations (颤动) of the pole itself. Nevertheless, the "ideal case" gives you a good idea of how high you could jump.

Relevant Words

handhold 握杆	high jump 跳高
pole planting 插杆	pull up 引体
push off the pole 推杆	standing high jump 立定跳高
swing up the leg 摆腿	

Lesson 13

> 滑冰运动与芭蕾舞有很多相似之处,在现代滑冰运动的训练中就大量地运用了芭蕾舞练习的很多动作技法。本文将芭蕾舞与滑冰运动进行了比较,归纳出很多相似之处,并探讨了芭蕾舞训练对滑冰运动员在形体、力量、平衡、表情、神态等方面的作用。阅读过程中读者如能将所读内容与所观看过的芭蕾舞表演和滑冰表演联系起来,会得到艺术之美的绝妙享受。

Making the Connections
—Ballet Classes Enhance Skating Technique in Many Ways

By Jacquelene Boucard, Anne Marine, and Debbie Pitsos
March 2005
Skating[1]

For years skating coaches have been encouraging their skaters to take ballet classes to aid in on-ice performance. And for years, parents and coaches have heard their skaters ask, "What has ballet got to do with skating?"

A fair question to be sure.

Though skating and ballet experts agree that studying ballet will enhance a skater's on-ice technique, it isn't always so obvious how this will happen. What is it specifically that is taught and practiced in ballet that relates to the elements on the ice?

Posture[2] and Power

Skaters require strong core muscles to connect the upper and lower body for controlled, powerful movements. They must be able to keep their shoulders over their hips throughout jumps, spins, footwork and edges[3] and be able to check their shoulders against their hips in Mohawks[4], three turns, brackets[5], rockers[6], counters[7] and choctaws[8]. Thus it is to the skater's benefit[9] to become aware of the feeling of twisting in the middle of the torso[10], and also the feeling of staying square[11].

Ballet teachers spend hours teaching students correct ballet

1. *Skating*《滑冰》,美国花样滑冰协会会刊,每月发行。主要介绍花样滑冰技巧、国际花样滑冰比赛的最新规则等。主要读者对象为花样滑冰专业人士。
2. posture /ˈpɒstʃə/ n. (身体的)姿态;体态
3. edge /edʒ/ n. 滑行线痕(花样滑冰的一种基本技术动作)
4. Mohawk /ˈməʊhɔːk/ 莫霍克步(前刃变后刃半周跳)
5. bracket /ˈbrækɪt/ n. 括弧型(花样溜冰的一种花式)
6. rocker /ˈrɒkə/ n. 内钩形(花样溜冰的一种花式)
7. counter /ˈkaʊntə/ n. 外钩形(花样溜冰的一种花式)
8. choctaw /ˈtʃɒktɔː/ n. 乔克托滑法(换脚转体180°)
9. to one's benefit 对某人有好处
10. torso /ˈtɔːsəʊ/ n. 躯干
11. to stay square 保持直立

posture, which is the same posture needed for skating—a neutral[12] spine with the shoulders over the hips. The ballet student is taught to engage the lower abdominal muscles while maintaining a neutral spine, thus learning to connect the upper and lower body for strong, powerful movements.

Balance and Body Lines

Maintaining a neutral spine is essential to both ballet technique and to performing on-ice elements. Ballet teaches the skater how to move the pelvis without losing balance or disconnecting the center in footwork sequences,[13] including pirouette[14] turns, jumps and leaps across the floor. With every movement, in either skating or ballet, there is a weight shift from one foot to the other, which causes a constant change in the center of balance.

Having a good sense of balance and a strong core is critical to a skater's alignment[15] and directly affects the skater's edge quality, footwork, jump preparation, landings[16] and spins.

Correct placement[17], power and quickness are addressed[18] in ballet classes through basic skills such as plies[19], tendus[20], degages[21], frappe[22], fouette[23] and grand battement[24]. These movements teach the basic "snap[25] through the hips, knees, ankles and feet" used for skating basics, such as power for stroking[26], pushing through the feet for jumps, and, of course, agility in quick footwork.

As the skater progresses in dance and skating, both disciplines focus on details of the basics—extension of body lines, flexibility while maintaining body alignment, quality of movement, and development of strength and confidence.

The skater learns to perform to different music rhythms and tempos, to count the beats of the music[27] and how style and carriage[28] change with the mood or theme of the music, thus establishing a dynamic range in presentation[29].

Expression and Emotion

While ballet is often thought of by skaters as one more thing to do, it is the ballet that teaches the skaters how to perform. Ballet can teach a skater how to interpret and express their music by telling a story or conveying an emotion through the connecting steps of their program. This is what makes the difference between a program that is all jumps with a lot of crossovers or stroking between the jumps, and a program that is interesting, and artistic.[30]

12. neutral /'nju:trəl/ *a.* 中立的；不歪不斜的
13. 通过练习芭蕾，滑冰运动员学习如何在移动臀部的一系列步法中保持重心。pelvis /'pelvɪs/ *n.* 骨盆
14. pirouette /ˌpɪruˈet/ *n.* 脚尖旋转
15. alignment /əˈlaɪnmənt/ *n.* （身体的）打开
16. landing /'lændɪŋ/ *n.* 落冰
17. placement /'pleɪsmənt/ *n.* 站位
18. address /əˈdres/ *v.* 进行；解决（问题等）
19. ply /plaɪ/ *n.* 弯曲（芭蕾动作）
20. tendu /'tɑːndjuː/ *n.* 并步跳（芭蕾动作）
21. degage /ˌdeɪgɑːˈʒeɪ/ *n.* 解脱，离开（芭蕾动作，活动脚往外延伸至离开地面几英寸的地方）
22. frappe /fræˈpeɪ/ *n.* 弹腿，击腿（芭蕾动作）
23. fouette /fweˈteɪ/ *n.* 古典芭蕾主要的旋转技巧之一，也称"挥鞭转"，指一腿伸出在空中急速划圈的单腿转。
24. grand battement 大靠合（芭蕾动作，活动脚和支撑脚有靠合的动作）
25. snap /snæp/ *n.* 快速移动
26. stroking /strəʊk/ *n.* 双腿交替向前滑，一条腿滑行时，另一条腿呈45度角向外后侧伸开。
27. …count the beats of the music 跟着音乐的拍子
28. carriage /'kærɪdʒ/ *n.* 姿态
29. …establishing a dynamic range in presentation 在表演中富于变化
30. 这使得（滑冰）节目具有趣味性和艺术性，与单纯的双腿交叉跳和跳跃中的摆动全然不同。

Comprehension Questions

1. What are the similarities between ballet and skating?
2. What elements do ballet classes help in enhancing skaters' on-ice techniques?
3. Why does a skater need strong core muscles?
4. What qualities are essential to skating which can be trained through basic skills in ballet classes?
5. What can a skater learn from ballet to improve his/her performance?

Background Reading

Ballet: An Introduction

Ballet is a form of dancing performed for theatre audiences. Like other dance forms, ballet may tell a story, express a mood, or simply reflect the music. But a ballet dancer's technique (way of performing) and special skills differ greatly from those of other dancers. Ballet dancers perform many movements that are unnatural for the body. But when these movements are well executed (完成), they look natural.

Ballet dancers seem to ignore the law of gravity (万有引力定律) as they float through the air in long, slow leaps. They keep perfect balance while they spin like tops (陀螺,一种玩具) without becoming dizzy (眩晕的,昏乱的). During certain steps, their feet move so rapidly that the eye can hardly follow the movements. The women often dance on the tips of their toes, and the men lift them high overhead as if they were as light as feathers.

The dancers take joy in (以……为快乐) controlling their bodies, and ballet audiences share their feelings. The spectators can feel as though they are gliding and spinning with the dancers. Simply by using their bodies, ballet dancers are able to express many emotions, such as anger, fear, jealousy, joy, and sadness. The lines of the dancers' bodies form beautiful, harmonious designs. Ballet technique is called classical because it stresses this purity and harmony (协调) of design.

In addition to the dance form called ballet, an individual dance work or performance using classical ballet technique is called a ballet. Any dance work involving a group of dancers may also be called a ballet even though it may not use classical ballet technique. For example, works of modern dance, musical comedy, and dance on television programmes may or may not include this technique, but many of them are called ballets. Classical ballet technique originally developed in France during the 1600's. Today, French words are used in all parts of the world for the various steps and positions of classical ballet.

Ballets are staged (上演) and performed by ballet companies. The artistic director of a company is in charge of staging a ballet. In some companies, he or she is also the choreographer (舞蹈指导), who arranges a ballet's dance movements and teaches them to the dancers. After a company decides to perform a ballet, the artistic director tries to produce a harmonious work of art by blending (合成,混合) all the parts of the ballet. These parts include the dancing, music, scenery, and costumes—all based on the ballet's story or mood. A ballet can be performed without music, scenery, or costumes. But most ballets use all three parts.

The choreographer, composer (作曲家), and scenery and costume designer work together as a team. But the dancing is the most important part of a ballet. The designer must plan scenery and costumes that allow the dancers space and freedom of movement.

Different ballet styles have developed in various countries. For example, the style that developed in the United States tends to be energetic and fast. Ballet in Russia is often forceful and showy (艳丽的), and French ballet is generally pretty and decorative. Ballet dancers travel throughout the world and adopt different features of foreign styles. As a result of these international influences, all ballet is continually being broadened and enriched.

Relevant Words

artistic impression 艺术印象	factor 难度系数
ice-skate 冰鞋	pairs skating 双人滑
short program 规定自由滑;短节目	short track speed skating 短道速滑
singles skating 单人滑	skate 冰刀

Lesson 14

英国草地网球协会(LTA)是英国网球运动的重要组织,历史上对英国网球的发展作出了巨大贡献。近年来,英国草地网球协会自己鼓吹的成绩受到了广泛质疑。本文就是将英国网球每年的花费与在国际网联排名中与英国相当的日本和巴基斯坦进行比较,对LTA提出了强烈批评。同时,作者从英国10多年未赢得戴维斯杯这一事实入手,批评了LTA的体制与管理问题。

LTA: Long-Term Aims or Leading Tennis Astray[1]?

By Neil Harman
September 29, 2005
The Times[2]

There are 40 more British men with a world ranking than three years ago, which suggests that David Felgate, the LTA's performance director, is working a minor miracle.[3] But if you consider that 18 of the present 71 have one ATP[4] point, which in some cases has been earned by losing 6-0, 6-0 on a tournament wild card[5], the picture becomes a little less well defined[6].

As in all things, a healthy dose of perspective is required.[7] Likewise, a letter to the Editor in The Times on Tuesday from Derek Bone, a former employee of the LTA, highlighted growing levels of disillusion[8] with "progress" in British tennis. Quoting John Crowther, the LTA's chief executive for the past eight years—who said that he had steered the "oil tanker of British tennis out of iceberg-infested water and into warmer seas"[9]—Bone wrote: "This is an assertion[10] for which he offered no evidence."

Today, the draw for the 2006 Davis Cup[11] will be made using the International Tennis Federation's rankings as part of the procedure. Great Britain lie 25th in the world, one place behind Pakistan and one ahead of Japan, and although Andy Murray[12] could tell you their No 1 players and their world rankings without turning a hair[13], most people would have to look it up. Takao Suzuki, of Japan, is ranked No 217;

1. LTA=Lawn Tennis Association 英国草地网球协会 lead... astray 领着……走入歧途
2. *The Times*《泰晤士报》,于1785年在伦敦创刊,是一份在全球享有很高声誉的日报,被誉为"现代新闻事业鼻祖","世界第一大报纸"等等。该报内容涉及国内外重大事件、金融、科学、教育、文体、法律等,其中国内外要闻和经济新闻的比重最大,这是它与通俗报纸鲜明的不同之处。销量为60万份左右,其读者对象主要是国会议员、政府官员、上层知识分子、企业家和金融界人士。
3. 比起3年前,又有40名英国男运动员进入世界排名,这意味着英国网球协会执行主管戴维德·费尔盖(David Felgate)实现了一个小小的奇迹。
4. ATP=Association of Tennis Professionals 国际男子职业网球联合会
5. wild card 外卡(直接进入正选赛资格)
6. well defined 清晰的,清楚的
7. 像任何事情一样,人们都期待美好的前景。
8. disillusion /ˌdɪsɪˈluːʒən/ n. 醒悟
9. ...he had steered the "oil tanker of..." 他指挥英国网球的这艘大船从冰山重重的大海中驶向安全而温暖的海域。infest /ɪnˈfest/ v. 大批出没于;侵扰
10. assertion /əˈsɜːʃən/ n. 断言;声明
11. Davis Cup 戴维斯杯网球赛(由国际网球联合会主办的每年一度的世界男子网球团体赛)
12. Andy Murray 安迪·穆雷(英国职业网球运动员)
13. without turning a hair 不动声色地

Aisam-Ul-Haq Qureshi, from Pakistan, is No 360. Neither the Japanese nor Pakistani federations receives a lump sum[14] of more than £25 million a year to assist with turning their tennis tankers around.[15]

Britain's worst Davis Cup defeat for a decade, by Switzerland in Geneva last week, can be offset by the fact that the opposition included a man being prepared for a place among the deities of the sport, but it was a hiding nonetheless.[16] The fact that of the six nations Britain may be drawn against today, the one they would least like to face is Serbia[17] and Montenegro[18] underlines[19] where they stand in the international order.

Britain have many players scrambling[20] at the bottom of the ladder, but not enough of them are showing signs of escaping these doldrums[21] and performing in a manner that might influence Jeremy Bates[22], the captain, to desist[23] from his present Davis Cup team of Greg Rusedski[24], Murray and... your guess is as good as any.

The LTA's decision to flood the tennis schedule with more domestic Challenger, Satellite and Futures events has achieved, in part, what was intended—to give British players a greater opportunity to earn more points while not having to travel the globe for their regular wallopings.[25] The downside[26] is that it has created too cosy an environment from which not enough have chosen to leave. Murray is the hope and although the 18-year-old will break into the top 100 today if he beats Robin Soderling[27], of Sweden, in the second round of the Thailand Open in Bangkok, he is a lone ranger in terms of international development that smacks of a failed and failing coaching structure[28].

For the LTA to deliver on its promise of 540,000 juniors playing regularly by 2009 and a 5 per cent annual growth in affiliated[29] club membership, Crowther insists that it has in place "a modern management structure with delegation to counties for delivery with professional, accountable managers.[30] The National Tennis Centre (scheduled to open next year at a cost of £40 million), the National Academies at Bath and Loughborough (we are still awaiting someone to emerge from those with international credentials), the High Performance Centres, together with Performance Clubs, will all play their part."

All very worthy. But for Britain not to have won a World Group Davis Cup tie in almost two decades—having had Tim Henman at the nation's disposal for ten years[31]—represents an unacceptable state of affairs.

14. a lump sum 一大笔(钱)
15. 通过比较了在国际网联排名中与英国相当的巴基斯坦和日本两个国家的资金投入，作者指责英国在网球上花费大量金钱，成绩上却无大的起色。
16. 近十年来，英国在戴维斯杯中最惨的失败就是上周在日内瓦被瑞士击败，对手中有一个人多年来就是向着运动的最高水平冲击。这虽然让英国能挽回点颜面，可无论如何都是一次惨败。offset /'ɒfset/ v. 抵消，弥补　deity /'deɪti/ n. 神，神性（这里指这项运动的最高水平）hiding /'haɪdɪŋ/ n. 鞭打；彻底的失败
17. Serbia /'sɜːbjə/ 塞尔维亚（原南斯拉夫联盟共和国的一部分）
18. Montenegro /ˌmɒntɪ'niːgrəʊ/ 黑山（原南斯拉夫联盟共和国的一部分）
19. underline /ˌʌndə'laɪm/ v. 突出体现
20. scramble /'skræmbl/ v. 爬行；攀登
21. doldrums /'dɒldrəmz/ n. 郁闷；无生气，意气消沉
22. Jeremy Bates，杰瑞米·贝兹（英国戴维斯杯队长）
23. desist /dɪ'zɪst/ v. 终止
24. Greg Rusedski 格雷戈·鲁塞德斯基（英国网球名将，以大力发球闻名网坛，外号"大力水手"）
25. 英国草地网球协会(LTA)决定通过国内的挑战赛、卫星赛和希望赛使国内赛事频繁化。这项决定已经在一定程度上实现了其初衷，即通过国内赛事使英国运动员获得更多的积分机会，让他们不用到世界各地比赛又屡遭失败。wallop /'wɒləp/ v. 击败
26. downside /'daʊnˌsaɪd/ n. 缺点；劣势
27. Robin Soderling 鲁宾·索德林（瑞典男子职业网球运动员）
28. that... structure 在国际赛事的开拓上，他(穆雷)是一个孤独的前行者，这说明了整个教练体系无论昨日，还是现在，都是失败的。ranger /'reɪndʒə/ n. 突击队员 to smack of... 让人想起，像（反面的东西）
29. affiliated /ə'fɪliːeɪtɪd/ a. 附属的
30. 克郎泽坚持认为一个现代的管理组织结构已经建立起来了，在这个结构下，总部往地区一级的组织派驻负责任的职业管理人员（来管理）。in place 到位　accountable /ə'kaʊntəbəl/ a. 有责任的
31. 亨曼已经为英国打了十年球了。Tim Henman 蒂姆·亨曼（英国网球运动员，被看做是英国网球的一面旗帜）

Comprehension Questions

1. How is the author's tone when he writes David Felgate is "working a minor miracle"?
2. What is Derek Bone's opinion on John Crowther's praise on his own contribution to British tennis?
3. What measures is LTA going to take to improve British tennis?
4. What is the meaning of the title according to the whole article?
5. Do you think LTA is leading British tennis astray? Why or why not?

Background Reading

An Introduction to LTA

The LTA is the governing body of British tennis. We are bound together by a lifelong passion for the game and united in our commitment to growing the sport of tennis throughout the country.

The Lawn Tennis Association (LTA) is committed to supporting tennis at all levels, from the grassroots (基层) of the game to success on the international stage. We work with clubs, schools and local authorities to make tennis accessible, affordable and attractive to everyone, regardless of age or background. We judge ourselves by the number of people enjoying tennis in Britain, and by the standard at which they play.

Our work and investment are based around our three priority areas: clubs, juniors and Performance. By building, growing and powering our Tennis Nation we are working towards our vision and mission.

Our vision is to make Britain a great tennis nation. Our mission is for more players and better players.

LTA Vision and Mission Statements

Working for tennis in Britain

We have around 200 staff based either in the 44 counties that make up the British tennis map, or in our central office at The Queen's Club in west London. We also have self-employed coaches, tutors and a vast network of volunteers in the counties.

We come from a wide range of backgrounds, including people from the business world as well as former coaches and players. Each of us brings new ideas and experiences that can help the organisation to grow and flourish. We have a broad remit and roles ranging from Coach Education and National Training to the financial and legal aspects of managing the game.

We also rely on a great team "out on the ground" who deliver tennis at a local level. Club development officers (CDOs) and tennis managers (TMs) are employed by the LTA to work with clubs, schools and local authorities to promote tennis across their county. Tennis managers (TMs) and tennis operations managers (TOMs) head up and direct the county activity.

Relevant Words

All-England Lawn Tennis Campionships 全英草地网球锦标赛
ATP(Association of Tennis Professionals) Tour 国际职业网球联合会巡回赛
Tennis Masters Cup 网球大师杯赛
Tennis Masters Series 网球大师系列赛
tier events 等级赛事
WTA(Women's Tennis Association) Tour 女子网球协会巡回赛

Lesson 15

世界杯足球赛赛场上是球员间的较量，而看台上的球迷则更多地体现了爱国主义和民族主义。本文未对本届世界杯的成绩做过多评论，而是另辟蹊径，从世界杯比赛中所体现的爱国主义和民族主义着手进行分析，描写了球迷们助阵的方式，剖析了球迷的观球动机和心态。从体育比赛入手，关注了种族歧视和移民问题，角度新颖独特，读来让人耳目一新。

Team Spirit, Yes, but Not Too Much

By Peter Berlin
July 1, 2006
International Herald Tribune[1]

Before each World Cup match, security guards at the stadiums search fans and confiscate[2] drinks, excess pens (more than two), deodorant sprays[3] and anything that might be a weapon.

If they find a flag, they shake it out and quickly assess it, tilting[4] their heads slightly the way people do when trying to guess measurements. If they judge the flag to be more than a meter deep by three meters, or 3 feet by 10 feet, it is impounded[5], to be collected after the game.

The vast majority of banners that fans carry at the World Cup are national flags, or variations[6] on them. The process of measuring them is clearly inexact or negotiable. Just before their game with Switzerland, South Korean fans unfurled[7] a flag that covered 20 rows.

Yet the message is clear: Patriotism[8] is nice, but only if it is kept in proportion.

Nationalism is the motor that drives the World Cup. The fans and their flags and shirts provide the backdrop[9] that reassures television audiences that they are watching a major event. The fans are happy to play their part.

Once only the English fans traveled in large numbers. Now the fashion for big-event tourism has infected every nation. Many even emulate[10] the bizarre English habit of traveling without tickets to cities where their team is playing to watch the match on giant screens while

1. *International Herald Tribune* 《国际先驱论坛报》，美国首要日报之一，其前身是1887年在纽约创刊的《纽约先驱报》。因立场中立，不受任何政治及商业利益制约，被誉为世界上"信息量最大"、"最具公信力"的新闻日报。由《纽约时报》全资拥有。
2. confiscate /ˈkɒnfɪskeɪt/ v. 没收
3. deodorant spray 体香喷雾器
4. tilt /tɪlt/ v. 倾斜
5. impound /ɪmˈpaʊnd/ v. 扣押；没收
6. variation /ˌveərɪˈeɪʃən/ n. 变形；变化
7. unfurl /ʌnˈfɜːl/ v. 展开；打开
8. patriotism /ˈpætrɪətɪzəm/ n. 爱国主义
9. backdrop /ˈbækdrɒp/ n. 背景
10. emulate /ˈemjʊleɪt/ v. (通过模仿)赶上，超越

drinking alcohol. Fighting among drunken fans away from the stadium has been the chief problem for the police at this World Cup.

The fans know that their uniformity creates an impressive effect at games: great blocks of orange, yellow, red or white. So do the shirt makers. In expressing their identities, the fans are growing increasingly homogenized[11]. The default[12] uniform is the national shirt, not just at games but all the time.

Either these fans pack a lot of shirts—and a typical shirt retails at more than $50—or that deodorant ban is a bad idea.

But those of Australia, Brazil, Croatia[13], Mexico, the Netherlands, Portugal, South Korea and the United States are also representing Nike[14]. Argentina[15], France, Germany, Japan and Trinidad and Tobago[16] shirts sport the Adidas[17] logo. Those of the Czechs[18], Iranians[19], Italians, Paraguayans[20], Poles[21], Saudi Arabians[22], Swiss and all five African entrants[23] advertise Puma[24].

The fans try to express their difference with jokey[25] accouterments[26]: orange clogs[27], blue and yellow Viking[28] helmets, inflatable[29] samurai[30] head-pieces[31] that say, "We are supporting our nation but we realize how risky nationalism can be."

Everywhere at this World Cup, there are reminders of the dangers of patriotism and its less-attractive cousin, nationalism, both in soccer's little bubble and in the wider world beyond. The most obvious symbol is the Berlin Olympic Stadium, which will stage the final on July 9 and was the home of Adolf Hitler's infamous[32] 1936 Olympics.

Before every World Cup game throughout the country, a banner covers the center circle. It reads, "Say No to Racism." Fans in northwestern Europe have come to accept that racial abuse of players is no longer acceptable. But during the recent European club season, there were well-publicized[33] incidents in which black players were abused in Spain and Italy and across Eastern Europe.

The change in behavior in northwestern Europe suggests that whatever their attitude toward new immigrants, most fans accept that their countries are changing color.

The dilemma[34] for immigrants, or members of minorities, is summed up by the Tebbit test, named after a right-wing[35] minister under former Prime Minister Margaret Thatcher[36] of Britain. Norman Tebbit was incensed[37] to see Pakistani, Indian or West Indian immigrants to Britain, or their children, supporting their countries of origin when they played England at cricket. He suggested that would-be

11. homogenized /həˈmɒdʒɪnaɪzd/ *a.* 一致的
12. default /dɪˈfɔːlt/ *a.* 默认的
13. Croatia /krəʊˈeɪʃjə/ *n.* 克罗地亚
14. Nike /ˈnaɪkiː/ 耐克(运动服装品牌)
15. Argentina /ˌɑːdʒənˈtiːnə/ *n.* 阿根廷
16. Trinidad and Tobago 特力尼达和多巴哥(大西洋岛国)
17. Adidas /əˈdiːdəs/ 阿迪达斯(运动服装品牌)
18. Czech /tʃek/ *n.* 捷克人
19. Iranian /ɪˈremjən/ *n.* 伊朗人
20. Paraguayan /ˌpærəˈɡwaɪən/ *n.* 巴拉圭人
21. Pole /pəʊl/ *n.* 波兰人
22. Saudi Arabian 沙特阿拉伯人
23. entrant /ˈentrənt/ *n.* 新加入者
24. Puma /ˈpjuːmə/ 彪马(运动服装品牌)
25. jokey /ˈdʒəʊkɪ/ *a.* 滑稽的
26. accouterments /əˈkuːtəmənts/ *n.* 穿着;饰物
27. clog /klɒɡ/ *n.* 木屐,木底鞋
28. Viking 指北欧海盗
29. inflatable /ɪnˈfleɪtəbəl/ *a.* 膨胀的;可充气的
30. samurai /ˈsæmʊraɪ/ *n.* 日本武士
31. head-piece 扎在头上的条形头巾
32. infamous /ˈɪnfəməs/ *a.* 声名狼藉的
33. well-publicized 广为人知的
34. dilemma /dɪˈlemə, daɪ-/ *n.* 进退两难
35. right-wing /ˈraɪtwɪŋ/ *a.* 右翼的
36. Margaret Thatcher 马格利特·撒切尔(英国前首相)
37. incense /ɪnˈsens/ *v.* 激怒

Britons be asked what cricket team they supported, and if it was not England, they should not be granted a passport.

As fans congregated[38] on the Champs Élysées[39] on Tuesday night to celebrate the victory over Spain, which was sealed by a late goal from the French icon[40], Zinédine Zidane[41], who is of Algerian descent, there were green Algerian flags waving amid the tricolors[42].

What could be more natural than a fan from some gray, rainy north European town then wanting to pretend to be Brazilian, and bring a little of the sunny, beautiful soccer of the equator into his soul?[43] When Brazil beat Ghana[44] on Tuesday, the number of non-Brazilians in yellow shirts may have outnumbered real Brazilians. If you want to see where the real Brazilian fans are, look for the section of the crowd refusing to do the wave. They are not there for fun.

At every game in Germany not involving the host, there have been Germans wearing Germany shirts, but there have also been many wearing shirts of other teams. As a general rule, they favor the underdog[45] or the more exotic[46] country.

Of course the World Cup also provides the opportunity to hate as well as love your neighbors. For example, England is, after all, not really a country at all. The majority of Welsh and Scottish fans and many in Northern Ireland can be counted on to support "whoever England is playing."

The habit of supporting "my enemy's enemy" is not limited to the British Isles. Argentina's 6-0 thrashing[47] of Serbia and Montenegro[48] gave great pleasure to its regional neighbors. Indeed, the national teams can barely keep pace with the break-up of the former Yugoslavia.

At this World Cup, Serbia and Montenegro qualified as one nation and arrived as two. The one Montenegrin player, a goalkeeper, Dragoslav Jevric, found himself playing for a country not his own.

"One chapter in our history is closing, and another, hopefully better, will open," said the Serbia and Montenegro team spokesman, Aleksandar Boskovic, sounding like the fan of any country eliminated[49] from the World Cup.

Time to order those Montenegrin two-headed eagle flags. Make sure they aren't more than three meters wide.

38. congregate /ˈkɒŋgrɪgeɪt/ v. 聚集
39. Champs-Élysées 香榭丽舍大街(位于巴黎市中心，西起凯旋门，东至协和广场)
40. icon /ˈaɪkɒn/ n. 偶像
41. Zinédine Zidane 齐内丹·齐达内(法国著名球星)
42. tricolor /ˈtrɪkələ/ n. 三色旗(特指法国国旗)
43. 一些球迷来自一贯阴雨连绵的北欧，他们在球场中装做巴西人支持南美球队，让赤道的阳光足球温暖自己的心灵，这难道不是再自然不过的事吗？ equator /ɪˈkweɪtə/ n. 赤道
44. Ghana /ˈgɑːnə/ n. 加纳(位于非洲西部，南濒几内亚湾)
45. underdog /ˈʌndədɒg/ n. 失败者
46. exotic /ɪɡˈzɒtɪk/ a. 外来的

47. thrashing /ˈθræʃɪŋ/ n. 鞭打(这里指沉重打击)
48. Serbia and Montenegro 塞尔维亚和黑山共和国(现已成为两个独立国家：塞尔维亚共和国和黑山共和国。在2006年世界杯上，塞尔维亚和黑山尚未分离，仍然作为一个国家参加比赛。)
49. eliminate /ɪˈlɪmɪneɪt/ v. 淘汰；排除

Comprehension Questions

1. What do security guards do before each world cup match? Why?
2. What kind of flag is not allowed in the stadium? How do the security guards deal with the flag not being allowed in the stadium?
3. What is the English habit that has recently spread to many other parts of the world?
4. What was the problem for Serbia and Montenegro at this World Cup?
5. What is the author's main attitude towards nationalism and patriotism in international matches?

Background Reading

Nationalism and Sport

Nationalism and sport are often intertwined (缠绕的), as sports provide a venue for symbolic competition between nations; sports competition often reflects national conflict, and in fact has often been a tool of diplomacy. The involvement of political goals in sport is seen by some as contrary to the fundamental ethos (精神) of sport being carried on for its own sake, for the enjoyment of its participants, but this involvement has been true throughout the history of sport.

The Olympic Games are the premier stage for nationalist competition, and its history reflects the history of political conflict since its inception (起初) at the end of the 19th century. The 1936 Summer Olympics held in Berlin was an illustration, maybe best acknowledged in hindsight (后见之明, 事后聪明), where an ideology (意识形态) was developing which used the event to strengthen its spread through propaganda (宣传). The boycott by the United States and politically aligned (排列) nations of the 1980 Summer Olympics and the Soviet Union of the 1984 Summer Olympics were part of the Cold War conflict.

When apartheid (南非种族隔离制度) was the official policy in South Africa, many sportspeople adopted the conscientious (本着良心的) approach that they should not appear in competitive sports there. Some feel this was an effective contribution to the eventual demolition (摧毁) of the policy of apartheid, others feel that it may have prolonged (延续) and reinforced (加强) its worst effects.

Relevant Words

bleachers （露天）看台	devotee 球迷
enthusiast 球迷	gallery 看台
grandstand （带顶蓬）看台	hooliganism 球迷闹事
riot 球迷闹事	root 助威
rooter 助威者	violence 球迷闹事

Part III

Sporting Memories

赛场风云

Lesson 1

雅典奥运会男子 200 米自由泳由于索普和菲尔普斯的竞争而备受关注。一个是澳洲飞鱼，一个是美洲神童。一个想继续自己的泳坛霸主地位，一个想打破前辈 7 金的神话。奥运会的游泳池中，两名游泳的绝代天才展开了巅峰对决。究竟谁能笑到最后，且看下文。

The Men's 200m Freestyle[1]

By Olympic Review's team of writers
October-November-December 2004
Olympic Review

The men's 200m freestyle had long been touted[2] as one of the faces of the Games and it certainly lived up to its billing[3]. The open-air main pool[4] at the Olympic Aquatic Centre[5] added to the atmosphere and also to the anticipation on a warm but breezy Monday evening in front of a packed crowd, giving the occasion a gladiatorial feel[6] as the competitors strode to the start.

The line-up featured four giants of the pool: Australian pair Ian Thorpe and Grant Hackett, Pieter van den Hoogenband of the Netherlands and the USA's Michael Phelps.[7]

Four years earlier in the corresponding race[8], van den Hoogenband had derailed[9] the previously unstoppable Thorpe express[10], pipping the home favourite for gold[11], while Phelps announced his arrival on the world scene by taking fifth place.

This time, world record holder Thorpe was slowest out of the blocks[12] as the defending champion[13] van den Hoogenband set the early pace, but the giant Australian had hauled himself back[14] within striking distance[15] by the first turn. Thorpe and van den Hoogenband were neck and neck[16] with Phelps lying third in the middle section of a race that, until the final 50 metres, was under world record pace. By that stage all the spectators bar none[17] were on their feet, urging the athletes on and as the swimmers began to tire in that last segment[18], it was the strength of Thorpe, the middle-distance specialist, that won through against van den Hoogenband, the out-and-out sprinter[19].

---

1. men's 200m freestyle 男子 200 米自由泳
2. tout /taʊt/ v. 吹捧
3. to live up to one's billing 名副其实
4. open-air main pool 露天主池
5. Olympic Aquatic Centre 奥林匹克水上运动中心
6. gladiatorial feel 角斗的气氛
7. 出场阵容由四大泳坛巨星组成：两名澳洲名将伊安·索普和格兰特·哈克特，荷兰的霍根班德和美国的迈克尔·菲尔普斯。
8. corresponding race 同一比赛
9. derail /diːˈreɪl/ v. 打败
10. Thorpe express "鱼雷"（索普的别号）
11. …pipping the home favourite for gold 击败了主场有望夺金的索普 pip /pɪp/ v. 打败；击败
12. out of the blocks 出发
13. defending champion 卫冕冠军
14. to haul back 追上
15. within striking distance 离……不远；可赶上的距离
16. neck and neck 齐头并进，不相上下
17. bar none 无例外
18. segment /ˈseɡmənt/ n. 段
19. out-and-out sprinter 不折不扣的短距离游泳选手

The Australian just missed the world record but set a new Olympic record of 1:44:71 as he stretched out one of his unfeasibly[20] long limbs[21] to touch the finish in first place ahead of the Dutchman in 1:45:23. Phelps finished just nine hundredths of a second back in third place to earn a bronze medal but still set a new national record in the process. His unheralded[22] team-mate Klete Keller was fourth. Hackett, a former 200m freestyle world record holder and dual gold medalist at the Sydney Games, but now more at home[23] in the 1500m where he would win a second successive gold later in the week, came home a creditable[24] fifth.

Thorpe revealed afterwards that he had turned to the Dutchman at the finish and said: "That's one-all now.[25] See you in Beijing."

"I hope we all will swim in Beijing," he told journalists. "It would be a great race. Pieter and I are good friends."

For his part van den Hoogenband refused to be downbeat[26] afterwards. "To be beaten by one of the best in my sport. Well that's the way it is," he said.

Phelps, who picked up his third of what would become a sensational[27] eight medals overall, was equally generous in defeat: 'How can I be disappointed? I swam in a field with the two fastest 200m swimmers of all time, and I was with them. It was fun. I had fun doing it.'

20. unfeasibly /ˌʌnˈfiːzəblɪ/ ad. 不可能地；难实施地（这里指特别地）
21. limb /lɪm/ n. 上肢
22. unheralded /ʌnˈherəldɪd/ a. 未被承认的(这里指不出名的)
23. to be at home 擅长
24. creditable /ˈkredɪtəbl/ a. 值得赞扬的；可称赞的
25. 现在是一平。
26. downbeat /ˈdaʊnbiːt/ a. 悲观的，忧郁的
27. sensational /senˈseɪʃənəl/ a. 非常好的,令人生畏的

Comprehension Questions

1. Who were the four giants competing in the men's 200m freestyle?
2. Who was the slowest to leave the start?
3. What achievement did Phelps make in the Sydney Olympics?
4. How did Phelps feel after being "beaten"?
5. Do you think American team will be able to continue their dominance at swimming in the Beijing Olympics?

Background Reading

Michael Phelps

Michael Phelps first appeared at the 2000 Summer Olympics in Sydney as the youngest American male swimmer in 68 years. He was only 15 and placed fifth in the 200m butterfly (蝶泳). While he did not win a medal, Phelps proceeded (继续进行) to make a name for himself (成名) in swimming shortly thereafter. Swimming the same event at the US Spring Nationals (美国春季全国赛) the following year, Phelps became the youngest swimmer ever to break a world swimming record at the age of 15.

Phelps's specialty (专长) is the shorter races of 100 to 400 meters in length. His records, world records and awards are almost too numerous to mention. He was named USA Swimmer of the Year (美国年度最佳游泳运动员) in both 2001 and 2003, and set an unprecedented five individual world records in one meet at the 2003 World Championships in Barcelona.

Phelps's dominance has brought comparisons (比较) to former swimming great Mark Spitz (马克·施皮茨), who won seven gold medals in the 1972 Summer Olympics. He was offered a $1 million bonus (奖金) by one of his sponsors (赞助者) if he could tie the record of seven gold medals in one Olympics. Phelps did not win the bonus, but he did win more medals than anyone else in a non-boycotted (非联合抵制的) Summer Games—eight in all, including six gold and two bronze. His golds came in the 100m and 200m butterfly, 200m and 400m individual medley (个人混合泳), the 4×100m medley relay (混合泳接力) and the 4×200m freestyle relay. His bronze medals were in the 200m freestyle and 4×100m freestyle relay.

Relevant Words

backstroke 仰泳	breaststroke 蛙泳
butterfly stroke 蝶泳	fin swimming 蹼泳
medley stroke 混合泳	starting block 出发台
swim lane 泳道	to purchase 抱水
to stroke 划水	to tread water 踩水

Lesson 2

他,被称为"中跑之王","英里之王",历史上 10 个最快的 1500 米纪录里他占了 7 个,10 个最快的 1 英里他拿了 8 个。他,一个绝对的中长跑统治者,却几度与奥运金牌无缘。在 1996 年至 2003 年的 83 场比赛中仅输掉了 3 场比赛——其中两场就是在奥运会比赛中。他就是摩洛哥中长跑名将希查姆•埃尔•盖鲁伊。96 年亚特兰大决赛最后一圈不幸绊倒,2000 年悉尼直道的最后几步无奈被超过。继连续两届饮恨后,盖鲁伊终于在 2004 年雅典打破奥运不赢的怪圈,一举拿下了 1500 米和 5000 米的金牌,实乃名至所归,为自己的十多年的田径生涯写下了最辉煌的一笔。

El Guerrouj[1] Wins Double Gold

By Olympic Review's team of writers
October-November-December 2004
Olympic Review

A couple of months before the Olympic Games, Hicham El Guerrouj revealed he was suffering from a breathing problem that could put his participation in doubt[2], a prospect that meant one of sport's greatest runners might never win the greatest prize.

El Guerrouj recovered and delivered the Olympic titles[3] that his reputation always suggested he should win, for once evading[4] bad luck at the critical moment.

In Atlanta in 1996, El Guerrouj was tripped[5] just before the bell[6] in the final of the 1500m and with it his chance went; in Sydney, he was beaten along the home straight[7] by Kenyan Noah Ngeny[8].

In Athens the Moroccan won the 1500m and 5000m double, a feat[9] achieved only once at the Olympic Games, in 1924 by the legendary[10] Flying Finn, Paavo Nurmi[11].

As El Guerrouj crossed the line after adding the 5000m to the 1500m, he waved two fingers about: eight years of pain and now two

1. El Guerrouj 埃尔•盖鲁伊(摩洛哥中长跑名将,雅典奥运会男子 5000 米和 1500 米双料冠军)
2. in doubt 悬而未决,还不能确定
3. to deliver the Olympic titles 如愿以偿地获得了奥运会冠军
4. evade /ɪ'veɪd/ v. 躲避,躲开
5. trip /trɪp/ v. 绊倒
6. before the bell 在铃响之前(这里指决赛的最后一圈)
7. home straight 终点直道
8. Noah Ngeny 诺阿•恩盖尼(肯尼亚中长跑运动员,男子 1000 米的世界纪录保持者)
9. feat /fiːt/ n. 功绩,战绩
10. legendary /'ledʒəndərɪ/ a. 传奇(式)的
11. Flying Finn, Paavo Nurmi 芬兰飞人帕亚沃•努尔米(他从 1920 年开始,连续 3 届奥运会参加 12 个项目共夺得 9 枚金牌和 3 枚银牌,是历届奥运会夺得金牌数最多的选手。)

sensational Olympic victories.

Since the late 1980s he has held world records for the 1500m and the mile[12], two of the epic distances[13], and he has won the 1500m world title on four occasions.

But at 30, the nagging[14] was starting to become worse: was the world's finest middle distance runner heading towards retirement without the gold that means the most? The answer he provided in the Olympic Stadium is one of the abiding memories[15] of these Games. No one was going to stop El Guerrouj this time.

The final of the 1500m was a classic. El Guerrouj took the lead with just under two laps left, attempting to kick away but always being followed by Bernard Lagat[16], of Kenya. With 90m to go, Lagat took over[17], but along the home straight El Guerrouj came back to edge back in front[18] to win in 3:34.18 from the Kenyan, who was second in 3:34.30, with Rui Silva[19], of Portugal, third in 3:34.68. El Guerrouj said: "I am very happy. This is a big moment for me. Now, at last, I am Olympic champion."

He celebrated with a dance, and then, on the final night of the track and field action, he was in a similar mood after winning the 5000m. His timing[20] was immaculate[21], waiting for his moment to pounce on[22] leader[23] Kenenisa Bekele[24], the 10,000m champion, with 50m to go. The Ethiopian had no response; a great champion was beaten by an even greater one. El Guerrouj won in 13:14.39. Bekele finished second, Eliud Kipchoge[25] of Kenya third in 13:15.10.

12. the mile 英里跑
13. epic distance 非同一般的距离，长距离
14. nagging /ˈnægɪŋ/ n. 批评的声音
15. abiding memory 永恒的回忆
16. Bernard Lagat 伯纳德·拉加特（肯尼亚中长跑名将）
17. to take over 接管，接任（这里指超过盖鲁伊领跑）
18. to edge back in front 渐渐追回跑在前面
19. Rui Silva 鲁伊·席尔瓦（葡萄牙中长跑选手）
20. timing /ˈtaɪmɪŋ/ n. 时间安排；速度控制
21. immaculate /ɪˈmækjʊlɪt/ a. 完美的
22. to pounce on 突然袭击（这里指突然前冲超过对手）
23. leader /ˈliːdə/ n. 领跑者
24. Kenenisa Bekele 科内尼萨·贝克勒（埃塞俄比亚的著名长跑运动员，男子万米世界纪录保持者，雅典奥运会和2005年田径世界锦标赛万米双料冠军）
25. Eliud Kipchoge 埃柳德·基普乔格（肯尼亚中长跑选手）

Comprehension Questions

1. What was the "bad luck" that kept Guerrouj away from the Olympic gold medals in the 1996 and 2000 Games?
2. Which athlete was the runner-up in the final of 1500m in the Athens Olympics?
3. According to the article, what gold medal means the most?
4. How did Bekele respond when he was defeated by Guerrouj?
5. What do the two Olympic gold medals mean to Guerrouj?

Part III Sporting Memories

Background Reading

Hicham El Guerrouj

Hicham El Guerrouj is a great legend (传奇人物) who made his mark in history. Born on September 14, 1974, he is a Moroccan middle-distance runner, the world record holder for the 1,500 metres (3:26.00), the mile (3:43.13) and 2,000 metres (4:44.79), and has been nicknamed (给……取绰号)"King of the Mile"(英里之王).

Guerrouj began his domination (统治) of the 1,500m in 1995. In the following years, he became the only middle-distance runner to win four consecutive (连续的) world titles in 1997, 1999, 2001, and 2003. Over a nine-year period, El Guerrouj raced in 86 finals at 1,500m and the mile and won 83 of those races. Hicham El Guerrouj often quoted Winston Churchill's famous words, "Never never never give up." But the Moroccan runner almost did give up, and who could blame him? El Guerrouj competed in the Olympics twice as the favourite (夺标呼声高的选手) in the 1,500 m, a race that requires endurance and finishing speed. Both times, the world-record holder practically (几乎) had a gold medal engraved (雕刻) with his name before the Games; both times, he lost. In 1996, with 430m to go, El Guerrouj was positioned (处于，位于) just behind the favourite, Noureddine Morceli. El Guerrouj's knee hit Morceli's heel. Morceli stumbled (蹒跚、跌撞前行) and El Guerrouj stepped on his heel, lost his balance and crashed to the ground. He finished the race, but ended up in last place. Between the Atlanta Olympics and the Sydney Olympics in 2000, El Guerrouj won 45 of 46 races at 1,500m and a mile. In the Sydney final, he faced his former pacesetter (领跑者), Noah Ngeny of Kenya. El Guerrouj took the lead after 900m and stayed ahead until the homestretch (终点直道). Ngeny caught up with El Guerrouj 50 metres from the finish and pulled ahead with 25 metres to go, as El Guerrouj had to settle for second place. El Guerrouj was doubled up in pain worse than he had ever felt in a decade of hard training. He wept and wept.

Tears of joy finally came in Athens. The middle-distance great finally overcame his Olympic jinx (厄运), winning not just one gold but two.

Relevant Words

abreast start 并排起跑	boxed in (中长跑)夹在人群里
crouch start 蹲踞式起跑	dead heat 同时到达终点
distribution of energy 体力分配	Golden League 黄金联赛
home bend 最后一个弯道	obstacle race 障碍赛跑
point of denouement 抢道起点	steady running 匀速跑

Lesson 3

作为英国知识界的双驾马车，牛津、剑桥之间的互不服气也算历史久远了。19世纪20年代，两个分别跻身于这两大名校的好友突发奇想，既然牛、剑在学术教育上互不服输，不如举行一次划船对抗赛来较量一番。赛艇就这样成为牛津、剑桥的另一种对抗。在岸边观战学生的加油声中，两艘船16只桨同时转动，揭开了第152届牛津、剑桥划船赛的序幕。虽然风强浪大，但两队仍然全力竞争。比赛以牛津大学胜利结束。

Oxford Conquer the Waves to Win Boat Race

By Christopher Dodd
April 3, 2006
The Independent[1]

Oxford took the 152nd Boat Race by storm[2] yesterday, in a race where fortunes turned halfway between Hammersmith Bridge[3] and Chiswick Eyot[4].

Winning the toss[5] and choosing the Surrey station[6] to give them the outside of the first bend[7] opened the door for[8] the Dark Blues[9], and being on the inside of the bend after Hammersmith, where the rough water hit the crews like a wall, closed the door behind them.

Cambridge were half a second ahead at the milepost[10] and settling to a rhythm which kept them alongside Oxford up to Hammersmith.

1. *The Independent*《独立报》，是英国一家简洁型报纸，创刊于1986年，隶属于汤尼·欧瑞利的独立新闻媒体公司，是英国最年轻的全国性日报。2005年11月的发行量为26多万份。该报在2004年英国媒体奖大会上被提名为该年度全国最好的全国报纸。
2. to take ...by storm 完全征服
3. Hammersmith Bridge 汉默史密斯桥（位于伦敦西郊）
4. Chiswick Eyot 奇斯威克小岛（位于泰晤士河中）
5. to win the toss 掷币获胜；抽签获胜
6. Surrey station 萨里湾站（萨里湾是泰晤士河上一段半圆的弧形，是整个划船赛程中最困难的地方。）
7. bend /bend/ n. 弯道
8. to open the door for 使……成为可能，为……提供机会
9. the Dark Blues 深蓝队[指牛津队员。因为牛津与剑桥均以蓝色作为自己学校的标志，各不相让，只好以颜色的深浅来区别，所以通常人们把剑桥队员称为"浅蓝队"(the Light Blues)，把牛津队员称为"深蓝队"(the Dark Blues)]。
10. milepost /ˈmaɪlpəʊst/ n. 里程柱

But the bend turned to Oxford's favour as they shot the bridge a second ahead.[11]

From there the cox Seb Pearce forced Cambridge into more exposed water. Suddenly wind and waves engulfed[12] the boats and both seemed to check[13].

There was no time for pretty rowing. In the words of Bastien Ripoll, Oxford's French stroke[14], "The key moment was along the island, in a washing machine."

The Dark Blues battled through this more effectively than the Light, and consolidated their lead[15] in a window of calm water along Duke's Meadows. They had six seconds on Cambridge at Chiswick Steps and 11 at Barnes Bridge.[16] The stuffing had been knocked out of Cambridge[17] by conditions.

This was a second win for Barney Williams, Oxford's president. "We were pushed really hard," he said, praising his crew, "who put their school on the back burner[18] despite the intensity of their studies. The commitment they put in really paid off.[19]"

He had particular praise for Jake Wetzel in the No 7 seat, his crew-mate in Canada's Olympic coxless four[20] two years ago. "For two years he backed me up and in that four he covered my back[21] every step of the way. I said to him before the race, 'I have your back'. He was a leader and he's a racer."

Tom Edwards, Cambridge's president, put a brave face on the defeat[22] of a crew which critics ranked with the great Light Blue winners of the 1990s. "I've had two years of trying to win this race, and it didn't happen," he said. "All credit to Oxford, they took it to us in the toughest part of the race round Hammersmith.[23] I was quite happy with our position in the crucial period at St Paul's, but we struggled in the conditions, and they dealt with the conditions better than us."

Oxford's French, British, and Canadian mixture beat a crew including the three Germans — Sebastian Thormann, Thorsten Engelmann and Sebastian Schulte — known as the Berlin Wall[24]. "Sometimes machines break," said Ripoll. Oxford's coach, Sean Bowden, in his ninth race, earned praise, while Cambridge's Duncan Holland, in his first, received a sobering[25] baptism[26].

152nd Boat Race: Oxford beat Cambridge by 5 lengths; 18 min 26 sec.[27]

Reserves race[28]: Goldie[29] beat Isis[30] by 4 and a quarter lengths, 19:09.

11. 但弯道变得有利于牛津队，使其以一秒的优势领先剑桥队。
12. engulf /mˈgʌlf/ v. 吞没
13. check /tʃek/ v. 停止
14. stroke /strəuk/ n. 尾桨手（决定全船划速的主要划手）
15. to consolidate one's lead 巩固某人的领先地位
16. 他们在 Chiswick Steps 领先剑桥 6 秒，在 Barnes Bridge 领先 11 秒。
17. to knock the stuffing out of sb. 极大地削弱某人
18. put their school on the back burner 把学业先搁置一边
19. 他们的付出确实得到了回报。
20. coxless four 无舵手四人划艇，四人单桨无舵手艇
21. to cover one's back 保护某人
22. to put a brave face on the defeat 在失败面前假装很勇敢
23. 我得称赞牛津队，他们在最艰难的汉哈默史密斯河段赶超了我们。
24. Berlin Wall 柏林墙（这里指剑桥队的 3 个德国舵手）
25. sobering /ˈsəubərɪŋ/ a. 使清醒的
26. to receive a baptism 接受洗礼
27. 牛津队以 5 个船身的距离取得胜利，成绩 18 分 26 秒。
28. reserves race 预备赛
29. Goldie 剑桥队
30. Isis 牛津队

Comprehension Questions

1. Which team won the toss at the beginning of the race?
2. When did Oxford overtake Cambridge?
3. What's the key moment consolidating Oxford's victory?
4. In what way did Cambridge's president think Oxford was better than them?
5. What do you think each side can benefit from the Boat Race?

Background Reading

The Oxford and Cambridge Boat Race

Oxford and Cambridge are the oldest and most famous universities in Britain, and there has always been a great rivalry (竞争, 竞赛) between the two institutions. But the most public competition between the two is the annual Boat Race.

The first boat race was the result of a challenge issued to Oxford by Cambridge in 1829. The Boat Race was started by two friends, Charles Merivale, a student at Cambridge and school friend Charles Wordsworth (nephew of famous poet William Wordsworth), an Oxford student. On March 29, Cambridge sent a challenge to Oxford beginning the tradition still followed to this day. Since then, the defeated team from the previous year challenges the opposition (对手) to a rematch (再次比赛). The race has became an annual event since 1856 (except during the war years).

There are nine people in a crew, eight oarsmen (桨手) and one cox, who steers, and gives commands to the rowers. Since 1836, the rowing "eights" have worn different shades (颜色深浅) of blue—Oxford wear dark blue and Cambridge light blue. As a result, the rowers are known as the Blues.

The average time taken to complete the course is 20 minutes, but Cambridge holds the record for the fastest time of 16 minutes and 19 seconds, achieved in 1998. Over the years that the two universities have gone head-to-head (并驾齐驱) on the river. The current score stands at 78 to Cambridge, 72 to Oxford, with one controversial dead heat (同时抵达终点) in 1877. There have been three occasions when one of the boats sank and forfeited (弃权; 放弃) the race.

Now the race attracts a massive (大规模的) crowd of 250,000 with live television audience of over 6,000,000 in the UK with a worldwide following of over 400,000,000 in 180 countries.

Part III Sporting Memories

Relevant Words

coxswain's seat	舵手座位	double sculls	双人双桨赛
favourable wind	顺风	hull	船身
interval rowing	变速划	oar	桨
rowing technique	划船技术	scull racing	无舵手赛艇比赛

Lesson 4

> 1979 年英格兰足总杯决赛的跌宕起伏成为 70 年代曼联大起大落的一个缩影。这场比赛临尽时，奇峰突起，堪称经典，是最值得回忆的一场足总杯决赛。阿森纳本有机会在 90 分钟内解决这场战斗，但曼联在比赛还剩 5 分钟时，背水一战，由戈顿·麦克奎因（Gordon McQueen）和萨米·麦克罗伊（Sammy McIlroy）连入两球，将比分扳为 2-2 平。最后时刻阿森纳队利亚姆·布莱迪 （Liam Brady） 送出精彩助攻，阿森纳队阿兰·桑德兰（Alan Sunderland）攻入制胜一球，使曼联饮恨温布利。

United Haunted by Ghost of '79

For Manchester United[1], the 1979 FA Cup[2] final against Arsenal[3] was like being sentenced to death, reprieved and then being run over by a bus[4].

By Henry Winter
May 19, 2005
The Age[5]

In a recent poll[6] of English fans, the 1979 FA Cup final between Arsenal and Manchester United was voted the 15th greatest game of all time.

The Wembley[7] showdown[8] of '79, memories of which have been stirred by the progress of Arsenal and United to this year's climax in

1. Manchester United 曼彻斯特联队[简称曼联。曼联前身为牛顿希思（Newton Heath），于 1878 年成立。]
2. FA Cup 英格兰足总杯 [The Football Association Challenge Cup, 简称足总杯（FA Cup），是由英格兰足球协会命名并主办的一项男子淘汰制足球杯赛。]
3. Arsenal 阿森纳队（于 1886 年成立）
4. ...like being sentenced to death ……如同被判了死刑，改为缓刑后被一辆公共汽车从身上辗过。reprieve /rɪˈpriːv/ v. 暂缓处刑，缓期执行
5. *The Age*《世纪报》，又译《时代报》，创刊于 1854 年，已有百年以上的历史，是一家具有全国影响的报纸，在澳大利亚维多利亚州首府墨尔本出版，发行量 25 万份，分平日版和星期日版。平日版为 32 版，星期日版为 160 版。该报现有 12 个驻外记者站，并且是澳大利亚各报中唯一在中国驻有记者的报纸。
6. poll /pəʊl/ n. 民意测验
7. Wembley 温布利球场（位于伦敦）
8. showdown /ˈʃəʊdaʊn/ n. 最后的较量，决战

Cardiff on Saturday, was not so much a classic final as a classic final five minutes[9]. The build-up[10] to the big day contained the usual stories, although no hint of the dramas that were to unfold[11].

Arsenal, which had required five attempts and most of January to bypass Jack Charlton's third-division Sheffield Wednesday in the third round, was troubled that its full-back[12], Sammy Nelson, might miss Wembley.[13]

For a joke, Nelson "mooned"[14] at Arsenal fans after scoring against Coventry. The FA was indignant[15] at such bare-faced cheek[16], although its two-match ban[17] left Nelson available for Wembley. United's manager, Dave Sexton, meanwhile, was out shopping, buying a watch for each of his United players (with his own money), which he presented on the eve of the final.

Sexton's[18] XI was considered by many the more attractive side, and neutrals[19] prayed for an early goal from Joe Jordan, Jimmy Greenhoff (prolific[20] in earlier rounds), Sammy McIlroy or Lou Macari to make Arsenal open up. Yet Terry Neill's men[21] had that Irish artist, Liam Brady, and were still fuelled[22] by the anger of losing out to Ipswich Town[23] the previous season[24]. Brady had given his loser's medal away and told teammates "we will be back next year".

Assisted by the recruitment[25] of Brian Talbot from Portman Road, Arsenal seized control on a sweltering day. Talbot even finished off a move begun by Brady (although it was part-claimed[26] by Alan Sunderland): 1–0. Then, just before half-time, Brady ghosted[27] away from Arthur Albiston and Martin Buchan, and crossed[28] —right-footed— for Frank Stapleton to head[29] past Gary Bailey[30], the keeper[31] enduring a wretched afternoon: 2–0.

Later, in the second half, with Arsenal fans chanting[32] "Ee-ay-addio, we've won the cup", Neill sent on the inexperienced Steve Walford for David Price as if the game was won. In the ITV studio, Jack Charlton informed the nation that this was the wrong move, that "the whole balance is upset". He added: "Arsenal might even be in trouble now."

How true. With five minutes remaining, Steve Coppell worked a free kick[33] to Jordan, who set up Gordon McQueen: 2–1. Then Coppell found the tireless McIlroy, who brilliantly eluded[34] David O'Leary and Walford before guiding the ball under Pat Jennings: 2–2. United celebrated. Arsenal looked drained[35], ready for defeat.

9. ...not so much a classic final... 与其说是经典决赛，不如说是最后5分钟经典。
10. build-up /ˈbɪldʌp/ n. 吹嘘，宣传造舆论
11. unfold /ʌnˈfəʊld/ v. 出现，发生
12. full-back n. 后卫
13. 阿森纳队曾进行了5次尝试，1月大部分时间里，在丙组第三轮阿森纳队和杰克·查尔顿带领下的谢菲尔德星期三队周旋。他们所担心的是后卫尼尔森也许不能参加温布利决赛。
14. moon /muːn/ v. 露出屁股（在公共场合暴露自己的屁股，作为一种恶作剧或不尊重的表示）
15. indignant /ɪnˈdɪɡnənt/ a. 愤怒的
16. bare-faced cheek 这里指露出的屁股。
17. two-match ban 停赛两场的判罚
18. Sexton 指戴夫·塞克斯顿(Dave Sexton)，曼联队主帅
19. neutral /ˈnjuːtrəl/ n. 中立者（这里指既不支持阿森纳也不支持曼联的球迷）
20. prolific /prəˈlɪfɪk/ a. 多产的（这里指进球多的）
21. Terry Neill's men 阿森纳队球员（Terry Neill 特里·尼尔，1976—1983 执教于阿森纳队）
22. fuel /ˈfjuːəl/ v. 刺激
23. Ipswich Town 伊普斯维奇城队（成立于1878年）
24. previous season 上个赛季
25. recruitment /rɪˈkruːtmənt/ n. 招募新球员
26. part-claimed 部分归功于
27. ghost /ɡəʊst/ v. 像鬼魂悄无声息地移动
28. cross /krɒs/ v. 将球大范围转移，传中
29. head /hed/ v. 头球攻门
30. Gary Bailey 加里·贝里（曼联的守门员）
31. keeper /ˈkiːpə/ n. 守门员
32. chant /tʃɑːnt/ v. 反复地叫喊；唱歌
33. free kick 任意球
34. elude /ɪˈljuːd/ v. 晃过
35. to look drained 看上去耗尽精力

Brady was shattered[36], fearing extra time[37], so he dug deep[38]. Socks rolled down, he dribbled[39] 40 metres, beating[40] Macari and Mickey Thomas, before releasing Graham Rix down the left. The cross came over, Bailey faltered, and there was the bubble-permed figure of Sunderland scoring at the far post.[41] United was stunned. "It was like winning the pools only to find you hadn't posted the coupon," lamented McIlroy. Over in the BBC studio, Lawrie McMenemy summed up United's roller-coaster[42] afternoon: "It was like being sentenced to death, being reprieved at the last minute — then walking from the courtroom and being run over by a bus."

Those present in the Arsenal dressing room talk reverentially[43] of the huge quantities of champagne downed. The famous trophy was rarely dry that weekend.[44]

When Neill returned home, his daughter glanced at the cup and inquired: "What's that grubby old thing?" It was soon in the neighbours' swimming pool.

Fast forward 26 years.[45] After obliterating[46] Newcastle United[47] in this season's semi-finals, Manchester United now has a chance to erase the painful memory of Sunderland.

36. shatter /ˈʃætə/ v. 垮掉
37. extra time 加时赛
38. to dig deep 深挖(这里指深入对方禁区)
39. dribble /ˈdrɪbəl/ v. 带球；盘球
40. beat /biːt/ v. 突破；带球过人
41. 一个传中，贝里脚步踉跄地扑救，这时桑德兰从后门柱(包抄)将球射入。falter/ˈfɔːltə/ v. 摇晃，踉跄 far post 远侧门柱，后门柱
42. roller-coaster 非常不稳定的；急转突变的
43. reverentially /ˌrevəˈrenʃəli/ ad. 虔诚地；谨慎地
44. 那个周末这著名的奖杯就没有干涸过。(这里指阿森纳队为庆祝胜利喝了很多香槟酒。)
45. 时光飞逝,26年过去了。
46. obliterate /əˈblɪtəreɪt/ v. 除去；淘汰
47. Newcastle United 纽卡斯尔联队

Comprehension Questions

1. What stirred the author's memories of the 1979 FA Cup?
2. How was Nelson punished after he "mooned" at fans?
3. What was the inappropriate move in Arsenal team in the second half?
4. Why did Brady dig deep within the last couple of minutes of the match?
5. Which football match is the most impressive in your memory?

Background Reading

Manchester United

Manchester United Football Club is one of the best-known sports teams in the world. The "Red Devils"(红魔) play in the FA Premier League (英格兰足球超级联赛，英超), the top level of professional football in England.

The history of United is also one of the most incredible (令人难以置信的) sporting stories. The seeds for its future success were sown when workers with the Lancashire (兰开夏郡) and Yorkshire (约

Part III Sporting Memories

克郡) Railway decided to form a team of their own in 1878. It became a professional football team in 1885, adopted its present name in 1902 and were crowned Division One (甲级联赛) champions just six years later. United followed up its league success the next year with an FA Cup victory. Although it won the league again in 1911, there followed a notably (特别地) barren (没有战果的) spell (时期) lasting until after the Second World War.

Sir Matt Busby (巴斯比) became manager in 1945 and his "Busby Babes" (巴斯比宝贝) won three league titles in the 1950s. However, tragedy struck on the return from a European tie (平局) in 1958 when an air crash in Munich claimed (夺走) the lives of eight United players and robbed the world of one of the most exciting teams of its era. United was returning from a match with Red Star Belgrade after a 3–3 draw (平局), which had earned them a place in the European Cup (欧洲冠军杯) semi-finals. Busby, along with Bobby Charlton and defender Bill Foulkes had survived (幸存) the crash. But it was to take another 10 years before Busby (and Manchester United) could replace his "Babes" with a winning team, and recover from the tragedy. It was in 1968 that Busby's European ambition was realised in their defeat of Benfica (葡萄牙本菲卡队) by 4–1 at Wembley Stadium.

Frequent success in cup competitions, including lifting the European Cup Winners' Cup (欧洲优胜者杯) in 1991, translated into league success in 1993 — the inaugural season (首个赛季) of the FA Premier League (1992—1993). The red machine went on to dominate English football, winning the Football Association Challenge Cup (英格兰足总挑战杯), or FA Cup, four times including three "doubles" of both League and Cup in 1994, 1996, and 1999. A win in the European Champions Club Cup (欧洲冠军俱乐部杯), or Champions League (欧洲冠军联赛), gave United an unprecedented (史无前例的) "treble" (三冠王) in 1999.

And there were further celebrations at Old Trafford (老特拉福德球场，曼联主球场) as United lifted the FA Cup for the 11th time in 2004 with a 3–0 win over Millwall (米尔沃尔队). Wayne Rooney (韦恩·鲁尼) arrived at Old Trafford in August 2004 to complete a formidable-looking front line and the England striker (前锋) won his first trophy at the club in February 2006, scoring twice in the 4–0 Carling Cup (卡尔林杯) Final against Wigan Athletic (维甘竞技队) at the Millennium Stadium (千禧球场).

Relevant Words

assist	助攻	banana kick	香蕉球
feint	假动作	goal kick	球门球
home team	主队	line-up	阵容
playmaker	进攻组织者	visiting team	客队
volley	凌空球	wall of players	人墙

Lesson 5

> 足球世界杯对于整个世界来说是一场狂热的盛宴。2006年德国世界杯决赛:法国对阵意大利,这是太过戏剧性的比赛。齐达内和马特拉济在常规时间各入一球,加时赛下半时风云突变,齐达内极不冷静的举动染红离场。在激动人心的点球大战中,特雷泽盖没有罚入,意大利以6-4夺得冠军!当大力神杯在意大利队员手中传递时,当满场的烟花点燃时,我们意识到:这届世界杯,带着人们的欢喜和遗憾,终告落幕了。但是足球的魅力却是永恒的!

Italy Wins 2006 World Cup Championship

By Grahame L. Jones
July 9, 2006
Los Angeles Times

BERLIN — Italy, embroiled in a domestic soccer scandal[1] that could sink some of its most famous clubs and throw its league into turmoil[2], won the World Cup here Sunday night amid extraordinary scenes at the historic Olympic Stadium.

The dramatic conclusion of the month-long tournament saw Coach Marcello Lippi's Azzurri defeat France, 5-3 on penalty kicks, after the teams had played to a 1-1 tie in two hours of regulation and overtime.[3]

It was the Italians' fourth world championship but their first since 1982, and the victory sparked[4] massive celebrations throughout Italy. "This is the most satisfying moment of my life," said Lippi, who thanked his players for providing it. "They gave absolutely everything they had. It is just a fantastic feeling."

Elsewhere, however, the result took second place to[5] a moment of

1. ...embroiled in a domestic soccer scandal 被卷入国内足球丑闻
2. ...throw its league into turmoil 使他们的足球联赛陷入混乱
3. 历时一个月的世界杯在一场极具戏剧性的决赛之后落下帷幕,两个小时的常规时间和加时赛中双方战成1-1后,马塞洛·里皮率领的"蓝衣军团"点球大战中5-3击败法国队。Marcello Lippi 马塞洛·里皮,意大利队主教练 Azzurri "蓝衣军团",意大利队别号(Azzurri 是意大利语,蓝色)penalty kick 罚点球 regulation /ˌreɡjʊˈleɪʃən/ n. 常规时间 overtime /ˈəʊvətaɪm/ n. 加时赛
4. spark /spɑːk/ v. 激发
5. to take second place to 逊色于

madness during overtime when France's captain Zinedine Zidane[6], one of the sport's most accomplished players, was ejected[7] for a blatant and bizarre foul[8].

The 34-year-old midfielder[9], a World Cup winner in 1998, was playing in the final match of his illustrious[10] career, which could have ended on a high note[11] with a second world title.

Instead, it ended in shame.

Just before the 110th minute, Zidane and Italian defender Marco Materazzi appeared to exchange a few words[12] when both were walking back toward the midfield. Suddenly, Zidane turned, lowered his head and butted Materazzi very forcefully in the chest.[13]

It was one of the most astonishing and unusual fouls in World Cup history.

The Italian player was left writhing[14] on the ground while goalkeeper Gianluigi Buffon rushed over to one of the referees and demanded to know whether he had seen the incident.

After consulting his assistants, referee Horacio Elizondo of Zidane, thus bringing to a sad conclusion of one of soccer's most glittering careers.

The game began dramatically, with two goals inside the first 20 minutes promising the crowd of 69,000 a night of unusual entertainment in what had been a low-scoring[15] World Cup.

France took the lead on a penalty kick in the seventh minute after Elizondo, somewhat controversially, judged that Materazzi had fouled French midfielder Florent Malouda as he tried to control the ball in the penalty area[16].

Zidane stepped up to take the kick and, just as Buffon dived to his right, the French icon chipped the ball and saw it strike the underside of the crossbar and bounce down just behind the line.[17]

It was also the first goal Italy had allowed an opponent to score during the entire tournament. The U.S. goal in Italy's 1-1 tie with the Americans was an own goal[18].

Unperturbed by the setback, Italy set leveled the score 12 minutes later, on a set piece.[19]

Argentine-born midfielder Mauro Camoranesi won a corner kick[20] off French defender Eric Abidal, and Andrea Pirlo sent an outswinger[21] into the throng[22] of players in front of the French net.

Materazzi climbed high above France's Patrick Vieira, pushing down on the Frenchman's shoulder, and headed the ball sharply past

6. Zinedine Zidane 法国队队长齐达内
7. to be ejected 被罚下场
8. a blatant and bizarre foul 明显的不可思议的犯规
9. midfielder /ˈmɪdfiːldə/ n. 中场队员, 前卫
10. illustrious /ɪˈlʌstrɪəs/ a. 杰出的
11. to end on a high note 高调结束
12. to exchange words 争吵; 吵架
13. 突然, 齐达内低头猛烈地撞击马特拉济的胸部。
14. writhe /raɪð/ v. 翻腾; 打滚

15. low-scoring /ˈləʊˈskɔːrɪŋ/ a. 进球不多的
16. penalty area 禁区
17. 齐达内走上前主罚点球, 当门将布冯扑向右侧的一霎那, 这位法国足球偶像一脚射门打在横梁下沿弹下, 刚好越过了球门线。
  to step up 走上前
  to take the kick 主罚点球
  to chip the ball 踢出一记吊射
18. own goal 乌龙球
19. 意大利在挫折面前泰然自若, 12分钟后在战术配合下将比分扳平。
  unperturbed /ˌʌnpəˈtɜːbd/ a. 泰然自若的
  set piece 事先布好的战术
20. corner kick 角球
21. outswinger /ˈaʊtswɪŋə/ n. 外弧线球
22. throng /θrɒŋ/ n. 群

French goalkeeper Fabien Barthez and the defenders guarding each post.[23]

Lippi, who had been biting his nails on the sideline until then, pumped his fists in the air in relief. It was 1–1. For the next hour and a half, it was a back and forth[24] affair, with each team failing to penetrate the other's defense[25]. Lilian Thuram was superb for France. Fabio Cannavaro was exceptional for Italy.

The closest anyone came to scoring was when Zidane (who else?) sent a pass out to Willy Sagnol on the right flank in overtime, then sprinted into the area and powered a goal-bound header off Sagnol's return cross.[26]

Goalkeeper Buffon, in a purely instinctive move, threw up an arm and barely managed to deflect the ball over the crossbar.[27] It was the save of the match.

23. 马特拉济高高跃起,力压着法国队员帕特里克·维埃拉的肩膀,头球攻门,球越过法国防守队员和门将法比安·巴特斯破网。
24. back and forth 来回的(这里指互有进攻的)
25. ...failing to penetrate the other's defense 相互间都不能突破对方的防线
26. 最接近的一次是在加时赛中齐达内(除了他还能有谁呢？)传球给右路的萨尼奥尔,然后插入禁区,接萨尼奥尔的回传,头球攻门。 right flank 右翼 goal-bound /gəʊl baʊnd/ *a.* 直飞球门的 return cross 横回传球
27. 门将布冯完全出于本能单掌将球托出横梁。

Comprehension Questions

1. Why is the final between Italy and France regarded as a "dramatic conclusion" of the 2006 World Cup?
2. When did Zidane commit a foul?
3. Which team scored the first goal of the match?
4. How many goals did Italy allow his opponents to score during the entire World Cup?
5. Do you think Zidane's illustrious career ended in shame? Why or why not?

Background Reading

Relive the 2006 FIFA World Cup

No other sporting event captures the world's imagination like the FIFA (Federation Internationale de Football Association) World Cup. Ever since the first tentative (试验性的,尝试的) competition in Uruguay (乌拉圭) in 1930, FIFA's flagship (旗舰) has constantly grown in popularity and prestige.

Germany 2006 will no doubt be remembered as the fans' FIFA World Cup. With millions of people attending public screenings of the event, the atmosphere in the host country was incredible, as people from all over the world took the official slogan (口号) "A time to make friends" to heart.

On the pitch, 32 teams battled it out for football's ultimate prize. Some bowed out (退出) after just three games while France fell at the final hurdle as Italy claimed the crown of world champions. Here are the official reviews of the performance of top 8 teams, listed in order of how far they got.

Winners: Italy

The Azzurri won the FIFA World Cup for the fourth time after holding their nerves (保持镇静) in a dramatic penalty shoot-out (点球大战). For their performances in the group stages, Round of 16 (16强), quarter-finals and semis, football fans all over the world would agree that Marcello Lippi's side were worthy winners of the competition.

Runners-up: France

Inspired by Zinedine Zidane, until his dramatic sending-off in the Final, Les Bleus (法国队) surprised everyone to reach the showdown in Berlin on 9 July. Although they looked shaky (不稳固的) in the group stage, it was in the knockout rounds (淘汰赛) that they really came into their own, defeating Spain, Brazil and Portugal with relative ease.

Third place: Germany

The highest scorers at the tournament captured the imagination of the public with a combination of fine football and a never-say-die (永不放弃) attitude.

Fourth place: Portugal

Luiz Felipe Scolari's outfit (阵容) were arguably the surprise package of Germany 2006, overcoming Mexico, the Netherlands and England en route (在途中) to the semi-finals.

Quarter-finalists:
Argentina

After some great performances in the group stages and a victory over Mexico in the Round of 16, the Albiceleste (阿根廷队,别号蓝白军团) were unlucky to lose to the hosts in a dramatic shoot-out.

Brazil

The world champions' attempt to secure their sixth FIFA World Cup success ended after a lacklustre (无光泽的) showing against France, a tournament to forget for the Seleção (巴西队).

England

Unlucky with injuries, unlucky from the spot. Once again, penalties proved to be the undoing (衰败的原因) of England, who failed to live up to their high expectations at this event.

Ukraine

Coached by Oleg Blokhin, the FIFA World Cup first-timers (首次参赛队伍) did extremely well in reaching the last eight, but found Italy too tough (强大的) an opponent in Hamburg.

Relevant Words

clean catching	（守门员）接高球	close-marking defence	盯人防守
diving header	鱼跃顶球	fair charge	合理冲撞
finger-tip save	（守门员）托救球	grazing shot	贴地射门
open football	拉开的足球战术	scissors shot	倒钩射门
spot pass	球传到位	total football	全攻全守足球战术

Lesson 6

> 2005年7月,当卫冕冠军费德勒步入全英俱乐部中央球场的时候,他的心中只有一个念头:创造历史。他出神入化的发挥,让罗迪克在比赛中每每望球兴叹,甘拜下风。最终,这位瑞士网球天才直落三盘战胜罗迪克,连续第三次捧起温网男单冠军奖杯。在温网的历史上,曾经有两位传奇人物在全英俱乐部的草地上实现过连续夺冠三次以上的伟绩,一位是瑞典球王比约博格,另一位则是老天王桑普拉斯。费德勒刚刚登上天王宝座,便成为第三位连续三次在温网夺冠的选手。目前,费德勒在草地上已完成36场连胜的纪录,这位新天王巨星正在创造新的网坛传奇。

Federer[1] Beats Roddick[2] to Win Wimbledon[3] Yet Again

By Christopher Clarey
July 4, 2005
New York Times

WIMBLEDON, England, July 3 — One by one, the former Wimbledon champions left Center Court[4] on Sunday and crossed the elevated walkway[5] that leads to the players' area, with its ample lawn[6] and circular tables. One by one, they were asked to put Roger Federer's third consecutive Wimbledon title in perspective.[7]

"For me, he's the most complete player[8] I've seen," said Richard Krajicek[9], the Dutchman who won here in 1996. "He reminds me of Pete Sampras[10], with a better backhand[11]. With Sampras, I always had the feeling his backhand could fall apart."

Boris Becker[12], who won here in 1985, 1986 and 1989, said: "He doesn't really have a weakness. He's comfortable from the back of the

1. Federer 罗杰·费德勒(Roger Federer,瑞士网球明星,现世界排名第一,被誉为天王)
2. Roddick 安迪·罗迪克(Andy Roddick,美国职业网球运动员,现世界排名第三)
3. Wimbledon /ˈwɪmbldən/ n. 温布尔登(英格兰东南部城市,是著名的国际网球比赛地。这里指温布尔登网球锦标赛,简称"温网",是网球运动中最古老和最具声望的赛事。)
4. Center Court 中央球场
5. elevated walkway 高架通道
6. ample lawn 大草坪
7. 他们逐一被邀请对费德勒取得温网三连冠发表看法。to put sth. in perspective 比较并做出正确判断
8. most complete player 最全面的选手
9. Richard Krajicek 理查德·克拉吉塞克(荷兰网球名宿,现已退役)
10. Pete Sampras 皮特·桑普拉斯(现役男子球员中夺得大满贯赛事冠军头衔最多的网球选手)
11. backhand /ˈbækhænd/ n. 反手
12. Boris Becker 鲍里斯·贝克尔(曾三次获得温网冠军)

court, he's comfortable at the net. And I think the other players have to learn from that."

John McEnroe[13], who won here in 1981, 1983 and 1984, later said on television, "People think I'm kidding or that I'm just talking him up[14] when I say he's the greatest talent of all time, but I believe that."

In the end, however, it was best to leave the floor to[15] Andy Roddick, the second-seeded[16] player here who, because of Federer, has yet to win Wimbledon and did not come close Sunday in a 6-2, 7-6 (2), 6-4 defeat, which required much less of the crowd's time and emotional energy than the classic best-of-three women's final[17] Saturday.

"You just have to sit back and say, 'Too good,' sometimes," Roddick said before turning his thoughts to the future. "Hope he gets bored or something. I don't know."

Roddick's light-hearted[18] responses after this latest disappointment was not the sort of post-match reaction[19] some of his less genial[20] predecessors, including McEnroe, might have had.

But it was one more sign of the depth of Federer's dominance on the game's original surface.

If Roddick had lost in the fifth set, 9-7, or even 7-6 in the fourth, he might have walked in with his chin down and his wit under wraps[21]. But it is difficult to kick oneself[22] when the goal seems so far out of reach[23].

Last year in the final, Roddick started as aggressively, and ended up winning the first set[24] and leading again in the third before losing in four generally competitive sets. But this year, all his sound and fury[25] ended up signifying nothing more than a 1-hour-41-minute rout[26].

"It's hard for him, you know," Federer said. "This is my best match maybe that I've ever played."

Federer, seeded No. 1[27], had an extra day of rest for this rematch[28] of last year's final; Roddick's semifinal victory over Thomas Johansson stretched over two days because of a rain delay[29].

But Roddick appeared to have no shortage of energy in the final. "There wasn't one point where I was tired," he said. "I was tired of him, but I wasn't tired."

What he lacked was the antidote[30] to Federer's variety of poisons[31]. Though he had beaten Federer just once in their nine previous matches, Roddick had not played him this season.

"He played head and shoulders above[32] what he played last year,"

13. John McEnroe 约翰·麦肯罗,(绰号"坏小子",被认为是在网球场上最能调动自己和观众情绪的选手)
14. to talk up 赞扬,吹捧
15. to leave the floor to 把发言权留给……
16. second-seeded player 二号种子选手
17. best-of-three women's final 三盘两胜制的女子决赛
18. light-hearted /ˌlaɪtˈhɑːtɪd/ a. 随便的,不经心的
19. post-match reaction 赛后反应
20. genial /ˈdʒiːnɪəl/ a. 亲切的,友好的
21. under wraps 受限制,受约束
22. to kick oneself 严厉自责
23. so far out of reach 遥不可及
24. set /set/ n. 盘
25. sound and fury 大吵大闹(这里指猛烈攻势)
26. rout /raʊt/ n. 溃败
27. seeded No. 1 一号种子选手
28. rematch /ˈriːmætʃ/ n. 重赛,同一对手间的第二次比赛
29. rain delay 因雨暂停,因雨延期
30. antidote /ˈæntɪdəʊt/ n. 解药,应对方法
31. variety of poisons 各种毒药(这里指费德勒的各种战术和技巧)
32. head and shoulders above 远远超出

said Roddick, who also lost to Federer in the semifinals here in 2003. "I probably played a more complete match this year. Last year, I played well in spurts, but I was really hit and miss. I feel like if I played the way I did this year versus the way I was playing last year, I'd probably win."

Unfortunately, he has to keep playing Federer, who gave him no true window of opportunity on Sunday but did offer one opening when Roddick broke him in the third game of the second set and then held his own serve to take a 3-1 lead.[33]

But Federer soon resumed firing timely serves, returns and spectacular passing shots to sweep the next three games.[34] Roddick saved two set points[35] on his serve in the 10th game to help earn a tie breaker[36].

On grass, Roddick wins a lot more than he loses, but he did not pose a threat in this match, dropping the first three points, scrambling back to 3-2[37] and then losing four in a row.

So much for the second set, and after a short rain delay, Federer broke Roddick in the seventh game with another backhand pass[38], and then held that advantage[39] to 5-4.

He opened with an ace[40], then came up with an ace on a second serve. A backhand error offered Roddick nothing more than a stay of execution[41].

Federer won the next two points, putting the finishing touch on his fifth major title with a first serve up the middle that Roddick could only lunge for and knock into the net.[42]

Federer shouted, closed his eyes and clenched his fists. Then he hunched[43] forward and tumbled to the grass, rolling on his back and covering his eyes.

After he returned to his feet[44], he was in tears, just as he was when he won here for the first time, in 2003. It has not been quite the triumphal season[45] he might have expected after dominating the sport in 2004.

Though he has lost only three times in 2005, two of those losses were in the first Grand Slam tournaments[46] of the year, in the semifinals of the Australian Open to the eventual champion Marat Safin[47] and in the semifinals of the French Open to the eventual champion Rafael Nadal[48].

When he arrived in London the week before Wimbledon, Federer said he felt fine, but he was hiding the truth.

33. 不幸的是,罗迪克还得不断和费德勒交锋。在星期日的决赛中,费德勒没有真正给他机会,但在第二盘第三局,费德勒确实拱手相让了一个发球局,罗迪克破发成功,并且保住自己的发球局,3-1 领先。 opening /ˈəʊpənɪŋ/ n. 发球局　break /breɪk/ v. 破对方发球局,破发　to hold one's own serve 保住自己的发球局

34. 但费德勒很快恢复了常态,打出一连串适时的发球,回击球和漂亮的穿越,狂扫接下来的 3 局。 passing shot 穿越球,超身球

35. set point 盘点

36. tie breaker 抢 7 局,决胜局

37. to scramble back to 3-2 磕磕绊绊地追回到 3-2

38. backhand pass 反手穿越

39. advantage /ədˈvɑːntɪdʒ/ n. 占先(平分后先得一分),优势分

40. open with an ace 以发球得分开局　ace /eɪs/ n. 发球得分

41. stay of execution 缓期执行(这里指费德勒的失误延缓了罗迪克的失败)

42. 接着费德勒一个漂亮的中路发球,罗迪克只能向前冲去回球下网,费德勒连得两分,完成了第五个大满贯赛事冠军的最后一击。 to knock into the net 回球挂网,回球下网

43. hunch /hʌntʃ/ v. 向前移动

44. to return to one's feet 重新站起来

45. triumphal season 获胜的赛季

46. Grand Slam tournaments 大满贯赛事

47. Marat Safin 马拉特·萨芬(俄罗斯职业网球运动员,2005 赛季澳网冠军)

He later said he was actually exhausted after going further at the French Open than before and then fighting to win in Halle[49], Germany, the following week.

"I called my conditioning trainer[50] and said: 'What's this all about? I'm so tired before the tournament,'" Federer said Sunday. "He said: 'Look, it's normal. It's all coming back at you now that you have a week off. The body needs time to sort of relax.' And I said, 'Well I hope this will be over soon, because otherwise the tournament is going to start.'

"I would start hitting in practice, and I couldn't move anymore. Then in the afternoon, I'd go to the city and walk, and I'd always have to sit down. I was really, really tired. Almost like a feeling I never had before."

But it all ended up feeling quite familiar at Wimbledon. His grass-court victory streak is now at 36, and he has joined Bjorn Borg and Pete Sampras as the only men to win three consecutive titles here since World War II.[51]

At least history poses a challenge to Federer on grass. For the moment, present company is not bothering him much. He lost only one set last year on his way to the title and lost only one this year.

Maybe, as Roddick suggested earlier, he could succumb to[52] ennui[53] and quit tennis, a notion Federer was quick to dismiss as he promised to press on[54].

"I won't get bored so quickly," Federer said. "So I'm sorry."

48. Rafael Nadal 拉菲尔·纳达尔（西班牙网球运动员，当今网坛最被看好的希望之星）
49. Halle 哈勒市（德国中部城市）
50. conditioning trainer 体能教练

51. 费德勒获得了草地36场连胜，也成功地夺得了温网三连冠，成为二战以来继博格和桑普拉斯之后第三位连续三度获得温网冠军的选手。grass-court victory streak 草地连胜 streak /striːk/ n. 连续（输或赢）
52. to succumb to 屈服于
53. ennui /ɒnˈwiː/ n. 厌倦
54. to press on 奋力前进

Comprehension Questions

1. Why did Federer's performance remind Richard Krajicek of Pete Sampras?
2. Why was Roddick tired of Federer?
3. What does the author imply when he writes "history poses a challenge to Federer on grass" in the first sentence of the third last paragraph?
4. How did Federer feel in the week before Wimbledon?
5. What has made Wimbledon the most prestigious tennis championships?

Part III Sporting Memories

Background Reading

The Wimbledon Championships

The Wimbledon Championships, commonly referred to as simply "Wimbledon", are one of the oldest and most prestigious tennis championships in the world. The very first Lawn Tennis Championships at The All England Lawn Tennis and Croquet Club (全英草地网球和槌球俱乐部) was an amateur (业余的) event in 1877. This match was limited and the only matches played were the Gentlemen's Singles. The Ladies' Singles competition began in 1884.

Wimbledon logo

By 1900, Wimbledon had become an international tournament. One of the interesting facts about Wimbledon is the amount of pride the English people take in the Championship. However, since the start of Wimbledon, only two British players, Arthur Gore and Fred Perry, have managed to win the Gentlemen's event.

There are five main events held at Wimbledon: Gentlemen's Singles, Ladies' Singles, Gentlemen's Doubles, Ladies' Doubles, and Mixed Doubles(混合双打). Matches in the Gentlemen's Singles and Gentlemen's Doubles competitions are best-of-five sets (五盘三胜制); matches in all other events are best-of-three sets. Most events are single-elimination (单淘汰制的) tournaments; in other words, a player who loses a single match is immediately eliminated from the tournament.

Wimbledon is held in the months of June and July, the weather usually cooperated, and however, there is usually a rain delay or two during the course of the Championship. The tournament is the third Grand Slam event played each year, preceded by the Australian Open and the French Open, and followed by the U.S. Open. Wimbledon is the only Grand Slam event played on grass courts. At one time, all of the other Grand Slam events were played on grass. But the other three abandoned (放弃) grass for the unfavourable (不利的) surface.

The nineteen courts used for Wimbledon are all composed purely of ryegrass (黑麦草). The main show courts, Centre Court and No. 1 Court, are used only for two weeks a year, during the Championships. The remaining seventeen courts, however, are regularly used for other events hosted by The All England Lawn Tennis and Croquet Club.

Away from the courts, Wimbledon fortnight (两星期) has become an annual flurry (骚动) of betting. Britain's legal off-course betting allows anyone over 18 to have a wager (赌注) on the matches.

Relevant Words

break point 破发点	double fault 双误
long drive 长抽	loop drive 弧圈球
mid-air return 空中拦击	net game 网前打法
service game 发球局	three straight 连胜3盘
to lose one's service 输掉发球局	volley 截击球

Lesson 7

温布尔登作为最为古老的大满贯赛事,在每一位职业球手心目中都占据着无法比拟的位置。2006年7月9日,温网比赛进入到最后一天,女双4号种子郑洁/晏紫经过三盘苦战以6-3/3-6/6-2击败了前世界第一的苏亚雷兹(Suarez)和帕斯奎尔(Pascual)的跨国组合,首次捧起温布尔登女双冠军,也是继澳网之后她们获得的第二个大满贯女双冠军。郑洁/晏紫的惊人夺冠,昭示了中国的网球水平正大跨步地提升。

Yan and Zheng Win China's First Wimbledon Title

By Pritha Sarkar
July 9, 2006
Daily Mirror[1]

LONDON (Reuters[2]) — Zheng Jie and Yan Zi captured China's first Wimbledon title on Sunday when they beat Virginia Ruano Pascual and Paola Suarez 6-3, 3-6, 6-2 in the women's doubles final.

The fourth-seeded pair[3] claimed their second major title of the year after winning the country's first grand slam trophy at the Australian Open in January.

Their win capped[4] a successful run for the world's most populous

1. *Daily Mirror*《每日镜报》,英国晨报。1903年创刊,1985年后更名为《镜报》,隶属于镜报报系公司。报纸内容融名人轶事、星相、犯罪故事、政治分析、笑话等于一炉。

2. Reuters /ˈrɔɪtəz/ n. (英国)路透社

3. fourth-seeded pair 女双4号种子

4. cap /kæp/ v. 完成;结束

nation at the grasscourt championships after Li Na had made her mark[5] in the women's singles draw earlier in the week.

Li was the first Chinese player to reach the singles quarter-finals at a grand slam, where her run was ended by Belgian Kim Clijsters.

Since Li Ting and Sun Tiantian's victory in the women's doubles at the 2004 Athens Olympics, China has made big strides[6] in women's tennis.

The players have benefited from their federation's push to produce world class competitors in time for the 2008 Beijing Games and Sunday's win proved China could achieve its target of landing an Olympic gold in tennis in two years' time.[7]

Zheng and Yan's win also prevented Ruano Pascual and Suarez from completing a career doubles grand slam. The unseeded[8] Spanish-Argentine duo[9] own eight major titles but have now fallen at the final hurdle at Wimbledon for the third time.

Zheng served for the match at 5-1 up in the third set but despite holding two championship points[10], she was broken thanks to some tenacious[11] hitting by Suarez.

The Chinese pair also saw four more match points go begging[12] in the next game as Suarez came back from 0-40 to hang on for dear life[13].

But it proved to be seventh time lucky for Zheng and Yan. A volley[14] winner ended the Centre Court contest after two hours and eight minutes and the beaming[15] Chinese pair celebrated their historic win with a warm embrace.

5. to make one's mark 使自己出名；榜上有名
6. to make big strides 取得很大的进步
7. 这对选手得益于中国网球协会为北京2008奥运会打造世界级运动员的不懈努力，星期日的夺冠证明了中国能够实现两年后夺得一枚网球奥运金牌的目标。push /pʊʃ/ n. 持续的努力 land /lænd/ v. 获得，赢得
8. unseeded /ˌʌnˈsiːdɪd/ a. 非种子的
9. duo /ˈdjuːəʊ/ n. 一对（这里指苏亚雷兹和帕斯奎尔的跨国组合）
10. championship point 冠军点
11. tenacious /tɪˈneɪʃəs/ a. 顽强的
12. to go begging 毫无用处
13. to hang on for dear life 拼命地坚持
14. volley /ˈvɒli/ n. 截击球
15. beaming /ˈbiːmɪŋ/ a. 喜气洋洋的；愉快的

Comprehension Questions

1. Where did Yan and Zheng rank in the world tennis standings before Wimbledon 2006?
2. Who was the first Chinese to reach the singles quarter-finals at a grand slam?
3. How many match points did Yan and Zheng obtain in the game?
4. How did Yan and Zheng celebrate their victory?
5. What do you think the perspective of Chinese tennis will be?

Part III   Sporting Memories

Background Reading

Historic Achievements of China's Women Tennis Players

1992: Li Fang reached the third round at the Australian Open, a Grand Slam record for Chinese players for 12 years.

1994: Li Fang reached the second round at the French Open, China's best result at the Roland Garros (罗兰·加洛斯体育场,这里指法国网球公开赛).

2000: Yi Jingqian leveled Li Fang's achievement at the Australian Open with a third round appearance.

2000: Li Na/Li Ting won China's first ever WTA (Women's Tennis Association, 女子网球协会,这里指女子网球协会巡回赛) doubles' title at the Tashkent (塔什干,乌兹别克斯坦共和国首都) Open in Uzbekistan (乌兹别克斯坦).

2004: Zheng Jie/Yan Zi made the quarterfinals at the Australian Open, becoming the first Chinese duo to reach the top eight at a Grand Slam event.

2004: Sun Shengnan, who teamed up with (与……合作) Latisha Chan Yung-Jan of Chinese Taipei, won the country's first Grand Slam trophy as they clinched the juniors' doubles title at the Australian Open.

2004: Zheng Jie squeezed into (挤进) the fourth round at the French Open, refreshing (更新,刷新) China's best performance at a Grand Slam event.

2004: Li Ting/Sun Tiantian seized the women's doubles gold medal at the Athens Olympic Games, the country's first tennis Olympic gold.

2004: Li Na was crowned at the WTA Guangzhou International, becoming the first Chinese to win a WTA singles title.

2005: Peng Shuai reached the semi-finals at the WTA Tier (等级赛事) II Sydney International by upsetting (意外地击败) the then world No. 3 Anastasia Myskina of Russia. She is the first Chinese to beat a world top-10 player and also the first to enter the semis of a Tier II tournament.

Relevant Words

```
ATP Tour    国际职业网球联合会巡回赛
(ATP = Association of Tennis Professionals)
Davis Cup    戴维斯杯(男子团体赛)
Federation Cup    网球联合会杯(女子团体赛)
Hopman Cup    霍普曼杯(男女混合团体赛)
International Series Gold    冠军系列赛
Tennis Masters Cup    网球大师杯赛
```

Lesson 8

棒球是美国男女老少生活中不可缺少的一部分。如果说棒球是美国的国球,那么洋基队则是国球具体而微的精神象征。1901年成立的纽约洋基队,不但是美国大联盟百年历史拿过最多世界冠军的老牌球队,更是大联盟一个世纪的缩影与精华。有人说,要了解美国人、要探究美国的历史,从洋基的队史上就可以看出端倪,因为,美国的历史少不了棒球,而谈到美国的棒球,就不能不谈到洋基队。细数洋基战史,26次拿下世界大赛冠军。下面我们一起再次领略洋基风采吧!

Yankees[1]' Victory Is Long Time Coming

By Tyler Kepner
July 5, 2005
New York Times

On the day George Steinbrenner[2] was born, a Yankees team with nine future Hall of Famers[3] lost a holiday doubleheader[4] in Washington. Seventy-five years later, another Yankees team loaded with star power[5] played one game that seemed like two.

YANKEES 13
ORIOLES 8

In the longest nine-inning game[6] in the majors[7] this season, the Yankees outlasted[8] the Baltimore Orioles[9], 13-8, yesterday at Yankee Stadium. Steinbrenner was not there, staying home in Florida with his family. After the Yankees needed 4 hours and 12 minutes to put away the victory, he might have needed a few more candles on his birthday cake.

"I'm sure it wasn't one he enjoyed watching," Manager Joe Torre said. "None of us did. The end of the game, I'm sure, put a smile on his face."

Held scoreless for five innings after an early 6-0 lead, the Yankees erupted for seven runs in the eighth.[10]

1. Yankees 纽约洋基队(美国大联盟百年历史上拿过最多世界冠军的棒球队)
2. George Steinbrenner 乔治·斯泰因布莱纳(纽约洋基棒球队老板)
3. Hall of Famers 加入美国职棒名人堂的球员
4. doubleheader /'dʌbəl'hedə/ n. 连赛两场
5. loaded with star power 球星云集   to be loaded with 装满
6. nine-inning game 一场九局的比赛;一场完全的比赛
7. majors 指 The major leagues,美国职业棒球联盟
8. outlast /aʊt'lɑːst/ v. 耐力胜过
9. Baltimore Orioles 巴尔的摩金莺队
10. 6:0 领先后,洋基队有5局未再得分。在第8局中,洋基队突然一举拿下7分。run /rʌn/ n. 得分

The rally erased a Baltimore comeback[11] that had put the Yankees down by two, and it brought back cozy memories of seasons not so tense.

"We're coming back the way we used to," said Bernie Williams, whose two-run bloop single[12] over first base scored the go-ahead run[13] in the eighth. "I think it's a great sign of good things to come."

The Yankees (42-39) have won five of their last seven games, coming from behind[14] four times and winning the other game, 1-0. It is a dangerous way to play, and emblematic of the Yankees' pitching problems.

Tanyon Sturtze made an emergency start yesterday because the Yankees had no viable replacement[15] for the injured Carl Pavano. The three relievers[16] who pitched after Sturtze were pitching for Class AAA Columbus[17] two weeks ago.

Sturtze lasted three and two-thirds innings, allowing four runs. Scott Proctor, Wayne Franklin and Jason Anderson followed him, and the mound[18] looked like a Petri dish[19] for Torre. The Yankees are experimenting with in-house bullpen[20] help before the July 31 non-waiver trading deadline[21], and yesterday Torre got a close-up look at the specimens.

The results were inconclusive[22] at best. Proctor walked in a run, then retired[23] four hitters[24] in a row before allowing a homer[25] to Jay Gibbons. Franklin struck out[26] Brian Roberts with a man on second[27] to escape a jam[28] in the sixth, but he gave up two runs in the seventh.

Anderson (1-0) earned the victory, but not without allowing a go-ahead two-run double[29] to Luis Matos in the seventh. Torre restored order in the ninth, using Mariano Rivera to finish it.

"We can't rely on games like this on a regular basis," Torre said. "We need to pitch effectively and control the game better than we did today."

As strange as it was for the Yankees, the game was just as bizarre for the Orioles. Their closer[30], the All-Star[31] B. J. Ryan, threw more pitches than their starter[32], Bruce Chen. Orioles Manager Lee Mazzilli summoned Ryan in a save situation in the eighth inning, which he had not done all season.

Ryan (1-2) failed, allowing five runs (four earned[33]) on three hits[34] and three walks[35], one intentional[36]. It was the 10th loss in 12 games for the Orioles, who lead the Yankees for second place in the American League East[37] by just a game and a half. But Mazzilli, after meeting with his players, said he was proud.

11. comeback /ˈkʌmbæk/ n. 奋起直追，东山再起
12. two-run bloop single 2 分的腾飞球一垒安打　bloop /bluːp/ n. 打到内外野之间的腾飞球　single /ˈsɪŋgl/ n. 一垒安打
13. go-ahead run 超前分
14. to come from behind（扭转比赛颓势）赶上来
15. replacement /rɪˈpleɪsmənt/ n. 替补队员
16. reliever /rɪˈliːvə/ n. 替补投手
17. Class AAA Columbus 三 A 哥伦布队
18. mound /maʊnd/ n. 投球区土墩
19. Petri dish 皮氏培养皿
20. bullpen /ˈbʊlpen/ n. 候补队员区，投手练习区
21. non-waiver trading deadline 交易球员的大限；731 交易大限（球季开始到 7 月 31 日之前交换球员没有必要交弃权书）　waiver /ˈweɪvə/ n. 弃权证书（这里指将球员合约提出特定指派或无条件释出大联盟球员的正式许可。）
22. inconclusive /ˌɪnkənˈkluːsɪv/ a. 不确定的
23. retire /rɪˈtaɪə/ v. 使（击球员）出局
24. hitter /ˈhɪtə/ n. 击球员
25. homer /ˈhəʊmə/ n. 本垒打
26. to strike out 使击球手三击不中出局
27. second /ˈsekənd/ n. 二垒
28. to escape a jam 脱离困境
29. two-run double 2 分双杀
30. closer /ˈkləʊzə/ n. 救援投手
31. All-Star 全明星
32. starter /ˈstɑːtə/ n. 先发投手
33. earned (run) 投手责任失分
34. hit /hɪt/ n. 安打
35. walk /wɔːk/ n. 四坏球上垒，自由上垒（投手投出四坏球而使击球手进到移到第一垒）
36. intentional (walk)（投手）故意送击球员上垒，故意保送
37. American League East 美国联盟东区

"You're down six runs to the Yankees in the second inning and you come back and score eight runs in this ballpark,[38]" he said to reporters. "It's pretty damn good. The bullpen did the job. They held them right where they were."

The Orioles might have won handily if not for Chen. Gary Sheffield smoked a three-run homer[39] to left off him in the first inning, and Hideki Matsui added a bases-empty blast[40]. In the second inning, Jason Giambi crushed the first of his two homers into the third deck in right.

It was 6-0 after two innings, but after a homer by Roberts in the third, Sturtze's stamina ran out in the fourth. A hit batter[41], a walk and a single brought in one run, and a two-out walk loaded the bases[42] for the No. 9 hitter, Sal Fasano.

Sturtze walked him with his 82nd pitch, making it 6-3 and bringing in Proctor from the bullpen.

"I just wanted to go as hard as I could as long as I could," Sturtze said. "That ended up being three and two-thirds. That's all I had."

With the Yankees leading, 6-5, in the sixth, Torre called for Franklin, a left-hander[43] so obscure[44] that Sturtze admitted he did not know his first name until he took the mound. Franklin used a backdoor slider[45] to strike out his first hitter, Roberts, and he punched the air on his way to the dugout[46].

"You don't want to make a mistake to the league's leading hitter," Franklin said, referring to Roberts and his .358 average. "That's why I got a little emotional right there. It was a one-run game."

But the Orioles quickly tied it in the seventh. Melvin Mora doubled and scored on a one-out single by Rafael Palmeiro. Anderson relieved Franklin, walked his first hitter and gave up Matos's two-run double on a curveball to put the Orioles ahead, 8-6.

Scoreless off three middle relievers, the Yankees had better luck off Steve Kline and Ryan. Giambi led off[47] the eighth with a homer, and after two singles, an intentional walk and a sacrifice bunt[48], Ryan walked[49] Alex Rodriguez on a 3-2 count[50] to force in the tying run[51].

"Every game has a moment, and I knew that was it right there," Rodriguez said. "Strikeout or pop-up[52], we might lose the game."

Instead, Williams followed the walk by looping a single just out of reach onto the grass near the foul line[53] in shallow right[54]. Two runs scored to put the Yankees ahead, 10-8, and they piled it on[55] from there.

38. 你们在第二局落后洋基队6分的情况下奋起直追，在场上连得8分。ballpark /ˈbɔːlˌpɑːk/ n. 棒球场

39. ...smoke a three-run homer 闷杀3分本垒打 smoke /sməuk/ v. [俚语] 杀死；谋杀

40. bases-empty blast 无人在垒的本垒打 blast /blɑːst/ n. 本垒打

41. hit batter 投球中身
42. to load the bases 占满垒

43. left-hander /ˈleftˈhændə/ n. 左撇子，左手投球
44. obscure /əbˈskjuə/ a. 不出名的
45. backdoor slider 从外侧投的滑球（由坏球区进好球区外侧）
46. dugout /ˈdʌɡaut/ n. 球员休息处，球员席

47. to lead off 开始；担任第一位击球员
48. sacrifice bunt 触击牺牲打
49. walk /wɔːk/ v. 保送上垒，使跑垒员跑垒
50. 3-2 count 三"球"两"击"，满垒
51. ...force in the tying run 追平了比分后强迫取分 force /fɔːs/ v. 强迫取分（当垒已满时击球员迫使跑垒员进垒而得分），迫使进垒
52. pop-up /ˈpɒpˌʌp/ n. 小腾空球
53. foul line 犯规线
54. shallow right 右侧迫近防守的位置
55. to pile sth. on 积累（这里指积分）

"Sometimes it's better to be lucky than good," Williams said.

He was referring to his hit, but he could have been talking about the team. The Yankees were not exactly good, but they had more staying power[56] than their sinking opponent[57], and they gave their owner the only thing he really cares about: a victory.

56. staying power 耐力,持久力
57. sinking opponent 体力下降的对手

Comprehension Questions

1. Why did the author say the Yankees played one game that seemed like two?
2. Why was this game not the one George Steinbrenner enjoyed watching?
3. Which team took the lead at the beginning of the game?
4. What did Williams mean when he said "Sometimes it's better to be lucky than good" (in the second last paragraph)?
5. Do you think Yankees are one of the best baseball teams in America? Why or why not?

Background Reading

The New York Yankees

America's most storied (历史上有名的) sports franchise (职业运动队), the New York Yankees, has a past the rest of Major League Baseball envies, and a present it fears. As a professional team based in the Bronx (朗克斯区), New York City, it has enjoyed more success than any other sports franchise. The Yankees has won 26 World Series (美国职棒世界大赛) in 39 appearances and featured (包含) such greatest players of all-time as Babe Ruth (贝比·鲁斯).

The team began playing as the Baltimore Orioles in 1901, was known as the New York Highlanders (高原人队) in 1903–1912, and changed its name to the New York Yankees in 1913.

The 1920s Yankees rested on the shoulders of Babe Ruth. The Boston Red Sox (波士顿红袜队) inexplicably (无法说明地；费解地) sold Ruth to New York after the 1919 season, and they soon regretted it. Ruth's stats (统计) were legendary 714 home runs, 2,174 runs, 2,210 RBI (Runs Batted In, 击球跑垒得分), 2,056 walks, a .342 average, and a mammoth (巨大的) .690 career slugging average (长打率). Ruth led the AL (American League, 美国联盟) in homers 12 times, in runs scored eight times, in total bases six times, in RBI six times, in walks 11 times, in batting once, slugging 12 times, and in on-base percentage (上垒率) 10 times.

The team continued to achieve success from 1941 to 1947 as they won 4 pennants (锦旗,象征职业棒球队获胜的旗帜) and 3 World Series titles. From 1948 to 1960, the club won ten AL pennants and seven World Series Championships, including five straight championships, a record unmatched to this day. The dynasty slumbered (沉睡,这里指没有战绩) from 1965 through 1993. With the exception of a brief, but unforgettably electric (令人兴奋的), flashback (重现) reign (统治) of five postseason teams, including consecutive World Series titles in 1977 and '78, the Yankees got lost in the crowd.

The franchise returned to dominance in the late 1990s, winning the World Series in 1996, 1998, 1999, and 2000 and AL Championships (美国棒球大联盟锦标赛) in 1996, 1998, 1999, 2000, 2001, and 2003.

Relevant Words

base runner	跑垒员	catcher	接手
diamond	棒球场	extra inning	（平局后）决胜局
pitcher	投手	shortstop	游击手
to advance	进垒	to force out	封杀出局
to steal base	偷垒	to swing	挥棒

Lesson 9

> 板球,一向被人们称为"绅士的游戏",是一项崇尚体育精神和公平竞争的运动。英国的体育爱好者把板球看做是英国的"国球",原因很简单,在半个世纪以来的世界板球大赛上,英国几乎届届夺冠。板球至今是英联邦国家最喜爱的运动,但在中国不是很盛行。中国板球协会在 2004 年加入了国际板球理事会,成为接纳会员(Affiliate Member)。下面我们一起了解一下板球比赛吧。

Somerset[1] Overseas Aides Increase Australia's Anxiety

By Ivo Tennant
June 16, 2005
The Times

Taunton (Australians won toss): Somerset beat the Australians by four wickets[2].

The Australians were beaten for the second time this week yesterday and, even though this was chiefly through centuries[3] by Graeme Smith and Sanath Jayasuriya, those two well-known sons of the Quantocks, it was still an occasion for much raucous[4] cider-pumping celebration[5]. Somerset had only defeated them once,

1. Somerset 英国萨默塞特板球俱乐部
2. ... beat... by four wickets 在无人出局的情况下赢 4 个球(回合) wicket /ˈwɪkɪt/ n. 一局,击球手的一回合
3. century /ˈsentʃərɪ/ n. 100 分
4. raucous /ˈrɔːkəs/ a. 喧闹的
5. cider-pumping celebration 开苹果酒庆祝

when Ian Botham excelled at Bath in 1977.

It should also be mentioned that Ricky Ponting[6] retired both himself and Matthew Hayden when they were on the verge of[7] making centuries. The Australians should have scored more than 342 for five on this excellent pitch.[8] Of greater concern than the defeat itself will be that some of their ground fielding[9] was not up to its customary standard[10]. Nor was some of the bowling[11]. Mike Kasprowicz conceded 89 runs[12] in his eight overs[13]. Yet Ponting was sporting[14] enough to lead his team into Somerset's dressing-room when they left the field.

"I am pretty embarrassed," Ponting said. "We shall sit down and talk about why we were not able to defend a total of 342. We weren't smart enough or good enough. We'll have our work cut out[15] against Bangladesh on Saturday the way we are playing."

Smith and Jayasuriya put on 197 in 23 overs. To travel in a chastened[16] state of mind after defeat by England at the Rose Bowl[17] and find the opposition's batting opened by two overseas cricketers[18] of such stature was all that the Australians wanted. This may have been a practice match, but they were still up against high-class performers who know them well.

If muscular strength was behind Smith's punched drives on both sides of the wicket[19], Jayasuriya's century counterpointed[20] this in that he used the pace of the ball to collect runs to third man[21] and long leg[22]. In the absence of Brett Lee, who will have a scan on his right shoulder, having left the field after bowling four overs, Shane Watson had little semblance of control[23] and even Glenn McGrath's figures[24] were less favourable than is normally the case.

Smith and Jayasuriya went in relatively quick succession[25] and the middle order initially did not excel. John Francis was bowled[26] round his legs[27] by McGrath, Keith Parsons played across the line and Ian Blackwell swung and missed at Watson's first ball when he returned at the old pavilion[28] end. The dismissal[29] of Matthew Wood, held at long-on[30], left an out-of-form James Hildreth to try to demonstrate his unquestioned talent. This he did to the extent of adding 54 off 26 balls with Carl Gazzard and achieving victory with 3.1 overs remaining.

The day had begun more favourably for the Australians. Hayden drove the first ball of the match for four and added 11 more boundaries

6. Ricky Ponting 里基·庞廷（澳大利亚板球队队长）
7. on the verge of 接近于，濒临于
8. 在这场精彩的比赛中，澳大利亚队本来不应该只得 342 分，使对方 5 个队员出局。for five 指 for five wickets their opponents have taken 对方有 5 个队员出局。pitch /pɪtʃ/ n. 板球场
9. ground fielding 接地滚球
10. customary standard 一般标准
11. bowling /'bəʊlɪŋ/ n. 投球
12. ...concede 89 runs 让对方得了 89 分
13. over /'əʊvə/ n. 回合（6 次投球为 1 回合），轮次
14. sporting /'spɔːtɪŋ/ a. 有体育道德的
15. to have one's work cut out 遭遇困难
16. chastened /'tʃeɪsənd/ a. 经磨练的
17. Rose Bowl 玫瑰碗球场
18. cricketer /'krɪkɪtə/ n. 板球队员
19. wicket /'wɪkɪt/ n. 三柱门
20. counterpoint /'kaʊntəpɔɪnt/ v. 与……进行对比
21. third man 三野手
22. long leg 左方较远球员
23. to have little semblance of control 几乎失去了控制
24. figure /'fɪɡə/ n. 数字（这里指得分）
25. in succession 接连地
26. bowled（击球手）被击杀（出局）（指投球手投球击中击球手方的柱门，将一个或两个横木击落）
27. leg /leɡ/ n. 击球手左后方
28. pavilion /pə'vɪljən/ n. 板球队员更衣室；(板球场旁供运动员和观众用的)建筑物
29. dismissal /dɪs'mɪsəl/ n. 出局
30. long-on n. 投手右后方

in an innings of 76 off 53 balls before he retired.[31] Ponting wanted to give others time in the middle as well, and departed having made 80 from 86 balls. Twice in succession he on-drove[32] Smith's off spin[33] for six, once into the River Tone.

Damien Martyn contributed 44 and Michael Clarke struck an unbeaten[34] 63 off 45 balls. In the absence of Andrew Caddick and with Gareth Andrew proving expensive, Smith gamely bowled himself towards the end of the Australians' innings.

Peter Anderson, the chief executive[35] for the past 17 years, will be leaving the club tomorrow without any opportunity for Somerset's members to give him a send-off[36]. Anderson will be succeeded by Richard Gould, 35, the commercial director[37] at Bristol City FC and son of Bobby Gould, the former Wimbledon manager. The position will be split into two roles, with Brian Rose, the former Somerset captain, running cricketing matters.

31. 澳大利亚队队员 Hayden 击中本次比赛的第一个球得 4 分，接着又将球直接击出场地 11 次，在出局之前投手投 53 个球,他总共拿下 76 分。for four 得 4 分。boundary /ˈbaʊndəri/ n. 击中或击过边界的球（击中边界的球,得 4 分；击出界外的球,得 6 分） innings /ˈmɪŋz/ n. 局（板球运动中，innings 指"局"，可以用作单数,也可以用作复数。
32. on-drive v. 击球
33. spin /spɪn/ n. 转球
34. unbeaten /ˌʌnˈbiːtn/ a. 未被击败的,未被打破的
35. chief executive 执行总裁,首席执行官
36. to give sb. a send-off 为某人送行
37. commercial director 商务总监

Comprehension Questions

1. What were the possible reasons for Australian's defeat?
2. Why was Brett Lee absent from the game?
3. In which team's favor did the game begin?
4. How did Jayasuriya counterpoint Smith's punched drives?
5. Cricket is regarded as a gentleman's game. What do you think?

Background Reading

Cricket

The origins of cricket are obscure （模糊不清的） and unrecorded. Many people believe it was invented by shepherds (牧羊人) who used their crooks (牧羊人用的曲柄杖) to defend the wicket gate to the sheepfold (羊圈).

Cricket is a team sport for two teams of eleven players each. A formal game of cricket can last from an afternoon to several days. Although the game play （玩法） and rules are very different, the basic concept of cricket is similar to that of baseball. Teams bat (击球) in successive innings and attempt to score runs, while the opposing team fields (接球) and attempts to bring an end to the batting team's innings.

The order in which the teams bat is determined by a coin toss. The captain of the side winning the toss may choose to bat or field first. All eleven players of the fielding team go out to field, two players of the batting team go out to bat. The remainder (其余的队员) of the batting team wait off the field for their turn to bat.

The bowler (投手) propels the ball (投球) with a straight arm from one end of the 22-yard pitch in an attempt to dismiss the batsman by hitting a target known as a wicket at the other end, or by causing the batsman to hit the ball into the air into a fielder's (接球手) grasp (抓住). The batsman attempts to defend the wicket with the bat and to score runs — the currency (流通,这里指跑动) of the game — by striking the ball to the field boundary, or far enough from the fielders to allow the batsman to run to the other end of the pitch before the ball can be returned. At least two bowlers must take turns, from alternating (交互的) ends; also, there are always two batsmen on the field, each to take a turn as required. When all but one of the batting team have been dismissed, the batting side's opportunity to score runs is closed, and the roles are reversed (对换). After all the players required to bat on both sides have done so either once or twice, the total number of runs accumulated (累积的) determines the winner.

Relevant Words

full toss　直投球
hat trick　帽子戏法,指击球手连击三球、次次击中目标(三柱门中的两个门),对方三名球员因此淘汰出局。
leg before wicket (lbw)　腿截球,(击球手)腿碰球(犯规)出局
ODI (One Day International)　一日赛
spin bowler　擅长投旋转球的球员
stonewall　打防守球
stump　门直柱,三门柱的一柱
The Ashes　"骨灰杯",英格兰和澳大利亚之间板球赛
twelfth man　第十二人,指替补队员
wicketkeeper　守门员,防守员,捕手

Lesson 10

阿姆斯特朗宣布将在第92届环法自行车赛(Tour De France)之后结束职业生涯,激起所有对手最后一次战胜他的欲望,但最终他赢得毫无悬念。一代车王以连续第7次夺冠完成自己的谢幕之作。组委会主席勒布朗不禁慨叹:在环法历史上将不会有人重续阿姆斯特朗的辉煌。23天的时间里,车手们从法国北部的弗罗芒蒂讷出发,经受了9个平路赛段,3个丘陵赛段,6个山地赛段的考验,翻越阿尔卑斯山、比利牛斯山,转战3607公里,围绕法国一圈,最终抵达巴黎香谢丽舍大街。赛事不仅给我们带来英雄主义的拼搏抗争精神,也将一个风景如画的浪漫国度清晰地展现在我们面前,环法赛已然成为一场不折不扣的视觉盛宴。

Uphill Racer

Grinding down[1] his rivals in the Alps and Pyrenees[2], Lance Armstrong[3] closed in[4] on his seventh straight win[5].

By Austin Murphy
July 25, 2005
Sports Illustrated[6]

This was why they had come, why they had camped out on the road to Pla-d'Adet[7]. This was why they put up with the hordes of Germans who poured over the border in RVs cloaked in the pink banners of the T-Mobile racing team.[8] This was why they endured the Americans, with their yellow bracelets and their confusing blend of friendliness and aggression, typified by the big blue banner that said, KICK ASS[9], LANCE.

They were the Basques[10], and this was their land. They came from

St.-Lary-Soulan, the village at the base of this menacing[11] peak in the Pyrenees, and from surrounding towns here in the South of France and across the nearby Spanish frontier. For this, the 15th and most brutal stage of the

1. to grind sb. down 压迫,使无力反击
2. Pyrenees /ˌpɪrəˈniːz/ *n.* 比利牛斯山脉,位于欧洲西南部
3. Lance Armstrong 兰斯·阿姆斯特朗,美国著名自行车运动员
4. to close in 逐渐接近
5. straight win 连胜
6. *Sports Illustrated*《体育画报》,创刊于1954年,周刊。美国传媒业巨头时代华纳公司旗下杂志,有超过300万的订户和2300万读者,主要通过图片的方式介绍体育明星和大众喜爱的赛事。
7. Pla-d'Adet 即 Saint-Lary-Soulan 圣拉里苏朗,位于法国南部
8. 正因为如此,他们容忍大批德国人开着休闲车来到他们的地界,车子上插满了粉红色的电信车队的旗子。horde /hɔːd/ *n.* 群,RV = recreation vehicle 休闲车,cloak /kləʊk/ *v.* 由……覆盖,T-Mobile racing team 德国电信车队
9. to kick ass [俗语]了不起,厉害
10. Basque /bæsk/ *n.* 巴斯克人,居住在西班牙和法国毗临比斯开湾的比利牛斯西部地区
11. menacing /ˈmenəsɪŋ/ *a.* 险恶的

173

Tour de France — the Pla-d'Adet was the sixth and final mountain the riders would climb this day — the Basques donned[12] their orange shirts, fortified[13] themselves with wine from goatskin bota bags[14] and hoped fervently[15] for good news.

And here it was. Powering up the mountain at the head of the field was a pair of riders, a Spaniard[16] named Oscar Pereiro and an American riding for Discovery Channel[17] whose face, incredibly, betrayed no suffering. Yes, the American was very strong, everyone knew that, but Pereiro was a pure climber on his home turf[18]. As the two cyclists neared the summit, the Basques crowded in, screaming for their boy. Epithets[19], and the odd[20] beverage[21], were thrown in the direction of the Discovery rider. One fan got too close and was run over by the motorcycle trailing the riders.

The American waited until he was safely inside the spectator barricades[22], in the final kilometer of the stage, before attacking. Rising out of his saddle[23], he dropped Pereiro with ease. As he crossed the finish line, he covered his face in disbelief, then raised his hands to the sky. "I'm in shock," George Hincapie[24] would say later. "I just won the biggest race of my life."

Sunday, July 17, was a very good day for Americans at the Tour de France. There was Hincapie, one of the nicest man in the peloton[25], followed on the podium by his friend Lance Armstrong, the overall leader, who had spent the afternoon wringing the last drops of hope[26] from his chief rivals. With a single mountain stage remaining in this year's Tour — and in his career — Armstrong held a lead of two minutes and 46 seconds over CSC's Ivan Basso[27], the brilliant young rider who spent the weekend launching furious, fruitless attacks against him. The Tour ends in Paris on July 24, the day after a time trial in which Basso is likely to lose still more time to Armstrong. The Texan[28] needs only to stay upright, it seems, to lock up his seventh straight Tour victory[29].

The story of how Armstrong and his Discovery teammates all but nailed down[30] number 7 is the story of how Hincapie rode away with the first Tour de France stage win[31] in his 11-year career: Discovery showed a willingness to call audibles[32], to chuck[33] the original plan if it wasn't working.

The Queens-born[34] 6'3" Hincapie has made a career of hiding his lamp under a bushel[35]. He has spent the last seven years sheltering Armstrong from headwinds and from crash-prone numskull sprinters.[36]

12. don /dɒn/ v. 穿上
13. fortify /ˈfɔːtɪfaɪ/ v. 增加体力
14. goatskin bota bags 西班牙羊皮水囊(外形为肾形,可以装酒、水等)
15. fervently /ˈfɜːvəntlɪ/ ad. 热切地
16. Spaniard /ˈspænjəd/ n. 西班牙人
17. Discovery Channel 美国探索频道车队
18. turf /tɜːf/ n. 地区;地盘
19. epithet /ˈepɪθet/ n. 带侮辱性的粗俗词语
20. odd /ɒd/ a. 出乎意料的
21. beverage /ˈbevərɪdʒ/ n. 饮料,这里指饮料瓶
22. barricade /ˈbærɪkeɪd/ n. 栅栏
23. saddle /ˈsædl/ n. 车座
24. George Hincapie 乔治·辛卡皮,美国探索频道车队的车手
25. peloton /peləˈtɔːn/ n. 主车群
26. to wring the last drops of hope 粉碎最后一丝希望
27. CSC's Ivan Basso 丹麦 CSC 车队车手伊凡·巴索
28. Texan /ˈteksən/ n. 得克萨斯人,指阿姆斯特朗
29. to lock up one's victory 锁定胜局
30. to nail down 赢得
31. stage win 赛段冠军
32. to call audibles 改变战术
33. chuck /tʃʌk/ v. 放弃
34. Queens-born 出生在纽约昆斯区的
35. to hide one's lamp under a bushel 不露锋芒
36. 7年来,他一直为阿姆斯特朗挡风,使其避开那些拼命加速导致撞车的蠢才。
headwind /ˈhedˌwɪnd/ n. 逆风
sprinter /ˈsprɪntə/ n. 速度很快的车手

His win on Sunday resulted from an impulsive decision he made 15 miles into the stage. When a group of riders broke from the peloton, he jumped it. At that morning's strategy meeting, team director Johan Bruyneel had stressed the importance of having as many Discovery riders as possible with Armstrong at the bottom of the final climb. Surely the breakaway would be reeled in before it reached the Plad'Adet, Hincapie reasoned, and joining it would put him in a strong position to pace his captain up that mountain.

We know how that worked out. The break stayed clear of the peloton, freeing Hincapie to ride for himself.[37] His victory, while surprising, was in character with[38] Discovery's week in the Alps and the Pyrenees. Things didn't always go as planned, but they turned out well in the end.

This was not Armstrong's strongest team ever, but it may have been his most resilient[39]. Certainly the team rallied gamely after its unscheduled snooze in the final kilometers of stage 8.[40] The course that day took the riders across the Rhine from Germany back into France and up the first truly challenging climb of the 92nd Tour, the Col de la Schlucht. Armstrong and his mates had scouted most of the other stages but not this one. The stiff ascent "blindsided"[41] them, Armstrong said. "We had no idea how hard that climb was. No clue."

As the peloton hit the steep grade[42] at 25 mph, it fractured[43]. Armstrong found himself in the lead group with all of his main rivals and no teammates. That's when the attacks began. T-Mobile's Alexander (Vino) Vinokourov attacked three times. Basso, Denis Menchov, Franciso Mancebo — everyone who was anyone in this race took a shot at the patron[44]. Everyone, that is, but T-Mobile's Jan Ullrich, who lived up to his reputation for tactical ineptitude[45]. Not only did Ullrich fail to attack Armstrong, but at one point he unwittingly[46] paced his rival[47], allowing the Texan to draft[48] behind him to return to the front. Though Armstrong chased down all but one of the attacks — he allowed T-Mobile's Andreas Klöden to escape — he suffered deeply doing so.

Discovery had been embarrassed. CSC's Bobby Julich said Armstrong's team had "imploded[49]." As Hincapie would later say, "Everyone started talking about how Lance didn't have a team. That pissed us off[50]."

Bruyneel did not raise his voice at the next morning's meeting. He didn't need to. Looking around the table, he told each of the riders

37. 冲出大部队使得辛卡皮可以完全按照自己的节奏骑行。
38. in character with 和……相称
39. resilient /rɪˈzɪliənt/ a. 充满活力的
40. 果然,探索频道车队在第八赛段的最后几公里突然表现低迷后,又不屈不挠地重整旗鼓。
41. blindside /ˈblaɪndsaɪd/ v. 使惊讶
42. steep grade 陡坡
43. fracture /ˈfræktʃə/ v. 分裂
44. patron /ˈpeɪtrən/ n. 老主顾,这里指阿姆斯特朗(因其多次参加环法赛并夺冠)
45. tactical ineptitude 不善战术
46. unwittingly /ʌnˈwɪtɪŋlɪ/ ad. 不知不觉地,无意地
47. to pace one's rival 为对手领骑
48. draft /drɑːft/ v. 利用车的尾流优势(紧跟在另一辆车的后面,以便利用其尾流里被减弱的空气压力的优势)
49. implode /ɪmˈpləʊd/ v. 内爆
50. to piss sb. off [俗语] 使恼火,变得生气

that what had happened the day before could never happen again.

For seven years Bruyneel has set the same template[51] for success: Have Armstrong take the lead in the first time trial. Keep him safe in the early, flat stages[52]. Then, on the final climb of the first mountain stage, sic him on his rivals[53]. Of course Armstrong does not redline[54] his engine at the valley floor. Rather, he tucks in[55] behind a line of teammates, who take turns spending[56] themselves on his behalf.

They take their turns in ascending order of strength. "We want the speed to constantly accelerate," says Armstrong. "We want to be shedding [rivals]." Discovery's mountain goats are sustained[57] by periodic radio[58] updates from Bruyneel in the team car: "Vino is dropped[59]! ... Landis is dropped! ... Ullrich has cracked[60]! Great job, boys. Keep it going!"

It is the team's custom to watch French TV between 10 and 11 p.m. for a replay of the day's highlights. "The boys like to see the amount of suffering they were dealing out[61]," says Armstrong. "It's good for morale."

Morale was excellent on the night of July 12. That day marked the Tour's first Alpine stage[62], which ended after the 22.2-kilometer (13.8-mile) ascent of a bear[63] named Courchevel. At the base of the climb the peloton consisted of some 70 riders. Then Discovery took over. First came Paolo Salvodelli, followed by Jose (Ace) Azevedo, then Hincapie. By the time Big George fell back, spent, only a dozen riders remained. Yaroslav Popovych took his pull, shedding four or five riders before punching the clock. That's when Armstrong delivered a burst of acceleration none of his main rivals could counter. One by one they wobbled[64] and cracked: Basso, Ullrich, Vino former U.S. Postal Service riders Floyd Landis (now with Phonak) and Levi Leipheimer (Gerolsteiner), all hemorrhaging[65] seconds that they would never get back.

What seemed like a routine day for Discovery had actually been a bit of a scramble.[66] Popovych crashed on a descent before Courchevel and was shaken as he began the climb. Azevedo wasn't feeling so hot. Jose Luis Rubiera, a brilliant climber, had a chest cold[67]. Two days later, on Bastille Day[68], Manuel (Triki) Baltran crashed and suffered a concussion[69] and had to abandon the race[70]. With the Pyrenees still ahead, Discovery was compromised. Armstrong's rivals took comfort[71].

On the eve of Saturday's mountain stage Armstrong asked Rubiera how he was feeling. The Spaniard said, "I'm afraid your last

51. template /'templeɪt/ n. 模式
52. flat stage 平路赛段
53. to sic sb. on sb. 让……袭击……
54. redline /'redlaɪn/ v. 停止操作
55. to tuck in 安置于;隐藏
56. spend /spend/ v. 疲倦,精疲力尽
57. sustain /sə'steɪn/ v. 支持;鼓舞
58. periodic radio 定期的广播节目
59. drop /drɒp/ v. 超过
60. crack /kræk/ v. 衰退;(在竞争中)失败
61. to deal out 分配,分担
62. Alpine stage 阿尔卑斯山赛段
63. ascent of a bear 艰难的上坡路段。bear /beə/ n. 艰难的事情
64. wobble /'wɒbəl/ v. 摇晃
65. hemorrhaging /'hemərɪdʒɪŋ/ a. 流失的
66. 看似平常的一天对于探索频道车队来说实际上是艰难混战的一天。scramble /'skræmbəl/ n. 费力的跋涉
67. chest cold 感冒
68. Bastille Day 巴士底日(7月14日,法国国庆日)
69. concussion /kən'kʌʃən/ n. 脑震荡
70. to abandon the race 退出比赛
71. to take comfort 感到安慰(心)

memories of me will be of a guy who was sick and struggling." Reminding his friend that they had won four Tours together, Armstrong said, "My memories of you won't have anything to do with this Tour."

At the base of Saturday's final climb, a steep, jagged[72] ascent to the Plateau de Bonascre, Armstrong found himself, once again, without teammates, and with the T-Mobile triad[73]: Vino, Klöden and Ullrich. At long last, after years of declaring that this would be the Tour in which Ullrich attacked Armstrong, the men in pink seemed poised to actually put a hurt on the patron. Sharing this view was the spectator who ran alongside[74] Armstrong shouting, "You are alone!"

"I looked around, "Armstrong said later, "and I thought, We're all alone."

What he meant was, they were all alone in their own worlds of pain. The T-Mobile riders had worked so hard to isolate Armstrong that they lacked the strength to attack on the final climb. It was the Texan who attacked them, and snuffed[75] their hopes.

Then Sunday was dominated by the heroics[76] of Hincapie, whose stage win called further attention to the strongest U.S. performance at any Tour de France. Before crashing out of the race, CSC's David Zabriskie, a Utahan, had worn the yellow jersey[77] for three days. Landis and Leipheimer joined Armstrong in the top seven as of[78] Monday. Chris Horner, an Oregonian riding in his first Tour, was having the time of his life, attacking in the flats and on the climbs. Though the future will look different for U.S. riders in France — not as yellow perhaps — there will be life after Lance.

72. jagged /'dʒægɪd/ *a.* 参差不齐的
73. T-Mobile triad 德国电信车队三人组合,指维诺、克罗登和乌尔里希三位车手
74. alongside /əˌlɒŋˈsaɪd/ *prep.* 与……并排
75. snuff /snʌf/ *v.* 扼杀
76. heroic /hɪˈrəʊɪk/ *n.* 英雄事迹
77. yellow jersey 黄色领骑衫,分赛段成绩领先者穿
78. as of 在……时

Comprehension Questions

1. Which stage is the most brutal of the Tour de France?
2. When did Hincapie earn his first stage win in his 11-year career?
3. How did Discovery keep their morale up?
4. What did Armstrong mean when he said, "We're all alone."?
5. What do you know about bike racing tactics?

Background Reading

The Tour de France

The Tour de France is by far the most prestigious of all cycling competitions in the world. It has long been a household name (家喻户晓) around the globe, even amongst people who are not generally interested in pro cycling (职业自行车运动). The Tour is to cycling what the FIFA World Cup is to football in terms of (就……而言) global popularity. Only the best cyclists in the world are chosen to compete and competitors must have an invitation to enter the race. It is also the world's largest annual pro sporting event, measured in the number of viewers.

The Tour is an epic long distance road bicycle racing held over three weeks in July in and around France. It has been held annually since 1903, interrupted only during wartime years.

The Tour is a "stage race" (分段赛), divided into a number of stages, each being a race held over one day. Although the number of stages has varied in the past, recently the Tour has consisted of about 20 stages, with a total length of between 3,000 and 4,000 km. Most stages take place in France, though it is very common to have a few stages in nearby countries, such as Italy, Spain, Switzerland, Belgium, Luxembourg and Germany as well as non-neighbouring countries such as the Republic of Ireland, United Kingdom (visited in 1974 and 1994) and the Netherlands. The three weeks usually include two rest days, which are sometimes used to transport the riders long distances between stages.

The itinerary (路线) of the race changes each year and alternates between clockwise (顺时针方向的) and anti-clockwise (逆时钟方向的) direction around France. To host a stage start or finish brings prestige, and a lot of business to a town. Whereas formerly each stage would start at the preceding stage's finish line, making a continuous course for the race, nowadays each stage can often start some distance from the previous day's finish, to allow more towns to share in the glory.

The Tour is immensely (非常) popular and important in France, not only as a sporting event but also as a matter of national identity (象征) and pride. Any Frenchman who has won the Tour becomes an object of public adoration (崇拜) in his native land. It is said that any rider who has worn the yellow jersey, even for a day, will never go hungry or thirsty again in France.

Relevant Words

bike grind 自行车竞赛	escort car 护车
feeding station 补给站	hill climb 爬坡赛
mass fall 多人摔倒	mountain bike 山地自行车
pace changing 车速调整	

Lesson 11

橄榄球运动是一项剽悍勇猛,集力量、速度、智慧和团队精神于一体的极具挑战性和刺激性的强者运动。它因为比赛中的高强度对抗、快速多变、观赏性强等特点,受到越来越多的人的喜爱。在我国,橄榄球运动是刚刚开展的新兴体育运动,英式橄榄球进入中国不过16年时间,而中国英式橄榄球协会的存在更是只有10年。我们一起来了解一下这"君子玩的野蛮运动"吧。

Williams Impresses to Put Bath[1] out of Reach[2]

By David Hands
October 10, 2005
The Times

Ospreys   20
Bath   27

Winning in Wales on wet Wednesdays was a staple[3] of the old Bath, the Bath that went on to dominate English club rugby for a decade. The new Bath had no objection to winning on a dry Sunday in Swansea[4] yesterday, particularly with the relatively inexperienced side they took to the Morfa Stadium to play the struggling Ospreys[5] in pool A[6] of the Powergen Cup.

The Welsh side, domestic champions last season, have scarcely taken flight at all in the present campaign and their lack of composure[7] at critical moments showed why.

They ran the ball[8] well, then let themselves down[9] in the tackle[10], losing so much confidence in the process that when they needed five points in injury time[11] to win the game, they opted for[12] a penalty attempt at goal[13] instead.

The result helped to reverse the cross-border[14] outcome of the cup's first weekend: where the

1. Bath 巴斯队,英国最成功的橄榄球队之一
2. out of reach 够不到(这里指巴斯队遥遥领先,对手无法追上)
3. staple /ˈsteɪpəl/ n. 主食(这里指家常便饭)
4. Swansea /ˈswɒnzɪ/ n. 斯旺西,威尔士南部市镇
5. Ospreys 威尔士鱼鹰队
6. pool A A组
7. composure /kəmˈpəʊʒə/ n. 冷静;沉着
8. to run the ball 跑动带球
9. to let oneself down 松劲;放松
10. tackle /ˈtækəl/ n. 擒抱;扑搂
11. injury time 伤停补时
12. to opt for 选择
13. penalty attempt at goal 罚踢射门
14. cross-border a. 越境的,跨境的

179

Welsh regions took the honours[15] 3-1, the English clubs did the same this weekend and it leaves Bath, beaten cup finalists[16] at Twickenham[17] last season, to slug it out[18] with Gloucester[19] on December 3 for semifinal place from their pool.

They are scarcely the masters of invention and were grateful to Olly Barkley, who suffered so much with his goalkicking last month, for kicking 14 points. But Tom Cheeseman, the young centre[20] (one of three Welshmen in the Bath starting XV[21]), did his long-term prospects no harm and Andy Williams, once an Osprey himself, scored the try[22] that put Bath just out of reach.

He did so from the wing[23], the position from which he scored a match-winning cup try against Gloucester last season, having moved from scrum half[24] after Frikkie Welsh left the field with a thigh strain[25]. But Bath also owed much to their lineout[26] and a brave effort by an inexperienced back row[27] against Welsh opponents including, for the first time this season, Ryan Jones, the Wales and Lions flanker[28].

Jones was replaced at half-time after bruising a shoulder, which gave Andrew Lloyd an opportunity to play against his former club as the Ospreys set about turning round a six-point interval deficit[29]. After Barkley's opening penalty, the Welsh side took the lead with an unusual penalty try[30]: Matthew Jones launched a diagonal kick from a penalty five metres from Bath's line and Richard Mustoe was taken out[31] early by two defenders[32] as he went for the catch[33].

Bath regained the advantage after James Scaysbrook stole an Ospreys lineout 15 metres out; his colleagues drove forward and switched play to the blind side[34], where Danny Grewcock gave Welsh the ball. The South African wing handed off[35] a tackler[36] to score.

But Bath were forced to defend sternly in the second quarter when Aled Brew was held up over the line. The visiting side's[37] scrum[38] was not as secure as it has been in recent years but the Ospreys could not make their territorial advantage count[39]. They made up for it with ten points in the first seven minutes of the second half, Damien Karauna — the New Zealander starting at full back[40] after only three days in the country — contributing to the move that allowed Mattew Jones to skip over[41].

Barkley nibbled away[42] at the lead, though, and Chris Malone added a dropped goal[43]. The crucial score came when Bath established a ruck[44] 35 metres out and Nick Walshe put Williams into space, the wing stepping two defenders and a head-high tackle[45] as he crossed.

15. to take the honours 领先
16. finalist /ˈfaɪnəlɪst/ n. 参加决赛的队
17. Twickenham 特威肯汉橄榄球场，位于英国伦敦西部
18. to slug it out 比出上下高低；决一雌雄
19. Gloucester 格洛斯特橄榄球队
20. centre /ˈsentə/ n. 正锋
21. starting XV 首发的15名队员
22. try /traɪ/ n. 达阵得分
23. wing /wɪŋ/ n. 边锋位置
24. scrum half 争球前卫，传锋
25. thigh strain 大腿肌肉拉伤
26. lineout /ˈlaɪnaʊt/ n. 列队争球；争边球
27. back row 后排，这里指后排队员
28. flanker /ˈflæŋkə/ n. 第三排边锋，侧翼前锋
29. ...turn round a six-point interval deficit 扭转失利6分的局面
30. penalty try 惩罚达阵；罚处达阵得分
31. to take out 除去；引开
32. defender /dɪˈfendə/ n. 后卫
33. catch /kætʃ/ n. 拾球；接球
34. blind side 狭窄边（争球点到边线较窄的一侧）
35. to hand off 推开
36. tackler /ˈtæklə/ n. 扑搂队员
37. visiting side 客队（这里指巴斯队）
38. scrum /skrʌm/ n. 司克兰；对阵争球
39. ...make their territorial advantage count 使他们的主场优势显现出来
40. full back 最后卫
41. to skip over 跳过，越过
42. to nibble away 蚕食（这里指一点点地向前移动）
43. dropped goal 落踢射门得分
44. ruck /rʌk/ n. 拉克；乱集团争球
45. head-high tackle 过高扑搂

The Ospreys, who have only two scratchy[46] home wins[47] to their credit this season, threw themselves back into the fray[48] and Shaun Connor was scythed down just short. His penalty goal took the home side[49] to within four points but he could not punish Salesi Finau when the Tonga wing threw the ball away at a lineout and was rightly penalised. Barkley promptly showed him how when Brew played the ball in an offside position[50] and the young fly half[51] made matters safe.

46. scratchy /ˈskrætʃi/ a. 拙劣的
47. home win 主场胜利
48. to throw oneself back into the fray 让自己重返战场
49. home side 主队
50. in an offside position 在越位的位置上
51. fly half 接锋，接球中锋

Comprehension Questions

1. How many years did Bath dominate English club rugby?
2. When did Bath secure a place in the semifinal?
3. Why was Jones replaced at half-time?
4. When did the crucial score come?
5. Do you know the difference between American football and rugby?

Background Reading

The Powergen Cup

The Powergen Cup is the national knockout (淘汰赛) cup involving 132 rugby clubs around the country, each fighting it out for the right to play on the hallowed (神圣的) turf (草场) of Twickenham for the Powergen Cup trophy.

First played in 1972, the competition has evolved (发展) over the years, and today in the age of professionalism, it still remains the premier (主要的) domestic club knockout trophy.

The Powergen Cup is considered to be a lucrative (赢利的) competition for the clubs, with television coverage (报道；覆盖率), a guaranteed £250,000 for each club and a prize fund of around £200,000 for the semifinalists. Additionally, winning the cup will give the victors automatic qualification for next year's Heineken Cup (喜力杯橄榄球赛).

There is a new format for the Powergen Cup as of the 2005—2006 season. Twelve rugby union teams from the Guinness Premiership and the four regional Welsh teams are entered into a pool system where they are put into groups of four consisting of three English teams and one Welsh team. Each team will play a match against each of the others. The winner of the pool will progress to the semifinals and so on.

Teams from the lower leagues are excluded (排除在外) and instead are given the chance to play for the Powergen National Trophy.

Relevant Words

basket pass 双手传球	conversion kick 追加(转换)射门
ground the ball 持球触地(得分)	
grubber kick 踢地滚球	in-goal 极阵,达阵(得分)区
maul 冒尔;围挤争球	place goal 定踢得分
shovel pass 低手拨传	try getter 持球触地得分手
unfield offside 持球越位	

Lesson 12

作为全球最著名的赛车运动之一,纳斯卡赛车以它的刺激和不确定性而闻名,在美国更是具有无可替代的地位,其每个赛季的首站比赛"戴托纳500"被称为"赛车界的超级碗"。赛车所提倡的"草根精神"、"速度"、"超越"以及它成功的商业运作都使这项赛事极具魅力。赛车先进的设备,赛道变幻的风云,车手高超的技巧、奋进的力量,吸引并感染着观众。纳斯卡已然成为全美观众人数增长最快的体育运动。一起来体验一下赛场上的风驰电掣吧!

Busch[1] Leaves Pack, and the Debris, in the Dust

By Dave Caldwell
July 25, 2005
New York Times

LONG POND, Pa., July 24 — When Kurt Busch grabbed the lead[2] from Jamie McMurray on the first lap Sunday, the race was pretty much over. Busch was the fastest driver by far, refusing to be unnerved[3] by debris on the track or the numerous crashes that slowed the race.

Busch, the defending Nascar Nextel Cup champion[4], won the Pennsylvania 500[5] with ease, leading for 131 of the 203 laps.

He pulled away[6] from the field three times on restarts in the last nine laps.

Sunday's victory was Busch's first since April 23, when he won at Phoenix[7], but he has rapidly re-established himself as a formidable[8] driver in the series[9]. He has all but locked up a place[10] in the 10-driver Chase[11] for the Nextel Cup in the past two races.

"This is a big momentum run for us," Busch said.

The victory was the second this year at Pocono Raceway[12] for

1. Kurt Busch 科特·布施[蓬斯克车队(Penske Racing)名将]
2. to grab the lead 夺取领先优势
3. unnerve /ʌnˈnɜːv/ v. 使失掉勇气;使身心交疲
4. defending Nascar Nextel Cup champion 纳斯卡纳克斯泰尔杯赛卫冕冠军。Nascar Nextel Cup 纳斯卡纳克斯泰尔杯赛;NASCAR (National Association of Stock Car Auto Racing) "纳斯卡",全美汽车比赛协会;defending champion 卫冕冠军
5. Pennsylvania 500 宾夕法尼亚500赛
6. to pull away 离开
7. Phoenix /ˈfiːnɪks/ n. 菲尼克斯国际赛车场
8. formidable /ˈfɔːmɪdəbəl/ a. 强大的,难以应付的
9. series /ˈsɪəriːz/ n. 系列赛
10. to lock up a place 取得名次
11. Chase /tʃeɪs/ n. 追逐赛
12. Pocono Raceway 波科诺赛车场

Jack Roush[13], the owner of Busch's Ford. Carl Edwards won the Pocono 500 on June 12 in one of Roush's cars. Mark Martin, another Roush driver, finished third Sunday, behind Rusty Wallace.

The race for second place between Martin and Wallace drew more attention than Busch did, partly because Martin and Wallace are veteran drivers in their late 40's who are planning to retire from Nextel Cup racing after this season.

Busch, who turns 27 on Aug, 4, scrubbed[14] much of the excitement from yet another long race at Pocono. Roush said Busch would probably drive the same car in the Allstate 400 at the Brickyard on Aug. 7 at Indianapolis[15], a flat track that is similar to Pocono.

"You're going to have races that are barnburners[16], and you're going to have races that are yawners[17]," Martin said, "and you can't panic when there is a yawner."

Busch does not seem capable of panicking. After leading 90 of the first 100 laps, he dropped to eighth place after a pit stop[18] at the 122nd lap. He climbed to third place with 60 laps scheduled to be run and trailed only Martin with 40 laps remaining.

A tire on Joe Nemechek's black Chevrolet[19] blew out[20] on Lap 164, sending him into the pits trailing thick clouds of smoke. The leaders pitted[21], and Busch lost the track position[22] he had gained by taking four fresh tires instead of two.

"Track position is obviously in favor of the two tires," Busch said. "But then, competitive lap times are in favor of the four tires, so can the four tires overcome the two?"

He found out quickly enough. Busch was in sixth place when racing resumed, but he picked off[23] Martin for fifth place within one lap, Kevin Harvick for third place within three laps and Edwards for second place within seven laps.

Busch passed Wallace for the lead, but the field had been frozen seconds before because of another yellow flag[24]. So, on the 183rd lap, Busch rocketed[25] past Wallace between the second and third turns of the unusual two-an-half-mile tri-oval[26].

"We just had to face reality," Wallace said. "I knew he had a fast car, and there was no way, with two tires, that I was going to beat his four tires with a car that dominant."

The racetrack, which had undergone repairs in the second turn after several drivers blew out tires in the June race here, did not seem to cause as much damage Sunday, but Wallace and Martin said they

13. Jack Roush 杰克·鲁什(纳斯卡车赛中拥有车队最多、实力最强的老板,前越野拉力赛高手)

14. scrub /skrʌb/ v. 除去

15. Indianapolis 印第安纳波利斯赛车场

16. barnburner /bɑːnˈbɜːnə/ n. 竞争激烈、令人兴奋的赛事

17. yawner /ˈjɔːnə/ n. 乏味的赛事

18. pit stop 检修加油站

19. Chevrolet /ˈʃevrəuleɪ/ n. 雪佛兰牌汽车

20. to blow out 爆裂

21. pit /pɪt/ v. (赛车比赛中停在再加油区)检修加油,停站

22. track position 赛道位置

23. to pick off 摘掉(这里指超过)

24. yellow flag 黄旗(危险通告,以及表示禁止超车的信号。主要提示赛场上发生了事故或车辆停止的情况。)

25. rocket /ˈrɒkɪt/ v. 飞速上升;猛然上升

26. tri-oval n. 三角椭圆形赛道

had spotted brake rotors[27] that had fallen from cars on the track.

Martin said one of the 13 caution periods was caused because someone had hurled a water bottle onto the track. Wallace said the second turn was really not that much better than it was in June, even though a set of rumble strips[28] had been replaced.

"Driving across the Tunnel Turn is like driving across railroad tracks," Wallace said, referring to the second turn by its nickname.

Sitting beside Wallace as a news conference, Martin smiled and said: "I would be sorely[29] surprised if they didn't try to take that bump out of there, unless they want to put a ski jump[30] in the front straightaway, too. It's pretty rough[31] over there."

Busch kept the lead as the race disintegrated[32]. Mike Wallace, Rusty's younger brother, smacked[33] the wall. Michael Waltrip wrecked, then wrecked again. The race was extended two laps, but another caution for debris ended the race.

Busch was not the only driver who had a good day.

Rusty Wallace hung onto fourth place.

Jimmie Johnson lost a lap early when he was pitting as a caution period started, but he rallied[34] to finish 12th and keep his lead in the overall standings[35].

"For a while there, I didn't think we were going to get back on the lead lap," Johnson said.

Tony Stewart was no threat to win the race but finished seventh and took over second place in the standings from Greg Biffle, who finished 17th.

But the top 10 stayed the same, and six races remain until the field for the Chase for the Nextel Cup is set.

Wallace and Martin have spots, for now, and they seem to be enjoying their final races against each other.

Busch seems to be preparing for another run to a championship, and nothing much, even debris, seems to, be getting in his way.

"You always have to race every lap for what it's worth[36], and until the checkered flag[37] drops, your job isn't done," Busch said. "That's the motto I keep. If it's not won and over yet, we keep digging[38]."

27. brake rotor 刹车盘
28. rumble strip 停车振动带（一种路面标志，车驶上即颤动作声以提醒司机减速）
29. sorely /ˈsɔːlɪ/ ad. 非常
30. ski jump 跳高滑雪台
31. rough /rʌf/ a. (路面)不平的
32. disintegrate /dɪsˈɪntɪɡreɪt/ v. 崩溃；瓦解（这里指比赛结束）
33. smack /smæk/ v. 猛撞
34. rally /ˈrælɪ/ v. 重整旗鼓，从挫折或不利处境中突然恢复过来
35. standing /ˈstændɪŋ/ n. 积分榜
36. for what it's worth 不管价值如何
37. checkered flag（赛车比赛时使用的）格子旗
38. to keep digging 坚持住；继续努力

Comprehension Questions

1. Why did the race for the second place draw more attention?

2. What could cause a caution period during the race?
3. Why did the second turn of the race acquire its nickname "Tunnel Turn"?
4. How do you understand Busch's motto?
5. What do you think has made car racing one of the most popular spectacular sports?

Background Reading

NASCAR

Nascar Racing is one of the most popular sports in America today. Nascar, an acronym (首字母缩略词) standing for "National Association for Stock Car Auto Racing", is a sanctioning body (核署机构) which oversees (监督) many types of racing across the country. The three top series under the Nascar banner are: Nextel Cup Series, Busch Series (布施系列赛) and Craftsman Truck Series (卡车赛). When most people say Nascar they are referring to the Nascar Nextel Cup Series.

A modern Nascar Nextel Cup race car has only a passing (非常的) resemblance (相似) to its "strictly stock (改装)" heritage. Based on four-door American made cars, Nascar cars are not the sleek (光滑的) open-wheel (双座开轮式) pointy-nosed (尖鼻子的) race cars that run Formula One, CART (卡丁车) or IRL Series (Indy Racing League Series, 印第车赛联合会系列赛).

Today, NASCAR is regarded as America's "hottest" or "fastest-growing" sport. Its popularity has exploded, which can be seen from the following facts in 2004.

More people paid money to personally witness the largely nondescript (无可名状的) Nascar race in the Irish Hills than purchased tickets to watch all five games of the NBA playoffs in Los Angeles and Auburn Hills.

More people packed the grandstands (看台) and perched (坐) atop (……顶) the buses and motorhomes (汽车移动房屋) at Michigan International Speedway than would fill Comerica Park for the 2005 Baseball All-Star Exhibition or Ford Field for the 2006 Super Bowl (橄榄球超级碗大赛).

More people showed up at isolated MIS for the DHL 400 (Nextel Cup Series 纳克斯泰尔杯赛的一场比赛) than at storied Indianapolis Motor Speedway, where world famous Formula One was making its only appearance of the year in the United States.

More people were on their feet, pumping their fists at the stock cars, than were cheering Phil Mickelson (菲尔·米克尔森, 美国高尔夫球运动员) and Tiger Woods (泰格·伍兹, 著名高尔夫球运动员) at the U.S. Open in New York.

Relevant Words

auto rally	汽车拉力赛	brake failure	刹车失灵
formula racing	方程式汽车赛	grid order	发车排位顺序
overhaul	大修；检查	stock car	改装赛车
tire degradation	轮胎磨损	to pile up	连环碰车

Lesson 13

英国皇家爱斯科(Royal Ascot)赛马会是世界上最著名的赛马盛会,也是英伦三岛上至君主、下至平民的狂欢盛事。英国是赛马王国,赛马和育马有着悠久的历史和很深的社会背景。在英国,赛马是除足球之外,观众人数最多的体育项目,每年的59项马赛,总会吸引包括英女王伊丽莎白二世在内的550多万名观众现场观战。2006年7月29日,赛马"旋风骏骥"在接近比赛终点时力挫"电极使者"和"真心呼唤",夺得了乔治国王6世和伊丽莎白女王钻石杯赛马大赛冠军。我们再一起回顾一下那惊心动魄的夺冠时刻吧!

Hurricane[1] Blows Away Rivals

By Eddie Fremantle
July 30, 2006
The Observer[2]

The King George VI and Queen Elizabeth Diamond Stakes[3] has been a race that has a history of producing the sort of finish that makes the hairs on the back of your neck rise[4]. Grundy's battle with Bustino in 1975 is the one most people cite and my favourite was The Minstrel's epic struggle with Orange Bay two years later, but Hurricane Run's thrilling victory from Electrocutionist[5] and Heart's Cry[6] was right up there with them.

Even though there were only six runners, this was the race of high

1. Hurricane /ˈhʌrɪkən/ n. 即 Hurricane Run,"旋风骏骥"(赛马的名字)
2. *The Observer*《观察者报》,是英国一家仅在周日发行的报纸,是英国《卫报》的姐妹报。该报创刊于1791年,是世界上首张周日发行的报纸。2005年该报建立了自己的博客网站,成为首家刊登自己内部决定的报纸。
3. The King George VI and Queen Elizabeth Diamond Stakes 乔治国王6世和伊丽莎白女王钻石杯赛马大赛
4. to make the hairs on the back of sb's neck rise 使毛骨悚然;使震惊
5. Electrocutionist /ɪˌlektrəˈkjuːʃənɪst/ n. "电极使者"(赛马的名字)
6. Heart's Cry "真心呼唤"(赛马的名字)

187

drama[7], some of it enacted[8] before it had even started. On Friday, Kieren Fallon failed in a last-minute bid to have his riding ban in this country overturned pending the outcome of conspiracy charges in a case that will not be heard until next year.[9] So Christophe Soumillon came in for the ride on Hurricane Run, trained by the brilliant French handler Andre Fabre.

Then, yesterday morning came the news that Electrocutionist was found to be stiff[10] and a doubtful[11] runner. It was not until after racing had started that Saeed bin Suroor and his Godolphin team were able to give the go-ahead[12] for Frankie Dettori's mount[13] to run.

Heart's Cry travelled from Japan to take his chance, bringing with him many fans from his native land. It is reputed[14] that a crowd of 175,000 massed[15] at Nakayama racecourse[16] when Heart's Cry became the first horse to lower Japanese hero horse Deep Impact[17] in the Grand Prix Arima Kinen[18] over Christmas, so it is rather doubtful that the visitors from the Orient[19] were impressed with Ascot's tiny — in comparison — gathering for the King George. None the less, the thrill that Heart's Cry gave his supporters in playing a huge part in this race will leave the visitors a marvellous memory to take back to Japan.

Electrocutionist's pacemaker[20] Cherry Mix[21], good enough to be runner-up in the Prix de l'Arc de Triomphe two seasons ago, set a strong gallop[22] pursued by Hurricane Run, sent off a shade of odds-on in his attempt to emulate[23] his sire[24] Montjeu by winning this race.

But when Electrocutionist and Dettori loomed[25] up to challenge for second place about half a mile out, it looked as though Hurricane Run was in trouble with his jockey[26] stoking[27] him along. Approaching the home turn, as Heart's Cry and Christophe Lemaire swept past him as well, his number really looked up.[28]

All was not lost, however, for Hurricane Run, because soon after taking the lead from Cherry Mix on the outside below the two-furlong[29] marker, Heart's Cry began to tire. And as Dettori tried to force Electrocutionist's head in front, so his mount started to hang away from the fence, head to one side, allowing Soumillon room for a late challenge on the inside with Hurricane Run responding gallantly[30] to his urgings.

With three in a line entering the final furlong, it was Hurricane Run's late thrust[31] that proved decisive, with Electrocutionist rallying bravely to snatch second. That overnight mishap may have contributed

7. high drama 动人的戏剧，令人提心吊胆的戏剧
8. enact /ɪ'nækt/ v. 表演
9. 星期五，骑师凯伦·法伦最后时刻申请取消英国禁赛，但败诉了。指控他阴谋诈骗的案件明年才会审理。Kieren Fallon 凯伦·法伦，爱尔兰骑师，to hear a case 审理案件
10. stiff /stɪf/ a. 烈性的
11. doubtful /'daʊtfəl/ a. 不可靠的
12. to give the go-ahead 允许
13. mount /maʊnt/ n. 坐骑，乘用马
14. repute /rɪ'pjuːt/ v. 号称
15. mass /mæs/ v. 聚集
16. Nakayama racecourse 日本中山赛马场，位于日本的本州岛千叶县
17. Deep Impact "大震撼"，又译"深度撞击"（一匹日本赛马的名字）
18. Grand Prix Arima Kinen 日本有马纪念大奖赛
19. Orient /'ɔːrɪənt/ n. 东方人，亚洲人
20. pacemaker /'peɪsˌmeɪkə/ n. 定步速的马；领头的马
21. Cherry Mix "红樱桃"（赛马的名字）
22. gallop /'gæləp/ n. 疾驰，飞奔
23. emulate /'emjʊleɪt/ v. 尽力赶上
24. sire /'saɪə/ n. 赛马的父亲（辈）
25. loom /luːm/ v. 隐约地出现
26. jockey /'dʒɒkɪ/ n. 职业赛马骑师
27. stoke /stəʊk/ v. 给（火或火炉）添加燃料，拨旺（这里指鞭打马，使其快跑）
28. 接近终点弯道时，骑师 Christophe Lemaire 驾驭"真心呼唤"疾驰超过"旋风骏骥"，而这时"旋风骏骥"夺冠的趋势却渐渐显现出来。
29. furlong /'fɜːlɒŋ/ n. 弗隆，英国长度单位，等于 201 米
30. gallantly /'gæləntlɪ/ ad. 漂亮地，勇敢地
31. thrust /θrʌst/ n. 冲刺

to his downfall but he still ran a race to make his connections proud.³²

Dettori said: 'He gave me everything he had' whilst Lemaire felt that Heart's Cry 'got a bit tired in the last 100 yards on his first run since March.' Heart's Cry's trainer, Kojiro Hashhiguchi, said: 'We will beat Hurricane Run on our home course if he comes over for the Japan Cup.'

Soumillon was, not surprisingly, ecstatic. 'I always thought he was the best horse in the world. If I lost today, I was the bad guy but I won so I am the good guy.' He certainly put a modest effort on Ouija Board³³ in the Eclipse³⁴ well behind him here.

Hurricane Run is now outright³⁵ favourite for the Arc at Longchamp³⁶ in October, when Fallon will be permitted to ride.

Hurricane Run runs in the colours of Michael Tabor, although he was joined on the podium to collect the 'piece of plate valued at £4500 for the winning owner' by his Coolmore partners, John Magnier and Derrick Smith. Tabor said: 'That was everything you like in racing. It is the best of racing.'

But, despite the fine efforts of Soumillon, there was the feeling that the Coolmore trio³⁷ will be smarting³⁸ about the enforced absence³⁹ of Fallon for a long while to come.

32. 前一晚上的霉运也许致使它（电极使者）没有夺冠，但它仍出色地完成了比赛，使马主及练马师引以为豪。
connections /kəˈnekʃəns/ n. 马主及练马师

33. Ouija Board 占卜（一匹英国赛马的名字）
34. Eclipse /ɪˈklɪps/ n. 日蚀大赛（赛马比赛）
35. outright /ˈaʊtraɪt/ a. 十足的；毫无疑问的
36. Arc at Longchamp 在法国巴黎的隆尚(Longchamp)马场举办的凯旋门大奖赛
37. trio /ˈtriːəʊ/ n. 三人组
38. smart /smɑːt/ v. 伤心；痛心
39. enforced absence 被迫缺席

Comprehension Questions

1. How many runners were there in the race?
2. How many people, reputedly, witnessed Heart's Cry's victory in Japan?
3. Which horse was the pacemaker for Electrocutionist?
4. When did the favor turn to Hurricane Run?
5. What do you think is the primary reason that horse racing survives as a major professional sport?

Background Reading

Horse Racing

The competitive racing of horses is one of humankind's most ancient sports, having its origins among the prehistoric (史前的) nomadic tribesmen (游牧部落) of Central Asia. For thousands of years, horse racing flourished (繁荣) as the sport of kings and the nobility. Modern racing, however, exists primarily because it is a major venue (地点) for legalized gambling (合法赌博).

Although horse racing is one of the oldest sports, its basic concept has remained unchanged over the centuries. It has developed from a primitive (原始的) contest of speed and stamina (体力；耐力) between two horses into a spectacle involving large fields of runners, sophisticated (精密的) electronic monitoring equipment, and immense sums of money, but its essential feature has always been the same: the horse that finishes first is the winner. In the modern era horse racing developed from a diversion of the leisure class into a huge public-entertainment business.

By far the most popular form of the sport is the racing of mounted thoroughbred (纯血马, 良种马) horses over flat courses at distances from three-quarters of a mile to two miles. Races are classified as stakes (有奖赛马), handicap (让步赛马) or allowance (让步赛马), and claiming events (参加比赛的马在赛后按议定价格出售的赛马会).

Stakes races usually involve horses of the same age and sex, all of which are initially assigned the same weight. Stakes races derive (得到) their name from the stake (赌金), or entry fee (报名费) that owners must pay.

Handicap races are events in which horses are assigned (分配；指派) specific weights based upon their race records. The horse considered superior is assigned the highest weight, with the less-acclaimed (成绩稍差的) horses receiving proportionately (成比例地) lighter handicaps.

Entries in allowance races are judged on their past performances. A track official, called the racing secretary, takes into account (考虑；顾及) the number of races won and money earned. Horses of about the same ability are matched against one another.

Claiming races are devices to sell horses. The selling price of the entered horses is stipulated (规定) before the race, whereupon a buyer may make a claim for (对……提出要求) that amount. The buyer takes possession of the horse (占有) at the completion of the race, regardless of its performance. If two or more interested parties claim the same horse at the same price, lots (抽签) are drawn to determine the winning offer. Knowledgeable owners and trainers may use claiming races to obtain, at bargain prices (廉价), horses whose former owners underestimated the potential of their horses.

Relevant Words

equestrian 马术	show jumping 超越障碍赛
dressage 花式骑术, 盛装舞步	steeplechase 障碍赛马
flat race 平地赛马	

Lesson 14

有着100多年历史的现代拳击运动常被误认为是一种伤残竞搏,事实上,拳击是力量、智慧和毅力的体现。说到底,这是勇敢者的游戏。小小拳台,不过十几平米,进,虽处处是险;退,却退无可退。倒下,再站起,这简单的动作里却蕴藏着自古以来最大的一种挑战:顽强拼搏并在逆境、绝境中勇于争胜。拳坛高手云集争霸,上演着一场场巅峰对决。第53届终极格斗大赛(UFC)上八对拳手终极PK,精彩绝伦。

Andrei Arlovski[1] Defends Heavyweight Title at the UFC 53

By Edward Pollard
September 2005
Black Belt[2]

ATLANTIC CITY, NJ — UFC 53: Hard Hitters, the Ultimate Fighting Championship's[3] latest event held at Trump Plaza[4] on June 4, 2005, was blessed with an enthusiastic live audience[5] and a thoroughly engaging fight card[6]. Two titles were up for grabs[7], and two key figures from *The Ultimate Fighter*[8], the UFC's reality TV show, were fighting in their first pay-per-view[9] appearances. In addition to the excitement of the heavyweight headliner[10] between Andrei Arlovski and Justin Eilers, the title bout[11] between middleweight champion Evan Tanner and former light-heavyweight challenger Rich Franklin would decide who will join welterweight champion Matt Hughes as the second coach for *The Ultimate Fighter* 2 on Spike TV[12].

Arlovski was the favorite to win against relative newcomer Eilers. Arlovski stalked his opponent[13] from the start and peppered him[14] with short, sharp blows that took their toll[15]. With less than a minute left in the first round, Eilers planted[16] his right foot to release a punch[17] and his knee gave out. This sent him sprawling in pain, clutching his leg and helpless to Arlovski's attack. Referee John McCarthy decided he was no longer fit to continue and gave Arlovski the TKO win[18] at four minutes 10 seconds.

The title bout between Franklin and Tanner was difficult to call[19],

---

1. Andrei Arlovski 安德雷·阿洛夫斯基,白俄罗斯重量级拳击运动员
2. *Black Belt*《黑带》,是一本美国格斗和武术类的杂志,1961年创刊,每月发行,是同类杂志中发行最早的刊物,提供传统武术的训练、器械、营养等方面的权威信息,适合黑带程度的学习者及对此运动有兴趣的读者阅读。
3. Ultimate Fighting Championship 终极格斗大赛(美国自由搏击赛的主要赛事,缩写为UFC)
4. Trump Plaza 特朗普大厦,位于纽约第5大道
5. live audience 现场观众
6. thoroughly engaging fight card 十分精彩的拳击节目单
7. up for grabs 供人公开争夺的
8. The Ultimate Fighter "终极拳霸",又译"终极斗士"(UFC组织和Spike TV联合推出的电视节目,缩写为TUF)
9. pay-per-view 按次计费
10. headliner /ˈhedlamə/ n. 明星,报纸头条中经常提到的人物
11. title bout 拳王争霸赛
12. Spike TV 美国斯派克电视台
13. to stalk one's opponent 悄悄潜近对手
14. to pepper sb. 向某人连续进攻
15. to take their (its) toll 造成损失
16. plant /plɑːnt/ v. 固定;站稳
17. to release a punch 出拳
18. TKO win 技术击倒获胜(TKO是technical knockout的缩写)
19. call /kɔːl/ v. 判定

since both fighters bring a degree of tenacity[20] and drive[21] to the octagon[22] that few of their peers can match. The two spent half of the first round sizing each other up[23] with jabs[24] and clinches[25] until Tanner hit Franklin with a straight right[26] that nearly ended the fight. However, Franklin managed to rebound[27] and hold the champ off[28] long enough to regain his equilibrium[29]. From that point on, the fight was his. He exposed Tanner's limited striking skills, avoided extended grappling exchanges[30], and ground away at[31] his face and body with a barrage of punches and kicks[32] that left the Oregonian's face a bloody, swollen mess. Despite the gore and lopsided[33] pace of the fight, Tanner forged ahead[34], looking for any way to avoid defeat. Three minutes 25 seconds into the fourth round, referee Herb Dean called a halt to the dismantling[35], awarding Franklin the TKO — and with it the middleweight belt and second coaching chair in the second season of *The Ultimate Fighter*.

As the light-heavyweight champion from the inaugural season of *The Ultimate Fighter*, Forrest Griffin had much to prove in the first fight of his UFC contract. His opponent, Canadian Bill Mahood, has a reputation for being a hard-nosed[36], stand-up fighter. It was almost surprising when Griffin, another stand-and-trade[37] stalwart[38], took the fight to the ground. From there, he quickly seized control and worked his way to a rear-naked-choke submission[39] in two minutes 18 seconds.

Karo Parisyan came as close to an instant loss as any fighter would care to. Welterweight Matt Serra caught him on the chin with a mighty blow[40] and almost knocked him unconscious mere seconds into their matchup[41]. However, judo stylist[42] Parisyan shook it off[43] and bought time[44] by grappling in the clinch to work his way back into the fight. When his head cleared, the Armenian phenom[45] began to show just how accomplished a judoka[46] he is by controlling Serra and taking him down[47] at will[48]. Parisyan's grinding elbow strikes added menace to his attack, but Serra avoided serious injury until the end of the third round. Parisyan won the unanimous decision[49] and thanked his recent coach Randy Couture.

Following up on his recent KO win[50] over Eilers, heavyweight Paul Buentello faced newcomer Kevin Jordan and demonstrated his ability to absorb punishment and win. Jordan made solid contact early in the round and came back several times during the fight. However,

20. tenacity /tɪˈnesɪtɪ/ n. 不屈不挠
21. drive /draɪv/ n. 干劲；攻击性
22. octagon /ˈɒktəgən/ n. 八角笼（指拳击、自由搏击等格斗项目的比赛场所）
23. to size up 估计；判断
24. jab /dʒæb/ n. 刺拳
25. clinch /klɪntʃ/ n. 扭抱
26. straight right 右直拳
27. rebound /rɪˈbaʊnd/ v. 重新振作
28. ...hold the champ off 在比赛中采取拖延战术。to hold off 拖延 champ = championship 锦标赛
29. equilibrium /ˌiːkwɪˈlɪbrɪəm/ n. 平衡
30. extended grappling exchanges 长时间的相互扭打。grapple /ˈgræpəl/ v. 扭打，格斗
31. to grind away at 加紧做，努力做（这里指不断地出拳）
32. a barrage of punches and kicks 连续的拳打脚踢
33. lopsided /ˌlɒpˈsaɪdɪd/ a. 倾向一方的；一边倒的
34. to forge ahead 渐渐赶上
35. call a halt to the dismantling 叫停把两个拳击手分开。to call a halt 命令停止，dismantle /dɪsˈmæntl/ v. 拆开，分解
36. hard-nosed /ˈhɑːd nəʊzd/ a. 顽强的
37. stand-and-trade 站着不动并出拳攻击对手（这里指拳击手实力较强，不用移动就能躲开来拳并出拳攻击）
38. stalwart /ˈstɔːlwət/ n. 顽强的人
39. rear-naked-choke submission 用裸绞制服对手。rear naked choke 裸绞（格斗中非常实用、致命的招式）
40. ...catch him on the chin with a mighty blow 一记重拳打在他的下巴上
41. matchup /ˈmætʃˌʌp/ n. 比赛
42. judo stylist 柔道大师
43. to shake off 摆脱
44. to buy time 拖延时间；争取时间
45. phenom /fɪˈnɒm/ n. 杰出运动员
46. judoka /ˈdʒuːˈdəʊkə/ n. 柔道运动员
47. to take down 摔倒（使对方臀部着地）
48. at will 随意；任意
49. unanimous decision（裁判员）一致的裁决
50. KO win 绝对胜利（对方数10不起），KO 是 knockout 的缩写

given enough space to operate, Buentello was more dangerous. Buentello's pile-driving⁵¹ right fist took Jordan to the ground, where he briefly assumed full mount. Jordan escaped only to get tangled up⁵² in his opponent's attack. A takedown⁵³ attempt on Buentello's left leg opened Jordan to a standing one-armed neck crank that ended in submission on the ground at the four-minute mark.

The Ultimate Fighter's Nate Quarry faced veteran⁵⁴ Shonie Carter and proved his mettle⁵⁵ with solid striking and fight strategy. Quarry punished Carter with elbow strikes in the clinch and repeated elbows to the side of his head on the ground. By the time Carter could escape and get back to his feet, he was dazed⁵⁶ and vulnerable to further direct hits, a couple of which sent him sprawling to his knees. He stood up but was so woozy⁵⁷ that referee Mario Yamazaki awarded Quarry the TKO win after two minutes 37 seconds.

David Loiseau allowed middleweight newcomer Charles McCarthy some time at the beginning to work toward a submission, but then he reversed his opponent and never looked back⁵⁸. Loiseau ended the match with a spinning back kick⁵⁹ that connected solidly with McCarthy's rib cage⁶⁰ knocking the wind out of him⁶¹ and making him double over in pain⁶². Loiseau took advantage of his opponent's lack of defense until John McCarthy stepped in to stop the damage at two minutes 10 seconds of the second round.

Welterweight man-in-waiting⁶³ Nick Diaz pummeled⁶⁴ Pancrase fighter Koji Oishi to a rapid TKO victory in one minute 24 seconds, perhaps finally securing a title shot for his next appearance.

51. pile-driving 打桩[这里指（拳）重的]
52. to get tangled up 纠缠
53. takedown /ˈteɪkdaʊn/ n. 摔倒
54. veteran /ˈvetərən/ n. 老手（这里指有经验的拳击手）
55. mettle /ˈmetl/ n. 勇气，斗志
56. dazed /deɪzd/ a. 头昏的，眼花的
57. woozy /ˈwuːzɪ/ a. 眩晕的
58. to look back 倒退
59. spinning back kick 反抢踢，后旋踢
60. rib cage 胸腔
61. to knock the wind out of sb. 打得……透不过气来
62. double over in pain 疼得弯下了腰，疼得蹲了下去
63. man-in-waiting 有望成为冠军的拳手
64. pummel /ˈpʌməl/ v. 用拳头打

Comprehension Questions

1. How long did Arlovski spend in beating his opponent?
2. Why was the title bout between Franklin and Tanner difficult to call?
3. What was the light-heavyweight boxer Bill Mahood famous for?
4. How did Parisyan recover from the setback and beat his opponent?
5. How did Buentello demonstrate his ability to absorb punishment?
6. What is Quarry's biggest weapon in the fight?
7. How did David Loiseau end the match?
8. Boxing is regarded as a controversial sport. Do you like watching it? Why or why not?

Background Reading

The Ultimate Fighting Championship

Started in 1993, the Ultimate Fighting Championship (UFC) brand is in its thirteenth year of operation as a professional MMA (mixed martial arts, 综合武术, 综合格斗) organization, giving martial artists of the world a chance to distinguish (使杰出, 使著名) themselves in a fighting environment with very few rules.

The UFC organization follows a rich history and tradition of competitive MMA dating back to (追溯到) the Olympic Games in Athens. About 80 years ago, a Brazilian form of MMA known as Vale Tudo (葡萄牙语, 无限制格斗) sparked (激起) local interest in the sport.

Then, the UFC organization brought MMA to the world. The goal was to find "the Ultimate Fighting Champion" with a concept to have a tournament of the best athletes skilled in the various disciplines (分支) of all martial arts, including karate (空手道), jiu-jitsu (柔道, 柔术), boxing, kickboxing (自由搏击), grappling (格斗), wrestling, sumo (相扑) and other combat sports (格斗项目). Fighters could be matched up against fighters of any style, and the match ended only when one fighter submitted. The winner of the tournament would be crowned (授予称号) the champion.

In January 2001, the UFC brand completely restructured (改组, 重建) MMA into a highly organized and controlled combat sport: the New Ultimate Fighting Championship, which is a series of international competitive mixed martial arts events televised several times yearly and available (可用的) live (现场直播) or tape-delayed (录像重播) on pay-per-view and other formats, seen domestically and internationally. It is committed to (致力于) providing the highest quality live event and television production available to entertain and engage viewers in a fascinating sport.

The elite (精英) level of the competitor also known as an "Ultimate Fighter". The UFC brings together the most talented (有才能的) martial arts experts in the world. UFC fighters come from the US, Canada, Brazil, Japan, Russia, Holland, England, etc. All UFC fighters have previous combat sports experience and many are world or Olympic champions. UFC athletes train up to six hours a day or more in preparation for an event. Almost all have studied martial arts as a lifelong vocation (终身职业) and many are college educated.

Relevant Words

weight category 体重级别	flyweight 特轻量级, 蝇量级
bantamweight 最轻量级	featherweight 次轻量级
lightweight 轻量级	welterweight 次中量级
middleweight 中量级	heavyweight 重量级
super heavyweight 超重量级	

Lesson 15

> 美国职业篮球联赛(NBA)是世界上篮球运动水平最高的职业联赛。NBA众星云集，吸引了全世界关注和期盼的目光。2006年6月20日，在NBA总决赛第六场上，韦德表现出色，又一次成为总决赛的主宰者，在最多落后14分的情况下带领迈阿密热火队奋起反扑，以95-92击败达拉斯小牛队，这样他们就以4-2的总比分击败小牛队夺取历史上的首个总冠军，热火队也因此成为史上第三支在0-2落后的情况下逆转夺冠的球队。

Heat of the Moment

Wade Leads Miami[1] to Its First NBA Championship: Heat 95, Mavericks[2] 92

By Michael Lee
June 21, 2006
The Washington Post[3]

  DALLAS, June 20 — Shaquille O'Neal arrived in Miami two summers ago emerging from a diesel truck[4], playfully squirting[5] fans with a water gun and assuring fans that he would deliver a championship for the Heat. He was only half right.

  O'Neal won his fourth NBA championship on Tuesday night, as the Miami Heat closed out the Dallas Mavericks in Game 6 of the NBA Finals with a 95–92 victory, but he was by no means the ringleader[6], the dominant force who bulldozed[7] through opposing defenses and wreaked havoc[8]. He quietly scored nine points and was relegated[9] to the bench in foul trouble, with a towel over his shoulder, most of the night.

  Didn't matter.

1. Miami 指 Miami Heat, 迈阿密热火队
2. Mavericks 指 Dallas Mavericks, 达拉斯小牛队
3. *The Washington Post*《华盛顿邮报》，1877年创刊，是美国很有影响的日报，发行量为100万份左右。其声望仅次于《纽约时报》，被称为美国第二大报。该报对联邦政府和国会活动的报道、评论、分析较多，而且时有"内幕"新闻透露，号称是美国政界人士必读的报纸，也是了解和研究美国内政外交的重要报刊之一。该报在70年代领先报道了五角大楼关于越南战争的秘密文件以及"水门事件"，从此声名鹊起。
4. diesel truck 柴油卡车
5. squirt /skwɜːt/ *v.* 喷射
6. ringleader /ˈrɪŋˌliːdə/ *n.* 魁首
7. bulldoze /ˈbʊldəʊz/ *v.* 奋力前进
8. to wreak havoc 造成严重破坏（这里指给对手造成威胁）
9. relegate /ˈrelɪɡeɪt/ *v.* 命令撤离

When Mavericks point guard Jason Terry's potential game-tying three-pointer rimmed out just before the buzzer, the man most responsible for this title—Dwyane Wade—grabbed the rebound.[10] Wade tossed the ball toward the rafters[11] and howled[12]. The Heat players stormed[13] the court, none bouncing higher than 36-year-old Alonzo Mourning, the gritty[14] veteran who fought for 14 years—and recovered from a near-fatal kidney ailment[15]—to reach this pinnacle[16]. O'Neal chased down Mourning then embraced him, the two giants bobbing[17] hysterically with joy. The finals, once O'Neal's playground, now belong to Wade. "I made that promise because of D-Wade," O'Neal said. "He's the best in the world."

The Heat may have lacked the athleticism[18] and overall skill of the Mavericks, a 60-win team in the regular season. But it had Coach Pat Riley, who had previously guided the Showtime Lakers[19] to four NBA championships. It had O'Neal, who won three consecutive titles (and three NBA Finals MVP[20] awards) with the Lakers. And, more importantly, the Heat had Wade. He was virtually unstoppable as the Heat won the final four games, willing his team to thrilling comeback victories with a 42-point performance in Game 3 and 43 points in Game 5. He scored 36 points and grabbed 10 rebounds on Tuesday and was named NBA Finals MVP.

"I have never had a player like this," said Riley, who coached Magic Johnson. "I have not been around a player who can absolutely, at times, beat five guys, and then at the same time make great plays to players. Dwyane is probably one of the most respected young players this game has had in a long time. I think he proved a lot in the last four games."

With the Mavericks trailing 93-90 with 26 seconds left, Dallas Coach Avery Johnson drew up a play for his star forward Dirk Nowitzki. Nowitzki caught the ball from above the three-point line, but when he drove inside, O'Neal came to help Udonis Haslem (17 points, 10 rebounds). Nowitzki then threw the ball to Erick Dampier. Dampier lost the ball to Wade, then wrapped him up for a foul.[21] Wade stopped, glared at the fans behind the Mavericks' basket and stomped to the foul line to seemingly put the game out of reach.[22] He missed two free throws with 10.3 seconds left, but Terry's miss meant that he didn't have to worry about it.

"I can't wait to get to Miami, man," Wade said, smiling at the podium afterward.

10. 小牛队的得分后卫贾森·特里 (Jason Terry) 在终场蜂鸣器响起之前投出可能追平比分的三分球, 球沿篮筐滚出篮外, 这时负责抢篮板球的德怀恩·韦德 (Dwyane Wade) 抢下篮板。rebound /rɪ'baʊnd/ n. 篮板球
11. ...tossed the ball toward the rafters 将球投向屋顶。rafter /'rɑːftə/ n. 椽架屋顶
12. howl /haʊl/ v. 狂欢
13. storm /stɔːm/ v. 猛冲
14. gritty /'ɡrɪtɪ/ a. 勇敢的; 坚韧不拔的
15. near-fatal kidney ailment 几乎致命的肾病
16. pinnacle /'pɪnəkl/ n. 顶点
17. bob /bɔb/ v. 上下跳动
18. athleticism /æθ'letɪsɪzəm/ n. 运动能力
19. Lakers 指 Los Angeles Lakers, 洛杉矶湖人队
20. MVP 是 most valuable player 的缩写, 最有价值球员

21. 韦德断下丹皮尔 (Dampier) 的球, 因此丹皮尔无奈用胳膊搂住韦德对其犯规。
22. 韦德停了下来, 怒视着小牛队篮后的球迷, 踏步走到罚球线, 好像要把比分拉大, 使对方回天乏术。

The parade on Biscayne Boulevard[23] that Riley promised the city when he took over as coach and team president 11 years ago is coming. Riley returned to the bench after a two-year coaching hiatus[24] to replace Stan Van Gundy, who stepped down[25] Dec. 12 for "family reasons." Riley took considerable heat[26] for reworking his team in the offseason[27], acquiring Antoine Walker, Jason Williams, James Posey and Gary Payton and practically establishing an all-or-nothing[28] proposition for his team. But those moves paid off in the postseason. Walker scored 14 points with 11 rebounds in the series clincher[29]; Williams had a huge Game 6 in the Eastern Conference Finals[30] against Detroit[31]; Payton hit clutch buckets[32] in Games 3 and 5; and Posey provided solid defense on Nowitzki and nailed a huge three-pointer and a runner in the lane in the final four minutes on Tuesday.

"We're a team that never complained about nothing that happened. We lost 30 games, we lost Shaq for 18 games early in the season. We were a team that didn't have an identity and then we had a coaching change so we had to switch then," Wade said. "We knew inside what this team was built for. That's what makes this sweet. No matter what in the locker room[33], it was always 15 strong."

The Heat became the third team to come back from a 2-0 deficit to win the NBA Finals, joining the 1977 Portland Trail Blazers[34] and the 1969 Boston Celtics[35].

Miami returned to Dallas with a 3-2 lead and Riley in a situation reminiscent of 1994, when he took the New York Knicks[36] to Texas with two chances to get one win against Houston[37]. The Rockets won the final two games to win the series. Riley said he wasn't even thinking about a Game 7 in Dallas when he boarded the charter flight[38] from Miami on Monday. "I packed one suit, one shirt and one tie," Riley said before the game.

As he sat on the podium, hair soaked in champagne, Riley folded his wet tie and said to himself, "That'll go well on eBay[39]." Then, Riley took time to reflect on the moment. "I would give up six [championships] for this one," said Riley, who won his first title since 1988 to become the fourth coach with at least five championship rings. "It's not disrespectful to any of them that I won. But after 18 years, and chasing, you keep chasing it, you get tired. So this gives me a sense of absolute freedom."

The Mavericks were the deeper and more talented team, but despite dethroning[40] the champion San Antonio Spurs[41] and slowing

23. Biscayne Boulevard 比斯肯大道(位于迈阿密市)
24. hiatus /haɪˈeɪtəs/ n. 间断
25. to step down 辞职;"下课"
26. to take heat 受到压力;被怪罪
27. offseason /ˈɒfˌsiːzən/ n. 淡季
28. all-or-nothing /ˈɔːləˈnʌθɪŋ/ a. 极端的;或者成功或者失败的
29. clincher /ˈklɪntʃə/ n. 关键时刻
30. Eastern Conference Finals 东部联盟决赛
31. Detroit 指 Detroit Pistons,底特律活塞队
32. to hit clutch buckets 投关键球

33. locker room 更衣室
34. Portland Trail Blazers 波特兰开拓者队
35. Boston Celtics 波士顿凯尔特人队
36. New York Knicks 纽约尼克斯队
37. Houston 指 Houston Rockets,休斯敦火箭队
38. charter flight 包机

39. eBay 易趣网

40. dethrone /dɪˈθrəʊn/ v. 击败
41. San Antonio Spurs 圣安东尼奥马刺队

down the Phoenix Suns[42] —teams with superior records to the Heat— they appeared too immature to grasp the challenge at hand in the Finals. The Mavericks won the first two games of the series and city officials were already preparing a parade through downtown. But they will likely be smarting[43] over how they blew a 13-point lead[44] with 6½ minutes left in Game 3, didn't show up for Game 4 and suffered from miscues[45], miscommunication and an absolute meltdown[46] after Game 5. "This is going to really hurt this summer," Johnson said.

Nowitzki led the Mavericks with 29 points and 15 rebounds. Mourning had eight points and six rebounds and took a sip of champagne for the first time in six years. His kidney ailment had forced him to give up alcohol. "My doctor will give me a doctor's note for this one," said Mourning, who became the first Georgetown center to win a title.

42. Phoenix Suns 菲尼克斯太阳队
43. smart /smɑːt/ v. 懊恼
44. ...blew a 13-point lead 领先 13 分变成落后。blow /bləʊ/ v. 挥霍
45. miscue /ˈmɪsˈkjuː/ n. 失误
46. meltdown /ˈmeltdaʊn/ n. 彻底垮台

Comprehension Questions

1. Why was O'Neal sitting on the bench most of the time of the match?
2. Who was named NBA Finals MVP in this match?
3. Why was Riley under great pressure as the coach of the Miami Heat?
4. How many points did Nowitzki score in the match?
5. Which basketball player do you like best in the NBA?

Background Reading

NBA's Greatest Moments
—Jordan Hits "The Shot"

It is known, in Chicago (芝加哥公牛队) and especially in Cleveland (克里夫兰骑士队), as "The Shot". It was replayed on television hundreds of times, to the agony (痛苦) of Cleveland fans and the ecstasy (狂喜) of Bulls supporters. It was only one basket, yet it played an integral (不可分割的) role in the fortunes of not one but two NBA franchises (运动队).

The Cleveland Cavaliers were one of the NBA's best young teams in the late 1980s, with a nucleus (核心) that included Brad Daugherty, Mark Price, Ron Harper, Larry Nance and John "Hot Rod" Williams. Under the guidance of coach Lenny Wilkens, the Cavs improved by 15 games to a franchise-best 57-25 record in the 1988-89 regular season and appeared poised (泰然自若的) to challenge for the NBA title.

Part Ⅲ Sporting Memories

In their way stood the Chicago Bulls, a young team led by Michael Jordan that was just beginning to mesh (有效配合;相互协调) into the unit that would dominate the NBA in the 1990s. The Bulls had finished fifth in the powerful Central Division (中央组) with a 47-35 record, but they had beaten the Cavs in a five-game playoff(季后赛) series the year before and were matched up against Cleveland once again.

Chicago stole the home-court (主场)advantage in the best-of-5 series by winning the opener (第一场) 95-88 and could have closed out the set at home, but Cleveland rallied for a 108-105 overtime win in Game 4 to set up a deciding game in Cleveland.

It came down to the closing seconds, and as he would so many times in his career, Jordan had the ball with the game on the line(危险中). Starting from the right side, Jordan dribbled (运球) toward the key (罚球区) and rose up for a jumper (跳投) from inside the circle. Craig Ehlo, one of Cleveland's top defenders, leaped out to block (盖帽) the shot, but Jordan seemed to hang in the air (停留在空中) until Ehlo was out of his way, then released his shot. As the ball nestled through (舒适地穿过) the net, Jordan pumped his fists in jubilation (庆祝), completing a video highlight for the ages.

Two years later, the Bulls won the first of five NBA titles they would win from 1991 through 1997. Cleveland, meanwhile, has yet to reach the NBA Finals.

Relevant Words

NBA 东部联盟球队	NBA 西部联盟球队
Atlanta Hawks 亚特兰大老鹰	Dallas Mavericks 达拉斯小牛
Boston Celtics 波士顿凯尔特人	Denver Nuggets 丹佛掘金
Charlotte Bobcats 夏洛特山猫	Golden State Warriors 金州勇士
Chicago Bulls 芝加哥公牛	Houston Rockets 休斯敦火箭
Cleveland Cavaliers 克里夫兰骑士	Los Angeles Clippers 洛杉矶快船
Los Angeles Lakers 洛杉矶湖人	Memphis Grizzlies 孟菲斯灰熊
Minnesota Timberwolves 明尼苏达森林狼	Detroit Pistons 底特律活塞
	Indiana Pacers 印第安纳步行者
Miami Heat 迈阿密热火	Milwaukee Bucks 密尔沃基雄鹿
New Orleans Hornets 新奥尔良黄蜂	New Jersey Nets 新泽西网
Phoenix Suns 菲尼克斯太阳	New York Knicks 纽约尼克斯
Portland Trail Blazers 波特兰开拓者	Orlando Magic 奥兰多魔术
Sacramento Kings 萨克拉门托国王	Philadelphia 76ers 费城76人
San Antonio Spurs 圣安东尼奥马刺	Toronto Raptors 多伦多猛龙
Seattle Supersonics 西雅图超音速	Washington Wizards 华盛顿奇才
Utah Jazz 犹他爵士	

Part IV

Glimpses of the Superstars

体坛明星

Lesson 1

> 姚明,中国职业篮球运动员,1998年入选国家青年队,1999年进入国家男篮。2002年他辅助上海大鲨鱼队获得CBA联赛冠军。同年在NBA选秀大会上,以状元秀身份被休斯敦火箭队首轮选中,位置是中锋,成为NBA历史上第一个未打过NCAA却在首轮第一顺位被选中的外国球员。姚明被公认为NBA最全面的中锋。他的身高优势使他可以轻松地在防守队员头上投篮。他灵活多变的进攻脚步和个人技术对于像他这种身高的运动员来说简直就是不可思议。目前他已成为当今世界上最优秀的中锋之一,并具有在近年内成为联盟中顶级中锋的潜力。

Yao Has Grown into One of NBA's Biggest Stars

By Jonathan Feigen
October 6, 2005
Houston Chronicle[1]

The possibilities have long since grown into expectations that tower like his face peering down from billboards[2] from Shanghai to the Southwest Freeway.

The shoulders are broader, the back stronger, but the weight on Yao Ming has increased, too.

There is a strange irony[3] in that he is measured by, of all things, how much he must grow.

For Yao, it always has seemed not enough for him to be the player he is but to become the player he can be. Because he is 7-6 with powerful legs and soft hands, he has somehow managed to overshadow himself.[4]

This is his blessing[5] and his burden. So when he is asked how great he can be, the topic is, like him, enormous.

Five seconds pass in silence.

Ten seconds.

Yao lets out a long, almost pained sigh[6]. He looks away, toward the ceiling, as if trying to avoid distraction to his search for the answer somewhere within him.

---

1. *Houston Chronicle*《休斯敦记事报》,是休斯顿最有影响的报纸。现发行量居全美第十位,平时达55万份,周日达78万份。
2. billboard /ˈbɪlbɔːd/ n. 广告牌
3. irony /ˈaɪərəni/ n. 讽刺
4. 姚明身高7尺6寸,双腿有力,两手灵活,可是他却往往低估了自己。overshadow /ˌəʊvəˈʃædəʊ/ v. 低估;小看
5. blessing /ˈblesɪŋ/ n. 福气
6. sigh /saɪ/ n. 叹息,叹气

Fifteen seconds. Twenty.

Finally he gives up.

"Ahhhh. I don't know," he said, his voice more hushed than in any other answer. "I don't know."

He never has enjoyed talking of himself and his potential for greatness. The entire topic is too immodest for him and the culture he has often said he must represent.

"The team goal is always the championship," Yao said. "That's everything. There's nothing else with that."

"But I really feel tired with thinking of how great can you be. That's a very far goal. You think about 10 years, and it's very tiring. I want to think about today, what I can do today, tomorrow, and that's it."

A struggle to stay laid-back[7]

The burdens would seem massive, but Yao, 25, has become a master at ignoring all that is expected of him. He lives on magazine covers and in television commercials.[8] But even beyond all that, he represents so much to so many in a nation long obsessed with how it is perceived[9].

So Yao has trained himself to look past[10] all that.

"I don't like to feel like somebody forced me to do something, so I like to think like those fans are our friends," Yao said. "It makes you better and them better."

But it would not matter if Yao preoccupied[11] himself with the demands of others. As often as athletes say they put more pressure on themselves than anyone else can, that is Yao's strength and weakness.

"Yao is a very harsh critic of himself[12], and I think that can lead to good things when guys are very, very tough on[13] themselves, and at times, he should worry less, have a shorter memory about mistakes[14]," Rockets coach Jeff Van Gundy said.

"Sometimes being a harsh critic of yourself serves a guy well. Most of those people are perfectionists[15], which I think Yao is."

"But if Yao plays 82 games, plays his minutes, he's going to have a heck of a lot more good times than bad.[16]"

Yao can be rough[17] on himself. In a game in Dallas[18] last season, he stopped running the court to literally[19] beat himself up, punching his right hand into his left after a bad play.

"There were two girls playing in Sacramento[20] this year, Chinese

7. laid-back /ˈleɪdbæk/ *a.* 自在的；随便的
8. 他频频出现在杂志封面或电视广告中。commercial /kəˈmɜːʃəl/ *n.* 广告
9. perceive /pəˈsiːv/ *v.* 认知，理解
10. to look past sth. 不去关心、过问某事
11. preoccupy /priːˈɒkjʊpaɪ/ *v.* 过分关注
12. 姚明对自己的批评极为严厉。
13. to be tough on sb. 对某人苛刻，严格
14. 有时他应该减少焦虑，不要总是对自己的过失耿耿于怀。
15. perfectionist /pəˈfekʃənɪst/ *n.* 完美主义者
16. ... he's going to have a heck of a lot more good times than bad. 他表现好的机会将比表现不好的机会多很多。heck /hek/ *n.* [俚语] 用以加强语意
17. rough /rʌf/ *a.* 粗暴的
18. Dallas 达拉斯（位于美国得克萨斯州东北部）
19. literally /ˈlɪtərəli/ *ad.* 真正地；确实地
20. Sacramento 萨拉门托（美国加利福尼亚州首府）

girls (Miao Lijie and Sui Feifei of the WNBA's Monarchs[21])," Yao said. "I heard the coach in Sacramento (John Whisenant) say their biggest problem with them is if they make a mistake on the court, they want to say 'sorry' to everybody. Maybe it is hard to understand for you guys, but I understand that. The culture is different. I was like that, but I changed a little bit, but not totally changed."

"We always say we have to learn from mistakes. That's why Chinese people make mistakes and keep thinking, thinking."

Yao would seem to have more reasons to reflect on his ability than most. But rather than reacting to pressure or expectations, Yao is conscientious[22] because that is his personality, Van Gundy said.

But Yao knows he is expected to dominate[23]. The Rockets can cite[24] his improvements in transition defense[25] or against the constant pick-and-rolls[26] he sees. He was third in the NBA in field-goal percentage[27].

But subtle improvements don't work for giants.

"Everybody wants a guy to make improvements by leaps and bounds[28], and that's not usually how it happens in the NBA," Van Gundy said. "Yao's improvement has been incremental[29]. Yao's made solid progress throughout his time in the league. The numbers[30] say it. He's done fine."

"Where is he at? He's a very fine player."

Better at the post

Though he can't quite bear to consider his potential, Yao clearly believes he has considerable room to grow. He once was happy just to be in the NBA. But he has played well enough to know he can do much more.

"When the Rockets drafted me as the No. 1 pick (in 2002)[31], I didn't know what level I should be, how many points, how many rebounds[32] I should average[33]," Yao said. "That year, I really didn't put a lot of pressure on myself. I thought maybe I could score seven, eight points, maybe get five, six rebounds. That's not really pushing myself too hard.[34] Then I watched people around me, like checking every year what they did. OK, I didn't touch that level yet."

"From my second year, I tried to push myself hard. I would say I've improved. I know every year is very important for me, because every year I must improve something."

This season, Yao expects his conditioning[35] to be greater and his

21. Monarch 君主队（WNBA 中的一支球队）
22. conscientious /ˌkɒnʃiˈenʃəs/ a. 努力的
23. dominate /ˈdɒmɪneɪt/ v. 起首要作用
24. cite /saɪt/ v. 引用；列举
25. transition defense 转换防守
26. pick-and-roll 掩护转身切入
27. field-goal percentage 罚篮得分的准确率
28. by leaps and bounds 飞快地
29. incremental /ˌɪnkrɪˈmentəl/ a. 增加的
30. numbers 指姚明在 NBA 比赛中的统计数字

31. When the Rockets drafted me as the No. 1 pick (in 2002)…当我在 2002 年成为首轮被火箭队选中的状元秀时……
32. rebound /ˈrɪbaʊnd/ n. 篮板球
33. average /ˈævərɪdʒ/ v. 分摊；按固定比例分担
34. 我真的没有把自己逼得太紧。
35. conditioning /kənˈdɪʃənɪŋ/ n. 体能

post moves³⁶ versatile³⁷ and honed³⁸. To others, if that does not reach dominance, it will not be enough.

"There's so much on him," the Rockets' Tracy McGrady said. "He has to not even worry about that, just go out be the best basketball player he can be and help his ballclub³⁹ win. Then there won't be that pressure. I don't think he's gotten that. But he's young, and he's improving every day."

As demanding⁴⁰ as measuring up to⁴¹ that charge might be, it is more manageable than growing into the pressure of possibility.

"I don't know how much pressure I need," Yao said. "What is the right amount? No one can tell you right now. But I know I need some pressure to push me forward."

"We will get an answer after maybe 10 years, after I retire."

Minutes earlier, that answer was too much for him to predict, draining to even consider.⁴² But suddenly, like a mine⁴³ with its treasure buried, all that potential seemed worth exploring.

36. post move 策应移动(中锋战术动作)
37. versatile /ˈvɜːsətaɪl/ a. 多方面的
38. hone /həʊn/ v. 改进, 完善
39. ballclub /ˈbɔːlˌklʌb/ n. 球队所属的俱乐部
40. demanding /dɪˈmɑːndɪŋ/ a. 苛求的
41. to measure up to 符合; 达到
42. 几分钟前, 那个问题对他来说太难预测, 更别说考虑了。
43. mine /maɪn/ n. 矿井; 矿山

Comprehension Questions

1. What is considered to be Yao Ming's blessing and burden?
2. Why do you think Yao Ming does not like talking of himself and his potential for greatness?
3. What is Yao Ming's attitude to people's expectations?
4. How has Yao Ming improved himself over the years in NBA?
5. Do you think culture affects a player's performance and behaviour on and off court?

Background Reading

Prodigal (浪子) Returns to Chinese Home

Before Yao Ming became the first Chinese basketball player to make it big, very big, in the National Basketball Association, there was Wang Zhizhi. And though Yao's cross-cultural hoop (篮球) dream continues, Wang's came to an end this week when he boarded a flight in Los Angeles in an apologetic (道歉的) mood and returned to his homeland for the first time in more than four years.

The dual (双重的), very carefully calculated (精心计划的) objective: to save his career and save face for Chinese sports leaders.

While Yao, the Houston Rockets center, is the towering (高大的) 7-foot-6, or 2.28-meter, symbol of China's inexorable (坚定的) rise to greater heights, Wang is the seven footer that China has been asked to forget: the pioneering sports soldier who went AWOL (擅离职守的) and whose NBA games were then banned (禁止) from being broadcast in China by the authorities.

While Yao is reassuring proof to his nation's leaders that you can still retain your sense of duty and perspective once you have your millions and your rudimentary (初步的) grasp of American slang, Wang has been the cautionary (谨慎的) tall tale (吹牛; 说大话). He is the young man given the precious first opportunity to play in the NBA who then failed to pay back (回报) his country and former minders (照顾人) for the privilege.

It is, of course, more complicated than that. But what mattered this week was that Wang gave in to China's gravitational pull (吸引力), and while it was easy to feel pity for a once-independent youth turned repentant (后悔的), it certainly looked like the wise move for Wang.

He was the piquant (开胃的) flavor of the month when he joined the Dallas Mavericks (达拉斯小牛队) in 2001, thereby fulfilling his own wildest dream and one held by the globally minded (着眼于全球的) NBA commissioner, David Stern, too. But for (要不是) all his fine offensive skills (进攻技术), the 28-year-old Wang could not find an NBA employer this season after unexceptional tours of duty with the Los Angeles Clippers (洛杉矶快船队) and Miami Heat (迈阿密热火队).

"I think Wang had gotten to a point in his career and personal life where he had no option but to reconcile (和解) with Beijing," said Brook Larmer, the Shanghai-based author of "Operation Yao Ming," a book that charts (勾勒出) Yao's and Wang's paths from very big cradles (摇篮) to the United States.

"Wang's immigration status in the United States makes it difficult for him to try to travel to Europe and play in a league there. He needed professionally, personally and politically to make amends (修正) with Beijing at some point before his career was really over. I do think it's good news both for him and Chinese basketball, but obviously it's not the kind of triumphant return (凯旋而归) he was hoping to make."

It took years to negotiate Wang's departure from China for the NBA. How strange that it took even more years to negotiate the return journey.

Wang was not quite in time to help his former army club team, the Bayi Rockets (八一火箭队), compete in the championship of the Chinese Basketball Association that has just started, but he did make it back in plenty of time for the 2008 Olympics in Beijing.

Relevant Words

action shot	行进间投篮	check defence	堵截防守
dribble charging	运球撞人	fake pass	假传球
glide running	滑步跑	half-court press	半场紧逼
in-bound	发界外球	jump hook	跳起钩手投篮
multiple free throw	连罚	poke away	(把球)捅掉

Lesson 2

凯莉·韦伯(Karrie Webb)是澳大利亚最成功的女高尔夫球选手,也是世界女子高尔夫球史上的顶尖选手之一。她于1994年开始职业高尔夫球生涯,1996年加入美国LPGA巡回赛。韦伯现已在7项主要锦标赛中夺冠,并赢得所有5项女子主要比赛。她在2006年卡拉夫特·纳比什克(Kraft Nabisco)锦标赛中的成功使她第一次进入女子世界高尔夫排名的前10位。她于2005年被列入高尔夫球名人堂,成为迄今为止进入名人堂在世的最年轻的高尔夫球运动员。

Karrie Needs Jack Target to Bowl at

By Trevor Grant
February 28, 2002
The Herald Sun[1]

For Tiger Woods, it's simple. Whenever he needs motivation, he snaps out of his lethargy by thinking of one man and one number.[2] Since he came to pro[3] golf in 1996, Woods has regularly said that his goal is to beat Jack Nicklaus's record of 18 major championships. It was once seen as a high-water mark no flood of great players could touch.[4] Now that Woods, at 26, has already bagged[5] six majors, few are prepared to maintain the line that the Nicklaus record is untouchable. But the pursuit of it is going to keep Woods occupied for many years to come[6].

Twenty-seven-year-old Australian Karrie Webb, who, in her own field, has matched the remarkable feats[7] of Woods and Nicklaus in winning a career Grand Slam well before the age of 30, has a little more trouble summoning a long-term objective.

Her problem has been that ever since she left her home town of Ayr in Queensland in 1994 with her blubs slung over her shoulder and a pro's

1. *The Herald Sun*《先驱太阳报》,是澳大利亚一家保守的报纸,创刊于1990年,隶属于默多克麾下的新闻集团。总部位于澳大利亚维多利亚州首府墨尔本。该报是澳大利亚最受欢迎的报纸,日发行量为55万多份,拥有读者150多万人。也是澳大利亚销量最大的报纸。
2. 当他需要动力的时候,他只要想到一个人,一个数字,他就马上从无精打采的状态中恢复过来。motivation /ˌməutɪˈveɪʃən/ n. 动力;动机 to snap out of it [非正式用语] 恢复;迅速从失望、痛快和自我怜悯等不健康状态恢复到平时的状况 lethargy /ˈleθədʒi/ n. 无精打采,无生气
3. pro /prəu/ n. 职业人员(这里指职业运动员) a. 职业的
4. 杰克·尼古拉斯(Jack Nicklaus)的18场不败的记录曾被众多优秀的高尔夫选手看做是无法企及的目标。
5. bag /bæɡ/ v. 将……纳入囊中;收获
6. many years to come 在未来的很多年
7. feat /fiːt/ n. 功绩;战绩;壮举

certificate in her pocket, Webb's goals haven't been able to keep up with her astonishing rate of achievement.[8] She has been getting ahead of[9] herself in the best possible way every year since.

In 1995 she played her first full pro season on the European Tour. Her goal was to survive financially. By the time she'd won the British Open and secured her player's card at the US qualifying school—finishing second while playing with a broken bone in her writst—she'd done more than enough to ensure she wouldn't be sleeping in the back of a Kombi van and dining at the greasy spoon[10] with the rest of the tour battlers.

The following year, she started out with a tentative[11] wish to win rookie-of-the-year[12] and match the effort of the previous year's top rookie in finishing in the top 40 on the money list[13]. By the end of the season she'd won four events and became the first rookie in men's or women's golf to pass the US $1 million mark.

From there, the momentum[14] has kept up its breathtaking pace, peaking last year at the LPGA Championship[15] when she became the first Australian golfer in history, and one of a rare few in the world, to achieve the career Grand Slam[16] of all four major championships.

As far-fetched as it sounds now, Webb, who has retained the endearing modesty of a shy country kid,[17] says initially she wasn't too sure if she would be able to feed herself as a pro golfer. "I don't know if people understand but I find it hard to believe what I've already achieved," Webb said yesterday, on the eve of her defence of the Women's Australian Open title at Yarra Yarra. "When I started out I didn't set a time limit. But I wasn't going to go out and battle for money. If it was a struggle to keep my card or stay financial, I wasn't going to do that to myself. I didn't know how I'd go in the US but I knew I'd be better than I first thought I'd be."

Now, as a winner of 26 events on the US Tour, including five majors, there's still much more to do, including a whole bunch of[18] majors. But she says goal-setting is still not easy. "For me it's really hard to set my higher goals. I had this trouble after getting the career Grand Slam last year. I don't have the same direct goals as Tiger. He had that goal (about Nicklaus) before he turned pro. As I'm going along people will tell me I've broken a record, but I wouldn't have a clue[19] what it was. I think what drives me is that I know how good I am and what I've achieved."

"I look back now and see I've won 26 times in the US and four

8. 自从1994年她擦干眼泪,怀揣着一张职业选手的证书离开位于昆士兰州艾尔(Ayr)的家乡,她的问题一直没有改变,即她的惊人的运动成绩总是超越她为自己制定的目标。blub /blʌb/ n. 哭泣 sling /slɪŋ/ v. 抛, 投掷
9. to get ahead of 胜过, 超过
10. greasy spoon [美俚] (供应廉价食物、卫生条件差的)下等餐馆
11. tentative /ˈtentətɪv/ a. 试探的, 尝试的
12. rookie-of-the-year 当年的新选手 rookie /ˈrʊkɪ/ n. 新手;新队员
13. money list 收入榜
14. momentum /məʊˈmentəm/ n. 动力;势头
15. LPGA Championship LPGA 锦标赛。此球赛于1955年开始举行, 其历史仅次于美国职业女子公开赛。
16. career Grand Slam 职业大满贯
17. 听起来似乎让人不能相信, Webb 还保有着一个害羞的乡下孩子可爱的谦虚。
far-fetched /fɑːˈfetʃt/ a. 不可信的, 牵强的
endearing /ɪnˈdɪərɪŋ/ a. 惹人喜爱的
18. a bunch of 一系列;一束

19. clue /kluː/ n. 线索;头绪

or five times elsewhere. To have won at least 30 tournaments by the age of 27 is more than I ever dreamed of. Even on my bad days, after calming down, I can reflect on what I've done and realise it's one bad day out of a really good career."

"Good"? There's that modesty again. Karrie Webb can now safely use the word "great" to describe her career.

Comprehension Questions

1. How does Tiger Woods stimulate himself to achieve a higher goal?
2. What has Webb's problem been?
3. How did Webb manage to participate in the golf seasons when she was not financially secured?
4. Why did the author think that Webb still retained modesty sounded far-fetched?
5. What kind of personality do you think Webb had in light of what she said, "It's one bad day out of a really good career"?

Background Reading

Woods's Pain Is All Too Apparent as He Struggles to Keep Focus on the Course

He's the No.1 golfer in the world, but fails miserably as a liar. Tiger Woods stood in front of a cadre of (一组) cameras, microphones and notepads at The Players Championship and told the world: "I'm always fine." But the white teeth that tried to crack through (挤出) his thin smile (浅浅的笑容) did little to hide the truth: he's terribly worried about his father.

Woods flew to California on Tuesday afternoon to be with "Pops". His father, Earl Woods, is struggling in his fight with prostate cancer (前列腺癌). The elder Woods was diagnosed with the disease in 1998; last year he was too ill to attend the Masters (大师赛), and this spring he wasn't able to attend the grand opening of the Tiger Woods Learning Center in Anaheim.

"Dad wasn't feeling well, and it's just the same stuff, just tried to go out there and hopefully make his spirits feel a little better," Woods said. "He's a very stubborn (顽固的) man, which is good. He's fighting as hard as he can. It was good to see. At least he's trying to hang in (坚持) there, which is a very positive sign."

Woods said his father's condition could affect his decision to defend his Masters championship. "It's just one of those things you have to deal with," he said. "Everyone has to deal with that at some point in their life, and unfortunately, right now, it's our time."

Woods and his father share a tight bond (纽带关系). His father set high standards for his son, which he wrote about in the 1999 book *Training a Tiger*. Woods said his father was surprised to see him. "He was happy. He said, 'What the heck (程度较轻的咒骂,无实意) are you doing here?' It was nice to hear that."

Darren Clarke, whose wife, Heather, is in England battling cancer, was paired (成对儿, 一起) with Woods for Thursday's first round.   Clarke admitted that he and Woods shared a few private moments. "We had a few chats," Clarke said, refusing to be specific. "Personal issues, but we had a good chat."

Woods shot a 72 in the first round but refused to blame the ordinary score on jet lag (时差) or lack of focus (注意力不集中).

"Today was just a matter of trying to hit the ball in the fairway (球座与终点间的草地) and didn't do a very good job of that. And I didn't make any putts (轻轻击球)," he said.

But he admitted that his father wasn't far from his thoughts (当他承认他总是想着父亲) . "It (此处指他对父亲的挂念) comes and goes," he said. "I don't think you'd be human if you didn't think about it. It happens, and obviously you need to let it go quickly and focus on the shot. Sometimes it's easier than others."

Padraig Harrington,   whose father died earlier this spring,   said the illness of a parent is difficult regardless of who you are.

"When it comes to a bereavement (亲人丧亡) in your family, you're just a normal person, same as everybody else," Harrington said. "It doesn't give you any ability to handle it any better or words of wisdom or anything like that. It's something you try to go through (经受) in private, and it isn't easy."

Woods missed a great chance to post a good score on the TPC at Sawgrass course that was weakened by overcast (阴云密布的) skies, sporadic drizzle (零星的小雨) and little wind. Davis Love III and Jim Furyk didn't waste their chances; playing in the same pairing, the two veterans (经验丰富的选手) shot seven-under-par 65s. They lead Robert Allenby, Bernhard Langer and Miguel Angel Jimenez by two shots.

"I was hitting it close to the hole," Love said. "Jim was making some nice putts and ... showing me every putt was makeable because the speed wasn't that fast and the greens were smooth."

Relevant Words

break 一杆球	backspin 缩杆
cue 球杆	cue ball 主球
extension 加长杆	foul stroke 犯规击球
maximum 满杆	side spin 偏杆
snooker 障碍球	top spin 高杆

Lesson 3

纳坦·罗宾逊(Nathan James Robertson)和盖尔·埃姆斯(Gail Emms)为英国羽毛球运动员,多次在混合双打的国际比赛中取得优秀战绩。在2004年雅典奥运会上,他们直接进入第二轮比赛,打败了德国混双选手。在四分之一决赛中他们以15—8和17—15的比分打败了中国选手晋级半决赛,并以优势击败丹麦选手。在决赛中他们不敌中国的张军和高凌,最后夺得银牌。

Silver Lining as British Pair's Fightback Falls Short[1]

By Paul Hayward
August 20, 2004
Daily Telegraph

British badminton's HQ[2] at Milton Keynes[3] was said to be overrun[4] and "overwhelmed" by excitement and media interest yesterday. It was a red-letter day[5] in Buckinghamshire but a Red Flag afternoon[6] in Athens, as a Chinese pair conquered Nathan Robertson and Gail Emms at the end of an epic struggle for gold in the final of the mixed doubles.

Milton Keynes requires quite a prod[7] to rouse it from its slumbers[8].

Normally it reserves its bunting for changes to the roundabout system or the building of a new numbered street.[9] "As the magic hour approached in Athens this afternoon, a media circus[10] overwhelmed us," declared the website of the Badminton Association of England. The trouble is, Robertson and Emms were overcome as well in a contest that should draw

1. 英国羽毛球双打选手屈居亚军,获得银牌。to fall short 不足;不合格
2. HQ (= headquarters) 总部
3. Milton Keynes 米尔顿·凯因斯(英国城市名,位于伦敦西北80公里)
4. overrun /ˌəʊvəˈrʌn/ v. 侵占(此处指挤满了记者)
5. red-letter day 大喜日子,特别快乐的日子
6. Red Flag afternoon 惹人生气的下午 red flag [比喻]惹人生气的事物,此处为双关语,暗指中国的国旗。
7. prod /prɒd/ n. 刺
8. slumber /ˈslʌmbə/ n. 睡眠
9. 通常该市只有在改变交通环岛系统或是新建一条新编号的街道时,才会在四处插上彩旗。bunting /ˈbʌntɪŋ/ n. 彩旗;彩带
10. media circus 各路媒体

many converts[11] to this intense, acrobatic[12] and raucous[13] sport.

The two darting[14], dashing[15] Britons finished up with silver medals after going down 15-1, 12-15, 15-12 in a contest that will have opened many eyes to the joys of the shuttlecock shuffle[16]. With typical British understatement[17], Andy Wood, their coach called it "an extremely significant" day for the sport, even though it was Jun Zhang (the man) and Ling Gao (the woman) who occupied the top of the medal podium.

"Badminton's coming home!" Robertson and Emms might have announced had they been able to capitalise on[18] an 11-8 lead in the third "game"—badminton's equivalent of a tennis set. Though the sport traces its origins to the fifth century BC, its modern foundations were laid by the British Army in India in the Victorian age.

When the Duke[19] of Beaufort introduced the game to royal society at his country estate—Badminton House in Gloucestershire—the resoundingly[20] English name was applied. Knowing this, we are entitled to[21] wonder why Robertson and Emms were the first British players to reach an Olympic final.

"I think we've had a fantastic tournament. We were seeded fourth[22], so really the best we could hope for was bronze. To get silver was amazing," declared Emms after mopping up copious tears.[23] "In the final we did everything we could, but it just didn't come off[24] today."

The Goudi Olympic Hall rocks with flags, chants[25] and generally exuberant[26] spectators. You walk in expecting to find all the atmosphere of a library and bounce out with ringing ears[27]. British and Chinese ardour clashed head on.[28] It was the Proms[29] against a Beijing rally. Great fun it was, too, until Zhang and Gao ambushed[30] the British couple and annexed[31] the first game 15-1.

These painfully one-sided[32] opening exchanges had the Union Flag brigade[33] squirming in their seats. As Zhang smashed the shuttlecock at Emms again and again he borrowed the sound effects of Bruce Lee, punching home his points with a terrible yelp.[34] It was badminton as martial art.

"I've never seen anyone come out so fast," Emms agreed. "He was smashing so hard in that first game, and I just wasn't ready. Fair play to them. They were confident and just blew us off the court. When that happens, you just have to accept it. Then get on with it." Robertson's attitude was: "Forget that and move on. And that's

11. convert /kən'vɜːt/ n. 皈依者
12. acrobatic /ˌækrə'bætɪk/ a. 杂技的;特技的
13. raucous /'rɔːkəs/ a. 混乱的;无序的
14. darting /'dɑːtɪŋ/ a. 速度很快的
15. dashing /'dæʃɪŋ/ a. 精力充沛的
16. shuttlecock shuffle 比赛中羽毛球在两队间飞来飞去
17. understatement /ˌʌndə'steɪtmənt/ n. 保守的陈述
18. to capitalise on 利用
19. Duke /djuːk/ n. 公爵
20. resoundingly /rɪ'zaʊndɪŋlɪ/ ad. 轰动地,成功地
21. be entitled to do sth. 有权做某事
22. We were seeded fourth ... 我们是第四号种子选手……
23. ... mopping up copious tears. 抹去汹涌而出的泪水。 to mop up 抹去 copious /'kəʊpɪəs/ a. 大量的
24. to come off 成功,实现计划
25. chant /tʃɑːnt/ n. 歌曲,旋律
26. exuberant /ɪɡ'zjuːbərənt/ a. 被喜悦充溢的
27. ringing ears 耳鸣
28. 英国人和中国人的热情发生了正面的冲突。 ardour /'ɑːdə/ n. 热情,激情
29. the Proms 逍遥音乐会(每年一度在英国伦敦皇家艾尔伯特大厅举行,是世界著名的音乐节之一。这里指英国观众发出的助威、喝彩声。)
30. ambush /'æmbʊʃ/ v. 伏击
31. annex /ə'neks/ v. 夺下
32. one-sided /ˌwʌn'saɪdɪd/ a. 不平衡的;一边倒的
33. Union Flag brigade 英国国旗队(这里指看台上挥动英国国旗的球迷们)
34. ... punching home his points with a terrible yelp. 击杀得分时总是大叫一声。 yelp /jelp/ n. 叫喊

exactly what we did. They caught us with speed in the first game.³⁵ "

The counter-surge was impressive, and soon the British duo were levelling the match at one game apiece.³⁶ In the deciding session they recovered from 3 –0 down to lead 7 –3 and then 11 –8 before the Chinese regained their hold³⁷ to win seven of the next eight points. "I must say the British team played excellently today," said Zhang with more grace than he showed on court (gamesmanship³⁸ is a major component of this deceptively belligerent³⁹ sport).

"We got so close, and when we came off my first emotion was to be absolutely gutted⁴⁰. I felt sick," Emms said. "It was so close and it could have gone either way. But now I've got an Olympic medal round my neck and my name has gone down in history so that can't be bad. This is more than I expected."

"We came here today to give the performance of our lives and our reward for it was the silver medal," Robertson continued. "We've been the best-prepared team I've ever been involved with. I don't think we lost control of the match. The last few points to win an Olympic gold are going to be hard ones, and the Chinese have had more experience of that situation. It was our first time in the final and they were a bit more positive at the decisive stage."

There was something faintly Henman-esque⁴¹ about their defeat: the slow start, the valiant⁴² response and the missed opportunity right at the end. The enthusing⁴³ about the silver medal was also a little overdone⁴⁴ (not that Henman ever exaggerates the merits of his quarter- and semi-final appearances at Wimbledon). The chance was there and then surrendered. You see this a lot in sport. People who have to fight their way back from such a calamitous⁴⁵ start rarely have the emotional reserves then to push on through to glory.

"This has given me an appetite for more," Emms promised. "We want to go out and win some more things." No prizes for noticing that Britain are performing best in the middle-class or middle-England sports: sailing, rowing, equestrianism⁴⁶, archery⁴⁷ and now badminton. England's rugby team win the World Cup. England's footballers seem doomed to go out in quarter-finals. It is a talking point, anyway.

Milton Keynes was doubtless subdued last night. The day started with this battle cry⁴⁸ from Lars Sologub, Britain's performance director: "We will do everything we can to 'go for gold', as it says on the seams of our Ben Sherman⁴⁹ suits." But the Red Flag flew over Buckinghamshire.

35. 他们在第一局中凭借速度打败了我们。
36. 当时现场激动的情绪令人难忘，很快这对英国选手夺回一局，将总比分扳平。
    counter-surge /ˈkaʊntəsɜːdʒ/ n. (情绪)高涨，激动
    duo /ˈdjuːəʊ/ n. 双人组合
    level /ˈlevəl/ v. 使相等，使平等
    apiece /əˈpiːs/ ad. 每个，每人，各
37. to regained one's hold 重新获得控制权
38. gamesmanship /ˈɡeɪmzmənʃɪp/ n. 比赛中为取胜而使用的不犯规的小动作
39. belligerent /bɪˈlɪdʒərənt/ a. 好战的
40. gutted /ˈɡʌtɪd/ a. 极度沮丧的
41. Henman-esque 像亨曼一样的。-esque 为后缀，意为"……样的"，"似……般的"。Henman，即 Tim Henman, 蒂姆·亨曼，英国著名网球选手，曾被看做是英国网球的一面旗帜。
42. valiant /ˈvæliənt/ a. 勇敢的，英勇的
43. enthuse /ɪnˈθjuːz/ v. 显出或表现热情
44. overdo /ˈəʊvəˈduː/ v. 夸张，过分强调
45. calamitous /kəˈlæmɪti/ a. 多灾难的，不幸的
46. equestrianism /ɪˈkwestrɪənɪzəm/ n. 马术
47. archery /ˈɑːtʃəri/ n. 箭术
48. battle cry 呐喊；战斗口号
49. Ben Sherman 英国著名制衣公司，其服装设计多采用英国国旗的图案和颜色。

Comprehension Questions

1. What was the British people's response to Robertson and Emms' victory in the Olympic badminton final?
2. What was the history of badminton in Britain?
3. What did the pair expect before the final match?
4. How did Emms evaluate the Chinese players?
5. What ambition did the pair have after the Olympic Games?

Background Reading

China Opens Door to Success for British Pair

Gail Emms and Nathan Robertson smashed and dinked (装饰) their way into the national consciousness when they contested an extraordinary Olympic badminton mixed-doubles final to earn silver medals in Athens last year.

They have remained at the forefront (最前部,最前线) of their sport and are now poised (准备) to bounce back into the public eye during a new year that brings the All England Championships and the Commonwealth Games (全英锦标赛和英联邦运动会).

They have chosen to push for (争取) greater success rather than rest on their laurels (桂冠) and will start favourites at both events, especially after their victory at the China Open. Winning in China is generally restricted to the Chinese, and Emms struggled to find a comparison that could shed light on (使……清楚明白地显示出来) the magnitude (巨大) of their triumph.

Emms, 28, is the driving force (驱动力) of a partnership that has stood the test of time (经受了时间的考验). "We have a brother-sister relationship—I nag (使他烦恼) him and sort out (整理) his life," she said. "We go out a bit and are happy in each other's company (陪伴), but we like to keep our distance. It keeps us sane (清醒) and stops us killing each other. I'm the boss on court because I can see things better, but sometimes he has to kick me up the backside (背后) if I'm not concentrating."

So how big was this Chinese thing? "It was a major breakthrough because we were the first English winners since the mid-Eighties and it was on live television with an audience of millions. I was on posters and magazines, and Nathan with his bandana (大手帕)—he has this Nadal (纳达尔,西班牙网球新星) thing going on at the moment—is a little bit different, so we got followed around a bit and got a few stares."

"But winning was enormous: we did it on their home soil, with their Olympics coming up—and they do like to make it as hard as possible for their opponents."

While admitting China is more to be endured than enjoyed, Emms believes Britain lags (落后) a long way behind when it comes to producing world-class athletes.

"I play more ladies doubles (女子双打) than mixed, with Donna Kellogg, but there's a huge gap between us and the top four. We got whipped (击败) in 25 minutes at the China Open and we're ranked seventh in the world. It was a case of dodging (避开, 躲避) the shuttles and hoping the opposition would fall over (希望结果会与现实相反). In singles, our lads struggle to break into the top 20 because they are tall and skinny, while the Koreans and Chinese are powerhouses with huge thighs."

"The Chinese also train so hard. There is such competition because it's a way out (出路). It gives them an added personal drive, which is something we need to instil (灌输) in our kids. That sort of discipline is not in our culture, but in China they have a room in a training centre, away from family, friends and mobile phones. Our kids want things to come too easily."

Fortunately, at a time when the participation by girls in sport is low, Emms was never dissuaded from pursuing a life in a tracksuit (田径服).

"Girls are a real disappointment," she said. "They are more worried about what they look like and won't work hard. That's why Kelly Holmes (英国田径名将, 在 2004 年雅典奥运会上获 1500 米和 800 米金牌) was so good. You see the tennis girls in their tight dresses and earrings, and the athleticism (运动员气质) gets lost in glamour (魅力). We can't all be Maria Sharapova (莎拉波娃, 俄罗斯网球运动员)."

Emms attended the sporty Dame Alice Harpur School, in Bedford. "I played hockey at school and a lot of my friends were picked for England at junior level. Luckily, that was my peer (同辈) group and they wanted to work hard and play for their country. I was never out of my PE kit (装备) and I'm glad, because I didn't feel odd or different as I wanted to play sport."

If it seems Emms is dominating the discussion, it is because Robertson, 28, was in Denmark, awaiting his partner's arrival. Despite their Olympic success, they play club matches and are easyJet's (英国一家以票价低廉而著称的航空公司) biggest customers—there are few business-class lounges in international badminton.

"We're not similar personalities," Robertson admitted later. "We enjoy playing and can go anywhere and have a laugh. It's hard doing the training, but there are not many people who have the chance of doing what we do."

They expect, injuries permitting, to be together for the foreseeable future. The big stages loom (隐约可见), and they can't wait.

Relevant Words

ace 直接得分的发球	alternate in service 换发球
crosscourt flight 封角近网球	deep high service 发高远球
dribble 连击	drive 平抽球, 快平球
drop shot 短吊, 轻吊, 短球	foul hit 发球犯规
right to serve 发球权	singles court 单打球场

Lesson 4

> 凯特·豪威(Kate Howey)是英国唯一一位参加过四次奥运会的柔道运动员。她在1992年巴塞罗那奥运会上获得女子柔道70公斤以下级的铜牌,在2000年的悉尼奥运会上获得此级别的银牌。因此她也成为唯一曾在柔道运动中获两枚奥运奖牌的英国女运动员。1997年她因为在柔道事业中的杰出贡献,被授予大英帝国勋章。在2004年雅典奥运会开幕式上,她担任英国奥运代表队的旗手。2004年她宣布退役。

Attack Is the Best Form of Defence for a Fighter in Search of Gold

By Nicolas Soames
August 7, 2004
Telegraph

Fighting Kate Howey is not a pleasant experience—ask anyone who has squared up to[1] her on the judo mat, whether in training or at the top level of competition. She always gets the first attack in[2]—she has probably won more contests in the first 20 seconds than any other fighter—forcing the opponent into a defensive mode from the start. Even after 15 years at the top of the international middleweight category[3]—an extraordinary length of time—she is still fiercely competitive.

This revealed itself in an incident on her 30th birthday last year. She, her brother and a friend were attacked outside a nightclub by three young men bent on[4] causing trouble. The friend went down and Howey (who is 5ft 6ins tall) sprang to his defence.[5] So surprised were the thugs[6] by the speed and ferocity[7] of her attack that they turned tail[8] and ran.

Howey dismisses it because as captain of the British Olympic team she normally presents the necessary control

1. to square up to [口语] 摆好与 …… 打架的架势;准备开打
2. 她总是率先进攻
3. middleweight category 中量级

4. to be bent on (upon) 打算;决心 (做某事)
5. 那位朋友先被打倒,身高5英尺6英寸的豪威跳起来去保护他。
6. thug /θʌɡ/ n. 暴徒;歹徒
7. ferocity /fəˈrɒsɪtɪ/ n. 凶狠;凶猛
8. to turn tail 逃跑;逃走

216

and authority, and activity of this kind is traditionally frowned upon in the disciplined world of judo.[9] But needs must.[10]

And this is how Howey, a Team Bath player, regards her appearance in the Athens Olympics. She is now 31 and perhaps not as explosive as she once was. Yet with a bronze from the Barcelona Olympics[11] and a silver from Sydney she had no choice but to hold out for[12] the gold in Athens.

"I've had my eyes on[13] only one thing for the past two years," she says. Her decision was underlined[14] after the controversy of the Commonwealth Games in Manchester when she was not selected. "I refused to go out on that note,[15]" she declares.

So she subjected herself to two further years of the rigours of full-time judo training under the experienced direction of her coach, Roy Inman[16].

Judo players are among the fittest all-round athletes in the Olympics. In addition to the physical demands, the vast range of judo techniques has to be maintained. Olympic preparation is particularly demanding.

Howey knows this only too well. She has been representing Britain at senior level since the age of 15 and has a wide range of throws[17] and a devastating armlock[18] that brought the silver in Sydney.

"I like getting things over[19] as quickly as I can—especially now," she smiles. Actually, she says that tests show she is in even better condition than she was at Sydney.

She has rarely returned from a competition empty-handed as her record shows: a gold, two silver and two bronzes from world championships, three silvers and five bronzes from European championships (the gold always eluded[20] her) and numerous other medals from A internationals[21].

She is positive about her chances in Athens in spite of a new group of younger fighters. "I've beaten everyone who will be at Sydney, so I'm not worried by any of them," she says. Among them is Holland's Edith Bosch, and the world champion, Masae Uen o, from Japan. Howey also thinks the fact that this is her last competition will concentrate her mind. Certainly, at one of the final training sessions at Bisham Abbey, one after another of her opponents was summarily upended.[22]

"She looks 31 coming on 21,[23]" commented Inman, and there was certainly no stopping Howey as she went nonchalantly[24] through her

9. 豪威不再考虑这件小事。作为英国奥运代表团的队长，她必须表现出克制和权威。而且纪律严明的柔道界是不会赞同这种做法的。
10. 但是需要防卫的时候，还是应该采取措施。
11. Barcelona Olympics 巴塞罗那奥运会(1992 年于西班牙巴塞罗那举行，从那以后夏季和冬季奥运会在不同的两个国家举行)
12. to hold out for [口语] 坚持
13. to have one's eye on 着眼于；密切注意
14. underline /ˌʌndəˈlaɪn/ v. 强调
15. 我不能在那种情绪下外出比赛。
    note /nəʊt/ n. 情绪；情感
16. 于是她在经验丰富的教练罗伊·英曼的指导下，作为全职运动员，又接受了两年严格的柔道训练。
    rigour /ˈrɪɡə/ n. 严格
17. throw /θrəʊ/ n. 摔(柔道中的技术动作)
18. armlock /ˈɑːmlɒk/ n. 锁臂(柔道中的技术动作)
19. to get over 结束，完成
20. elude /ɪˈluːd/ v. 躲避

21. A internationals 甲级国际比赛
22. 在比萨姆·阿比(Bisham Abbey)进行的最后一场训练中，她轻松地把对手一个个放倒。
    summarily /ˈsʌmərəlɪ/ ad. 草率地；立刻 upend /ʌpˈend/ v. 打倒；放倒
23. 她看起来就像今年31，明年21。(意思是豪威的状态越来越好。)
24. nonchalantly /ˈnɒnʃələntlɪ/ ad. 冷静地

repertoire[25]: uchimata[26] (inner thigh throw) tomoe-nage[27] (whirling throw) and straight into an armlock; then seoi-nage[28], the shoulder throw, and finally her trademarked morote-gari[29], the double leg grab[30], her highest scoring technique for many years. It is clear that even now no one can touch her in the UK.

However, she is too intelligent to hang on for a couple more years.[31] In the past year she has been one of the regional co-ordinators[32] for the cadet[33] squad (11 to 17-year-olds) and has started to prepare for a judo coaching career. It is one of a number of options, but the most likely.

"The standards of international sport are getting higher and we have to start to prepare earlier, at grassroots[34] level," Howey explains with quiet confidence. But first comes Athens.

25. repertoire /ˈrepətwɑː/ n. 全部技能（此处指她的全部技术动作）
26. uchimata 挑内股（足技）
27. tomoe-nage 巴投（柔道中的技术动作）
28. seoi-nage 背负投；肩背投
29. her trademarked morote-gari 她的招牌动作双手刈
30. leg grab 足技（柔道中的技术动作）
31. 然而，她又非常明智，不会再多等上几年。to hang on 等待
32. regional co-ordinator 地区协调员
33. cadet /kəˈdet/ n. 军官学校学生
34. grassroots /ˈɡrɑːsruːts/ n. 基础；根源

Comprehension Questions

1. Why is fighting Kate Howey not a pleasant experience?
2. What can be frowned upon in the world of judo?
3. Howey said, "I've had my eye on only one thing for the past two years." What does the "only one thing" refer to?
4. Why is the Olympic preparation for judo contests particularly demanding?
5. What are Howey's technical characteristics like according to the news report?

Background Reading

Kate Howey

Retired Judo champ Kate Howey has been winning medals since her teens (十多岁). In 15 years of competing, she has been awarded an MBE (英帝国勋章) and won Bronze and Silver medals at the Olympics, the World Championships and the European Championships.

However, in all this time she has never been tempted to take drugs. Here she tells why:

"Judo has been part of my life from an early age. When I was really young I used to watch my dad go to Judo classes, and I always wanted to join him."

"I finally got my chance at seven years of age. My parents paid for me to attend classes as a birthday present and I've been going ever since."

Part IV Glimpses of the Superstars

"I got my first medal at just 16... that's 15 years ago now. Since then, I've had many fantastic achievements, like winning the Silver medal in the Sydney Olympics or the World Championships."

"But in all this time I've never been tempted to take anything—I think this proves you can get there without the use of drugs."

"The necessity of eliminating drug-use in sport is something that I feel very strongly about. It makes me so angry when athletes take drugs to improve their game. I think that anyone who is caught should be banned for life (终生禁赛)."

"It has a negative effect on everyone around them. We are all doing exactly the same amount of work, the fact that someone might win because they have cheated and taken drugs is completely unacceptable."

"That's why I am always happy to be tested. The way I see it, the more tests are held, the more people will be caught and the less athletes will be tempted to try it."

"But even if it wasn't for the risk of being caught, I can't get my head around (理解) why people would want to do it. You're not just being unfair to other athletes, you're also not being true to yourself."

"I wouldn't want to stand on a podium knowing that I had got there by taking drugs—it would not mean anything. You would have no sense of achievement."

"It is the pursuit of athletic achievement that has kept me going all these years. I'd advise anyone interested in Judo—or any other sport—to keep a goal in their head and keep reaching for it. My ultimate (最终的) dream was to win a gold medal in the Olympics. This ambition kept me going all these years and I always kept this goal in my mind whilst training or competing."

"It's also important to have support from the people around you. I have been very lucky, my family have supported me throughout and this has helped me enormously."

"Obviously it is not always easy and support from your friends and family can help you through the difficult periods."

"But if you really want to achieve in sport, you need determination. You can't give up the first time you experience a set-back (阻碍, 挫折)."

"Of course it's also vital that you enjoy it in the first place. If you're interested in a particular sport, look for a local club and join it. If you enjoy it, then stick to it and keep focused on your goal."

Relevant Words

arm-hold 臂扼法; 固臂	bend back a finger 反指关节
compound win 综合获胜	degree 段
execution of the throw(ing) 做摔的动作	floating technique 浮技
foot throw 足技	grip avoiding 拒抓
groundwork 寝技	hip technique 腰部摔法; 腰技

Lesson 5

> 被中国人昵称为"老瓦"的瓦尔德内尔是一位瑞典乒乓球运动员,生于 1965 年。由于早年在乒乓球上显示的天赋,他又被称为"乒乓球台上的莫扎特"。瓦尔德内尔 15 岁就取得了欧洲锦标赛冠军,80 年代初到中国参加了训练营,与中国结下了不解之缘。在中国,他是最受欢迎的瑞典人和最受欢迎的运动员之一,被称为"乒坛常青树"。他打了 20 多年乒乓球,但年龄并没有阻挡他的体育生涯,他仍然可以和小他 10 多岁的新生代选手抗衡。

For "Table Tennis Mozart," Few High Notes[1]

By Christopher Clarey
August 23, 2004
International Herald Tribune

Outside in the suffocating[2] heat, a pair of Swedish women in their blue and gold jerseys[3] with the three crowns on the back were searching in vain for tickets in a city where millions of tickets remain unsold.

Inside, in the cool of the Galtasi sports hall, their nation's off-again, on-again obsession, Jan-Ove Waldner, was searching in vain for another crack at a gold medal.[4]

Waldner's nickname is "the Mozart[5] of table tennis," a reference to his once-precocious[6] genius and once-prolific[7] output of victories and innovative shots.

But perhaps it's time for a new sobriquet. Mozart died before he turned 36. Waldner, whose very name can give his former rivals a faraway[8] look, will be turning 39 in early October, with no intention of even retiring until the end of next season but every intention of making this his final Olympics.

It is his fifth in a row, which means that he has been there since the beginning for his sport at the Games, in 1998 in Seoul, and it is his longevity combined with his stellar résumé[9] and deadpan[10] creativity that still make him a magnet[11] in Athens for autograph[12] seekers, many of them Chinese, who know their table tennis icons when they see them.

---

1. high note 赞美
2. suffocating /ˈsʌfəkeɪtɪŋ/ *a.* 使人窒息的
3. jersey /ˈdʒɜːzɪ/ *n.* 运动衫
4. 在凉爽的 Galtasi 体育馆内,瑞典人民的偶像、比赛成绩时好时坏的瓦尔德内尔正在徒劳地向夺取金牌做着努力。
   obsession /əbˈseʃən/ *n.* 使人着迷的人
   crack /kræk/ *n.* [口语] 尝试
5. Mozart /ˈməʊtsɑːt/ 莫扎特(奥地利作曲家)
6. precocious /prɪˈkəʊʃəs/ *a.* 早熟的
7. prolific /prəˈlɪfɪk/ *a.* 多产的
8. faraway /ˈfɑːrəweɪ/ *a.* 恍惚的;出神的
9. stellar résumé 辉煌的个人简历
   stellar /ˈstelə/ *a.* 主要的;显著的
10. deadpan /ˈdedpæn/ *a.* 面无表情的;不带感情色彩的
11. magnet /ˈmæɡnɪt/ *n.* 吸引力
12. autograph /ˈɔːtəɡrɑːf/ *n.* 签名

"Without a doubt, he's the No. 1 player in the history of the sport," said his coach, Peter Sternesborg. "Think about it. He played his first big final in 1982 in the European championship when he was 17 years old. Here, 22 years later, he is playing in the semifinals of the Olympics."

In between, there was a gold medal in men's singles in 1992 and a silver medal in the 2000 Games in Sydney. But if there is going to be another medal in Athens it will have to be bronze. Because Waldner, despite the nonstop racket generated by a block of Swedish supporters and the big buzz generated by his run through the draw, looked a shade too slow and a shade too confused on Sunday to put much of a dent in the fist-clenching approach of his semifinal opponent, Ryu Seung Min of South Korea.[13]

Ryu, causing Waldner a world of trouble with his deceptive serve, won four games to one with relative ease. "I met a player who was faster and quicker than the Chinese," Waldner said.

Waldner should know. He has been playing the Chinese for so long that some of those who used to be his rivals are now China's national-team coaches.

There is a bit of bias[14] in Waldner's celebrity. The Chinese might recognize Waldner, but only a few Swedish aficionados[15] could recognize the top Chinese players. But then the turnover rate is high when there are millions of aspiring champions in the pipeline[16].

"You can say he is competing against his fourth or fifth generation of Chinese players," said Waldner's older brother, Kjell-Ake, who is head coach of the Swedish team. "But it's also true that there is so much competition within the Chinese team that they don't have the same possibility to have very long international careers."

China's two top singles players here, Wang Liqin and Wang Hao, are 26 and 20, respectively, and the younger Wang beat the elder Wang on Sunday to reach the final against the Ryu, 22.

None of them were close to being born when Waldner walked into a club in Stockholm with his brother at the age of 6 and began taking swings at[17] a celluloid[18] ball that was bouncing well above his head, which was down around table level.

That was shortly after Stellan Bengtsson became Sweden's first world champion in singles in 1971. "That was maybe the reason for my brother to start," Kjell-Ake said.

But his brother, who began playing regular Swedish league matches at the age of 11, would build on Bengtsson's solid edifice[19]

---

13. 尽管瓦尔德内尔得到了一批瑞典人的支持，从没有停止过比赛，尽管他的比赛抽签结果激起一片欢腾，但在周日的比赛中瓦尔德内尔看上去还是有点太慢，太茫然，对于他的半决赛对手、频频举拳以示胜利的韩国选手柳承敏（Ryu Seung Min）也没有构成多大的威胁。shade /ʃeɪd/ n. 少量，少许 dent /dent/ n. 凹痕（这里指瓦尔德内尔对柳承敏的影响）

14. bias /ˈbaɪəs/ n. 偏见

15. aficionado /əˌfɪʃəˈnɑːdəʊ/ n. 球迷

16. pipeline /ˈpaɪplaɪn/ n. 管道（这里指国际乒坛就像一个巨大的管线，每年涌现大量的新人）

17. to take swings at sth. 挥击某物

18. celluloid /ˈseljulɔɪd/ n. 赛璐珞

19. edifice /ˈedɪfɪs/ n. 大厦；大建筑物

and go higher, much higher. By age 16, he received the prize of a Porsche[20] for winning a tournament in Germany but was still unlicensed[21] to drive it. His most dominant moment came between 1989 and 1993, when Sweden won consecutive world team championships.

At his peak, Waldner inspired a mixture of dread[22] and worship[23] in the opposition[24], well-reflected in some of the writings of Matthew Syed, a former British No. 1 who often suffered from Waldner's sleight[25] and speed of hand.

"The variety of strokes that Waldner is able to unleash flow in a sequence that seems to defy logic, as if by pure instinct,[26]" Syed wrote in a 1999 piece in *The Times of London*. "His playing narrative is more akin to[27] James Joyce than Jane Austen. Yet like Austen's prose, Waldner's stroke-making is deployed[28] with unrivaled subtlety[29] and grace."

He walked on court Sunday with the hint of a smile to roars[30] from the Swedes, his haircut still boyish—short-cropped with a part down the middle—but the slightest hint of a paunch[31] showing under his uniform.

But though he arrived in Athens with only a world ranking of 20, he arrived feeling healthy and confident, as the opposition would soon discover as he defeated world No. 2 Ma Lin of China in the third round and the European champion Timo Boll of Germany in the quarterfinals.

But there can be no doubt that the pendulum[32] that once was swinging Sweden's way has now come back in earnest[33]. The Chinese are in position to sweep all four Olympic events, just as they did in Sydney.

Chen Qi and Ma Lin already have won the men's doubles; Wang Nan and Zhang Yining already have won the women's doubles. On Sunday, Zhang Yining defeated Kim Hyang Mi of North Korea in four straight games[34] to win the women's singles title.

All that remains is the men's gold medal, and Wang Hao will be a slight favorite against Ryu in the final, while Waldner will face China's and the world's No. 1 player, Wang Liqin, in the third-place match.

The Swede won't be doing it much longer, which is why two Swedish fans were left without tickets in the midday Athens heat.

---

20. Porsche /ˈpɔːstʃi/ n. 保时捷汽车
21. unlicensed /ʌnˈlaɪsənst/ a. 没有驾驶执照的
22. dread /dred/ n. 畏惧
23. worship /ˈwɜːʃɪp/ n. 崇拜
24. opposition /ɒpəˈzɪʃən/ n. 对手一方
25. sleight /slaɪt/ n. 手法；技巧
26. 瓦尔德内尔的各种击球手法毫无逻辑可循，似乎他打球完全依靠直觉。unleash /ʌnˈliːʃ/ v. 解放，释放 defy /dɪˈfaɪ/ v. 蔑视，挑衅 instinct /ˈɪnstɪŋkt/ n. 直觉
27. be akin to 同……近似
28. deploy /dɪˈplɔɪ/ v. 展开，配置，部署
29. subtlety /ˈsʌtltɪ/ n. 精妙
30. roar /rɔː/ n. 大声喊叫
31. paunch /pɔːntʃ/ n. 大肚子
32. pendulum /ˈpendjʊləm/ n. 钟摆
33. in earnest 认真地；急切地
34. four straight games 连续四盘比赛

Part IV Glimpses of the Superstars

Comprehension Questions

1. Why was Waldner compared to Mozart?
2. How many Olympic Games had Waldner participated in before the Athens Olympics?
3. Why was Waldner seen as an icon by some Chinese fans?
4. What are Waldner's advantages and disadvantages in playing against a much younger player?
5. Do you know any Chinese table tennis player having an international career as long as Waldner's? Why can (or cannot) he/she play for a long time?

Background Reading

The Lightening of Jan-Ove Waldner

Jan-Ove Waldner is the Mozart of table tennis, because he can play many different compositions (组合) on the table. That's a brilliant metaphor (比喻) which turns up (出现) in many newspapers.

"He is indeed a little bit like the Mozart from the film Amadeus", says Jens Fellke, the former practise-mate (陪练) of Waldner.

I also approached his brother Kjell-Ake (38) for this interview. The other Waldner is national women coach of Sweden.

Jan-Ove Waldner (35) did many interviews in his life. That could be noticed very well during this interview. He solves supposed ignorance (无知) of the reporter by supplying necessary information without a worrying face. Nevertheless relatively little interested table tennis players know much about him. That's why this interview about and with Jan-Ove Waldner took place.

Jan-Ove Waldner was born in Stockholm on October 3th in 1965. Like in many Swedish families, both parents had a job. Mother was a shop assistant and father was graphical (绘图的) assistant at a newspaper.

Jan-Ove didn't need to check in a club. Together with his brother he is asked to play at Sparvagen during a little tournament in spring holidays when he was six years old. His parents noticed that he and his brother had very much fun on table tennis. They drove both brothers soon for practising and matches. Little Jan-Ove developed very fast. Faster than in tennis and football, sports for which he was gifted (有天赋的) too. On his ninth he became already Swedish Champion in his age group. He finished off his nine years taking ground school, to start playing table tennis as a professional on his fifteenth. On his sixteenth he won his first Porsche, which he might drive two years later.

Development

The Waldner at the age of 15, was another one than the Waldner now. His brother Kjell-Ake: "Jan-Ove plays nearer on the table than twenty years ago to gain time and energy. And he has improved his backhand (反手技术) all the time. But if you play on his level, it's necessary."

Jan-Ove thinks naturally the level is higher than when he started: "Table tennis has become much faster. Service-receive (接发球) is now more important than ever. Because there are less rallies (回合), it's important to start attacking after the service."

Passion

"His passion for table tennis is enormous", declares writer Fellke the long career of Jan-Ove Waldner. "It is incredible how he can maintain his way of life all this time. He practises more than ever ever to keep his level."

Jan-Ove: "I still have very much fun when I play. But I also had fun all the times I played for the national team. The atmosphere has always been very good. Many of the players are friends of mine. Moreover it fascinates me to keep an high level of concentration. All of my successes I reached by being able to concentrate very well."

Relevant Words

accelerated loop	前冲弧圈球	accuracy	命中率
advantage server	发球者占先	all cut	以削球为主的战术
amplitude of swing	挥拍的幅度	angle shot	斜线球
angle the drive	抽出角度来	attack on both side	两面攻,左右开攻
backhand chop	反手削球	backhand drive	反手抽球

Lesson 6

> 斯蒂芬妮·赖斯(Stephanie Rice),澳大利亚昆士兰的一名游泳运动员,现年17岁。在2006年墨尔本举行的英联邦运动会女子200米和400米混合泳比赛中击败多位著名奥运选手,分别以2:12.90和4:41.91的个人最好成绩获得这两个项目的金牌,确定了她在强手如林的澳大利亚游泳队中的新星地位。

Taste of Future as Rice Comes to Boil

By Richard Hinds
March 18, 2006
Sydney Morning Herald[1]

Microphones were thrust in her face. Responses were demanded. She had come to Melbourne on an important mission and performed with great authority. Now the media wanted a piece of this powerful woman by the name of Rice.

Not Condoleezza[2], although last night, she, too, would take her turn[3] at the podium, presenting the medals for the women's 50-metres breaststroke[4]. The woman they wanted to hear from was Stephanie Rice, whose starring role[5] at the pool the previous evening had been almost as unlikely as that of the US Secretary of State.

Which is why, the day after Rice had shocked everyone but herself by winning the 200m individual medley[6], the questions still flowed. Most pertinently[7]: Who was this bubbly[8] young woman from Brisbane with statuesque[9] good looks, a Luna Park smile[10] and a kick like a mule[11]?

1. *Sydney Morning Herald* 《悉尼先驱晨报》,1831年创刊于悉尼。原名为《悉尼先驱报》(*The Sydney Herald*),是澳大利亚至今连续出版的最古老的报纸,主要面向中上层社会读者。它与《世纪报》(*The Age*)一起,被誉为澳大利亚最有影响的报纸,在世界上也有一定声望。目前,它的发行量约达30万份。
2. Condoleezza Rice 美国国务卿赖斯。当时她正在墨尔本进行国事访问。
3. to take one's turn doing sth. 轮到某人做某事
4. breaststroke /ˈbrest-strəuk/ *n.* 蛙泳
5. starring role 主要角色
6. individual medley 个人混合泳
7. pertinently /ˈpɜːtnəntlɪ/ *ad.* 相关地
8. bubbly /ˈbʌblɪ/ *a.* 兴奋的;闪耀的
9. statuesque /ˌstætʃuˈesk/ *a.* 雕像一般的;轮廓极美的
10. a Luna Park smile 开心的笑容。Luna Park 为澳大利亚的娱乐场所,入口为一个张嘴大笑的小丑。此处比喻赖斯的笑容非常开心。
11. a kick like a mule 强有力的踢水 mule /mjuːl/ *n.* 骡子

There was no point calling her agent.[12] Unlike the gilt-edged[13] stars of the Australian swimming team, the 17 year-old does not have one. Not yet. There were some offers last year as she nudged her way towards[14] her first national team. But Rice did not want the distraction. "She'd just left school and her training was getting pretty full on,[15]" Rice's mother Raelene Hickey said. "She didn't want anything extra on her plate.[16]"

So, yesterday, it was left first to Rice in an intense pre-breakfast round of interviews, then to her mother, to give us the *Stephanie Rice Story*. It turned out, in the broad details[17], to be a familiar tale.

Talented young swimmer makes the necessary sacrifices—rises early, gives up teenage pursuits, battles occasional illness and fatigue—to follow her dream, all the time supported by a similarly self-sacrificing[18] mother. Although it is the every-swimmer story, it does not make Rice's performance in beating overwhelming[19] favourite[20] Brooke Hanson and a third Australian, Lara Carroll, any less remarkable.

Almost since she first learned to swim as an 18-month-old baby, she has demanded to be near water. "I just took to[21] it, just loved it," she says. "I wanted to keep going back again and again."

In a refreshing reversal of the "ugly parent syndrome"[22], when she was 10, Rice begged her mother to take her to an élite[23] coach who would push her much harder than they did at the local 25m pool. So she became a member of one of renowned coach Vince Raleigh's "underling squads[24]" at Indooroopilly.

It was then the ritual that would last seven years began.[25] The alarm would always ring at 4.45 am. By 5.05, Rice and her mother would start the 25-minute drive from Clayfield to Indooroopilly. As Rice trained, her mother would drive home, grab some breakfast and prepare Rice's lunch, before picking her up at 7.55 am.

Then they would drive from the pool to Clayfield College, Rice scoffing[26] her breakfast in the car. Finally, her mother would return during a free period or after school to take her to the pool again. Sometimes Raelene would clock five hours in the car each day, six days a week.[27]

Yet, like most swimming parents, Raelene recounts those journeys fondly[28]. "You'd get up at three for your own kids," she says. "She's finished school now and she's got her licence[29]. But you'd still do it if you had to."

12. 打电话给她的经纪人是没有用的。
13. gilt-edged /ˈgiltedʒd/ a. 最好的，最优秀的
14. to nudge one's way towards 跻身进入
15. ... her training was getting pretty full on. 她的训练计划安排得很满。
16. 她不想处理多余的事情。on one's plate 等待处理
17. in broad details 在大多数细节上
18. self-sacrificing /ˈselfˌsækrɪfaɪsɪŋ/ a. 有自我牺牲精神的
19. overwhelming /ˌəʊvəˈwelmɪŋ/ a. 势不可挡的，强有力的
20. favourite /ˈfeɪvərɪt/ a. 有获胜希望的
21. to take to 喜爱
22. 同其他运动员感受的"丑恶父母综合症"相比，赖斯的成长故事恰好相反，因此令人感到新奇。"丑恶父母综合症"指一些运动员从小被父母逼迫从事运动。refreshing /rɪˈfreʃɪŋ/ a. 新奇的 reversal /rɪˈvɜːsəl/ n. 翻转；倒转；逆转
23. élite /eɪˈliːt/ a. 优秀的；最好的
24. underling squad 下属小队
25. 就在那时，赖斯开始了她一成不变的生活。这种生活持续了7年。ritual /ˈrɪtʃuəl/ n. 不变的模式
26. scoff /skɒf/ v. 吃光
27. 有时Raelene每天在车内度过的时间长达5个小时。每周6天皆是如此。clock /klɒk/ v. 计时
28. fondly /ˈfɒndlɪ/ ad. 充满柔情地
29. license /ˈlaɪsəns/ n. 执照（此处指驾驶执照）

Part IV   Glimpses of the Superstars

For Rice, there has been the usual sacrifices—like giving up hockey in Year 11 for fear of injury. When she was 15, Rice suffered glandular fever[30] and, as an asthmatic[31], she sometimes struggles in the winter. "But she has always been very focused," says Raelene.

So much so that, during the Games in 2002, Raelene remembers her daughter making a vow[32]. "She said, 'The next Commonwealth Games, I'll be finished school by then and I think that will be the time for me'."

Yet, having earned her place in the team by finishing third at the national championships, Rice snuck under the guard of her rivals.[33] Hanson admitted she had been looking at Carroll in the opposite lane[34] unaware Rice was ploughing ahead.

She might not be the last to get lost in Rice's wash. Raelene and her husband, Allan Hickey, Rice's sister Courtney, father Warren Rice and grandfather Jack Rice flew from Brisbane to watch the race. In the blur of interviews and drug-testing that followed, they had only a few minutes to celebrate the moment with the winner.

Yet they left feeling it would not be the last gold medal to savour[35]. "No one really expected it, but she did," said Raelene. "I think this is just the start."

30. glandular fever 腺热, 功能性高烧
31. asthmatic /æs'mætɪk/ *n.* 哮喘病人
32. 赖斯在游泳上倾注了太多的精力和时间, 在 2002 年英联邦运动会上, Raelene 还记得赖斯的誓言。
33. 在全国游泳锦标赛上, 赖斯名列第三, 逃过了对手的防备。sneak /sniːk/ *v.* 潜行, 隐藏
34. lane /leɪn/ *n.* 泳道; 跑道
35. savour /'seɪvə/ *v.* 细细品尝

Comprehension Questions

1. What did Condoleezza Rice do during the 2006 Commonwealth Games?
2. What was people's response to Rice's victory?
3. What was Rice's life pattern when she received the training of coach Vince Raleigh?
4. What do you think contributed to Rice's success?
5. Do you think it is worthwhile to be a professional athlete since so many personal interests and pursuits have to be sacrificed?

Background Reading

Rice Steals Show with Unlikely Win

Australia's only gold medal on the opening night at the pool came from the most unlikely source. Not from Libby Lenton, who in recent weeks has been portrayed (描绘) as some kind of superwoman with a shot (企图) at seven golds, but from 17-year-old Stephanie Rice, who caused a major stir when she shot from obscurity (不出名) to win the 200-metres individual medley.

227

After a 20-year-old Scottish woman, Caitlin McClatchey, had punctured the Australian women's aura (光环) of invincibility (战无不胜) in a little less than two minutes by motoring (快速游过) past Lenton in the final stages of the 200m freestyle, it fell to the quiet Queensland teenager to cause a second upset as the unlikely leader of an Australian trifecta (三连胜) in the medley.

Rice, on her first national team, was perhaps the least likely of the Australian women to triumph on a night usually decorated heavily with Australian gold. But she showed a formidable (令人生畏的) turn of speed to kick away from (甩掉, 摆脱) the favourite, Brooke Hanson, and the fancied (被看好的) youngster, Lara Carroll, who led at the last turn.

Upon touching just ahead of the formidable Hanson in a personal best and Games record time of two minutes, 12.90 seconds, Rice looked about to burst into tears and embraced Hanson.

"I had no idea if I was first, second or third, it was so close," Rice said afterwards. "It's a dream." With Hanson second and Carroll third, it was the medal sweep (席卷奖牌) that most Australians had expected, but in a different order.

It helped to ease the shock of McClatchey's victory, which started the Games on an entirely different note than was anticipated. It came after weeks of mad predictions that the Australian women would have a monopoly (垄断) on gold and that Lenton had a shot at history by surpassing the six gold medals won by Susie O'Neill in Kuala Lumpur and Ian Thorpe in Manchester.

She can simply get on with her Games, and will meet Olympic champion Jodie Henry in the highly anticipated 100m freestyle and world champion Jess Schipper in the 100 butterfly. There will be no easy swims.

Lenton's wide smile as she received her silver medal suggested she was not remotely bothered about defeat, and indeed the 21-year-old clocked (计时) a time that would have delivered gold at the Athens Olympics and at last year's world championships.

"I know a lot of people expected me to win tonight but it was my first 200-metre in an international meet, so to come up with that performance, I'm really really happy," said Lenton, who raised expectations at the world titles by setting a Commonwealth record in leading off (开始) the 4×200 metres freestyle relay.

She was not the only Australian for whom Caitlin McClatchey was not a household name (家喻户晓) before she qualified fastest for last night's final.

McClatchey, a specialist in the 400m freestyle who lives and trains at Loughborough in England, was as incredulous (怀疑的, 不轻信的) as the parochial (眼界狭窄的) Melbourne crowd after finishing off an absorbing (引人入胜的) race by springing from Lenton's shoulder in the closing stages to touch in 1:57.25, a new Commonwealth Games record.

"I can't believe it, it's fantastic," said the 20-year-old, who came to some prominence (突出, 显著) when she won bronze in the 400m at the Montreal world titles. "A gold medal, and it's not even in my major event."

England's Melanie Marshall took the bronze medal, destroying Australian hopes of a sweep in the first event.

Teenager Bronte Barratt and Linda MacKenzie, the renowned fighter who was considered the main

Part IV Glimpses of the Superstars

danger to Lenton's chances after coming from behind to win at the trials, were relegated to (下降到) fourth and fifth respectively.

And so, after Scotland the Brave (《苏格兰勇士》, 苏格兰民歌) rang out (演奏完毕) at the Melbourne Sports and Aquatic Centre when everyone had expected to hear Advance Australia Fair (《前进,美丽的澳大利亚》,澳大利亚国歌), it fell to a 17-year-old from Queensland to kick-start Australia's gold medal haul in the pool.

Relevant Words

false start 出发犯规	forward thrust of the instep of foot 脚背发力
medley relay race 混合接力	negative split 后半程加速游
oblique shoulder 斜肩	push out horizontally 向水平方向蹬出
recovery of legs 收腿	scissors kick 剪式打腿动作
shortened pull 划水动作短促	twist the body around 半转体动作

Lesson 7

> 雅娜·皮特曼(Jana Pittman)是一名澳大利亚田径运动员,专攻 200 米和 400 米跨栏。她的明星运动生涯始于 1999 年世界青年锦标赛澳大利亚选拔赛。2000 年她成为第一个在国际田联和国际奥委会举办的田径比赛中同时获得 400 米跑和 400 米跨栏金牌的女运动员。在 2002 年英联邦运动会和 2003 年的世界锦标赛上曾获 400 米跨栏金牌。在 2006 年英联邦运动会上她打破该运动会 400 米跨栏纪录,获得该项目的金牌,并在 4×400 米接力赛中赢得金牌。但由于她的私生活备受争议,她被澳大利亚人戏称为"话题女王"。

Jumping a Self-made Obstacle Course

By Jenny McAsey
August 10, 2002
The Australian[1]

Jana Pittman was spinning out of control, taking a scattergun approach to life.[2] One part of her wanted to run fast. Another part wanted to become a minister of religion[3]. Or maybe a doctor or a physiotherapist[4].

The teenage Sydneysider[5] named the rising star of international athletics, whose coach believes she will be "the greatest track athlete Australia has ever produced", had moved out of home, was partying hard[6], studying at university, attending church and training.

Sixteen months ago, Pittman, who has become the darling[7] of Australian athletics after stunning victories in the Commonwealth Games 400 meters hurdles[8] and 4 × 400 meters relay, was a little girl lost who had taken on too much.

"All the bits of me I thought I'd held together just fell apart. I was completely lost, I didn't know myself," recalled Pittman this week as she soaked up[9] the adulation[10] at welcome-home parades in Melbourne and Sydney. "I was very confused. I was a teenager growing up in a world I didn't really understand."

Her inner turmoil spilled out in late March last year,[11] just after she won the 400 meters hurdles at the national titles in Brisbane in a sluggish time. The normally bubbly Pittman poured her heart out,

---

1. *The Australian*《澳大利亚人报》,是澳大利亚第一份全国性报纸,也是澳大利亚最具影响力的全国性报纸,创刊于 1964 年,隶属于默克多的新闻集团,报社总部位于悉尼。该报平日版的发行量为 13 万份,拥有读者 40 多万,周末版的发行量为 32 万份,读者达 90 多万人。为了吸引年轻读者,报社开设了免费网站,供读者浏览。
2. 皮特曼随意地对待生活,不知如何是好。
   scattergun /ˈskætəɡʌn/ *n.* 机关枪
3. minister of religion 牧师
4. physiotherapist /ˌfɪziəʊˈθerəpɪst/ *n.* 理疗师
5. Sydneysider /ˈsɪdnɪˌsaɪdə/ *n.* 悉尼人
6. party hard 花很多时间参加聚会
7. darling /ˈdɑːlɪŋ/ *n.* 宠儿
8. hurdles /ˈhɜːdlz/ *n.* 跨栏
9. to soak up 经历;享受
10. adulation /ˌædʒʊˈleɪʃən/ *n.* 阿谀奉承,谄媚
11. 去年三月她就向外界吐露了内心的迷惑

Part IV Glimpses of the Superstars

declaring she feared the onset of chronic fatigue syndrome and was reassessing her future.[12] "I just feel really, really tired all the time," she said.

It was a cry for help from an over-achiever[13] who had taken on the world in 2000, competing at the Olympics when only 17, then winning the 400 meters hurdles and 400 meters at the world junior championships[14] while also doing her HSC[15]. She had been whisked to Monaco by the International Athletics Federation, lauded as the world's best junior athletes, and made headlines when she danced with Prince Albert.[16]

After the euphoria died down, Pittman crashed back to earth.[17] She admits she was vulnerable and mindful of the fall from grace of teenage tennis star Jennifer Capriati.[18] "That went through my mind. But the way I did it was I just got really fat. I ate everything and I went out all the time."

Her plea for help was heard by her then coach, Jackie Byrnes, who was concerned about her erratic[19] behaviour. Athletics Australia also stepped in.[20] Within two days of the national titles, an urgent meeting was held to ensure one of Australia's brightest talents was given guidance and support to get her life in order. It was a pivotal point[21] in the runner's career.

"I've told her she can do the 400 meters hurdles at the 2004 Olympics, in 2008 she can do the 400 metres flat[22] and in 2012 she can do the 800 metres, and get a gold medal in all three," says Byrnes, who also coached sprinter[23] Melinda Gainsford-Taylor.

Without that rescue meeting, attended by Pittman, her parents, Jackie and Brian Byrnes, and AA head coach Keith Connor, her prodigious[24] talent might have been wasted. They agreed to a plan, and the next week Pittman moved to the cocoon-like[25] environment of the Australian Institute of Sport[26] in Canberra to be coached by Craig Hilliard. She lived on-site and was put under a curfew[27] but responded positively to the discipline.

"It was the biggest decision I've ever made," Pittman said. "But I knew I needed a change of environment. Keith [Connor] said, 'You need some control, we need to basically lock you up and knock it out of you,' and it didn't take too long. It only really took two months at the institute and I was ready to rock and roll[28] again."

Hilliard's coaching suited her and off the track[29] she formed a steady relationship with 30-year-old Rohan Robinson, a 1996 Olympic

12. 平日活泼开朗的皮特曼露心扉，坦言她害怕会患上慢性疲劳综合症，并且正在重新衡量自己的未来。
13. over-achiever /ˈəʊvəˌəˈtʃiːvə/ n. 成就过多的人
14. world junior championships 世界青年锦标赛
15. HSC (Higher School Certificate) 高中毕业证
16. 她曾被国际田径联合会邀请到摩洛哥，被赞誉为世界上最优秀的青年运动员，并且她和摩洛哥阿尔伯特王子跳舞也成为头条新闻。whisk /wɪsk/ v. 迅速移动，挥动 laud /lɔːd/ v. 赞美，称赞
17. 当浮华散尽，皮特曼回落到现实中。euphoria /juːˈfɔːriə/ n. 精神欢快，兴高采烈
18. 她承认她极为脆弱，而且牢牢记着少年网球明星珍妮弗·卡普里亚蒂 (Jennifer Capriati) 盛名之后的衰落。
19. erratic /ɪˈrætɪk/ a. 不稳定的；奇怪的
20. 澳大利亚田径协会也插手帮助。
21. pivotal point 转折点，关键点
22. 400 metres flat 400 米跑（与跨栏跑相对）
23. sprinter /ˈsprɪntə/ n. 短跑运动员
24. prodigious /prəˈdɪdʒəs/ a. 巨大的；惊人的
25. cocoon-like /kəˈkuːnlaɪk/ a. 像茧一样的（意为"封闭的"）
26. the Australian Institute of Sport 澳大利亚体育学院（位于堪培拉）
27. curfew /ˈkɜːfjuː/ n. 宵禁（此处指规定皮特曼晚间不得外出）
28. rock and roll 摇滚（此处意为"参加聚会"）
29. off the track 田径场外，训练之余

400 metres hurdles finalist[30]. With a stable lifestyle, everything started to gel[31]. After almost a year away from the stress of competition, she emerged eight kilograms leaner, stronger and more emotionally mature. In the past six weeks, she has lowered her personal best in the hurdles three times, from 55.20 seconds to 54.14 seconds, the second-fastest time in the world this year.

As the statuesque Pittman stood next to Ian Thorpe outside Sydney Town Hall[32] on Thursday, and then spoke impressively to the large crowd, it was hard to believe that, like Thorpe, she is only 19. She has the potential to be as big a talent in her field as Thorpe is in his, but wants to do it her way.[33]

Can she be as good as Cathy Freeman[34]? "I'm hoping I can do better. You can't set your limits on something like that.[35] I'd like to be the next Jana Pittman, if you know what I mean."

30. finalist /ˈfaɪməlɪst/ n. 参加决赛的选手
31. gel /dʒel/ v. （想法）更清晰，更稳定；各部分紧密结合
32. Sydney Town Hall 悉尼市政厅
33. 她有潜力，像索普一样在各自的领域里成为天才的运动员，但她却希望以她自己的方式发展。
34. Cathy Freeman 卡西·弗里曼（澳大利亚土著运动员，曾在悉尼奥运会获400米金牌）
35. 你不能像那样局限自己的目标。

Comprehension Questions

1. What approach did Jana Pittman take to her life?
2. What was Pittman's response to people's flattery and admiration in Melbourne and Sydney?
3. Why did Pittman suffer the inner turmoil?
4. How did Pittman's coach and Athletics Australia help Jana out of her dilemma and put her life in track?
5. Do you know the life story of Jennifer Capriati? Can you compare her experience and Pittman's?

Background Reading

Forget the Dramas, the Soap Operas, This Is a Love Story

In the end there was no drama, just sheer brilliance and the return of a champion athlete named Jana Pittman.

Pittman had promised to let her spikes (鞋钉，此处指跑鞋) do the talking and on Thursday night they did in emphatic (断然的；高调的) fashion with the defending Commonwealth champion (英联邦运动会卫冕冠军) smashing the Games 400m hurdles record to win what will be known as her career-saving gold medal. Two horror years of injuries and self-doubt disappeared in one lap around the MCG, with Pittman dominating her seven rivals to stop the clock at 53.82sec.

Any doubts about whether Australia was behind the hurdles champion evaporated （消失）before, during and after the race, with Pittman the queen of the 'G (运动会女王).

"This is the greatest experience of my life and it was the Australian crowd that lifted me," an emotional Pittman said.

Part IV Glimpses of the Superstars

"When I came out on the track I tried so hard to not smile, and stay focused. But I couldn't help it. I heard that roar and it made me so proud to be Australian."

"It was sensational. I tried so hard to keep a low profile (保持低调) before this race. I am such a misunderstood person. I just thought if I do my talking on the track, I can turn that around (扭转人们对我的误会). I am such a proud Aussie (澳洲人) and I want to be there for everybody."

"Tonight showed that the people of our country love their sport, love their heroes."

It was the Pittman of old as she sprang from the blocks in lane six and put her stamp on the race after two hurdles.

By the end of the back straight (非终点直道) she was cruising and the race was basically over. A slight stutter (步履不稳) at the final hurdle not a problem given silver medallist Natasha Danvers Smith (55.17) was 5m away and Scotland's bronze medallist Lee McConnell (55.25), out of the picture (没在电视画面之内).

"I felt electric (兴奋;刺激) down the back straight. I've never felt like that before. It was pretty sensational," Pittman said. "In some ways I feel a lot of relief because I was very nervous."

"I wanted it so much it was ridiculous, but I knew I had to do the process to get the outcome and the hardest part was trying to keep focus on the start line because the crowd was pretty amazing."

Pittman revealed she had read Olympic champion Cathy Freeman's column (专栏) in the *Herald Sun* (墨尔本当地报纸), which had explained how she handled the pressure of the Sydney Olympics.

"It was about keeping it simple and that's what I did," she said.

Her recent hamstring (肌腱) tightness meant she was forced to put aside her dream of breaking Debbie Flintoff-King's national record of 53.17 in front of 83,000 screaming fans in the final of the Commonwealth Games.

After so much time devoted to Pittman and her off-field dramas, Thursday night showed it was time to focus on the athlete again.

At 23, Pittman is already a two-time world junior champion, a world youth champion, world champion, Olympic finalist and two-time Commonwealth champion.

In the past two years she had lost faith in her body and mind because of the injuries and the associated problems after changing her life around following the Athens Olympics debacle (溃败) in 2004.

After a knee injury ruined that campaign—she miraculously (奇迹般地) made it to the final and finished fifth—she parted with coach Phil King and hooked up with her fiance(未婚夫), English 400m hurdler Chris Rawlinson.

Defending her world title in Helsinki (赫尔辛基，芬兰首都) last year was supposed to be her redemption (救赎), but a back injury three weeks out forced her out.

The lead-up to (在……之前) these Games has been filled with injuries and drama involving her row (口角) with Tamsyn Lewis.

Rawlinson admitted in the lead-up that Pittman needed to win gold for her confidence and to ensure her longevity (资历) in the sport. On Thursday night the world was told Jana Pittman, the athlete, is back.

Relevant Words

cross-country race 越野跑	decathlon 十项全能
marathon 马拉松	pole vault 撑竿跳
putting the shot, shot put 推铅球	sprint 短跑
throwing the discus 掷铁饼	throwing the hammer 掷链锤
throwing the javelin 掷标枪	triple jump, hop step and jump 三级跳

Lesson 8

> 萨莎·科恩(Sasha Cohen)是美国著名花样滑冰运动员,也被公认为是当今世界最优雅的滑冰运动员。她在 2002 年盐湖城冬奥会上名列第四,并在 2003-04 赛季达到个人事业的巅峰:她在三项大满贯赛事中夺冠,在美国全国锦标赛和世锦赛上获第二名。在当年的世锦赛上她第一个使用后外勾点冰三周的技术动作。2006 年科恩第一次获得全美冠军,在 2006 年都灵冬奥会上获银牌,在同年的世界花样滑冰锦标赛上获铜牌。

After Falling, She Rises and Shines

By Sally Jenkins
February 24, 2006
The Washington Post

Turin, Italy—There was no way to prettify[1] it. Everyone fell. On such a night, when the Olympic gold medal in figure skating went to practically the only woman left standing, it seemed right that silver was awarded to the one who did the best job of getting back up again.[2]

There will be a lot of argument as to whether Sasha Cohen deserved her medal. But there is none here. Cohen didn't skate well in the women's long program at the Palavela and she virtually donated the gold medal to Shizuka Arakawa of Japan. But there was something worthwhile, memorable even, in Cohen's performance anyway. It's not often an athlete watches her heart fall out on to the ice, but finds a way to pick it back up again.

Cohen fell in warmups. She fell on her first triple jump[3] of the night, a lutz[4], when she lost her balance and landed on the back of her exquisite[5] little red dress. And then she almost fell again, on a triple flip[6], when she staggered[7] and put both hands on the ice. But somehow Cohen managed to steady herself on that ice, so scarred with skid marks, and stayed upright.[8]

1. prettify /ˈprɪtɪfaɪ/ v. 美化,使漂亮,粉饰

2. ... it seemed right that silver was... 银牌应当之无愧地颁发给了那个摔倒后继续比赛、并且是滑得最好的运动员。

3. triple jump 三周跳
4. lutz /lʊts/ n. 后外勾点冰一周跳(卢茨跳)
5. exquisite /ˈekskwɪzɪt/ a. 高雅的;精致的
6. triple flip 后内点冰三周跳
7. stagger /ˈstæɡə/ v. 摇晃,蹒跚
8. 无论如何,科恩还是设法在冰面上稳定下来,身体保持直立,但对横滑行的痕迹却心有余悸。 skid /skɪd/ n. 横滑行

From that moment on, she began counterpunching.[9] The triples began landing cleanly, like uppercuts.[10] Triple loop[11]. Triple flip. Triple toe[12]. And then two more triple salchows[13]. Five triple jumps in all, before she ended her four-minute free program[14], and skated to the sideboard[15] where she mouthed[16] something to her coach, John Nicks, that looked like, "I tried."

No one would land more triples among the final group of contenders. Not Arakawa, and not the bronze medallist Irina Slutskaya of Russia, who fell hard on her own triple flip, and also skipped other planned jumps.

"I was able to take one step at a time. I was able to believe when everything looked a little dark and gray," Cohen said.[17]

The fact that skaters wear mock evening gowns makes it hard to appreciate what Cohen did. Maybe if her knees were bloody. Maybe if she wasn't such a royal figure in her garnet[18] and gold dress, and maybe if the score[19] of "Romeo and Juliet" hadn't been playing while she was working, it would be easier to convey the grit[20] of her performance. Think of it this way: How often does a quarterback[21] throw two interceptions[22] in the first quarter but come back to throw three touchdowns[23] and make the playoffs? What Cohen did was something similar.

She was fortunate, of course, that most of her rivals skated poorly. "I think it was a gift," Cohen acknowledged. But in that light[24], Cohen's refusal to give up was all the more critical, and instructive.

It partially redeems what has been a frustrating pattern of losses for her.[25] In several major competitions now, Cohen has gone into the free skate as the leader, only to yield medals by falling.[26] She has lost two national titles this way. At the Salt Lake Olympics in 2002, she was in third place after the short program, but failed to medal when she tripped up.[27] She won the short program at the 2004 World Championships, but two-footed a triple in the free skate to lose the gold.[28]

In the short program earlier this week, she laid down a little bit of near-perfection on the ice, to stand in first place.[29] She was ebullient[30] afterward, and it seemed all of her old habits were forgotten. But she turned reclusive[31] on Wednesday, skipping two practice sessions to stir rumors[32] that she was injured.

According to Nicks, she was simply tired and balked at[33] returning to the ice.

9. 从那一刻开始，她的状态开始改善。counterpunch /ˈkauntəˌpʌntʃ/ v. 回击
10. 三周跳落地干净利落，就像拳击手打出的上钩拳。
11. triple loop 后外结环三周跳
12. triple toe 三周点冰
13. triple salchow 后内结环三周跳
14. free program 自由滑项目
15. sideboard /ˈsaidbɔːd/ n. 滑冰场边的挡板
16. mouth /mauθ/ v. 做口形；无声地说
17. 科恩说："我那时只能采取一个措施。当情况不利的时候，我还能相信自己。"
18. garnet /ˈgɑːnɪt/ n. 深红色
19. score /skɔː/ n. 音乐
20. grit /grɪt/ n. 勇气，刚毅；不屈服的精神
21. quarterback /ˈkwɔːtəbæk/ n. (橄榄球)四分卫
22. interception /ˌɪntəˈsepʃən/ n. 中途夺取，拦截
23. touchdown /ˈtʌtʃdaun/ n. 触地得分
24. in that light 从另一个角度看
25. 这为她部分地挽回了最初令人沮丧的失败局面。
26. 科恩在自由滑中已经处于领先地位，但跌倒使她丧失了奖牌。在本句中，动词不定式短语表示意料之外的结果。
27. to trip up 绊倒，使失败
28. ... but two-footed a triple in the... 但在自由滑的三周跳中却双脚着地，痛失金牌。
29. 在本周初的自由滑项目中，她降低了在冰上的完美标准，首先要确保自己不摔倒。
30. ebullient /ɪˈbuliənt/ a. 热情高涨的；兴高采烈的
31. reclusive /rɪˈkluːsɪv/ a. 隐遁的，隐居的

Cohen has changed coaches three times and moved from California to New York and back again, in an attempt to cure her bouts with nerves,[34] and solidify her skating. Finally, she returned to her first coach, Nicks, who seems to best understand and accept her temperament[35]. "Sasha Cohen, moody[36]?" he said earlier this week, with gentle sarcasm[37].

It may be that something inside Cohen is temperamentally unsuited to the compressed tensions of figure skating performances.[38] An Olympic gold medal is a single opportunity that is just four minutes long, and which only comes every four years. But it has been fascinating to watch Cohen try to cure herself of her competitive vulnerability[39].

All Olympic athletes talk about delivering their personal bests. But the fact is, it's a hard thing to offer up on command in the cooker of an arena with a gold medal at stake,[40] and Cohen couldn't quite do it. But she can take home something else, and that is the personal knowledge she acquired in those terrible four minutes, the knowledge that while she fell, she would not quit.

"I think as a person I matured," she said. "I was strong through it all. I'm happy with it and just really ecstatic to come home with a medal."

"Personally, the next time I skid out on a patch of bad ice, I hope I recover with half the heart.[41]"

32. to stir rumors 引起谣言
33. to balk at 畏缩，回避
34. 试图用勇气提高比赛成绩。bout /baut/ n. 回合，较量
35. temperament /ˈtempərəmənt/ n. 性情；性格
36. moody /ˈmuːdi/ a. 情绪化的，喜怒无常的
37. sarcasm /ˈsɑːkæzəm/ n. 挖苦，讽刺
38. 科恩的性情有那么一点与花样滑冰表演本身特有的紧张压力不适合。
39. vulnerability /ˌvʌlnərəˈbɪlətɪ/ n. 弱点
40. But the fact is, it's a hard thing to...with a gold medal at stake ... 但事实上，在气氛紧张的竞技场上，当众人都在对金牌觊觎的时刻，呈现个人最佳水平极为困难。at stake 在危险中，处于成败关头
41. ... I hope I recover with half the heart. 我希望我能恢复现在状态的一半就很好了。

Comprehension Questions

1. Why was Cohen's performance considered "something worthwhile and memorable"?
2. What did Cohen say to her coach after her performance?
3. What is the author's attitude to Sasha Cohan's remark, "I was able to take one step at a time. I was able to believe when everything looked a little dark and gray"?
4. Why did Cohen change coaches and the training sites frequently?
5. What is the fundamental reason for Cohen's falls on the ice?

Background Reading

Meissner Is Golden at Worlds

Calgary, Alberta—Add Kimmie Meissner to the list of teenage American champions that includes

Michelle Kwan, Tara Lipinski and Sarah Hughes.

Add another huge disappointment to Sasha Cohen's resume (履历).

The 16-year-old Meissner pulled off (努力实现,赢得) one of the biggest upsets in World Figure Skating Championships history with the performance of her life Saturday. She joined Kwan and Lipinski among U.S. teens who won a world crown, and Hughes, of course, was the 2002 Olympic champion at age 16.

"I am so happy with myself; it's an awesome (非常好的) feeling," said Meissner, who was sixth last month in Turin. "I really wanted to do my best at the last competition of the season—smooth sailing right through my program (在比赛中一帆风顺)."

While she soared, Cohen hit rough ice from the beginning, adding to a distressing (悲伤的) trend for the U.S. champion. Another free skate with an international gold medal in reach (伸手可及), and another flop (摔倒) for Cohen.

"It's frustrating and disappointing," said Cohen, who landed only two clean jumps and fell on her final one, a salchow (后内结环一周跳). She also was credited (相信,认为) for a jump combination she never completed. "But I know I gave it my best effort."

"A few years ago, I used to cry, but I used up all my tears. I am disappointed."

Japan's Fumie Suguri was second, adding to her nation's medals haul in international events this season. Shizuka Arakawa won the Olympics when Cohen blew her lead after the short program, and Mao Asada won the Grand Prix championship.

Meissner was as sensational (引起轰动的) as Cohen was weak. She landed seven triple jumps, including two triple-triple combination—the only ones of the day—just a few minutes after Cohen self-destructed (自我毁灭,此处指摔倒).

Even before Meissner was done with (完成) her final spin (旋转), she was smiling widely, knowing she couldn't have done any better. She lingered (逗留) on the ice, her arms raised to the rafters (体育馆上排的座位), where she was certain her mother was sitting "because she can't stand (忍受) to be too close to the ice."

"This blows the rest of the programs out of the water (她的出色表现使其他选手黯然失色)," she said, still breathless over a routine that earned a personal-best 129.70 points, easily the most (最高分) in the free skate. That gave Meissner nearly a 10-point margin (差额) over Cohen, who'd led her countrywoman by 5.58 after the short program.

Meissner carried an American flag around the ice after receiving her medal. She stood at attention (立正站立) on the top of the podium and sang "The Star-Spangled Banner," (《星条旗》,美国国歌) the smile never fading (脸上一直挂着笑容).

It was another big letdown(失望) for Cohen, whose career is marked by faltering (衰退) in the major internationals. In Turin, she felt she was given a gift when she won silver despite a mediocre (普普通通的) free skate.

Cohen also slipped (下跌,滑落) from third to fourth in the 2002 Olympics, has two runner-up (亚军) finishes at worlds, and has never beaten Michelle Kwan at nationals (国内比赛).

"I struggled through it," she said. "The quality wasn't there. I didn't really feel on (我感觉自己的

Part IV Glimpses of the Superstars

状态不佳). I'm a little tired."

　　Meissner's gold and Cohen's bronze gave the United States the most medals at the event. Evan Lysacek won a men's bronze, Tanith Belbin and Ben Agosto got bronze in ice dancing.

　　Emily Hughes scored a personal-best 104.84 in her free skate, securing a top 10 in her first senior worlds. It was a nice way to finish off (结束) the year in which she was third at nationals, seventh in Turin and then eighth here.

Relevant Words

arabesque spin　燕式旋转	bracket jump　括弧跳
camel spin　燕式旋转	cartwheel lift　侧翻举
change-double-three　双刃变"3"字形	chassé step　侧快滑步
death spiral backward outside　后外螺旋线	half loop jump　后外结环一周跳(异足起落)
prescribed pattern dance　规定成套舞蹈	

Lesson 9

> 安德烈·阿加西(Andre Agassi)，美国职业网球运动员，1995年4月10日首次登上球王宝座，前世界排名第一。他也是现今唯一一位职业金满贯(Career Golden Slam)男子单打网球运动员。阿加西擅长底线抽击，而且具有极强的接发球能力，打法适合各种场地。他被誉为90年代中期最佳底线球员，曾与前球王桑普拉斯(Peter "Pete" Sampras)主宰了90年代的男子网坛。

Andre the Mastermind[1]

By Chip Le Grand
January 24, 2004
The Australian

There is an Andre Agassi match that Craig O'Shannessy has watched 200 times. It is not one of the Agassi-Sampras classics.[2] Not even an Agassi-Rafter[3] epic[4]. It is a match against Scott Draper[5] in the final of a relatively minor ATP[6] tournament six years ago, a match Draper probably wishes he hadn't seen the first time.

O'Shannessy is a tennis coach from Albury, NSW[7], now plying[8] his trade in the US. Every time he takes charge of a new player he sits them down to watch the Agassi-Draper match.

It is not to show them Agassi's phenomenal return of serve or precision forehand.[9] Anyone who has watched Agassi can appreciate these things. It is not to teach them about footwork[10] and fundamentals[11], though Agassi's are as good as anyone's.

It is to show them how Agassi thinks through a point and outthinks an opponent.[12] To reveal the workings inside that neatly shaved head which some time today will be plotting the demise of another hapless opponent en route to another Australian Open title.[13]

Any player can do the work Agassi does; the work on court, the work in the gym, the work dragging tyres up that oft-mentioned[14] hill behind his Las Vegas home in preparation for another Australian summer. But even if they did the work, it would not be enough. Just like the generation of basketballers who wanted to be like Mike[15], today's players need to think like Andre.

---

1. mastermind /ˈmɑːstəmaɪnd/ *n.* 智多星；大智的人
2. 这场比赛并不是阿加西和桑普拉斯之间的一场经典鏖战。Sampras，即Pete Sampras，皮特·桑普拉斯，美国著名职业网球运动员。在ATP职业赛生涯中，连续六年(1993—1998年)名列年终世界排名第一。
3. Rafter，即Patrick Rafter，帕蒂克·拉夫特，澳大利亚职业网球运动员(1991—2002年)，前世界排名第一。
4. epic /ˈepɪk/ *n.* 史诗；可写成史诗的事迹(这里指精彩的比赛)
5. Scott Draper 斯各特·德瑞普(澳大利亚职业网球运动员兼高尔夫球运动员)
6. ATP (Association of Tennis Professionals)国际职业网球联合会的缩写
7. NSW (New South Wales 的缩写)新南威尔士(澳大利亚的一个州)
8. ply /plaɪ/ *v.* 从事(某项)工作；经营
9. 这并不是向他们展示阿加西出色的接发球或精准的正手球。phenomenal /fɪˈnɒmɪnəl/ *a.* 非凡的；杰出的

"If I could take off his skull and look inside his brain at what is going on, that's when you'd understand where every shot goes, why it is going there and how well he understands his opponents," O'Shannessy said. "He understands his opponents much more than his opponents understand their own game."

If only.[16] Like the rest of us, O'Shannessy has no direct access to Agassi's inner thoughts and processes. But what O'Shannessy has been doing this Australian Open, along with fellow coach Alan Curtis, is to chart with computer software the patterns in Agassi's shots and strategies.[17]

They are no closer to finding a foolproof way to beat Agassi.[18] For all the hours spent in the stands of the Rod Laver Arena, they have exposed no glaring[19] weakness in his game.

What they have discovered is a better understanding of what Agassi does and why he does it. Against Czech qualifier Tomas Berdych in the second round, for example, O'Shannessy and Curtis discovered an extraordinary grouping of Agassi returns[20] whenever he was receiving on his backhand[21] from the deuce court[22]. Nearly every return landed slightly to the backhand side of the Czech, and well inside the sideline[23]. He did not hit one winner[24].

What O'Shannessy and Curtis realised was that the game's best returner of serve had decided not to attack the serve directly, but to draw his opponent into rally[25] after rally. From there, the percentages were always with Agassi.[26] With every shot, Agassi would slightly improve his position and Berdych would lose ground. And so on until he faltered, or Agassi found an open court[27].

Against Thomas Enqvist yesterday, one of only a few current players to have a winning record against Agassi before this match, the plan was brutally simple. Computer grouping of his return revealed his key objective was to rally on the backhand side. Then at a moment invariably[28] of Agassi's choosing, Enqvist would be sent scurrying[29] across court. Enqvist has a great forehand, but he only got to use it at the least opportune times.[30]

Enqvist did not win a point until the fourth game and ended up in a 6-0 6-3 6-3 rout[31].

"Usually I have been able to play pretty well against him," Enqvist said. "Against another player, he is going to give you a few chances to get back into the match. When Andre is up, he will not give you anything."

10. footwork /ˈfʊtwɜːk/ n. 步法；脚步动作
11. fundamental /ˌfʌndəˈmentl/ n. 原理；原则（这里指基本功）
12. 这是为了向他们显示阿加西是如何通过一个得分去思考并且智胜对手的。
    outthink /aʊtˈθɪŋk/ v. 智胜；以思维敏捷胜过
13. 这是为了向他们显示那个头顶光光的脑袋在不停地思考。没准儿今天又会盘算着如何阻止一个倒霉蛋对手获得澳网冠军。本句为省略句，句首省略了 It is。 workings /ˈwɜːkɪŋz/ n. 工作方式 plot /plɒt/ v. 策划；密谋 demise /dɪˈmaɪz/ n. 终结；结束 hapless /ˈhæpləs/ a. 倒霉的，不幸的
14. oft-mentioned /ˌɒftˈmentʃənd/ a. 经常提到的
15. 此处的 Mike 指 NBA 巨星迈克尔·乔丹 (Michael Jordan)。
16. 要是能这样就好了。
17. O'shannessy 在今年的澳网期间所做的就是和他的同事阿兰·克蒂斯 (Alan Curtis) 教练一道，借助电脑软件将阿加西的击球和战术用图表的方式展现出来。chart /tʃɑːt/ v. 制图
18. 他们完全没能找到一个简单易行的办法击败阿加西。
    foolproof /ˈfuːlpruːf/ a. 有效的；简单的，连笨人也能做的
19. glaring /ˈɡleərɪŋ/ a. 明显的
20. return /rɪˈtɜːn/ n. 回击球
21. backhand /ˈbækhænd/ n. 反手
22. deuce court 右区
23. sideline /ˈsaɪdlaɪn/ n. 边线
24. winner /ˈwɪnə/ n. 制胜球
25. rally /ˈræli/ n. 连续对打；对网
26. 这样，阿加西的得分率总是很高。

What both these examples show is the depth to which Agassi constructs his points.

After Agassi beat Yevgeny Kafelnikov to win the 2000 Australian Open, he was asked about the points he had won with two stunning drop shots[32]. The answer provided a glimpse into the Agassi psyche[33]. "He's a good mover and plays five metres behind the baseline. I thought if I could get him to come in a bit, it would make my power game more effective."[34]

The endgame[35] was not the drop-shot winner, it was keeping Kafelnikov closer to the baseline in rallies so Agassi could hurt him with his ground strokes[36]. With Agassi, it is not the winner you see which is necessarily doing the damage. For every shot a purpose, but the purpose is not always immediately clear.

The great advantage Agassi has is that not many players think about tennis this way. They think mainly of their own game. They come into post-match press conferences and speak of it in isolation, as if one opponent is interchangeable[37] with the next.

With Agassi, no two game plans are the same. Paradom Srichaphan beat him in their only meeting at Wimbledon and will require a different strategy altogether when the pair meet tomorrow. Agassi's game starts with the weaknesses of those he plays. For him, tennis is a zero-sum game[38]. When he comes into post-match press conferences, he talks about his opponents, for they are foremost in his mind.

"You go out there with a real clear awareness as to what it is you need to do, what it is you need to worry about, the dynamic you want to set up from the baseline," he explained after thrashing[39] Enqvist. "When you play each other so many times, you are sensitive to those subtle changes that happen throughout the course of a match. You constantly feel like you are making adjustments to get it back to the terms[40] that you are looking for."

"I felt like when he hit a good ball, I was staying strong on my shots. I wasn't letting him back me up[41]. When I got control of the point, I felt like I was keeping control. Thomas has a big game. If I'm not hitting the ball sharply and I'm not moving well, he can let one ball go and get a big advantage in the point."

Agassi can be beaten, even at Melbourne Park. When Pat Rafter played here in 2001, he matched Agassi shot-for-shot and thought-for-thought before severe cramping[42] set in[43]. But to find the

27. open court 空档(这里指阿加西找到了对手的漏洞所在)
28. invariably /ɪnˈveərɪəblɪ/ ad. 不变地,总是
29. scurry /ˈskʌri/ v. 急跑;急转
30. Enqvist 的正手技术极好,可是他只能在最不恰当的时机得以施展一二。Thomas Enqvist 托马斯·恩奎斯特,瑞典网球运动员。opportune /ˈɒpətjuːn/ a. 恰好的;时机适宜的
31. rout /raʊt/ n. 溃败
32. drop shot 放小球;短球;网前球
33. psyche /ˈsaɪki/ n. 心理状态;想法
34. 他移动迅速,擅长在底线5米后打球。我想如果我把球打进内场,我的力量会发挥得更有效。baseline /ˈbeɪslaɪn/ n. 底线
35. endgame /ˈendɡeɪm/ n. 比赛最后阶段
36. ground stroke 击触地球,打落地球
37. interchangeable /ˌɪntəˈtʃeɪndʒəbəl/ a. 可以相互替换的;雷同的
38. zero-sum game 零和游戏(指一个参与方的收益相等于另一参与方的损失,变化净额永远是零)
39. thrash /θræʃ/ v. 击溃;彻底打败
40. term /tɜːm/ n. 条件
41. to back up 倒退,后退(这里指退到后场接球)
42. cramp /kræmp/ v. 抽筋,痉挛
43. to set in 开始,出现

last time Agassi did lose in Melbourne, you need to go back five years. Too long you might think, for a tennis player to have any recollection[44] of how it felt.

  Not so with Agassi. In that neatly shaved cranium[45], there is a special compartment[46] even for this. "I'm way[47] too experienced not to realise how on the line you play, you walk, every single match," he said. "I don't know how it looks from the outside. I can tell you that it is hard work and I'm absolutely relieved every time I put together[48] a good match here."

44. recollection /ˌrekəˈlekʃən/ *n.* 回忆,回想
45. cranium /ˈkremiəm/ *n.* 头颅
46. compartment /kəmˈpɑːtmənt/ *n.* 隔间;部分
47. way /weɪ/ *ad.* 在很大程度上;非常
48. to put together 完成;创造

Comprehension Questions

1. Which match does Craig O'Shannessy always ask his new trainees to watch?
2. What does O'Shannessy think his new trainees can learn from this match?
3. What makes Agassi distinguished from other tennis players?
4. What have O'Shannessy and Curtis found in the charted patterns of Agassi's shots and strategies?
5. What do you think is the foremost factor for an athlete to win?

Background Reading

Agassi Feels Pinch (压力) in Swift Exit

  When his latest and quite possibly last French Open began on Tuesday, the ageing but still eager Andre Agassi was playing too quickly, rushing his serves and his shots. By the end, he was moving too slowly, the inflamed (发炎的) sciatic nerve (坐骨神经) in his lower back sounding alarms in his right hip and down his right leg.

  It has been quite some time since Agassi had the right balance on the world's most famous clay (粘土) court, and his 7-5, 4-6, 6-7 (6-8), 6-1, 6-0 loss to the Finnish qualifier Jarkko Nieminen did nothing to restore (恢复) his equilibrium (平衡).

  "I mean, if I feel this way, it's impossible," Agassi said after stumbling in the first round at the French Open for the second consecutive year.

  Even at two sets to one up, Agassi had been feeling sharp pain for several games and was already considering walking to the net and retiring. "To serve was painful; to move, to stand, then even to sit," he said.

  It was hard to watch for those who have seen him at his best. At the age of 35, Agassi has experienced the range of emotions here on the dusty rectangle (长方形,指网球场地) that was built to provide a grand stage for the four French musketeers (士兵,此处指网球运动员) to defend the Davis Cup in the 1920s.

Agassi has been playing at Roland Garros so long that centre court is now named for Philippe Chatrier, a former president of the French Tennis Federation who died in 2000 and whom Agassi called "a bozo (家伙)" in his less-diplomatic youth.

Agassi made his breakthrough in a grand slam event at the French Open, reaching the semi-finals at age 18, and he cemented (巩固) his place in the game's history when he won here in 1999—it was the one grand slam title missing from his resume.

The mixture of joy and shock on Agassi's face when he finally won is hard to forget, but it will also be hard to shake the memories of the past two years.

"It's not something where we're figuring that it's time to stop," Gil Reyes, Agassi's long-time conditioning (体能) coach and close friend, said. "We just know that we have to make some adjustments maybe to make sure that he goes out in the manner he deserves."

He added: "I hope it's not a doctor who decides it's time for him to finish."

For the last two seasons, Agassi has been bothered by recurring (复发的) pain in his right hip, a problem he said had recently been traced to his sciatic nerve. The condition kept him away from Wimbledon last season and he almost missed this year's Australian Open.

He had a cortisone (可的松) injection in the nerve in February, but was convinced he could make it through the French Open without another injection.

With Wimbledon looming (临近) next month, Agassi said it was time for another injection, and he has been told he can have as many as three in a year.

"If I'm getting a few months out of it, it's fair enough for me," he said.

But the prospect of regular painkillers also raises the question of whether it is time to start thinking about life after competitive tennis. Agassi is clearly weary (厌倦) of discussing retirement, but at this stage of his career, he must deal with it in every interview. He refuses to set a date, but he came closer to a timetable this week. "I'll assess the necessary components at the end of the year," he said. "But I can't afford to pollute the potential of my winning matches or tournaments with sitting on the fence (迟迟不做决定), with where I am, what I'm doing, why I'm doing it."

On Tuesday, Agassi set a men's record for the open era by playing in his 58th major, surpassing Michael Chang, Jimmy Connors, Ivan Lendl and Wayne Ferreira. But that will not be why this year's French Open will stick (深陷) in his memory.

Relevant Words

chopped ball 削球	defensive volley 防御性截击空中球
drop volley 空中轻轻截击使球刚过网就落地	forty-love 三比零
hit the ball on the run 奔跑中击球	long swing 大抡拍
pass 超身球	punch volley 短平击球
money point 一场中的决胜分, 赛点(西方称法)	
net ball 落网球;不过网的球;擦网球	
outside approach shot 开放式随上球,外角上网反弹球	

Lesson 10

迈克尔·舒马赫(Michael Schumacher,1969—)著名德国一级方程式赛车车手,被称为二代车神。随着与法拉利车队合约的到期,2007年赛季法拉利的车手阵容及天王接班人成为F1时下最热门的话题之一,而舒马赫也将在最近几个月决定是否退休。但据说法拉利车队已经提供了一纸为期两年、价值8660万美金的合约,正等着舒马赫签署。

Schumacher's Race Not Over Yet as New Talent Arrives on Grid

By Alan Jones[1]
March 31, 2006
The Age

He may be the oldest bloke[2] in Sunday's formula one race[3] at Albert Park[4], but I'm not convinced we have seen the end of Michael Schumacher's winning ways.

He could come down a couple of notches[5] and still be better than most drivers going around in a grand prix[6] car. He is that good at all facets[7] of formula one.

Knowing Michael, I believe that as long as he has made up his mind to keep putting his bum[8] in car then he'll be a competitive force; he knows no other way. And more than anyone, Michael will know the moment when he's had enough[9] and he'll be the first to say goodbye. I can't ever imagine the Ferrari[10] management needing to tap Michael on the shoulder and say it's time to go.

While last season was bleak[11] by their own standards, Schumacher and Ferrari have made a fresher start to 2006 with the new V8 rules. And they have won at Albert Park four of the past six years.

And I know that championship leader Fernando Alonso has wisely not written Schumacher off this weekend, suggesting that he might be his strongest challenger.[12]

Just how competitive Schumacher and Ferrari will be may depend on cool weather, given that this year's race is a month later than usual. Ferrari's Bridgestone tyres are often not at their optimum[13] in cooler

1. Alan Jones 于 1980 年赢得了世界赛车锦标赛冠军。
2. bloke /bləuk/ *n.* [俚语]人,家伙
3. formula one race 一级方程式赛车
4. Albert Park 公园名,位于墨尔本市中心,以景色优美著称。
5. 他的水平可能有所下降。
   notch /nɒtʃ/ *n.* [口语]等,级
6. grand prix 国际汽车大奖赛
7. facet /ˈfæsɪt/ *n.* 方面
8. bum /bʌm/ *n.* [口语]屁股
9. have enough (of) 受够了,再忍受不住了
10. Ferrari /fəˈrɑːriː/ *n.* 法拉利(车队名)
11. bleak /bliːk/ *a.* 没有希望的;惨淡的
12. 并且据我所知,联赛领先人物阿隆索(Fernando Alonso)很明智,没有预先断定舒马赫将在本周末的比赛上失利,说明舒马赫也许仍是他最强有力的挑战者。
13. at the optimum 在最佳状态

conditions but I'm sure they have options to overcome that on a track at which they have a huge data bank.

In a career that I hugely admire, I have only once seen something with Schumacher that I don't quite understand. Just why didn't he push to force his way past teammate Felipe Massa in Malaysia two weeks ago—and why didn't Ferrari invoke[14] the usual team orders?

The answers are not something Ferrari is willing to share.

In any case, time will not wait for Schumacher and while he contemplates[15] the best moment to walk away from F1, he faces the increasing challenge from the young charges[16].

The latest of those is German Nico Rosberg, who at 20 years of age is the most promising rookie since Alonso.

His father Keke, world champion with Williams in 1982, was one of the hardest I raced against and if Nico has inherited any of that fire then he will have a bright future.

After races in Bahrain[17] and Malaysia, I'm impressed by Rosberg, who is already a step ahead of his father—he's taller and better looking.

I believe Rosberg has the bravado[18] and talent to keep teammate Mark Webber honest this year and that can only be a good thing for the competitiveness of the Williams team.

I was a little surprised to hear that after the Malaysian GP, Rosberg had received a mild rebuke[19] from the team because he squeezed[20] Webber for room at the start and into turn one. Mark showed he is more than capable of looking after himself and I encourage Nico to show the drivers that he will not be an easy touch[21].

As long as he doesn't punt[22] his teammate off, then I think Williams should be careful not to discourage Rosberg from having a go[23]—it will stand him in good stead[24] the first time he is charging into turn one against someone such as Schumacher.

One of Rosberg's strengths is the enormous amount of international racing and test mileage[25] he has completed from karting[26] through the junior categories[27] and now F1. And he is a bright young lad.

Over recent years, the Williams team has made all its new drivers sit an engineering test[28] paper to evaluate their understanding of formula one and Williams technical director Patrick Head tells me that young Nico topped the class.

How things have changed. I would have flunked[29] any such test

14. invoke /ɪn'vəʊk/ v. 行使；实行

15. contemplate /'kɒntəmpleɪt/ v. 凝视；沉思
16. young charges 被照料的孩子（这里指年轻的选手）

17. Bahrain /bɑː'reɪn/ n. 巴林岛

18. bravado /brə'vɑːdəʊ/ n. 表面上的自信；虚张的勇气

19. rebuke /rɪ'bjuːk/ n. 指责；谴责；非难
20. squeeze /skwiːz/ v. 挤；紧握

21. easy touch 有求必应的人，容易受骗的人
22. punt /pʌnt/ v. 踢（从手中扔下而未着地的足球）
23. to have a go 进行尝试
24. to stand sb. in good stead 给某人好处，对某人有利
25. mileage /'maɪlɪdʒ/ n. 里程数
26. kart /kɑːt/ v. 开赛车
27. junior category 少年组
28. to sit a test 参加考试

29. flunk /flʌŋk/ v. 失败；考试不及格；放弃

paper in my day at Williams, so I'm glad this is only a recent innovation.

No doubt Rosberg's engineering intelligence would be invaluable in a post-race de-brief[30], but I'm unconvinced it would assist any driver to go quicker through a flat-in-fifth-gear 220 km/h corner. Sometimes the thicker[31] the driver, the quicker he is—I know I would have flunked Patrick Head's test paper. But technology now rules[32] F1 and Rosberg is part of the future of the sport.

30. post-race de-brief 赛后汇报情况
31. thick /θɪk/ *a.* 愚笨的;愚钝的智力上缺乏灵活性的
32. rule /ruːl/ *v.* 裁决;决定

Comprehension Questions

1. What was Schumacher's performance in recent years' races?
2. What adjustments have Ferrari management and the auto racers made to revert the bleak performance?
3. Why was Rosberg rebuked by his teammates?
4. Which strength of Rosberg's is mentioned in the text?
5. In pushing the teammates to force the way forward, Schumacher was compared with Rosberg. What was the writer's real intention?

Background Reading

Michael Schumacher: "We Can Now Be Confident for Other Races"

Sepang (雪邦国际赛车场,位于马来西亚)—With temperatures in the high thirties, even the ice cool Michael Schumacher had to take a break from the media scrum (争抢) that surrounded him as he spoke to the media for the first time since finishing second in last Sunday's opening race. "I was very happy with the result in Bahrain. We were not expecting to be in a position to fight for the win, even if we thought we could be up there looking to finish on the podium (领奖台)," said the Scuderia Ferrar Marlboro driver. "It was very close and we just missed the win, but we can now be confident for other races this season."

A year can make a big difference in terms of car performance as Schumacher reminded his audience. "Last year we had one of our worst races of the season in Sepang and this year we have good reason to be optimistic that we can leave here happy. Tyres will be a key factor this weekend and that is the big question mark. But I think we should be strong here on this front. As for the engine, all we can do is open the vents (排气口) on the bodywork (车体) more to improve cooling (冷却)." On the engine front, Felipe Massa needed an engine change after the first race and David Coulthard's Ferrari engine also had to be replaced. "Naturally, I am a little bit concerned (担心的)", admitted Michael. "But we have checked everything and to date (到目前为止), it is looking good. So there is no reason to be worried."

Schumacher's best memory of Bahrain was the return to form (恢复状态) which seems to have been confirmed. "Driving the new car was great. It was good to be back fighting again and I liked the new qualifying (合格的，有资格的) format. I think those people who were on the podium and Jenson Button, who finished fourth in Bahrain, will be the ones fighting for the championship this year. The fact that we tested in Bahrain in February obviously helped a bit in that we immediately found the right set-up (计划，安排). But the question is did the others have more potential in their cars or not: I don't think so, so the testing we did was not really an advantage in the race. So there is no real reason to be less confident here in Malaysia, other than (除了) there are five cars that are very close here, so a little mistake could make the difference between first and tenth. It will be interesting to see."

Relevant Words

automotive engine system 引擎系统	combustion chamber 燃烧室
crankshaft gear 曲轴齿轮	crankshaft 曲轴
cylinder head 汽缸盖	detonation 爆震
displacement 排气量	engine 引擎
float level 浮筒油面高度	four-stroke cycle 四行程引擎

Lesson 11

兰斯·阿姆斯特朗(Lance Armstrong)是一名退役的美国公路自行车赛职业车手。他于1992年开始职业自行车生涯,1999年世界排名第七,并于当年获得环法大赛的车手总成绩冠军。之后直到2002年,他又连续三次夺冠。到2003年为止,阿姆斯特朗共8次参加环法,4次夺得总冠军,15次夺得赛段冠军。他在1996年10月参加世界顶级公路赛时被诊断患了癌症,但经过3个月的化疗和一年多的停赛休养,阿姆斯特朗于1998年2月康复,并在其后创造了环法大赛四连冠的奇迹,被人们称为"环法英雄"。自从阿姆斯特朗在比赛中成绩领先穿上黄色领骑衫之后,有关他服用禁药的传言就没有中断过。但是,每站比赛后药检的科学数据却显示:在他的尿样中,只含有十亿分之零点二的合成类固醇,远远低于国际自行车联合会规定的尿检中十亿分之十以上合成类固醇为断定车手是否服用违禁药物的标准。

Armstrong Blames "Setup[1]" for Charges

By Agence France-Presse
August 27, 2005
International Herald Tribune

Facing the most serious doping allegations[2] of his career, Lance Armstrong has vehemently[3] denied the charges[4] and attacked what he called lapses[5] in antidoping protocol[6] that allowed a French newspaper to gain access to his stored urine samples[7] from the 1999 Tour de France[8].

Armstrong said on Thursday that something was wrong with an antidoping system that allowed his six-year-old urine samples to be retested after they were supposed to have been stored anonymously[9].

"This thing stinks[10]," he said. "It's not good for me. The unfortunate thing is that you're dealing with something you could be faced with the rest of your life. Protocol wasn't followed, and there was no backup sample[11] to confirm what they said was a positive[12] test."

He said he believed many were at fault[13], from L'équipe[14],

1. setup /ˈsetʌp/ *n.* 骗局
2. doping allegation 服用兴奋剂的断言
3. vehemently /ˈviːəməntli/ *ad.* 激烈地,强烈地
4. charge /tʃɑːdʒ/ *n.* 控诉;指控;控告
5. lapse /læps/ *n.* 失误;疏忽
6. antidoping protocol 反兴奋剂协议
7. urine sample 尿样
8. Tour de France 环法自行车赛
9. anonymously /əˈnɒnɪməslɪ/ *ad.* 不具名地,化名地
10. stink /stɪŋk/ *v.* 讨厌透顶
11. backup sample 储备样本
12. positive /ˈpɒzɪtɪv/ *a.* 阳性的
13. at fault 该受责备的;有罪的
14. L'équipe《队报》,法国报纸

the French sports daily that published the allegations on Tuesday, to the French laboratory involved, the French sports minister[15] and the World Anti-Doping Agency[16].

"There's a setup here and I'm stuck in the middle of it[17]," Armstrong told The Associated Press. "I absolutely do not trust that laboratory."

L'équipe reported on Tuesday that new tests of six urine samples that Armstrong provided during the 1999 Tour had resulted in positive results for the red-blood-cell-booster EPO[18].

Armstrong's comments came after Dick Pound, head of the World Anti-Doping Agency, said officials had received the lab results and would review them. Armstrong also said that although Pound might trust the lab that tested the samples, "I certainly don't."

On Thursday night, Armstrong elaborated[19] on that distrust on the CNN television interview program "Larry King Live[20]."

"A guy in a Parisian[21] laboratory opens up your sample—you know, Jean-François so-and-so[22]—and he tests it—nobody's there to observe, no protocol was followed—and then you get a call from a newspaper that says 'We found you to be positive six times for EPO,'" he said. "Well, since when did newspapers start governing[23] sports?"

Armstrong acknowledged that he was frustrated by the report and the difficulty of proving his case. "All I can do is come on this stage and tell my story and be honest," he said. "I've always done that. Since this stuff's rolled out[24], I sleep great at night. I don't have a problem looking at myself in the mirror."

Armstrong questioned the validity[25] of testing samples frozen six years ago, how those samples were handled since, and how he could be expected to defend himself when the only confirming evidenc—the A sample[26] used for the 1999 tests—no longer exists.

He also asserted[27] that officials at the suburban Paris lab had violated World Anti-Doping Agency regulations for failing to safeguard the anonymity of any remaining B samples it had.

"Nowadays, we all want clean sport[28]," Armstrong told Larry King. "And fortunately, an organization called WADA has come along[29] and has really governed the world of antidoping. They have set about a protocol and a code that everybody has to live by.[30]"

The lab, he added, "violated the code several times."

L'équipe reported on Friday, however, that the lab had kept the

15. sports minister 体育部长
16. 世界反兴奋剂机构,简称 WADA
17. to be stuck in 陷入

18. the red-blood-cell-booster EPO 红血球增长剂 EPO

19. elaborate /ɪˈlæbəreɪt/ v. 详尽阐述
20. Larry King Live 电视节目名称, Larry King 访谈直播。Larry King 节目主持人名。
21. Parisian /pəˈrɪziən/ a. 巴黎的;巴黎人的
22. so-and-so 某某人,某某
23. govern /ˈɡʌvən/ v. 监管;管理

24. to roll out 出现

25. validity /vəˈlɪdəti/ n. 有效性;合法性;正确性
26. A sample A 瓶中的样本(运动员的尿样收集后被分置在 A 瓶和 B 瓶中。如果 A 瓶中的样本检测呈阳性,运动员可提出申请检测 B 瓶中的样本。)
27. assert /əˈsɜːt/ v. 断言;声称
28. clean sport 不服用兴奋剂的"纯净"体育
29. to come along 出现
30. 他们(WADA)制定的条约和条例每个运动员都要遵守。

samples anonymous. The newspaper said its reporters had matched the samples' numbers with the names and numbers in the data from the original 1999 test.

  The French report appears stronger than previous doping allegations raised against Armstrong, Pound said.

  "There's been an awful lot of rumor and accusation about him for a number of years, always of the he-said, she-said variety,[31]" he said. "This appears—I haven't seen the documents myself—to have some documentary connection. That's a lot more serious. It's got to be taken more seriously."

  "If he had one, you could say it was an aberration[32]," Pound said. "When you get up to six, there's got to be some explanation."

  Pound said that the lab is accredited[33] by the International Olympic Committee and that he trusts it handled the samples properly. Pound also questioned the need for two samples to confirm a positive test.

  "You can count on the fingers of one hand the times a B sample has not confirmed the result of the A sample,[34]" he said. "It's almost always a delaying tactic[35]."

  Armstrong said that contradicts WADA's own drug-testing policy.

  "For the head of the agency to say he actually doesn't believe in the code," he said, "if your career is riding on the line, wouldn't you want a B sample?"

  "The French have been after me forever", he said, "and 'Whoops!' There's no B sample? The stakes are too high."

  Pound said the lab had asked WADA months ago if the agency was interested in reviewing its findings[36] and that he had agreed. He said the agency did not expect names to be connected to the findings, but only wanted to see whether the leftover[37] samples from 1999 would show riders had used EPO. "They said it's simply research," Pound said.

  Armstrong said he had submitted 17 test samples in 1999 and wants to know what happened to the 11 others.

  Armstrong, a cancer survivor, believes the accusations have also been fueled by French resentment of his unprecedented cycling success.[38]

  "The story has been too good to be true for them from the very beginning," he said. "Consider my situation: Here is a guy who comes back from a death sentence. Why would I dope?"

---

31. 近几年来对他的谣言和谴责多得可怕，都是"据说"这一类的。

32. aberration /ˌæbəˈreɪʃən/ n. 失常

33. accredit /əˈkredɪt/ v. 授权，认可

34. 你可以扳手指算算 B 瓶不能证实 A 瓶结果的次数。(意为 B 瓶的结果大多数情况下与 A 瓶检测结果一致。)

35. delaying tactic 缓兵之计

36. finding /ˈfaɪndɪŋ/ n. 检查得出的结论（此处意为药检结果呈阳性）

37. leftover /ˈleftˌəʊvə/ a. 剩余的

38. 阿姆斯特朗是一名癌症幸存者，他相信是因为法国人嫉妒他在自行车赛上取得的前所未有的成功，才会对他有这些指控。resentment /rɪˈzentmənt/ n. 怨恨，愤恨

Comprehension Questions

1. What did Armstrong vehemently deny?
2. Whom did Armstrong believe should be blamed?
3. What was Armstrong's response to the French laboratory's statement that he used EPO to boost the red blood cells?
4. Did Pound think the report of the French newspaper valid or not? Why?
5. Based on the knowledge you have obtained from the article, can you name some of the rules concerning anti-doping tests set about by WADA?

Background Reading

The Wheels of Change Turn for Lance Armstrong's Mom, Too

When Linda Armstrong Kelly sent son Lance a copy of her first book, she was worried what he might think.

"Most of the stuff in that book he did not know," she says. "I didn't know if he was going to be embarrassed or mad at me, but I knew I had to write the truth."

One night after a speaking engagement (应邀发表演讲), she got an e-mail from the seven-time Tour de France winner. "Mom, I just finished the book," he wrote. "I couldn't put it down. I had no idea what you have been through (经历). I've been crying while I've been reading it. It answers so many questions I've wondered about."

Immediately, Kelly says, she felt a great sense of relief. "We underestimate (低估) our children and what they think and believe. It was very healing (有治疗功用的) for me." Because she wrote about economic hardships and her life as a teen (十几岁的) mother, Kelly has been able to reach (沟通,交流) others, much the way her son has reached thousands of cancer survivors through his foundation. "The book, *No Mountain High Enough*, was very healing for me," she says by phone from her Texas home. "I wanted to help people so they don't feel ashamed or alone. I felt those things all those years through teenage pregnancy, job declines and challenges. I felt if someone read my story they might think, 'She made it. I can, too.'"

Kelly's example, in fact, was impressed upon her son at an early age. After a particularly tough day at work, she came home and shared her frustration with Lance. "He was in seventh or eighth grade and he said, 'Why don't you quit your job?'" Ever the role model (榜样), Kelly turned to him and said, "Son, don't ever quit."

"I've realized through my experiences you've got to treat others the way you'd like to be treated."

She also learned how valuable support is.

"This has been a long, long journey," she says of Armstrong's rise from BMX biker (小轮自行车手) to cycling icon (偶像). "It didn't happen overnight." Still, Kelly wasn't a pushy parent.

Part IV Glimpses of the Superstars

"Parents have to find something their children are passionate about. Don't make it your goal, make it their goal—whatever it is, sports, music, chess. Your children are dependent on you and your attitude. Follow their passion and do what you can to help them through it."

Kelly's method? She and Armstrong would plan early in the week what they'd do on the weekend—participate in a race, for example. "If he didn't want to get up on Saturday morning, he didn't get off the hook (脱身,此处意为必须起床). He made a commitment. I'm a hard ass," she says with a laugh. "I'd make him go... your word is good." Despite years of frustration, Armstrong kept at cycling and eventually succeeded. Kelly's part? She got him to the races and served as his best cheerleader (啦啦队队长).

Interestingly, he could have gone in another direction. "He loved swimming and running and doing triathlons (三项全能运动;铁人三项)," she says. "One day his swim coach pulled me aside and said, 'Lance could get a scholarship for swimming if he'll give up triathlons'" Kelly talked to her son and he said he didn't want to do it. She understood and told him she would support his decision.

When cycling took hold (扎根;最终确定), she agreed to work weekends to fund his passion. "Cycling is a very expensive sport and we didn't have a lot of money," she says. "But we were a tag team (小团体). I am walking testimony (活生生的例子) that if you make sacrifices for your children they will pay off (回报). I'm living a happy, healthy life. I believe you don't measure your success by the car you drive or the education you've got but by the children you raise and their contribution to society."

When Armstrong retired from professional cycling last year, Kelly was filled with mixed emotions (百感交集). "This is all he has been doing for 20 years," she explains. "To see him announce his retirement was a very emotional experience, but he prepared himself for what he's doing today. His humanitarian (人道主义的) work makes me proud."

Giving back (回馈,回报), she says, is something he learned by watching others. "Out of the blue (突然地;出乎意料地), Lance decided to start a foundation. 'Mom, I want to give back.'"

Bouts with testicular cancer (睾丸癌) that had spread to his lungs and brain threatened to end his cycling career but Kelly never believed they would end his life. "I never gave up hope that he would beat that disease," she says. "I attribute (归因于) that to the positive attitude we both have. I get up every day and realize I have choices. I can either collapse (崩溃) or choose to turn it into an opportunity."

Because she had Lance when she was a teenager, Kelly says "I also grew up with him. We've been very close."

Neither, however, would judge the other's dates (约会对象). "It's not important what you say but how you say it," she says. "I would say, 'I get bad vibes (心灵不沟通)' or 'I get great vibes (心灵相通).' But that's up to him. I'm not somebody who will tell you how I feel about someone."

Besides, Kelly says, if a parent starts offering advice once his or her child is an adult, "it's too late. You have to do the job of a parent before it gets to that"

When she met Ed Kelly five years ago, Lance didn't weigh in (介入). He just knew mom had picked the right man. ("I had been married several times before," she says. "I'm an overachiever in that area.") Introduced by a mutual friend, Ed and Linda had plenty in common. He had lost his wife of 30 years to breast cancer; she struggled through Lance's illnesses.

When they married, he insisted she quit working. "I was blown away (惊讶). My job and career were important to me. I loved being around people."

A global account manager (账目经理) for Telecom, she came up the ranks without a college degree.

Still, the idea of retirement intrigued (吸引) her. Kelly agreed, realizing other opportunities were waiting. Ed Kelly, in fact, suggested she write the book. "He thought it was time I put my stories down in print."

Public speaking, as a result, has also become a big part of her new life. Nerve-wracking (非常伤脑筋的)? Not in the least (一点也不). "I'm from Texas," she says proudly. "We dress up like show dogs."

Like Lance, she realizes success is possible in any arena "as long as you're passionate about it. You've got to find something you're passionate about."

She is, of course.

And she's very proud of her son.

Every Mother's Day, she gets the biggest gift of all—a phone call. "That means more than anything to me. Time is the one thing we don't have enough of."

Spending time with him and her three "bonus" kids (此处指 Ed Kelly 的子女) and grandchildren is the best, she says. Watching Lance excel (优秀) in other arenas is even more fun.

A political career for Lance Armstrong? "You know," mom says with no small degree of pride, "I wouldn't be surprised."

Relevant Words

cycling track 赛车场,(自行车等的)倾斜赛车场	
indoor velodrome 室内自行车赛场	road cycling 公路自行车赛
track cycling 场地自行车赛	sprint 追逐赛
pursuit 争先赛	

Lesson 12

> 麦克斯·施密林(Max Schmeling)(1905—2005)生前为德国重量级拳击运动员,1932获得世界重量级拳击冠军的称号。曾与美国黑人拳击运动员乔·路易斯(Joe Louis)两度交手。施密林在第一次比赛中战胜路易斯,开始被纳粹德国利用,成为希特勒宣扬的"白人优化论"中雅利安人的代表,从而使这场拳击比赛蒙上了政治意义。尽管人们认为施密林与纳粹有关联,并被德国和美国的宣传媒体所利用,但事实证明他在二战中曾经解救过犹太人。直至今日他仍是德国体育界的传奇人物。

German Boxing Legend Max Schmeling

By Louie Estrada
February 5, 2005
The Washington Post

Max Schmeling, 99, the former world heavyweight[1] boxing champion from Germany whose two bouts[2] with Joe Louis in the years leading up to World War II symbolized and ultimately debunked[3] the Nazi's claim to racial superiority[4], died on February 2 at his home in Hollenstedt, Germany. No cause of death was given.

Mr. Schmeling, a tall, swarthy[5] figure, became the first professional fighter to knock out[6] Louis when the two first met in a non-title[7] match at Yankee Stadium in June 1936. At the time, few people expected Louis, a young, undefeated African American boxer known as the "Brown Bomber," to lose to the German fighter, who held the world heavyweight title in the early 1930s.

The upset was the high point in the career of Mr. Schmeling, who had become the first German to hold the world heavyweight title in 1930 when, in a controversial bout, Jack Sharkey—ahead on judges' scorecards——was disqualified for a low blow[8] in the fourth round.

Mr. Schmeling, who once fought for the German equivalent of[9] $5 a fight, was considered over the hill[10] when he knocked out Louis in the 12th round of their first bout.

He then returned to Nazi Germany a national hero and became a symbol of Hitler's master race[11] theory. Although not a member of the

---

1. heavyweight /ˈheviweɪt/ n. 重量级运动员;重量级
2. bout /baʊt/ n. 回合,较量
3. debunk /diːˈbʌŋk/ v. 揭穿;拆穿假面具,暴露
4. racial superiority 人种优越论(希特勒宣言雅利安人是最优秀的种族。)
5. swarthy /ˈswɔːði/ a. 黝黑肤色的;黑色的
6. to knock out 击倒(使对方在规定的时间内不能起立而获胜)
7. non-title /ˌnɒnˈtaɪtl/ a.不争夺冠军(或锦标)的;非冠军(或锦标)赛的
8. low blow 低击(击腰带以下,犯规),腰下拳(击腰带以下部位的拳)
9. equivalent of 相当于;等同于
10. to be over the hill 上年岁的;走下坡路的
11. master race 优等民族

Nazi Party, Mr. Schmeling appeared to bask in[12] the attention and gratitude of the Third Reich[13]. He received a personal appointment[14] from Hitler to serve as an adviser to youth athletic groups. It was a tumultuous[15] time, however, as German troops invaded Austria and the scope of the persecution of Jews[16] began to surface.

Mr. Schmeling, who denied he was an anti-Semite[17], later said that he was exploited by the propaganda machinery[18] of the Nazi regime[19] and explained how he once pleaded with Hitler to allow him to retain his Jewish manager, Joe Jacobs.

In boxing, "We are not conscious of Protestants[20], Catholics, Jews or Negroes.... We are interested only in boxing. It was clear from Hitler's stony silence that he did not like this at all, but I insisted that I needed Herr[21] Jacobs and that so much of what I had achieved in the United States was due to him," Mr. Schmeling said in a 2003 interview with *the Sunday Times* in South Africa.

In 1993, two researchers reported that in 1938, Mr. Schmeling hid two Jewish teenagers from Nazi violence during Kristallnacht[22], when Jews were targeted for killing. The teenagers' father, a friend of Mr. Schmeling's, asked the boxer to hide his sons until the violence subsided[23].

Still, Mr. Schmeling, known as "The Black Uhlan[24] of the Rhine[25]," was widely seen as a Nazi boxer. The buildup[26] to the rematch between Mr. Schmeling and Louis in 1938 reached epic proportions as the two became the human faces of their respective countries' ideals. In one corner, there was Louis and democracy; in the other, Mr. Schmeling and Fascism[27]. Louis, now the world champion, was eager to avenge his only loss. Reviled[28] in the U.S. media as a Nazi, Mr. Schmeling faced protesters at his New York hotel and jeers[29] in the streets.

Before 80,000 people in Yankee Stadium, Louis made good[30] on his promise to finish Mr. Schmeling quickly. Louis stalked[31] Mr. Schmeling at the opening bell, then unleashed a fury of power punches to the body and head that buckled[32] the former champion. A kidney punch[33] from Louis broke Mr. Schmeling's vertebra[34]. Once a skilled counter-puncher[35] compared to the great Jack Dempsey[36], Mr. Schmeling was left bloodied and severely beaten when the fight was stopped a little more than two minutes into the first round.

It would be Mr. Schmeling's last major fight and would be remembered as one of the greatest sports events of the 20th century. Millions around the world listened to a blow-by-blow[37] account on the

12. to bask in 享受乐趣,得到满足
13. Third Reich 第三帝国(指希特勒统治下的纳粹德国)
14. personal appointment 亲自任命
15. tumultuous /tjuːˈmʌltjuəs/ a. 喧嚣的;混乱的
16. persecution of Jews 迫害犹太人
17. anti-Semite /ˌæntɪˈsiːmaɪt/ n. 反犹分子
18. propaganda machinery 宣传机器
19. regime /reɪˈʒiːm/ n. 政权;政体;政权制度
20. Protestant /ˈprɒtɪstənt/ n. 新教徒
21. Herr /hɛə/ n. 先生,阁下(在说德语的地区,加于人的姓或职称之前的礼貌称呼)
22. Kristallnacht [德语]水晶之夜(指 1938 年 11 月 9—10 日德国纳粹党杀害犹太人和抢劫犹太人财产的事件。因暴行后到处是砸碎的玻璃,故有此名。)
23. subside /səbˈsaɪd/ v. 平息;衰减;沉淀
24. Uhlan /ˈuːlɑːn/ n. 枪骑兵(先是属于波兰军队,后来又属于前德国军队的骑兵)
25. the Rhine 莱茵河
26. buildup /ˈbɪldʌp/ n. 累积;集结
27. Fascism /ˈfæʃɪzəm/ n. 法西斯政权
28. revile /rɪˈvaɪl/ v. 辱骂;斥责
29. jeer /dʒɪə/ n. 嘲笑;讥讽;戏弄
30. to make good 成功;实现
31. stalk /stɔːk/ v. 慢慢走近
32. buckle /ˈbʌkəl/ v. 使屈服
33. a kidney punch 对肾打出的一拳
34. vertebra /ˈvɜːtɪbrə/ n. 脊椎骨
35. counter-puncher /ˈkaʊntəˈpʌntʃə/ n. 善于反击的拳击手
36. Jack Dempsey 美国拳击运动员,被认为是拳击史上最有实力最凶狠的重量级拳王之一。
37. blow-by-blow a. 极为详细的

radio.

Mr. Schmeling, who soon fell out of favor with[38] Germany's leaders, eventually was drafted[39] into the Army. He trained as a Nazi parachute infantryman[40] and participated in the aerial invasion of the Greek island of Crete[41]. At one point, he was reported to have been killed while trying to escape British soldiers. Then news came that he was actually in an Athens hospital, recovering from a tropical ailment[42], according to one news report. At the hospital, Mr. Schmeling was promoted to sergeant[43] and awarded the Iron Cross of the second class.

In 1947, after he was cleared of any war crimes, Mr. Schmeling attempted a comeback with a lackluster[44] performance in Kassel, Germany, that failed to impress observers about whether he could again seriously challenge for the title. He had hoped to fight in a series of exhibition bouts in the United States, but his travel visa request was denied after Rep[45]. John R. McDowell of Pennsylvania protested that Mr. Schmeling should not be permitted in the country because of his Nazi service.

Nearly destitute[46], Mr. Schmeling used his ring earnings[47] to buy a Coca-Cola bottling plant in Germany, which he turned into a profitable business. He also operated a farm, where he raised animals for their furs.

"We were the victims of bad propaganda," Mr. Schmeling said at a reunion with Louis in Chicago in 1954. "There never was any bad feeling on my part." The two remained friendly. In 1981, he helped pay for Louis's funeral.

Mr. Schmeling was born in Brandenburg, Germany, the son of a merchant marine officer. He enjoyed wrestling and soccer before taking up boxing as a teenager. He fought as an amateur, then turned professional, eventually winning the European championship.

His wife, the former German film actress Anny Ondra, died in 1987.

38. to fall out of favor with 失宠于
39. draft /drɑːft/ v. 征兵，入伍
40. infantryman /ˈɪnfəntrɪmən/ n. 步兵
41. Crete /kriːt/ n. 克里特岛（希腊东南沿海的一个岛屿，古希腊文明的发源地之一）
42. tropical ailment 热带疾病
43. sergeant /ˈsɑːdʒənt/ n. 中士
44. lackluster /ˈlækˌlʌstə/ n. 无光泽，暗淡
45. Rep. (Representative 的缩写) 众议院议员
46. destitute /ˈdestɪtjuːt/ a. 穷困的，潦倒的
47. ring earnings 在拳击场上赚得的钱

Comprehension Questions

1. What do you expect to learn about Schmeling in the following parts of the text after reading the first paragraph?
2. What was Schmeling's sporting performance before he fought against Louis?
3. What did Schmeling's victory over Louis bring to him in Germany?

4. What may attest Schmeling was not an anti-Semite and he was exploited by the propaganda machinery of the Nazi regime?
5. Can you give a brief account of Schmeling's life based on the newspaper report?

Background Reading

Kristallnacht

Kristallnacht is a German word with the meaning of Crystal Night. It is also called Night of Broken Glass or November Pogroms (大屠杀), the night of November 9–10, 1938, when German Nazis attacked Jewish (犹太人的，犹太族的) persons and property. The name Kristallnacht refers ironically (讽刺地) to the litter of broken glass left in the streets after these pogroms. The violence continued during the day of November 10, and in some places acts of violence continued for several more days.

The pretext(借口，托辞) for the pogroms was the shooting in Paris on November 7 of the German diplomat(外交官) Ernst vom Rath by a Polish-Jewish student, Herschel Grynszpan. News of Rath's death on November 9 reached Adolf Hitler in Munich, Germany, where he was celebrating the anniversary of the abortive (失败的) 1923 Beer Hall Putsch ([德语] 起义, 暴动). There, Minister of Propaganda (宣传) Joseph Goebbels, after conferring (协商) with Hitler, harangued (向……做长篇讲话) a gathering of old storm troopers (纳粹党突击队员), urging violent reprisals (报复) staged to appear as "spontaneous demonstrations (自发组织的示威游行)." Telephone orders from Munich triggered pogroms throughout Germany, which then included Austria.

Just before midnight on November 9, Gestapo ([德]盖世太保, 纳粹秘密警察) chief Heinrich Müller sent a telegram to all police units informing them that "in shortest order, actions against Jews and especially their synagogues (犹太教会堂) will take place in all of Germany. These are not to be interfered with." Rather, the police were to arrest the victims. Fire companies stood by (坐视不管) synagogues in flames with explicit (清楚的) instructions to let the buildings burn. They were to intervene (干涉) only if a fire threatened adjacent (附近的) "Aryan" (雅利安人, 在纳粹德国指犹太人以外的白种人) properties.

In two days and nights, more than 1,000 synagogues were burned or otherwise damaged. Rioters (暴徒) ransacked (掠夺, 洗劫) and looted (掠夺, 抢劫) about 7,500 Jewish businesses, killed at least 91 Jews, and vandalized (摧残, 破坏) Jewish hospitals, homes, schools, and cemeteries (公墓). The attackers were often neighbours. Some 30,000 Jewish males aged 16 to 60 were arrested. To accommodate so many new prisoners, the concentration camps (集中营) at Dachau, Buchenwald, and Sachsenhausen were expanded.

After the pogrom ended, it was given an oddly poetic name: Kristallnacht—meaning "crystal night" or "night of broken glass." This name symbolized the final shattering (破坏) of Jewish existence in Germany. After Kristallnacht, the Nazi regime (政权) made Jewish survival in Germany impossible.

The cost of the broken window glass alone came to millions of Reichsmarks (德国马克). The

Reich(德意志帝国) confiscated(没收,充公) any compensation claims(赔偿金) that insurance companies paid to Jews. The rubble(碎石,瓦砾) of ruined synagogues had to be cleared by the Jewish community. The Nazi government imposed a collective fine(集体罚款) of one billion Reichsmarks (about $400 million in 1938) on the Jewish community. After assessing the fine, Hermann Göring remarked: "The swine(卑贱的人) won't commit another murder. Incidentally(附带地,顺便提及) ... I would not like to be a Jew in Germany."

The Nazi government barred(禁止) Jews from schools on November 15 and authorized local authorities to impose curfews(宵禁令) in late November. By December 1938, Jews were banned from most public places in Germany.

Relevant Words

```
arm feint      手臂虚晃,手臂的假动作
awarding of points   判分,给分
bobbing and weaving   低头闪躲(然后摆出进攻的姿势)
direct hit     直接命中的一拳(击)
flatten        击倒对方使其在规定时间内不能起立
hit and away   (且战且退的)逃避战术
pinning        压住来拳;张开手套压住对方拳头进行阻挠,阻挠
right hook     右钩拳
```

Lesson 13

> 斯蒂芬·布拉布里(Steven Bradbury),原澳大利亚速滑运动员,现已退役。他在 2002 年的盐湖城冬季奥运会上创造了历史,为澳大利亚乃至南半球国家赢得了第一枚冬季奥运会金牌。事实上,他的这枚男子速滑 1000 米金牌出乎所有人的意料。在半决赛中,对手冲撞在一起,令名列最后的他幸运地闯入决赛。决赛中其他四名选手又在最后一个转弯处相撞,布拉布里成为唯一一个站着闯过终点线的运动员。虽然他被称为是"最幸运的金牌得主",布拉布里在获胜后表现出的诚实和谦卑却使他赢得了所有人的喜爱和尊敬。

Accidental Hero

By Greg Baum
February 18, 2002
The Age

Steven Bradbury did not fall off his skates, but he fell on his feet. Yesterday the short-track[1] skater from Brisbane became Australia's first Winter Olympics gold medallist, and one of the most improbable, bizarre[2] and comical[3] winners in Olympic history. No last laugh was ever heartier.

Bradbury looked to have been skated out of the 1,000 metres when he finished third in a quarter-final[4], but survived when second-placed Canadian Marc Gagnon was disqualified[5] for pushing. In a semi-final, he was a long last[6] with a lap[7] to go, only for the other four skaters to trip[8] one another and leave him as the winner.

Against incalculable odds[9], the final ran an identical course. Bradbury was tailing off[10] last when, on the last corner of the last lap, 15 metres from the finish, the four other skaters cannoned[11] into each other and crashed to the ice. As the old cliché goes, Bradbury had only to stand up to win.

Bradbury was not implicated[12] in

1. short-track /ʃɔːtˈtræk/ a. 短道的
2. bizarre /bɪˈzɑː/ a. 奇异的
3. comical /ˈkɒmɪkəl/ a. 好笑的,滑稽的
4. ... he finished third in a quarter-final 在四分之一决赛中他排名第三
5. disqualify /dɪsˈkwɒlɪfaɪ/ v. 使丧失资格
6. a long last 最后一名,远远地落在其他选手后面
7. lap /læp/ n. (跑道的)一圈
8. trip /trɪp/ v. 跌倒,绊倒
9. 出乎所有人的意料
10. to tail off 在数量上逐渐减少 [此处意指(由于速度而被)落在人后]
11. cannon /ˈkænən/ v. 撞击;相撞
12. implicate /ˈɪmplɪkeɪt/ v. 牵扯进

260

the collision; he was in what an American commentator called a 'unique vantage[13] spot' for a winner. Booing filled the stadium, not for Bradbury, but for the pile-up that made fall guys of certain medallists and possibly cost American Apolo Anton Ohno the gold medal.[14] Bradbury's first instinct was to think: "Oh, hang on... this can't be right... I think I won!" His next was to expect a re-race.

Then he had to deal with a piqued[15] spectator who told him to wipe the smile off his face. Bradbury told him some home truths[16] about winners and grinners[17].

Short-track skaters race tightly and frenetically[18] around a 111-metre track, making for many thrills and regular spills[19]. Knowing he was at a pace disadvantage in the semi-final and final, Bradbury said he had deliberately sat back[20] and waited for the tumbles[21]. "It's the nature of the sport, especially at the Olympics," he said.

"Maybe not four guys. But I was expecting two to go down in the final, and maybe to get a bronze.[22]"

Ohno was judged second and Canadian Mathieu Turcotte third. Ohno had six stitches[23] inserted in his leg and Turcotte had a cut on his posterior[24] that made it painful for him to sit down. These were injuries added to insults.

"No one feels great when it happens," said Turcotte, "but it happens." But none begrudged[25] Bradbury.

Bradbury owns the Revolutionary Boot Company in Brisbane, supplying skating boots to, among others, Ohno. On Friday, Bradbury had e-mailed Ohno to say: "If you win gold, make sure you give me a mention[26]!"

Now he could plug himself, live, prime-time, in the US.

Neither Bradbury nor his sport are in the mainstream of Australia's sporting consciousness. None the less, his victory is destined to far outlive[27] its moment. Already the puns have started. Soon enough, anyone who has victory fall into his or her hands will be said to have "done a Bradbury."[28]

This was just Australia's third Winter Olympics medal of any colour.[29] Bradbury was a member of the short-track relay team that won the first, a bronze, at Lillehammer in 1994 in similar circumstances when more fancied teams crashed. Zali Steggall won a bronze in the women's slalom[30] at the last Olympics in Nagano[31].

Bradbury smiled sheepishly throughout the medal presentation, surprised himself by knowing all the words to "Advance Australia

13. vantage /'vɑːntɪdʒ/ n. 优势，有利情况
14. 体育馆内响起一片嘘声，但观众们嘲笑的不是布拉布里，而是那些倒在一起并很可能夺冠的滑冰运动员。这次跌倒也可能使美国运动员阿波罗·安通·奥诺丢掉了就要到手的金牌。
  booing /'buːɪŋ/ n. 嘘声
15. pique /piːk/ v. 生气；愤怒
16. home truth 难以接受的事实
17. grinner /'grɪnə/ n. 露齿而笑的人
18. frenetically /frə'netɪklɪ/ adv. 疯狂地，狂热地
19. spill /spɪl/ n. 跌倒
20. to sit back 宽舒地休息；放松
21. tumble /'tʌmbl/ n. 跌倒；摔跤；翻跟头
22. 但我希望两个人能够在决赛中被淘汰，这样也许我还能得到一块铜牌。
23. stitch /stɪtʃ/ n. 缝针
24. posterior /pɒs'tɪərɪə/ n. 臀部
25. begrudge /bɪ'grʌdʒ/ v. 嫉妒

26. to give sb. a mention 提及某人

27. outlive /aʊt'lɪv/ v. 比……耐久；经受住
28. 当一个人的成功从天而降的时候，人们就会说他做了一件布拉布里做过的事情。
29. 这是澳大利亚曾经获得的第三枚冬季奥运会奖牌。of any colour 指金银铜奖牌的颜色。
30. slalom /'slɑːləm/ n. 障碍滑雪
31. Nagano /nə'gɑːnəʊ/（日本）长野（1998年第18届冬奥会举办地）

261

Fair", called the result "unbelievable" and "freakish"³², but was not going to apologise for it, nor give back his medal.

"I wasn't the fastest skater on the ice tonight," he said. "I was obviously not the most deserving guy. I had a lot of luck on my side. But I won't take the race for the one-and-a-half minutes it was on. I'll take it for the ten years of hard work that I put in. I'll take it as a reward."

Bradbury, 28, is in his fourth and last Olympics. He won world championship relay gold in 1991 and Olympic bronze in 1994. But he also twice suffered horrific injuries.

After a crash in 1994 in Canada, he lost four litres of blood, had 111 stitches in his leg and was lucky to live. Two years ago, after crashing headlong³³ at training, he broke two vertebrae³⁴ and had to wear a halo brace³⁵ for a month.

Last night was a swing to those roundabouts.³⁶

Bradbury celebrated into the small hours³⁷ in a pub called—what else?³⁸—the Last Lap.

32. freakish /ˈfriːkɪʃ/ a. 怪异的
33. headlong /ˈhedlɒŋ/ ad. 头向前地
34. vertebrae /ˈvɜːtɪbrə/ n. 椎骨
35. a halo brace 颈箍
36. 昨夜他的运气有了一个大逆转。swing /swɪŋ/ n. 改变
37. into the small hours 直到凌晨 small hours 复数形式表示午夜之后的时间。
38. What else? (酒吧) 还能叫什么名字呢?

Comprehension Questions

1. Why is Steven Bradbury remarked as one of the most improbable, bizarre and comical winners in Olympic history?
2. What happened to Steven Bradbury in the quarter-final and semi-final?
3. What made Bradbury deliberately sit back and wait for the tumbles in the semi-final and final?
4. How did the Australians view Bradbury and his sport before and after his victory at the Winter Olympic Games?
5. How did Bradbury evaluate his victory?

Background Reading

Ohno Zone Interview—Steven Bradbury

Ohno Zone: Australia isn't known as a Mecca (麦加; 人人渴望去的地方) for winter sports. How did you get started in short track speedskating?

Steven Bradbury: My father was a speed skater and I was introduced at a young age. Short track has never been a popular sport in Australia but it has been around (存在) a long time. The first short track world champion in 1978 was Australian.

I grew up in Sydney and moved to Brisbane at age 15. Brisbane has been the home of most of

Part IV Glimpses of the Superstars

Australia's best skaters over the last 10 years. The rink (冰场) utilised has the best ice conditions in Australia (still not very good though).

OZ: *What is the status of short track as a sport in Australia? Did it become more popular after your success in the 2002 Winter Olympics?*

SB: Short track experienced an overwhelming (不可抗拒的) number of kids wanting to skate right after SLC 2002. The ice time, number of coaches and number of skates was not enough. Many of the kids did not continue with the sport but maybe 15% did. I hope to see at least one of them go on to be a champion skater.

OZ: *U.S. fans really enjoyed your commentary (解说) on NBC during the 2003 World Cup in Salt Lake City. How did this opportunity happen and do you expect to repeat it?*

SB: I'm glad they enjoyed it, I did too. I was not sure how it would go but this is good feedback (反馈) and NBC is keen to have me back next year and probably the 2006 Olympics as well.

OZ: *You had a couple of life-threatening (危及生命的) accidents as a skater. Steven broke his neck in a 2000 training accident, and nearly bled to death in 1994 when he was impaled (刺穿, 刺住) on a competitor's blade (冰刀), cutting his femoral artery (股动脉). What made you continue? Did you ever have fear after those experiences?*

SB: Fear was never a consideration. I continued because I had not satisfied myself. I had great chances to win gold in Lillehammer (in) 1994 and Nagano (in) 1998 but either skated badly or had bad luck. Breaking my neck 18 months before Salt Lake resulted in a change of attitude. I had been to three Winter Olympics and not done my best at any of them. That became my goal for Salt Lake, simply to do my best, do that and I could walk away, no regrets. Everyone knows the result, I did my best and probably should have finished 9th, but good fortune stepped in (插手帮忙) and I was there to pick up the pieces.

OZ: *Who are your favorite up and coming skaters on the world scene?*

SB: Enjoy watching J.P. Kepka when he is rocking (摇晃). Jon Eley the tall skinny British kid is interesting to watch. (Tatiana) Borodulina the young Russian girl is definitely one to watch. Monette's brute force (强力) skating style is great to watch.

OZ: *Are you still involved in making boots (冰鞋) for skaters?*

SB: Yes, I'm still involved with RBC, not making boots anymore though. We are planning on moving into a factory in the next 6-12 months and then making our mark on the standard boot market. Check out (查看) our boots, ankle boosters (踝关节调压器) and other products at www.rbcsport.com.

OZ: *Your teammate Stephen Lee described RBC's world headquarters as being a "shed (工棚) in someone's backyard." Is that accurate?*

SB: That is Clint Jensen's backyard, my business partner in RBC. Our operation is pretty small and needs to be to satisfy the sport's elite (精英; 优秀运动员). Handmade boots and attention to each individual's needs is what sets us apart from (有别于) other companies. We have big plans for growing the company but will always maintain our attention to detail.

OZ: *How long has Apolo been an RBC customer? How did that happen?*

SB: I think Apolo's first pair of RBC's was in late 1998. The now ex-US (前美国的) coach Stephen

263

Gough has been a long-time friend of mine and knew the quality of our boots, he guided Apolo in the right direction. Whilst being one of the world's best skaters, Apolo is undoubtedly a fussy (爱挑剔的, 难取悦的) little bugger (家伙, 小伙子) when it comes to his boots. Actually he has recently received a new pair. We are waiting for his feedback, but not holding our breath!

OZ: I heard you decided to become a firefighter (消防员) after retiring from competitive skating. How did you decide you wanted to be a firefighter, and how is it working out?

SB: I have always wanted to become a fireman. I have been accepted and have been on the waiting list about 15 months now. This is a good thing because I'm still doing a lot of promotional (宣传的) work and corporate (集体的) speaking, but when the time is right I'll be there.

OZ: Just for fun—let's play Short Track Survivor (生存者, 一个娱乐节目的名称): You, Apolo, Fabio, Jiajun, Dong Sung, Monette, Smith, Gagnon, and that little Korean guy Ahn live in a house in the Alps (阿尔卑斯山). Who's the first one voted off (投票放弃)? Who is the last one standing?

SB: The first one off—easy, that's Rusty Smith. Once he is out, there might be a few seconds of silence. On second thoughts I have not heard Dong Sung sing yet, but I imagine he's not that good.

Everyone knows who the last man standing is! On Survivor it would be no different!

Relevant Words

change lanes 换道	side step 侧滑步
curved stroke 滑弧线	qualifying times 资格成绩
demote 降级	start 起
enter the curve 进入弯道	
International Skating Union (ISU) 国际滑冰联合会	
skating of prescribed movement 按规定图形滑行	

Lesson 14

> 纳迪娅·科马内奇(Nadia Comaneci)是一名前罗马尼亚体操运动员,被公认为是20世纪最伟大的运动员之一。她在1975年的欧洲锦标赛上就已崭露头角,赢得4枚金牌。在1976年的蒙特利尔奥运会上,她不仅成为奥运会史上第一个获得满分10分的体操运动员,还赢得3枚金牌、1枚银牌和1枚铜牌,共7次获得完美的10分,当时她年仅14岁。在此后的1980年奥运会上,她又获得4枚奥运奖牌。1989年她移居美国,继续关注体操,并从事慈善事业。由于她为体育做出了杰出的贡献,她两次获得国际奥委会颁发的奥林匹克勋章。

Still a Perfect 10

By Paul Ziert
April–June 2005
Olympic Review

There have been many remarkable women athletes during the 109-year history of the modern Olympic Movement, but few have had the global impact of the young girl from rural Onesti, Romania, named Nadia Comaneci. Even today, almost 30 years after her greatest triumphs[1], you need only mention the word "Nadia" and sports fans around the world know instantly to whom you are referring.

The 1976 Olympic Games opened in Montreal with some uncertainty hanging over[2] them. Memories of the massacre of 11 Israeli athletes at the 1972 Munich Games still lingered in many people's minds[3] and 26 African nations had boycotted[4] the Montreal Games. With the modern Olympic Games becoming a global forum to protest geopolitical[5] issues, many sports pundits predicted tough times ahead for the Games.[6]

1. triumph /ˈtraɪəmf/ n. 成功
2. to hang over 笼罩;威胁
3. 在1972年的慕尼黑奥运会上,11名以色列运动员惨遭屠杀,这一幕仍存留在很多人的记忆之中。massacre /ˈmæsəkə/ n. 残杀,屠杀　linger /ˈlɪŋɡə/ v. 徘徊,逗留
4. boycott /ˈbɔɪkɒt/ n. 联合抵制
5. geopolitical /ˌdʒiːəʊpəˈlɪtɪkəl/ a. 地理政治的,地缘政治的
6. 许多体育评论家预测这届奥运会将面临一段艰难的时期。pundit /ˈpʌndɪt/ n. 批评家;评论家

However, on the first full day of the women's gymnastics competition, everything changed. Nadia Comaneci stepped up to the uneven bars[7] and did something no other Olympic gymnast had ever accomplished. She scored a perfect score of 10. Her perfect score in the Olympic Games, sport's biggest stage, resonated[8] throughout the world. This moment of "perfection" changed gymnastics, the Olympic Games and her life forever. This mark, in fact, was so unexpected that the electronic scoring system[9] could only display the score as a 1.00. Comaneci says, "Even today, not many people remember how many medals I won, but they still remember that first perfect 10."

After scoring seven perfect marks during the course of the competition, Nadia left Montreal with five Olympic medals (three gold, one silver and a bronze) and super stardom[10]. American sports writer Frank DeFord said: "Had she scored a 9.999, nothing would have changed, but the 'Perfect 10' changed everything. Nobody had the foggiest[11] idea who she was or where she had come from, but she became the icon of the Games."

Three months before her 1976 Olympic Games triumph, the American public witnessed a preview[12] of Nadia's expertise[13] when she competed in the 1st American Cup, in Madison Square Garden in New York City. There, she easily won the competition and scored two perfect 10's in the process. Comaneci shared the winner's podium with a young American, Bart Conner, who was celebrating his 18th birthday that very day. Twenty years later, Nadia and Bart would become husband and wife.

From 1976 until 1980, Nadia struggled with the demands of celebrity[14], puberty[15] and gymnastics. Although during this time she won two of three successive[16] European All-Around titles and four World Championships medals, her personal struggles dominated the media coverage of her.[17]

Nevertheless, Nadia managed to arrive in Moscow for the 1980 Games with completely new exercises and the competitive desire to delight the world again. However, she made a mistake on the uneven bars in the first round of optional exercises[18], which seemed to eliminate her chance of defending her All-Around Olympic title[19]. After a prolonged judging of her balance beam routine[20], which took 28 minutes to resolve, Comaneci took home the silver medal behind her Soviet rival, Elena Davydova.[21] By the end of the Games, Comaneci had earned two gold and two silver medals for Romania.

7. uneven bars 高低杠
8. resonate /ˈrezəneɪt/ v. 回响；反响
9. electronic scoring system 电子计分系统
10. stardom /ˈstɑːdəm/ n. 明星地位
11. foggy /ˈfɒgɪ/ a. 模糊的，不清晰的
12. preview /ˈpriːvjuː/ n. 预审，预看
13. expertise /ˌekspɜːˈtiːz/ n. 技能
14. celebrity /sɪˈlebrɪtɪ/ n. 名声，名誉
15. puberty /ˈpjuːbɜːtɪ/ n. 青春期
16. successive /səkˈsesɪv/ a. 接连的；连续的
17. ... her personal struggles dominated the media coverage of her. 但媒体主要报道的却是她个人奋斗的故事。
18. optional exercise 自选动作
19. All-Around Olympic title 全能奥运冠军的称号
20. balance beam routine 平衡木项目规定动作
21. 科马内奇获得银牌，金牌被前苏联运动员埃莲娜·戴维多娃 (Elena Davydova) 摘走。

The impact of this brilliant performance was reduced, partly because the US-led boycott restricted some countries' television coverage[22] of the Games and partly because nothing could have possibly matched her historic perfection of 1976. Comaneci says: "Many people say to me, 'I guess you didn't do very well in 1980. What happened?' Well, actually, I got two golds and two silvers, I don't think that is too bad."

After the 1980 Moscow Games, Nadia was rarely seen outside the Communist bloc of nations[23]. Her last official competition was at the World University Games in 1981 in Bucharest[24] where she won gold medals in every event; nevertheless, Nadia saved her retirement announcement for early 1984.[25] It was at this retirement party that Juan Antonio Samaranch[26], then President of the IOC, awarded her the Olympic Order[27] for her illustrious[28] career in the sport of gymnastics.

Life in Romania under President Nicolae Ceausescu[29] had become increasingly difficult even for the young woman who had put the country on the map[30]. "I was rarely allowed to travel outside of Romania, except to Moscow, and once I went to Cuba," Comaneci recalls. Therefore, it was surprising that she was allowed to attend the 1984 Los Angeles Games as a guest of chief organiser, Peter Ueberroth[31].

Finally, in November 1989, Nadia escaped from her homeland as she crossed the border to Hungary and then on to Austria. After making contact with the US Embassy in Vienna, Comaneci was given political refugee status[32] and she boarded a plane for New York City. It was only three weeks later that the Romanian revolution began. To this day, many Romanians salute Nadia for her willingness to risk her life for freedom.[33] Comaneci eventually made her way to Montreal[34] where she lived with Romanian friends, until September 1991 when she moved to Norman, Oklahoma[35], to be with her old acquaintance and new boyfriend, Conner. With the fall of Communism in Romania and the growing pains[36] of the new democracy, the Romanian gymnastics programme was struggling to obtain the funds necessary to retain[37] the level of performance they had learned to expect. Therefore, in 1995, Nadia donated USD100, 000 to the Romanian Gymnastics Federation to help the gymnastics team prepare for the Atlanta Games.

In April 1996, she married Conner, a two-time US Olympic gold medallist, in a lavish[38] state wedding in Bucharest. The Lido Hotel was renamed "Hotel Nadia" for the month of April and became her residence[39] so that she and Bart could host the more than 100 guests

22. television coverage 电视转播
23. Communist bloc of nations 共产主义阵营的国家
    bloc /blɒk/ n. 政治组织，集团
24. Bucharest /ˈbjuːkərest/ n. 布加勒斯特（罗马尼亚首都和最大城市）
25. 纳迪娅直到1984年初才宣布退役。save/seɪv/ v. 保留
26. Juan Antonio Samaranch 胡安·安东尼奥·萨马兰奇(1920— ，西班牙人，1980年至2001年间任国际奥委会主席)
27. Olympic Order 奥运勋章
28. illustrious /ɪˈlʌstrɪəs/ a. 杰出的
29. Nicolae Ceausescu 尼古拉·齐奥塞斯库(1918—1989，罗马尼亚政治家，1989年遭杀害)
30. to put a place on the map 使一个地方出名
31. Peter Ueberroth 彼得·尤伯罗斯(1984年任洛杉矶奥运会组委会主席，首创了奥运会商业运作的"私营模式"，改变了奥运会赔钱的历史)
32. political refugee status 政治难民的身份
33. 现在仍有很多罗马尼亚人赞扬纳迪娅甘冒生命的危险争取自由。
34. Montreal /ˌmɒntrɪˈɔːl/ n. 蒙特利尔（加拿大魁北克省南部的一个城市）
35. Oklahoma /ˌəʊkləˈhəʊmə/ n. 俄克拉何马州（美国中南部的一个州）
36. growing pains 发展时期(尤指初期)的困难
37. retain /rɪˈteɪn/ v. 保持，保留
38. lavish /ˈlævɪʃ/ a. 盛大的
39. residence /ˈrezɪdəns/ n. 住处

who came to celebrate their union. More than 10,000 Romanians lined the streets of Bucharest to cheer for their legendary heroine[40] on her wedding day. The 20th century ended with Nadia being named in many lists of important contributors to society. In Austria, at the famous Vienna Opera House, she was awarded the World Sports Award of the Century. She also made the list of People magazine's "100 Most Important Moments of the Century," and ABC Television and Ladies Home Journal's "50 Most Significant Moments in Television History".

Even 30 years after her greatest sports moment, Nadia continues to be in demand[41]. She recently signed a four-year sponsorship contract that includes annual donations to the Nadia Comaneci School of Gymnastics in Onesti and the Nadia Comaneci Children's Clinic in Bucharest. Although she helps out with many different charities[42], Nadia remains very active in three in particular. She is the Co-Chairman of the Board of Directors of the Special Olympics International[43], a Vice-President of the Muscular Dystrophy[44] Association and a founding member of the Laureus Sports Foundation.

She travels all over the world to promote the values of sports to disenfranchised[45] children. In 2004, Comaneci was awarded the IOC Olympic Order for the second time. IOC President Jacques Rogge honoured her on this occasion for her continuing work to promote sports, especially gymnastics, all over the world. She says, "I have worked with Nelson Mandela[46], and I have heard him say, 'sport has the power to change the world,' so I am happy to use my celebrity to help others."

Although many wish to freeze Nadia in the one very special moment in time when she made global history by scoring the first perfect 10, she would be the first to say, "I rarely look back at either the good times or the bad ones. I prefer to live in the present, and my present couldn't be more perfect."

40. heroine /ˈherəʊɪn/ n. 女英雄；女主角

41. in demand 非常需要的；受欢迎的

42. charity /ˈtʃærɪtɪ/ n. 慈善机关（团体）

43. Special Olympics International 国际特奥会（为智力残疾的人举办的奥运会）

44. dystrophy /ˈdɪstrəfɪ/ n. 萎缩

45. disenfranchise /ˌdɪsɪnˈfræntʃaɪz/ v. 剥夺权利

46. Nelson Mandela 纳尔逊·曼德拉（南非前总统）

Comprehension Questions

1. What was the political background of the 1976 Montreal Olympic Games?
2. How did Comaneci's perfect score of 10 change her life forever?
3. For what reasons was Nadia Comaneci awarded the Olympic Order twice?

Part IV Glimpses of the Superstars

4. Why is Nadia Comaneci considered having an global impact on the development of the Modern Olympic Movement?
5. Based on Nadia Comaneci's life story, can you elaborate the relationship between politics and the Olympic Games?

Background Reading

Love for Her Son Drives Olympic Medalist on

Oxana Chusovitina is an extraordinary combination: gymnast and mother. The 1992 Olympic gold medallist has a career remarkable for its longevity (时间长), and a son, Alisher, 6, who in 2002 was diagnosed with acute (急性的) lymphocytic (淋巴细胞的) leukaemia (白血病).

At 30, Chusovitina is unique in a sport in which older competitors are becoming more common but, for so long, youth has ruled.

The World Artistic Gymnastics (竞技体操) Championships, starting today at the Rod Laver Arena, will be the ninth for the veteran from Uzbekistan (乌兹别克斯坦), apparently a record in itself. Yet Chusovitina has also had a rare motivation (动力).

At the World Championships three years ago in Debrecen (德布勒森), Hungary, she admitted she was competing to raise the money for her son's cancer treatment in Germany.

The family had no health insurance, and Uzbekistan no specialist oncology (肿瘤学) facilities.

"If I don't compete, then my son won't live, it's as simple as that," said Chusovitina at the time. "My son underwent an operation today, and the only reason he managed to get that treatment is because I am earning money. I have no choice."

Yesterday at Melbourne Park, Chusovitina said the situation was much improved. Alisher is now, she explained through an interpreter, "going very well".

He requires three blood tests each month, but otherwise (但在其他方面), he is just another child. Chusovitina insists she is competing in Melbourne out of desire rather than desperate need, but she thanked the international gymnastics community, which for several years at her competitions has raised €120,000 ($A193,000) for Alisher's care.

With her husband, Bakhodir Kurpanov—a former Olympic wrestler—at home with Alisher in Cologne, Chusovitina will continue competing as long as she is able.

She won gold at the 1992 Barcelona Olympics as a member of the former Unified Team (独联体队), and the triple world champion is now defending the vault (跳马) title she won in California in 2003.

Chusovitina's challengers include many gymnasts nearly half her age, but she is undaunted (无畏的). Indeed, Australia's head women's coach, Peggy Liddick, considers Chusovitina an inspiration and a role model (榜样) who is "every bit as good" now as when she won Olympic gold 16 years ago.

"When you are on the podium, nobody's asking you whether you are 15 or 30," Chusovitina said. "What matters is who can do great gymnastics. As for my plans—if everything is all right I'm looking forward to competing in Beijing in 2008, and then who knows? Maybe I will continue, it depends."

Gymnasts from 53 nations will contest the world championships, which start with today's men's qualifications, and continue until Sunday.

Relevant Words

aerial tinsica 侧空翻	half leg circle （鞍马）摆越
angle jump 屈体前手翻，山下手翻	magic traveling 全旋移位
back rest to forward swing dismount 后撑前摆下	free forward seat circle 腾身前回环
cross one hand balance 单手倒立	non-executed part 没有完成的动作
half-turn somersault 空翻转体 180°	roll forward through prone position 鱼跃

Lesson 15

乔治·贝斯特(George Best, 1946—2005)北爱尔兰足球运动员,曼联史上最伟大的前锋,曾被誉为"足球界的梵高"、"世界上最好的球员"。他1961年加盟曼联,1963年至1974年间出任曼联前锋,凭借其独特的天赋协助曼联在1965年和1967年的足球联赛冠军赛(Football League Championship)中获胜,并捧得1968年的欧洲杯。1968年他被评为"欧洲足球先生",并被英格兰足球记者协会评选为年度最佳球员。他在曼联比赛中个人进球纪录至今尚未有人打破。他的速度、平衡能力、双脚带球、射门精确度和在整个防守中自由穿梭的能力无人能及。然而,他的私生活一直为人诟病。酗酒、好赌和放纵女色令他早早地结束了足球生涯。因肺部感染而导致多个器官衰竭,他于2005年11月25日病逝于伦敦,终年59岁。他曾使无数男孩子钟情于足球,并向人们展示足球运动与众不同的魅力。贝斯特是曼联史上永远的7号。

Flawed Best Had It All

By James Button
November 26, 2005
The Age

(The champ in his Manchester United days in 1968. Photo: Peter Kemp)

To many he was the best of the best, but booze[1], fame, and more booze brought out the worst in the soccer champ[2], reports James Button.

The boy with the Beatles mop[3] ran along the goal line[4] from the corner flag[5]. He swerved[6], feinted[7], and deceived three or four defenders[8]. From a seemingly impossible angle, he drove the ball high into the net.

As the crowd erupted, a young reporter in the Manchester United press box[9] asked if anyone had caught the exact time of the goal. "Never mind the time, son," said an older voice. "Just write down the date."

The date was in the 1960s, although the exact day is not recorded, perhaps because George Best conjured many goals[10] like that in the

1. booze /buːz/ n. 烈酒
2. champ /tʃæmp/ n. [非正式用语] 冠军
3. 这个留着披头士扫把发型的男孩
4. goal line (足球)球门线
5. corner flag 角旗
6. swerve /swɜːv/ v. 突然转向
7. faint /feɪnt/ v. 做假动作
8. defender /dɪˈfendə/ n. 防守队员
9. press box 新闻记者席
10. ... conjure many goals 像变戏法似地射入许多进球

decade he held British football under his spell.[11]

But the magic has long since been lost to alcoholic decline.[12] Overnight Best was in London's Cromwell Hospital, surrounded by friends and family expecting the worst[13].

"I am afraid Mr Best is coming to the end of the long road of his ill-health," said his tearful consultant, Professor Roger Williams. "There is no change, just deterioration. I have to tell you that his hours are numbered now.[14]"

By Best's bedside were his father, Dickie, 87, two sisters and a brother who had flown from Belfast[15] to be with him.

His son Calum, 24, was there, as was his agent Phil Hughes, who told a newspaper on Sunday that Best had shrunk to 44 kilograms and looked like a "broken sparrow[16]".

Former teammates Sir Bobby Charlton and Denis Law visited to make their farewells.

Best had been on a life-support machine[17] for a week after suffering an acute lung infection[18], but his health had been in intermittent[19] crisis for more than five years after a lifetime of heavy drinking[20].

After a liver transplant[21] in 2002, doctors warned that more drinking would kill him, and Best vowed to fight the alcoholism[22] that had cut short his career[23] in the early 1970s. Within a year, he was back on the booze.[24]

Last Sunday a picture of Best looking gaunt[25] and yellow, with tubes attached to his body, was published on the front page of the News of the World. Best allowed the photo to be taken, as a warning about the dangers of alcohol, along with a message saying: "Don't die like me."

Best, whose mother also died an alcoholic[26], grew up on a poor Protestant housing estate[27] in Belfast. He came to Manchester United as an awestruck 17-year-old[28] and left having played 466 games, scored 179 goals—a remarkable number for a winger[29]—and helped the club win two league championships[30] and a European Cup[31].

Yet the more famous he became, the more he drank, until Manchester United sacked[32] its star in 1974, when he was 27. Best, who was reduced to tears[33] by the sacking, drifted[34] from club to club in Britain and the US but never regained his old form[35].

He also played 37 times for Northern Ireland but was rarely seen on the world stage, as the tiny province was too weak to make many

11. ... he held British football under his spell. 他将英国足球置于他的魔法之下。
12. 然而，酗酒导致他自身运动能力下降，这种魔力已经消失很久了。
13. ... expecting the worst 等待最坏的结果（死神的降临）
14. ... his hours are numbered now. 他剩下的时间不多了。
15. Belfast 贝尔法斯特（北爱尔兰首府及最大城市）
16. sparrow /ˈspærəʊ/ n. 麻雀（此处为比喻用法）
17. life-support machine 呼吸机
18. acute lung infection 急性肺感染
19. intermittent /ˌɪntəˈmɪtənt/ a. 间歇的，断断续续的
20. heavy drinking 过度酗酒
21. liver transplant 肝脏移植
22. alcoholism /ˈælkəhɒlɪzəm/ n. 酗酒
23. ... cut short his career 缩短了他的运动生涯
24. 不到一年，他又开始恢复到从前的酗酒状态。
25. gaunt /ɡɔːnt/ a. 瘦骨嶙峋的
26. alcoholic /ˌælkəˈhɒlɪk/ n. 酗酒者，酒鬼
27. housing estate 居住区，住宅区
28. 17岁那年，他怀着敬畏的心情来到曼联。
29. winger /ˈwɪŋə/ n. （足球）侧翼运动员
30. league championships 联赛
31. European Cup 欧洲杯
32. sack /sæk/ v. [俚语] 解雇
33. ... was reduced to tears 痛哭流涕
34. drift /drɪft/ v. 漂泊，辗转
35. ... regained his old form 恢复旧时的状态

major competitions.

He was devastatingly fast, "with feet as sensitive as a pick-pocket's hands[36]", wrote Sunday Times journalist Hugh McIlvanney in a 1992 article that also describes the press box incident recorded above.

"His control of the ball under the most violent pressure was hypnotic[37]. The bewildering repertoire of feints and swerves, sudden stops and demoralising spurts, exploited a freakish elasticity of limb and torso, tremendous physical strength for so slight a figure.[38]" Argentinian champion Diego Maradona called Best his idol. Brazil's incomparable Pele[39] said Best was the best player he ever saw play.

Best, twice married and twice divorced, once boasted to McIlvanney[40] that "If I had been born ugly, you would never have heard of Pele." He was saying, presumably, that he could have been even greater, had drinking and wild living not done him in.[41]

Blessed with pop-star looks—he was called the "fifth Beatle"—he was a showman on the field and shambolic off it, though his wit and charm, especially towards women, were legendary.[42]

Asked once if he had wasted his life, he famously said: "I spent a lot of money on booze, birds and fast cars. The rest I just squandered[43]."

Best liked to tell the story of a bellboy who brought breakfast to his hotel room in the early 1970s. He saw Best drinking champagne in bed with the then Miss World[44] and several thousand pounds of cash won from a night's gambling, and exclaimed: "George, where did it all go wrong?[45]"

In the end the jokes weren't funny. Best spent Christmas 1984 in jail after receiving a three-month sentence for drink-driving, assaulting a police officer and failing to answer bail[46]. Last year he copped[47] another drink-driving charge and his wife, Alex, a former air hostess, divorced him for adultery[48].

He will be remembered by most as a glorious wasted talent, an early case of a footballer destroyed in part by the pressures of superstardom[49]. British television personality[50] and former sports journalist Michael Parkinson once said: "The only tragedy George Best has to confront is that he will never know how good he could have been."

This week the British media remembered him at his best.[51] In *The Observer*[52], journalist Bill Elliott described his 1976 World Cup game for Northern Ireland against Holland, then nearly the world's greatest

36. ... with feet as sensitive as a pick-pocket's hands 他的双脚像小偷的手一样灵活
37. hypnotic /hɪpˈnɒtɪk/ a. 催眠的，催眠术的
38. 他迷人的个人技能，如假动作、突然转向、疾停和让人无可奈何的冲刺，全部出自他异常柔韧的肢体。他身材矮小，但身体里却蕴含着巨大的能量。
elasticity /ˌiːlæˈstɪsɪtɪ/ n. 弹力，弹性
39. Pele 巴西球王贝利
40. McIlvanney 英国著名作家
41. 大概他是想说，要是没有酒精和放荡生活给他带来的负面影响，他可能会更优秀。to do sb. in 伤害，杀害
42. 上天赐予他一副明星的面庞，因此他被戏称为"披头士乐队中的第五名成员"。在足球场上他是明星，球场下他生活毫无节制，然而他有着传奇般的智慧，特别是对女人，有着巨大的吸引力。
shambolic /ʃæmˈbɒlɪk/ a. 混乱的、纷乱的或无组织的
43. squander /ˈskwɒndə/ v. 浪费，挥霍，乱花钱
44. then Miss World 当年的世界小姐
45. 怎么会这样？哪里出了差错？
46. ... answer bail 在保释期间每天向警察局报告每天的行踪
bail /beɪl/ n. 保释；保证金
47. cop /kɒp/ v. [俚语]被警察抓住
48. adultery /əˈdʌltərɪ/ n. 通奸，通奸行为
49. superstardom /ˈsjuːpəstɑːdəm/ n. 超级明星的身份
50. personality /ˌpɜːsəˈnælɪtɪ/ n. 名人
51. 本周，英国媒体缅怀了当年处于最佳状态的贝斯特。
52. *The Observer*《观察者报》

side[53], with Johan Cruyff[54] acknowledged as the world's best.

Asked by Elliott before the game if Cruyff was greater than him, Best, whose greatest days were already behind him[55], promised to "nutmeg[56]" the Dutchman the first chance he got.

Five minutes into the game, Best—who had run onto the pitch carrying a red rose that a blonde woman had handed to him as he emerged from the tunnel—took the ball wide[57].

Instead of going straight for goal he turned infield, "weaved his way past at least three Dutchmen and found his way to Cruyff. He took the ball to his opponent, dipped a shoulder twice and slipped it between Cruyff's feet. As he ran round to collect it and run on, he raised his right fist into the air."[58]

He had answered the journalist's question.

53. ... then nearly the world's greatest side 当时几乎是世界上最强的劲旅
54. Johan Cruyff 约翰·克鲁伊夫（著名荷兰足球运动员）
55. 已经江河日下，失去了最佳的状态
56. nutmeg /'nʌtmeg/ v. [口语]将球从对方球员的两腿间传过或踢过
57. ... took the ball wide 他将球远远地带离球门区
58. 他没有直接带球射门，相反他却绕到场内，"绕过至少三名荷兰队员，将球带到克鲁伊夫附近，他两次沉肩，把球从克鲁伊夫的双脚间带过。然后他绕过克鲁伊夫，再次控球，继续带球前进，同时将右拳举向空中。"

Comprehension Questions

1. How do you understand the older reporter's advice of not minding the time but just writing down the date (in the third paragraph)?
2. What shortened George Best's career as a footballer?
3. Why did Best allow the picture showing his ill looks published on the front page of the *News of the World*?
4. How did George Best answer the journalist's question about who was the greater footballer, him or Cruyff?
5. How do you evaluate George Best as a footballer and as a man?

Background Reading

Maradona in Intensive Care (重病特别护理) amid Overdose Reports

Former Argentina soccer star Diego Maradona is heavily sedated (给……服镇静剂) in intensive care following a crisis of hypertension (高血压) or high blood pressure, his doctors said today.

Maradona, who has long been in therapy to battle a drug addiction (毒瘾) that has left him a bloated (发胀的；浮肿的) shadow of his former self, was admitted to (接收进入) a Buenos Aires clinic after being taken ill.

Part IV Glimpses of the Superstars

Doctors said he was breathing with the help of a respirator (呼吸器) and his condition was "reserved" (有所保留, 意即情况不乐观).

"Diego Armando Maradona has been admitted to intensive care... because of a crisis of hypertension (高血压) related to myocardium (心肌层)," a statement issued to reporters outside the clinic said.

"He also had respiratory difficulties and so is aided by a respirator, as a result of which he is permanently sedated (镇静的)."

"His initial haemodynamic (血液动力的) reaction is moderately favourable," the statement added.

Maradona's family doctor Alfredo Cahe refused to comment on media reports that the former soccer star had taken a cocaine overdose (过量服用可卡因), saying an update (最新声明) on his condition would be issued on Monday.

Family, friends and well-wishers (祝福者) flooded to the Suizo-Argentina clinic on Sunday evening as news of the 43-year-old's condition spread.

One teary-eyed fan held aloft (高高地) a photograph of Maradona in his soccer-playing prime (黄金时期).

A banner read "Diego, Argentina loves you", while passing cars honked their horns.

Television channel Todo Noticias said Maradona had fallen ill after taking a drug overdose but gave no source for the report.

Maradona had earlier attended a soccer game at his former club Boca Juniors' stadium in the Argentine capital before being taken ill and whisked (迅速移动) to the clinic in an ambulance.

Maradona is regarded as one of the finest players to have graced (为……增辉) the game, leading Argentina to World Cup victory in 1986.

His supporters are so fanatical (狂热的) that some 20,000 people as far afield as(远在) Vietnam and Iceland have become members of the "Church of Maradona".

He has also been honoured with a musical (音乐剧) about the ups and downs of his turbulent rags-to-riches life (从赤贫到暴富的生活).

However, drug use off the pitch marred (损害, 糟踏) Maradona's career, and he is often barely intelligible (可理解的) in interviews screened (放映) on Argentine television.

Relevant Words

direct (indirect) kick	直接(间接)球	free kick	任意球
hat-trick	帽子戏法	throw in	掷界外球
heading	顶球	overhead kick	倒勾球
kick-off	开球	sending-off	罚下场

Part V

Sporting Mosaic

体坛多棱镜

Lesson 1

在宣布北京赢得2008年奥运会主办权的当天,《时代》周刊记者 Jessica Reaves 采访了资深奥林匹克报道记者 Barry Hillenbrand。Jessica 的问题可谓直奔主题:投票结果出乎人们意料吗?投票结果公正吗?北京作为一个城市对奥运会组织者来说有没有特别的吸引力?北京能办好这届奥运会吗?奥运场馆设施开始建造了吗?且看 Barry 如何作答。

Beijing Gets the Games

By Jessica Reaves and Barry Hillenbrand
July 13, 2001
Time[1]

(Students celebrate at Beijing's Millennium Monument)

Beijing lands the 2008 summer Olympics. TIME's Olympic veteran Barry Hillenbrand weighs in[2] on the IOC's decision—and what it means for athletes and spectators.

After years of frustration[3], Beijing got its good news Friday: Olympic committee members announced the Chinese city had won its long-standing[4] bid to host the 2008 summer Games.

IOC officials gave the nod[5] to anxious Chinese officials, at 10 p.m. local time, choosing Beijing over chief rivals Toronto[6] and Paris. Istanbul[7], Turkey and Osaka, Japan had also placed bids.

What will the first Chinese Olympics be like? How did China nail down[8] their bid? TIME international correspondent Barry Hillenbrand

1. *Time*《时代》周刊,于1923年在纽约创刊,是一份世界性新闻周刊,有世界"史库"之称,每期发行量约500万份之多。该周刊除在纽约出版外,还有大西洋、亚洲、拉丁美洲、南太平洋等国外版,以报道国际国内新闻为主,并辟有多种栏目。它的指导思想是旨在使"忙人"能够充分了解世界及美国大事。它针对国内外重大事件提供背景材料,进行分析解释,这种新闻报道方式不同于美国报纸传统的"客观"报道,成为解释性报道的先驱。
2. to weigh in 谈论
3. frustration /frʌsˈtreɪʃən/ n. 挫败,挫折
4. long-standing /lɒŋˈstændɪŋ/ a. 长期存在的;长久持续的
5. to give the nod [口语] 批准;许可;选中
6. Toronto /təˈrɒntəʊ/ 多伦多(加拿大第一大城市)
7. Istanbul /ˌɪstænˈbuːl/ 伊斯坦布尔(土耳其最大的城市和港口)
8. to nail down 明确,把……弄清楚

has covered[9] four Olympics for TIME (most recently the 2000 summer games in Sydney). He spoke with TIME.com Friday morning after the announcement.

TIME: Was today's vote a real surprise to anyone?

Barry Hillenbrand: No. Everybody knew that Beijing was the leader on the basis of the fact that they'd been the runner-up[10] in the 1993 vote that gave Sydney the 2000 Games.

So Beijing had that fact working in their favor. They also had IOC president Juan Antonio Samaranch[11] wanting to bring China into the fold[12]—that's the geopolitical[13] angle on why we should have China as the host.

The other primary argument was that to some extent, it was also just Asia's turn this time around. The 2000 games were in Sydney; they'll be in Athens in 2004, then in Italy in 2006 for the winter games.

Listening to the Chinese officials talk about the vote before it happened, you definitely got the sense they were going to be extremely annoyed if they didn't win the bid this year. Do you think the IOC members were bullied[14] or pressured to make this decision?

I don't think so. The IOC membership is the most independent (106 independent people) voting body you'll ever find. It's made up of 106 people who can vote and do whatever they please.

But it's certainly true that Beijing wasn't happy in '93 when they didn't get the vote. They were eminently[15] confident then, and they didn't get it and went into a sulk[16] and didn't apply for the next round. And this decision was enormously important for China as a nation. They want to show the world they're a big, important nation and that they can do this right.

Does Beijing, as a city, have something that makes it especially attractive to Olympic organizers?

Not especially. On a number of fronts[17], Beijing is less attractive than Toronto and Paris.

Paris had the backdrop[18] of the century—for example, they were planning to hold the equestrian[19] events in the Tuilieries[20]. It would

---

9. cover /ˈkʌvə/ v. (记者)采访、报道
10. runner-up /ˌrʌnərˈʌp/ n. 在竞争中居第二位者
11. IOC president Juan Antonio Samaranch 国际奥委会主席胡安·安东尼奥·萨马兰奇
12. to bring ... into the fold 把……引入行列中
13. geopolitical /ˌdʒiːəʊpəˈlɪtɪkəl/ a. 地理政治学的
14. bully /ˈbʊlɪ/ v. 威吓
15. eminently /ˈemɪnəntlɪ/ ad. 异乎寻常地;非凡地
16. to go into a sulk 生气;发脾气
17. front /frʌnt/ n. 重要方面
18. backdrop /ˈbækdrɒp/ n. 背景
19. equestrian /ɪˈkwestrɪən/ a. 马术的
20. Tuilieries 杜勒丽花园 (Parc des Tuileries),位于巴黎市中心,与协和广场(Pl. de Concorde)、巴黎歌剧院(即加尼埃歌剧院)、马德莲教堂(Sainte Marie Madeleine)、罗浮宫(Palais du Louvre)等相邻。

have been spectacular. And Toronto had a very compact[21], very interesting site proposal.

But Beijing will mount[22] credible[23] games because they'll have great audiences and spend a lot of money making sure the structures are good. They'll do a wonderful job on the technical front. It's the spirit and soul that I'm worried about.

With that misgiving[24] in mind, what do you think these games will be like?

These games will be highly stylized[25]. You're going to get packed[26] houses, but packed with subdued[27] crowds, just as they were in Nagano and Seoul. Asian crowds are just different—there's not going to be the spontaneity[28] that makes the Olympics special. And that's a real problem, not only for the spectators but for the athletes as well.

In Sydney, for example, the crowds were incredibly vocal[29], and would chant, and go crazy. And this made every venue and every event incredibly exciting for the crowds and for the athletes. I fear that's one of the things will be lacking in China.

Has Beijing started construction on any facilities for the Games?

That's one of the last things they worry about in China. Rest assured[30] that everything will be built on time and to specifications. The Chinese will do very well on the specifics[31]: seating, logistics, et cetera[32].

There is one other potential problem: security and inflexibility. The great thing about Sydney was that if things weren't working according to plan, the Australians bent the rules and improvised[33], with wonderful ease. That just isn't going to happen in China.

What we saw in Beijing after the vote was announced is a pretty good indicator of what we're going to see in 2008: A lot of flags, a lot of national pride and a lot of staged celebrations.

21. compact /kəm'pækt/ a. 紧凑的
22. mount /maʊnt/ v. 进行
23. credible /'krɛdɪbəl/ a. 可靠的
24. misgiving /mɪs'gɪvɪŋ/ n. [常作复] 担忧
25. stylized /'staɪlaɪzd/ a. 程序化的
26. packed /pækt/ a. 拥挤的（此处指挤满观众的）
27. subdued /səb'djuːd/ a. 驯服的；克制（感情、欲望等）的
28. spontaneity /ˌspɒntə'neɪətɪ/ n. 自发性
29. vocal /'vəʊkəl/ a. 使用嗓音的（这里指观众情绪高涨，不断欢呼喝彩，呐喊助威。）
30. to rest assured 放心；确信无疑
31. specific /spɪ'sɪfɪk/ n. 细节
32. et cetera /ɪt'setərə/ [拉丁语] 以及其他等等
33. improvise /'ɪmprəvaɪz/ v. 临时发挥；即席创作

Comprehension Questions

1. Which other countries also placed bids to host the 2008 Olympic Games apart from Beijing?
2. Was the interviewee, Barry Hillenbrand, really surprised that the Games will go to Beijing in 2008? Why is this?

Part V   Sporting Mosaic

3. Why does Barry Hillenbrand think that the decision for Beijing to host the Games is "an enormously important one for China"?
4. Does Barry Hillenbrand think the facilities for the Games will be constructed in time?
5. Will hosting the Olympic Games give China a sporting advantage in 2008? Would you expect China to win more medals than it ever has before?

Background Reading

Mission of the Organising Committee (组织委员会)

The organisation of the Olympic Games is entrusted (委托) by the International Olympic Committee (IOC) to the National Olympic Committee (NOC) of the country of the host city as well as to the host city itself. The NOC forms, for that purpose, an Organising Committee for the Olympic Games (OCOG) which, from the time it is constituted, communicates directly with the IOC, from which it receives instructions.

The OCOG executive body includes: the IOC member or members in the country; the President and Secretary General of the NOC; and at least one member representing, and designated by, the host city. In addition, it generally includes representatives of the public authorities and other leading figures (重要人物).

From the time of its constitution (建立) to the end of its liquidation (解散), the OCOG must comply with (遵守) the Olympic Charter, the contract entered into between the IOC, the National Olympic Committee and the host city (Host City Contract) and the instructions of the IOC Executive Board (执行委员会).

Nowadays, these Organising Committees have turned into enormous administrative entities employing hundreds of people. The Organising Committee starts its work with a period of planning followed by a period of organisation which culminates (达到最高点) in the implementation (履行) or operational phase (实施阶段).

A Few Aspects of an Oraganising Committee's Work

—To give equal treatment to every sport on the programme and ensure that competitions are held according to the rules of the International Sports Federations (IFs, 国际单项体育联合会);

—To ensure that no political demonstration (示威游行) or meeting is held in the Olympic City or its surroundings (周围地区);

—To choose and, if necessary, create the required installations (设施): competition sites, stadiums and training halls; to arrange for the required equipment;

—To lodge (提供住宿) the athletes, their entourage (随行人员), the officials;

—To organise medical services;

—To solve transportation problems;

—To meet the requirements of the mass media in order to offer the public the best possible information on the Games;

—To organise cultural events that are an essential element of the celebration of the Olympic Games;

—To write the Final Report on the celebration of the Games in the two official languages and distribute it within two years after the end of the Games.

Relevant Words

Association of National Olympic Committees (ANOC)
国家/地区奥林匹克委员会协会

Association of National Olympic Committees of Africa (ANOCA)　非洲国家/地区奥林匹克委员会协会
Pan American Sports Organisation (PASO)　泛美体育组织
Olympic Council of Asia (OCA)　亚洲奥林匹克理事会
European Olympic Committees (EOC)　欧洲国家奥林匹克委员会总会
Oceania National Olympic Committees (ONOC)　大洋洲国家奥林匹克委员会总会

Lesson 2

> 古希腊城邦间连年混战，人民深感厌恶，大家渴望能有一个休养生息的和平环境。于是，古希腊各城邦达成协议，决定在奥运会举办期间停止一切战争，这就是著名的"奥林匹克神圣休战"。它的期限最初为1个月。停战期间，凡是参加奥运会的人都将受到保护，不容侵犯。
>
> "奥林匹克神圣休战"体现了人们追求和平的美好意愿，对现代奥运会和国际社会产生了深远影响。1993年10月25日，在联合国大会上，全体代表一致通过了由国际奥委会倡议的"奥林匹克休战"提案：在奥运会期间和奥运会前后各1周时间内，各成员国放下武器，停止战争，让全世界在和平的气氛中，欢度4年一度的奥林匹克节日。
>
> 在2006年都灵冬季奥运会即将到来之际，联合国呼吁成员国切实做到并积极监督"奥林匹克休战"的实施情况，促进世界和平。

U.N. Urges Members to Uphold[1] Olympic Truce[2]

By the Associated Press
Nov 3, 2005
The New York Times

UNITED NATIONS (AP)—The U.N. General Assembly[3] urged all 191 member states on Thursday to observe a truce during the upcoming[4] Turin Olympics and to promote peace through sports.

The resolution calling for the traditional "Olympic Truce" during the Feb. 10–26 games and the Paralympic Winter Games[5] that follow in the Italian city from March 10–19 was adopted by consensus[6]. So was the resolution promoting the "International Year of Sport and Physical Education[7]."

Italy's deputy U.N. Ambassador Aldo Mantovani, who introduced the truce resolution, said it had a record 190 co-sponsors and stressed that "since ancient times the idea of the Olympic Games has been closely associated with that of peace."

Venezuela[8] went along with the resolution but expressed a reservation[9] because it mentioned a document adopted by world leaders at September's U.N. summit committing them to efforts to fight poverty, human rights abuses and terrorism. Some felt that document had been watered down[10] because it didn't include a definition of terrorism that rules out[11] attacks on civilians[12].

---

1. uphold /ʌpˈhəʊld/ v. 确保
2. Olympic Truce 奥林匹克休战
3. U.N. General Assembly 联合国大会
4. upcoming /ˈʌpˌkʌmɪŋ/ a. 即将来临的
5. Paralympic Winter Games 残疾人冬季奥运会
6. consensus /kənˈsensəs/ n. 一致通过
7. International Year of Sport and Physical Education 国际运动与体育年
8. Venezuela 委内瑞拉（位于南美洲）
9. reservation /ˌrezəˈveɪʃn/ n. 保留意见
10. to water sth. down 削弱
11. to rule out 禁止
12. civilian /sɪˈvɪljən/ n. 平民

While acknowledging the ancient origin of the truce, the resolution also incorporated the issues of today's world—"the maintenance of peace, the promotion of development, the fostering[13] of dialogue, cooperation, and understanding among various cultures and civilizations."

The resolution declares that a truce would "encourage a peaceful environment" and ensure "the safe passage of participation of athletes and others at the games."

The origins of the truce come from the ancient Greek tradition of ekecheiria, or "Olympic truce," declared to stop war between the sides of participating athletes and ensure safety throughout the duration of the games.

The General Assembly revived[14] the appeal for an Olympic Truce in 1993 after an appeal from the International Olympic Committee allowed athletes of war-torn[15] Yugoslavia, which was on the brink of[16] breaking up[17], to participate in the 1992 Barcelona Olympics.

A complementary[18] resolution, declaring an international year of sport and physical education, calls for member states to hold conferences and employ sports "as a means to promote education, health development and peace."

It also calls for the appointment of sports celebrities[19] as spokespeople to promote the resolution's message.

Adolf Ogi, special adviser to U.N. Secretary-General Kofi Annan on promoting sport for development and peace, told a news conference he hoped sports would give children in an impoverished[20] village in Thailand that he just visited a better future.

"Sports and physical education play a major role in the achievement of economic goals," Ogi said. "This resolution gives me hope, hope for a better world."

When asked how the cash-strapped[21] organization proposes to pay for programs being created under the resolution, Ogi remained optimistic without providing any specifics.

"We will find a solution," he said.

Israeli Ambassador Dan Gillerman gave an example of how athletic competition also encourages dialogue between nations, citing[22] Qatar's[23] building of a soccer stadium in Israel.

"The local team is composed of Jewish and Arab Israeli players representing an opportunity for our countries to enhance relationships on a people-to-people basis," Gillerman said.

13. foster /ˈfɒstə/ v. 促进
14. revive /rɪˈvaɪv/ v. 使振奋；使更生
15. war-torn /ˈwɔːtɔːn/ a. 受战争蹂躏的
16. on the brink of 将要；将陷于
17. to break up 散开；分离（这里指南斯拉夫国家解体）
18. complementary /ˌkɒmplɪˈmentərɪ/ a. 补充的
19. celebrity /sɪˈlebrɪtɪ/ n. 公众人物
20. impoverished /ɪmˈpɒvərɪʃt/ a. 穷困的
21. cash-strapped /ˈkæʃstræpt/ a. 缺钱的
22. cite /saɪt/ v. 引用；举……为例
23. Qatar 卡塔尔（位于西亚）

Comprehension Questions

1. What did the U.N. General Assembly urge all 191 member states to do on Thursday?
2. Why did Venezuela express a reservation regarding the resolution?
3. Why would some people feel that the document was "watered down"?
4. What "issues of today's world" were incorporated into the resolution?
5. In your opinion, is the concept of an Olympic Truce workable in today's international climate?

Background Reading

The Olympic Truce

The ancient Olympic truce protected athletes and pilgrims (游客) traveling to and from the games. Participating city-states were restricted from military actions and legal disputes for the duration of the games. In the modern Olympics, the truce is not legally binding, but the spirit of peace inherent (固有的; 天生的) in the truce is honoured.

"May the world be delivered from crime and killing and be free from the clash of arms (武器)."

—From the early Olympic truce

Longing for Peace

After an interruption of eight years due to the First World War, the Olympics made a welcome return in 1920 in Antwerp (安特卫普，比利时第二大城市). This Belgian city was chosen to host the Games in recognition of how severely and bravely it had suffered during the war. The Antwerp games were notable for many things, not the least of which was the release of hundreds of doves (和平鸽) during the opening ceremony, symbolising (象征) the return of peace to the continent of Europe. Since then, the releasing of doves has become a permanent part of opening ceremony protocol (方案).

The Ancient Olympic Truce

The Greek word for truce (ekecheiria) means "the holding of hands" and "the break of hostilities." The Olympic truce began in 824 BC as a month-long "Holy Treaty" between king Iphitor of Elis (厄利斯), King Lykourgos of Sparta (斯巴达), and King Kleosthenes of Pisa (比萨). The terms of the truce were engraved (雕刻) on a bronze discus (铁饼) that was kept in the Temple of Hera (赫拉神庙) in the Altis at Olympia. The official terms of the truce were:

- Neither armies nor weapons were allowed to enter Elis;
- Attendees (参加者) whose city-state was at war could travel safely through hostile (敌对的) areas;
- No death penalties were allowed.

In order to spread the news of the truce before the start of the Olympic festival, three heralds (使者) decked (戴着……的) with olive wreaths (橄榄枝编成的环) and carrying staffs (旗杆) were sent out from Elis to every Greek state. It was the heralds' responsibility to reaffirm the date of the festival (each city-state had its own calendar system), to invite the inhabitants to attend, and to announce the Olympic truce. Because of this, they came to be known as the "truce-bearers" (spondophoroi). These heralds were also the official warrantors (保证人) of the truce and full-time legal advisors (法律顾问) to the Eleans (伊利斯).

Although the Games themselves lasted for five days, the truce was in effect for one month. Later it was extended to two and then three months to protect visitors coming from further away. Even though the truce ended after the Games, the ongoing neutrality (中立) of Elis, which was achieved through the negotiation of treaties with other city-states, was indispensable (不可缺少的) to the success of the quadrennial (四年一次的) truce.

Relevant Words

残疾人奥运会比赛的分类	
Spinal Cord Injury 脊髓损伤类	Amputee 截肢选手类
Cerebral Palsy 脑瘫选手类	Mentally Handicapped 智障选手类
Visually Impaired 视障选手类	Others 其他类

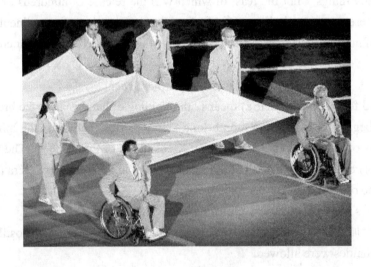

Lesson 3

新科"女飞人"凯丽·怀特(Kelli White)在2003年巴黎田径世锦赛上先后获得100米和200米的金牌。她在100米赛后提供的尿样却在兴奋剂检测中出了问题,国际田联属下的反兴奋剂试验室发现其尿样含有"莫达芬尼"——一种类似于麻黄素功效的刺激物成分。

尽管怀特声称是为了治疗睡眠不规律才"误服"的,但国际田联拒绝接受怀特的解释,最终判其"有罪"。国际田联"收金牌"之心非常坚决,怀特将面临禁赛处分,还将失去12万美元的世锦赛奖金和"首位包揽100米、200米世锦赛冠军的美国人"的荣誉。

本文作者认为,无论服用兴奋剂是由于疏忽还是故意为之,都是不可原谅的。怀特的行为在美国的田径史上写下了不光彩的一页。

The Kelli White Follow Up

By Mary Nicole Nazzaro
August 30, 2003
American Track & Field

Of course everyone has by now heard the latest, and certainly the worst, round of bad news for the United States at the World Track and Field Championships. I was in a cafe in the Third Arrondisment[1] on Saturday afternoon, a block away from a road where the men's marathon was to be contested. I glanced at a copy of L'Equipe, France's daily sports newspaper, on a coffee table near the front door of the cafe. "Une Affaire Kelli White?"[2] it said. I turned to the story

and all I can say is, even my poor French, left over from a couple of years of high school classes, was enough to decipher[3] the story: White had tested positive for a stimulant[4], and the incident was being investigated by the IAAF[5].

L'Equipe scored a major journalistic coup[6] by breaking the story, which according to IAAF Senior Vice-President Arne Ljungqvist only

1. Third Arrondisment 巴黎的一条街道名

2. "Une Affaire Kelli White?" [法文] = "An Affair Kelli White?" "凯丽·怀特丑闻?"

3. decipher /dɪ'saɪfə/ v. 解读;辨读
4. stimulant /'stɪmjʊlənt/ n. 兴奋剂

5. IAAF 国际田联(International Association of Athletics Federations 的缩写)

6. coup /kuː/ n. 出乎意料的行动

reached his ears on Friday afternoon. And coming on the heels of my congratulatory column yesterday about White and her coach,[7] I have to confess that this hurts. Whether or not White was purposely doping[8]—an allegation[9] she emphatically denied at a press conference late Saturday night at the Stade de France—it's a major black mark on the U.S. sprinting program[10] and for White personally in this, her breakout[11] international season.

To her credit[12], White did not run the 4×100 relay on Saturday night so as not to jeopardize[13] the U.S. result in the event she is disqualified[14] from the world championships. And at her press conference, she didn't just read a prepared statement, but answered questions from the media as well. The press conference room was packed fuller than a Paris metro train[15] at rush hour, but White did her best to answer the questions and keep her cool.

It wasn't always pretty, though. White said that the drug detected by her doping test after the 100-meter final, modafinil[16], was prescribed to her because she and several other members of her family suffer from narcolepsy[17], a sleep disorder. But when asked to identify the members of her family who also have the disorder, White declined. Asked why she had never before disclosed that she has narcolepsy, she said "I would never tell reporters my medical history. I think that's a personal, private issue." White also declined to name the supplements she listed on her doping control form. (She did not list modafinil or its American brand name, Provigil, on the form.) The word among some of the assembled media afterwards was that she came off[18] looking as though she had something to hide.

Her explanation for why she did not list Provigil on her doping control form should serve as a warning to every athlete in every sport who undergoes drug testing. In her prepared statement, she said she did not write Provigil on the form "because I had no idea that Provigil contained a banned substance." But every athlete knows that the IAAF list of banned substances is not comprehensive and that "related substances"—in this case, a stimulant—can trip up[19] the doping tests. Athletes must seek medical exemptions for any type of medication,[20] even if they don't think it's on a list of banned substances. There's just no excuse for ignorance at the world-class level, no matter what.

It's doubly hard to take because White has one of the most experienced coaches in the sport in Remi Korchemny[21]. It's been so exciting to see White move up to the world-class level this year and become

7. 我昨天刚刚写了一篇专栏文章祝贺凯莉·怀特和她的教练。
8. dope /dəʊp/ v. 服用兴奋剂
9. allegation /ˌælɪˈɡeɪʃən/ n. 断言；宣称
10. sprinting program 短跑项目
11. breakout /ˈbreɪkaʊt/ a. 首次，初次
12. to one's credit 值得赞扬某人的是……
13. jeopardize /ˈdʒepədaɪz/ v. 危害
14. disqualify /dɪsˈkwɒlɪfaɪ/ v. 取消资格
15. metro train 地铁列车

16. modafinil 莫达芬尼[一种治疗发作性睡眠病（一种无法抑制的阵发性嗜睡或突然的沉睡）的药物]
17. narcolepsy /ˈnɑːkəʊlepsɪ/ n. 嗜眠发作

18. to come off 结束

19. to trip up 失败（这里指没有通过兴奋剂检测）
20. 对于任何药品，所有的运动员都应该先咨询是否可以服用 exemption /ɪɡˈzempʃən/ n. 免除；解除；豁免
21. Remi Korchemny 柯奇尼（前乌克兰著名田径教练，当时指导凯莉·怀特）

Korchemny's first individual world champion—and heartbreaking to see this incident tear it all down[22]. The IAAF's upcoming investigation could result in as much as a two-year suspension[23] in addition to disqualification from this world championships.

22. to tear it all down 把它全毁了
23. suspension /sə'spenʃən/ n. 禁赛

White was asked on Saturday night whether she thinks she has a chance to keep her two gold medals from the 100 and 200.

"Deep in my heart, I do believe [I will]," she said. "I worked very hard to earn them, and I'll work very hard to keep them."

I would love to believe every word she said. Unfortunately for her and for us too, it's out of our hands[24] now.

24. out of one's hands 不受某人控制

Comprehension Questions

1. What is the "latest, and certainly worst, round of bad news for the United States" to which the journalist refers?
2. What substance had Kelli White allegedly tested positive for?
3. Has Kelli White admitted any wrongdoing on her part and how does she explain the existence of the substance that she tested positive for?
4. What must athletes do when taking any form of medication that might contain banned substances?
5. The IAAF's investigation could result in a two-year suspension for Kelli White in addition to disqualification from the World Championships. What in your opinion would be a fair sanction for this alleged offence?

Background Reading

A Piece of Anti-Doping History: IAAF Handbook 1927–1928

In 1928 the IAAF became the first ever International Sport Federation to ban the use of doping products. As detailed in the 1927–1928 IAAF Handbook, historic discussions took place at the time of the 1928 Olympic Games in Amsterdam. This Handbook details for the first time a ban on doping practices in the sport of athletics.

Within the selected pages of the Handbook you will find two main sections dealing with the topic of Doping. Section 13 details the decision by the IAAF Congress accept a rule prohibiting the use of doping products in athletics.

"*The Congress voted unanimously (一致地) that such a rule should be introduced, whereupon a lively discussion ensued (紧接着进行) as to the text to be adopted in this respect*".

The discussions then continued on the second day of meetings which can be found in section 22. It was at this time that the final wording of the rule was accepted.

"Doping is the use of any stimulant not normally employed to increase the poser of action in athletic competition above the average. Any person knowingly acting of assisting as explained above shall be excluded from any place where these rules are in force or, if he is a competitor, be suspended for a time or otherwise from further participation in amateur athletics under the jurisdiction (权限) of this Federation".

The IAAF is proud to have been the first International Federation to prohibit the use of doping products, nearly 78 years ago. The rules and procedures in the field of anti-doping certainly have changed drastically (极度地;极大地) since this time.

The IAAF is equally proud that today we are recognised as one of the leading organisations in the modern fight against doping in sport. It would be a safe bet that at the time of drafting these rules in 1928, the IAAF congress would not have imagined a staff of 11 people working within the IAAF Medical and Anti-Doping Department to combat doping in athletics.

The vast majority of our athletes compete in clean an honest manner without resorting to (利用;采取) doping. The IAAF will do all it can to continue implementing and improving its anti-doping programme in order to protect the efforts of these clean and true athletes.

Relevant Words

anti-doping 禁止使用兴奋剂
doping test 兴奋剂检测
elevated result 化验结果超标
in-competition test 比赛期间进行的检查
out-of-competition test 赛外检查(也称飞行检查)
random test 随机检查

Lesson 4

> "2012年奥运会举办地是伦敦!"国际奥委会主席罗格的声音从遥远的新加坡传到了伦敦。狂喜犹如从天而降,这个古老沉静的城市瞬间变成了欢乐的海洋。
>
> 中长跑名将霍姆斯和其他运动员代表以及数以万计的群众聚集在伦敦市中心特拉法加广场,一张张激动的面孔上写满了惊喜。
>
> 广场中心树起了一个电视大屏幕,电视直播把观众带到了2012年奥运会申办投票现场。当罗格打开信封准备宣布最后结果时,喧闹的广场陷入一片紧张的沉寂之中,人们都屏住了呼吸。
>
> 当罗格最后说出"伦敦"时,广场先是一阵短暂的寂静,人们似乎不敢相信自己的耳朵,接着迸发出震耳欲聋的欢呼。香槟酒在人群上空喷洒,烟火燃放起来,天空中飘满彩色的纸屑,人们在相互拥抱庆祝,尽情挥洒着喜悦。

Tears of Joy as Holmes[1] Leads the Celebrations

By Tom Knight
July 7, 2005
Daily Telegraph

The shock, disbelief and unconfined[2] joy that gripped[3] Kelly Holmes was mirrored in 12,000 faces yesterday as Trafalgar Square[4] rocked[5] with the excitement of the Olympic triumph. A veteran of three Games, Holmes's emotions were laid bare on a day of excruciating tension.[6]

Holmes took to the stage alongside fellow Olympians including track legend Steve Cram, sailors Sarah Webb and Ben Ainslie, 800 metres runner Jo Fenn, paralympian[7] Danny Crates, curling gold medallist Rhona Martin and Dame Mary Peters in the minutes before the International Olympic Committee's decision on the 2012 host city was announced on the giant screen.

With the sort of reverence[8] that will not be in evidence[9] in 2012, it was the Capital Radio presenter, Katy Hill, who told the crowd: "We're going across to Singapore and the big man, Jacques Rogge.[10]" She meant the IOC president, Jacques Rogge, but Hill and the assembled Olympians had to maintain their dignity for a few minutes

---

1. Kelly Holmes 凯丽·霍姆斯(英国中长跑名将,在2004年雅典奥运会上获女子800米和1500米金牌)
2. unconfined /ˌʌnkənˈfaɪnd/ a. 无限制的
3. grip /ɡrɪp/ v. 抓牢;控制
4. Trafalgar Square 特拉法加广场(位于英国伦敦市中心)
5. rock /rɒk/ v. 撼动
6. 在这样一个极度紧张的日子里,三赴奥运赛场的老将霍姆斯完全不掩饰自己的情感。excruciating /ɪkˈskruːʃieɪtɪŋ/ a. 极度的
7. paralympian /ˌpærəˈlɪmpiən/ n. 残疾人运动员
8. reverence /ˈrevərəns/ n. 尊敬
9. in evidence 明显的
10. 现在我们连线到新加坡和大人物雅克·罗格。

more as a rendition of the Olympic anthem[11] played out from the Raffles Hotel complex[12] in Singapore.

Then, as Rogge began to open the envelope, Holmes squeezed both eyes shut and clasped[13] her hands as if in prayer. The eyes of the crowd were locked on the screen and the yellow-jacketed workmen leant over the scaffolding[14] across the front of the National Gallery[15].

As Rogge edged[16] closer to naming the winning city, Holmes buried her head in Cram's shoulder and the rest of the athletes closed their eyes and held hands.

Finally, the word "London" unleashed myriad[17] emotions from on stage and around the windswept[18] landmark[19].

Holmes and Cram leapt[20] in the air, hugged and kissed. The crowd went wild as music blared[21] and blizzards of[22] confetti[23] cascaded[24] on the celebrations.

Cram said: "Kelly and I were shivering on that stage. We thought it was the cold weather before we realised that it was through sheer[25] nerves."

By the time Holmes wove her way[26] through the massed ranks of the media, she was wiping away tears. "I was getting emotional about how I felt at an Olympic Games and I realised that a whole new generation are going to feel the same thing," she said.

"This will change the face of Great Britain for ever. The Games are going to be so huge and the effects will be felt here for generations to come. The Olympic spirit is so powerful that anyone who has not experienced it doesn't know what's going to hit[27] them.

"It will change so many people's lives in this country. Children are going to say they want to be part of the Games and it will change the perception of sport around the country. In schools, there will be more facilities and people will get off their sofas to get involved in sport.

"But this isn't just about the athletes. It is about the fans, the volunteers and officials. We have to show the world that we can have the best Games ever. And we will. For me, the Olympic Games were the best thing ever. I feel excited for those children who will be there in 2012."

Peters, the 1972 Olympic pentathlon champion, was 66 yesterday and could not have had a better birthday present. "It was a very emotional moment," she said. "We were so frightened because we knew that Paris had been talked about so much. We were all shaking with emotion and I feel very proud to be British."

11. Olympic anthem 奥运会歌
12. complex /ˈkɒmpleks/ n. 综合楼
13. clasp /klɑːsp/ v. 紧握
14. scaffolding /ˈskæfəldɪŋ/ n. 台架
15. National Gallery 国家美术馆（位于特拉法加广场北边）
16. edge /edʒ/ v. 徐徐移动
17. myriad /ˈmɪrɪəd/ a. 数不清的
18. windswept /ˈwɪndswept/ a. 暴露在风中的
19. landmark /ˈlændmɑːk/ n. 地标性建筑（这里指特拉法加广场）
20. leap /liːp/ v. 跳跃
21. blare /bleə/ v. 大声鸣响
22. blizzards of 大量的
23. confetti /kənˈfetɪ/ n. 五彩纸屑
24. cascade /kæˈskeɪd/ v. 瀑布般地落下
25. sheer /ʃɪə/ a. 全然的
26. to weave one's way 迂回行进

27. hit /hɪt/ v. 影响

Everyone was hugging everyone else as Olympians, officials and journalists struggled to come to terms with the enormity[28] of what had just happened.

Even the normally understated[29] director of performance at UK Sport, Liz Nicholl, was letting her emotions show. But Nicholl knew there was not a lot of time to enjoy the triumph. By 9.30 this morning, she will be chairing meetings to establish the way forward for the country's elite[30] sportsmen and women.

If Britain puts money into all 28 sports contested in 2012, for instance, Nicholl believes another ₤20 million a year, on top of the current annual spending of ₤98 million, could be required.

Nicholl said: "This is the best thing to happen to British sport and it has the power to unite everyone in sport behind a shared goal. We know we can deliver a wonderful Games. UK Sport's role is to deliver a successful team.

"We've already done a lot of work on this. We know how much we need to move sports into the medal zone and the view is that a place among the top five countries in the world is the highest we can aspire[31] to. The next 12 months is the critical time because, for some of the sports, if you delay it any longer they will not be able to move from where they are now to where they need to be.

"Our commitment to the IOC and the world is producing a top-class team to win medals."

Prime Minister Tony Blair assured the IOC that London's preparations would start the day after the decision on the host city was made. According to Steve Martin, the deputy chief executive of the British Olympic Association, everything is in place to make that happen. Martin said: "We need to crack on[32] with realising young athletes' dreams in 2012."

Already planned by the BOA is a meeting with all the country's sports, Lottery[33] funded or otherwise, the performance directors and the directors of the nation's sporting institutes.

Exciting the movers and shakers yesterday was the realisation that sport has now moved to the top of the political agenda. As Mike Calvin, deputy director of the English Institute of Sport, said: "The Government know that sport works. This is a great day for sport in this country and we can, at last, make things happen. There are some good people in the system but the system has often held them back. Now the shackles[34] are off."

28. enormity /ɪˈnɔːmɪtɪ/ n. 巨大；无限
29. understated /ˌʌndəˈsteɪtɪd/ a. 不夸张的；含蓄的
30. elite /eɪˈliːt/ a. 精英的，非常优秀的
31. aspire /əsˈpaɪə/ v. 期望
32. to crack on 继续
33. lottery /ˈlɒtərɪ/ n. 彩票
34. shackle /ˈʃækəl/ n. 束缚

Comprehension Questions

1. Who did Kelly Holmes take to the stage with minutes before the International Olympic Committee's decision on the 2012 host city was announced?
2. Who made the announcement regarding who was to host the 2012 Games?
3. In terms of sporting achievement for the 2012 Games what position does Britain aspire to?
4. According to Liz Nicholl, what is UK Sport's commitment to the IOC and the world?
5. What kind of a positive impact do you think hosting the 2012 Olympic Games will have on sports development in Britain?

Background Reading

Olympic Hosts London and Beijing Sign Partnership Agreement

BEIJING (AFP)—London Mayor Ken Livingstone signed an agreement with his Beijing counterpart Wang Qishan to promote the two cities and deepen trade links in the run-up (准备阶段) to the next two Olympic Games.

With Beijing hosting the 2008 Games, and London taking over the responsibility four years later, Livingstone's three-day China visit that began Sunday has focused very much on the world's biggest sports event.

"Our cities will have particular opportunity to cooperate because they are holders of the next two Olympic games," Livingstone said in a statement.

"We hope this agreement will foster (培养) an environment in which London and Beijing can become closer business partners and develop a deeper cultural understanding through the exchange of tourists and students."

The two mayors plan to work together to encourage "business and trade links, tourism, educational exchanges and cultural relations between the two capitals, benefiting both cities," the statement said.

London only has similar partnership agreements with New York, Moscow, Berlin and Paris, said the statement released by a public relations firm handling Livingstone's visit.

Beijing mayor Wang had also been invited to London in early 2007 for a meeting of European mayors, according to the statement.

Livingstone is being accompanied on his China visit by a large delegation of mostly business and finance leaders, as well as London Olympics organizing committee chairman Sebastian Coe.

"My purpose in Beijing is clearly to see what we can learn from the way Beijing has prepared for the Olympic Games," Livingstone told reporters as he visited Tiananmen Square on Sunday.

"But also it's much more than that. We want to try and build very strong links between London and Beijing."

Lesson 5

在2005年世界杯资格赛中,英格兰队惨败给北爱尔兰队,年少气盛的鲁尼(Wayne Rooney)狂怒之下对队长贝克汉姆(David Beckham)恶语相向。一旦冷静下来又后悔不迭,连忙飞往贝克汉姆效劳的皇家马德里队道歉。余下的资格赛不可轻视,英格兰队也不乏精兵强将,且看总教练埃里克森如何调遣。

Rooney Says Sorry to Beckham

By Henry Winter
October 3, 2005
Sunday Telegraph[1]

Wayne Rooney, the Manchester United attacker[2], yesterday flew to Spain to apologise personally to David Beckham, Real Madrid's[3] England captain, for swearing at[4] him during the sulphurous defeat[5] to Northern Ireland in Belfast[6] last month. Rooney was scheduled to have dinner with Beckham after Madrid's match last night.

Rooney's flight of contrition[7] will be welcomed as it should remove any heat from England training this week. After a collection of[8] stupid fouls at Windsor Park[9], Rooney was ordered to calm down by Beckham, but the teenager responded with a mouthful of invective[10]. Rooney continued his rant[11] in the dressing room at half-time.

The yellow card that accompanied Rooney's excess[12] in Belfast means that he is suspended from Saturday's World Cup qualifier[13] with Austria, but he will train with the team and return to the line-up[14] against Poland, also at Old Trafford[15], a week on Wednesday.

Another United player, Alan Smith, returned to the England fold after a brief spell in purdah for refusing to represent his country in August's friendly against Denmark.[16]

Smith, who missed last month's internationals against Wales and Northern Ireland, is included as a midfielder[17] in Sven-Goran Eriksson's 24-man squad.

Smith regains his place, and the head coach's favour, ahead of

1. *Sunday Telegraph*《星期日电讯报》,创立于1961年,系英国大报《每日电讯报》的姊妹报,是一份综合性报纸,被认为是保守党的媒体之一。
2. attacker /əˈtækə/ n. 前锋
3. Real Madrid(西班牙)皇家马德里队
4. to swear at 辱骂
5. sulphurous defeat 惨败
6. Belfast /belˈfɑːst/ 贝尔法斯特(英国北爱尔兰首府)
7. contrition /kənˈtrɪʃən/ n. 悔悟
8. a collection of 一系列的
9. Windsor Park 温莎公园球场(位于贝尔法斯特)
10. a mouthful of invective 满嘴脏话
11. rant /rænt/ n. 瞎闹
12. excess /ɪkˈses/ n. 过分(的行为)
13. qualifier /ˈkwɒlɪfaɪə/ n. 资格赛
14. line-up /ˈlaɪnʌp/ n. (比赛时球员的)阵容
15. Old Trafford 老特拉福德体育场(位于英国曼切斯特郊区)
16. 另外一名曼联队的球员阿伦·史密斯也回到英格兰队。之前他因为拒绝代表国家出战八月对丹麦的一场友谊赛而短暂地消失了一段时间。
17. midfielder /ˈmɪdfiːldə/ n. 中卫

more established midfield talent such as Scott Parker and Danny Murphy, who have been overlooked despite their good form for Newcastle United[18] and Charlton Athletic[19] respectively[20]. Michael Carrick and Owen Hargreaves are absent injured.

With Eriksson committed to returning to 4-4-2, rather than the 4-5-1 that misfired[21] in Belfast, central midfield[22] options will be limited for Smith. Beckham is expected to move back to the right with Steven Gerrard and Frank Lampard forming the central-midfield bulwark[23].

Unless Eriksson deploys[24] Ledley King to anchor[25] a forward-looking[26] three-man think tank[27] of Beckham, Gerrard and Lampard, Eriksson will need to introduce a left-sided presence[28] such as Joe Cole or Kieran Richardson.

Having watched Emile Heskey struggle up front for Birmingham City at Arsenal yesterday, Eriksson has turned to Peter Crouch as his likely partner for Michael Owen in the absence of Rooney.

Darren Bent, the prolific striker who scored twice for Charlton on Saturday in front of Eriksson, retains his place.

Newcastle's manager, Graeme Souness[29], insisted that Owen "should be fine" after missing the weekend's game against Portsmouth with a dead leg acquired running into[30] defender Steven Taylor in training.

In defence, Sol Campbell makes a welcome return. England have missed the Arsenal stopper's[31] steadying presence, particularly with Rio Ferdinand prone to lapses[32] in concentration.

One of the great debates this international week will be which two centre-halves[33] are chosen from the gifted collection of Campbell, Ferdinand, John Terry and Jamie Carragher.

Fulham's[34] manager, Chris Coleman, watched Ferdinand at close hand on Saturday and he believes England's best central-defensive[35] axis does not necessarily include the United man.

"I think the one obvious choice at the moment is John Terry," Coleman said. "For me, he's the best and most reliable centre-back[36] in the country.

"Sol Campbell is obviously coming back from injury and is going to want to stake a claim. He's got great experience, and if he gets back to form, I wouldn't look any further than him.

"Rio's a fantastic centre-back, but when you've got three centre-backs like Rio, Sol and John Terry, it's a difficult choice."

---

18. Newcastle United 纽卡斯尔联队
19. Charlton Athletic 查尔顿队
20. respectively /rɪˈspektɪvlɪ/ ad. 分别地
21. misfire /ˈmɪsˈfaɪə/ v. 不奏效
22. central midfield 正中场
23. bulwark /ˈbʊlwək/ n. 堡垒
24. deploy /dɪˈplɔɪ/ v. 调度
25. anchor /ˈæŋkə/ v. 打自由人(清道夫)的位置
26. forward-looking /ˈfɔːwədˈlʊkɪŋ/ a. 有远见的
27. think tank 智囊团
28. ...introduce a left-sided presence ……在左侧安插一名球员
29. Graeme Souness 索内斯(当时纽卡斯尔联队的主教练)
30. ...a dead leg acquired running into 因为撞到……而使小腿受伤 dead leg 小腿伤
31. stopper /ˈstɒpə/ n. 盯人中卫
32. lapse /læps/ v. 失误
33. centre-half /ˈsentəhɑːf/ n. 中后卫
34. Fulham 富勒姆队
35. central-defensive /senˈtrəl dɪˈfensɪv/ n. 中场防守
36. centre-back /ˈsentəbæk/ n. 中后卫

Eriksson has dropped defenders Stephen Warnock and Matthew Upson, while injury precludes³⁷ the selection of Gary Neville, Wayne Bridge and Kieron Dyer.

37. preclude /prɪˈkluːd/ v. 妨碍

Comprehension Questions

1. Why did Wayne Rooney feel the need to apologise to David Beckham?
2. What did David Beckham order Wayne Rooney to do at Windsor Park and why?
3. Which players are out injured for England's next match (including those players whose selection was precluded by injury)?
4. According to Chris Coleman, who is the best and most reliable centre-back in the country?
5. The FIFA World Cup is one of the most popular international sporting festivals. Does it dampen your interest when your home country is not involved, or do you channel your support towards another team?

Background Reading

FIFA World Cup Qualification

FIFA World Cup qualification is the process a team must go through to qualify for the FIFA World Cup Finals, or, more commonly known as the FIFA World Cup or Football World Cup. FIFA World Cup is a global event, and qualification is used to reduce the large field of participants (about 200) to a practical number.

Qualifying tournaments are held within the six FIFA continental zones (Africa, Asia, North and Central America, South America, Oceania, Europe), and are organized by their respective confederations. For each tournament, FIFA decides beforehand the number of spots awarded to each of the continental zones, based on the relative strength of the confederations' teams (and, some may argue, political considerations).

The hosts of the World Cup receive an automatic berth (席位) in the finals. Unlike many other sports, results of the previous World Cups or of the continental championships are not taken into account. Until 2002, the defending champions also received an automatic berth, but starting from the 2006 World Cup they also need to enter qualifying.

Over the years, the World Cup's qualification has evolved, from having no qualification at all in 1930, to a three-year process in 2006. The qualification format was basically the same throughout the history of the World Cup. The teams have been grouped continentally, and playing for a fixed number of berths.

Currently, 32 places are available in the final tournament. One of them is reserved for the host nation (if two nations host the competition jointly, each is awarded a place).

Qualification in all zones ends at approximately the same time, in September-November of the year preceding the finals.

In all group tournaments, 3 points are awarded for a win, 1 for a draw, and none for a loss. FIFA has regularized the list of the tie-breakers (决胜赛) for teams that finish level on points:

1. greater number of points obtained in matches between the tied teams;
2. goal difference in matches between the tied teams;
3. greater number of goals scored in matches between the tied teams;
4. goal difference in all group matches;
5. greater number of goals scored in all group matches;
6. a play-off on neutral ground, with extra time and penalties if necessary.

Relevant Words

关于伤病的词(1)

broken pelvis 骨盆骨折	broken ankle 踝骨折
broken collarbone 锁骨骨折	broken leg 小腿骨折
broken toe 脚趾骨折	broken shoulder 肩部骨折
bruised shin 胫骨撞伤	bruised thigh 大腿撞伤
bruised jaw 下巴撞伤	bruised rib 肋骨撞伤
bruised head 头部瘀伤	calf strain 小腿扭伤
chest injury 胸部受伤	concussion 脑震荡
dead leg 小腿受损	damaged shoulder 肩部受伤
damaged foot 脚受伤	damaged heel 脚后跟受损
damaged knee cap 膝盖骨受损	damaged knee cartilage 膝盖软骨受损
damaged cruciate ligaments 十字韧带受损	damaged elbow 肘部受损

Lesson 6

2001年埃里克森(Sven-Göran Eriksson)作为欧洲足球最受欢迎的主教练之一开始执掌英格兰队帅印。可以说,在他的带领下,英格兰队的比赛纪录是出色的。然而,在2006年德国世界杯资格赛中,英格兰队以0-1败给"小弟"北爱尔兰队,这让埃里克森遭受了一场前所未有的信任危机。他不仅遭到英国媒体的口诛笔伐,甚至有些失望的球迷起哄要求其下课。在这种情况下,著名球员欧文(Michael Owen)挺身而出,表达了对主教练绝对的信心和支持。

Owen Restates His Case for Doing It the Eriksson Way

By George Caulkin
October 4, 2005
The Times

Michael Owen not only intends to prove his own fitness this week, but also that of Sven-Göran Eriksson. In issuing a staunch[1] defence of the England head coach, whose position has been questioned after abject[2] displays[3] by his team against Northern Ireland, Wales and Denmark, the forward[4] tried to defuse[5] a controversy[6] last night that has impinged upon[7] a faltering[8] World Cup qualifying campaign.

"There has been a lot written about supposed disharmony[9] in the dressing-room," Owen, who missed Newcastle United's 0-0 draw away to Portsmouth on Saturday with a dead leg, said. "Nothing could be further from the truth.[10] This is a tight squad, with a firm belief in ourselves and in Sven-Göran Eriksson and the coaching staff. Team spirit will be important over the coming days. Rest assured, it is as strong as ever."

"The players are fully behind the manager. His record in competitive games is outstanding and people seem to have forgotten that the defeat against Northern Ireland was his first in a qualifier in over four years. Perhaps we have got used to a certain level of success under Sven. I have not changed my belief that he is the right man to lead us to [next summer's finals in] Germany and achieve success

---

1. staunch /stɔːntʃ/ *a.* 坚定的;忠诚的
2. abject /ˈæbdʒekt/ *a.* 拙劣的
3. display /dɪˈspleɪ/ *n.* 表现
4. forward /ˈfɔːwəd/ *n.* 前锋(这里指 Michael Owen)
5. defuse /ˌdiːˈfjuːz/ *v.* 除去危险
6. controversy /ˈkɒntrəvɜːsɪ/ *n.* 争论;辩论
7. to impinge on/upon 危害
8. faltering /ˈfɔːltərɪŋ/ *a.* 蹒跚的;跌跌撞撞的
9. disharmony /dɪsˈhɑːmənɪ/ *n.* 不和谐;不一致
10. 这完全不是事实。

there."

Owen's bullishness[11] should not be interpreted as complacency[12]. There is a collective recognition that last month's historic 1–0 defeat in Belfast was far from the required standard. "This is our chance to put things right," he said, "and I'm confident we will. I can't wait to get on to the Old Trafford pitch [against Austria on Saturday] and I'm sure the rest of the lads[13] are the same.

"There was a lot of criticism after that game [against Northern Ireland] and we have to take it on the chin[14]. We know the performance was not acceptable, both as a team and as individuals. There was a lot of frustration at the way we performed in Belfast. We let ourselves and the fans down[15]. We are determined to react in the most positive way and channel that frustration into[16] much better performances."

Owen, who was praised by Graeme Souness yesterday for his "huge impact" at St James' Park[17], will be assessed by England's medical staff when he reports for duty[18] today, but expects to be available for Saturday's game against a dishevelled[19] Austria team and for Poland four days later. He is "convinced" that England will collect the two victories that would ensure their participation in the finals next summer.

"I'm really pleased with how my Newcastle career has started and was looking forward to building on those promising first few games," Owen said. "However, I'm confident I'll be fit for Saturday. It was just a dead leg picked up in training and shouldn't affect me too much in the next few days. In any case, the anticipation of two huge games ahead of us against Austria and Poland will speed along my recovery."

11. bullishness /ˈbʊlɪʃnes/ n. 断言；坦率直言
12. complacency /kəmˈpleɪsənsɪ/ n. 安心；满足
13. lad /læd/ n. [口语] 伙计；家伙
14. to take it on the chin [俚语] 勇敢而又平静地面对责难
15. to let ... down 让……失望
16. to channel ... into 把……化为
17. St James' Park 圣詹姆斯球场（纽卡斯尔联队的主场）
18. to report for duty 报到
19. dishevelled /dɪˈʃevəld/ a. 混乱的；慌乱的

Comprehension Questions

1. What is Michael Owen intending to do this week?
2. Why has England head coach Sven-Göran Eriksson's position been questioned?
3. Has the England football team lost many qualifiers in the last four years?
4. What does Michael Owen say about his Newcastle career in this article?
5. Can you think of any other sports teams or individual players who have succeeded despite widespread criticism from the fans and media?

Part V   Sporting Mosaic

Background Reading

Sven-Göran Eriksson

Sven-Göran Eriksson joined England as National Team Coach in January 2001, having won the Italian League and Cup double in 2000 with Lazio (意大利拉齐奥队).

Eriksson's first game in charge was the 3–0 victory against Spain at Villa Park in a friendly international on 28 February 2001. Four subsequent (后来的) wins in consecutive (接连的) games ensured that Eriksson achieved the most successful start of any England coach.

Admired and respected by fellow managers, players and fans, Eriksson is known for his astute (机敏的) tactical (善于策略的) awareness and his calm, reassuring style.

Under Eriksson, England qualified for the World Cup in one of the most dramatic campaigns in the Three Lions' (三狮军团, 英格兰队的别称) history. Having reached the quarter-finals in the Far East, Sven's men then qualified for Euro 2004 without losing a game.

They went on to the quarter-finals of the European Championship, but eventually lost out to hosts Portugal on penalties after an epic encounter in Lisbon.

Qualifying for the World Cup Finals in Germany got under way with a 2–2 draw in Austria, followed by victory in Poland. England won their next five qualifiers before losing in Belfast to Northern Ireland.

Qualification was assured by victory over Austria at Old Trafford and England rounded off (结束) 2005 with an amazing 3–2 friendly win over Argentina.

England's second World Cup journey under Sven ended with a heart-breaking defeat on penalties in the quarter-finals after a 0–0 draw.

Prior to the tournament, on Monday 23 January 2006 it was announced that Sven would be leaving his role as England Head Coach after the World Cup.

Relevant Words

关于伤病的词(2)

facial injury 面部受伤	groin strain 腹股沟扭伤
gashed leg 腿部划伤	gashed head 头部划伤
hip injury 臀部受伤	pulled hamstring 韧带拉伤
stubbed toe 脚趾骨折	sprained wrist 腕关节扭伤
sprained ankle 踝扭伤	strained neck 脖子扭伤
strained wrist 手腕扭伤	strained ankle ligaments 踝韧带扭伤
strained knee ligaments 膝盖韧带扭伤	twisted knee 膝盖扭伤
twisted ankle 踝扭伤	torn hamstring 韧带撕裂
torn groin muscle 腹肌撕裂	torn calf muscle 小腿肌肉撕裂
thigh strain 大腿扭伤	

Lesson 7

体育明星是怎么"炼"成的？美国少年冰球运动员们的训练生活也许会给你一些答案。他们小小年纪，不仅要离开家庭，告别父母，参加训练及比赛，同时又要兼顾学业。是什么动力促使并支持他们选择并面对这一切的呢？那就让我们走进少年冰球运动员 Zach Redmond 的生活，去寻找这个答案吧。

Junior Hockey[1] Players Chase Dream in America's Heartland[2]

By Dirk Lammers
January 14, 2006
The Associated Press[3]

SIOUX FALLS, S.D.[4] —Zach Redmond spends his weekday mornings in high school classes like most 17 year olds, but the rest of his daily schedule sounds more like a tale from a Canadian province than America's heartland.

After grabbing lunch at his host family's[5] home, the Sioux Falls Stampede defenseman[6] heads to the hockey rink for practice. Monday and Wednesday afternoons are spent in the weight room, and weekends are filled with home games or road trips to other Midwest cities.

"It's quite a bit, but I guess you just have to look at it like it's going to pay off[7] for you in the end," said Redmond, of Traverse City, Mich. "It's not too bad."

Nearly everyone who's played the game has dreamed of becoming the next NHL[8] star, but it's an NCAA Division I[9] scholarship that Redmond and most of his United States Hockey League peers are after.

The USHL[10] is the only Tier 1[11] junior league in the United States, and the talent level is on par with[12] Canada's Major Junior leagues, said USHL president Gino Gasparini.

But while the NCAA classifies the major Canadian circuits[13] as professional, the 16- to 20-year-olds who compete in the USHL can

1. 由于冰球（ice hockey）在美国和加拿大非常流行，所以在这两个国家，说到 hockey，一般就是指冰球；为了区别，曲棍球就被称为 Field Hockey。而在欧洲和其他国家，则将场地曲棍球简称为 hockey，冰球称为 ice hockey。
2. heartland /ˈhɑːtlənd/ n. 中心地带
3. *The Associated Press* 美联社，即美国联合通讯社的简称。英文简称 AP，是由各成员单位联合组成的合作型通讯社。1892年成立于芝加哥。
4. Sioux Falls, S.D. (Sioux Falls, South Dakdta) 苏福尔斯，位于（美国）南达科他州。
5. host family 提供寄宿的家庭
6. defenseman /dɪˈfensmən/ n. 防守队员
7. to pay off 回报
8. NHL = National Hockey League （美国）全国冰球联合会
9. NCAA Division I 美国大学体育协会第 1 区
10. USHL (United States Hockey League) 美国冰球联合会
11. Tier 1 第一级别
12. on par with 与……一样；相当于
13. circuit /ˈsɜːkɪt/ n. 巡回赛

maintain college eligibility[14], Gasparini said.

Redmond was playing Midget[15] Major AAA hockey for Detroit Compuware when he was drafted by both the Stampede and the Plymouth (Mich.) Whalers of the Ontario Hockey League. He said he chose South Dakota over his home state because playing in the OHL would have nixed[16] his chance of nabbing[17] a Division I scholarship.

Gasparini said the USHL's goal is to develop players' skills and maturity in a well-supervised environment, and billet housing[18] is a big part of that philosophy.

Billeting is a time-honored[19] tradition in junior hockey, but one probably more recognized north of the border, said Gary Weckwerth, the Stampede's owner and chief executive officer.

Each year, families in USHL cities such as Waterloo, Iowa, and Kearney, Neb., open their homes to players, receiving no more than a monthly food stipend[20] and game tickets in return[21].

Teams scrutinize[22] host families with interviews and background checks so parents sending their loved ones to an unfamiliar city can feel more at ease, Weckwerth said.

"The thought of putting them in a hotel room or sharing an apartment with four other guys is just incomprehensible," he said. Some of the Stampede's billet families are recent empty-nesters[23], while others have sons who play youth hockey.

Redmond's host parents, Carley and David Strand of Sioux Falls, fall a bit into each category. Their teenage daughter left for college this year, and their 11-year-old son, Jonathan, is a goalie.

Some of the Strands' friends have billeted Stampede players and enjoyed the experience, so the family decided to give it a try this season.

The Strands have held Stampede season tickets for the past five years, but hosting Redmond has taken their intensity[24] to another level, Carley Strand said. The family has traveled 90 miles south to Sioux City, Iowa, for away games and now watches most road games over the Internet.

"My friends, they don't get it," she said. "They're not into hockey and they're like, 'Get a life. All you do is hockey'."

Weckwerth said billeting is also a great experience for young players such as Jonathan Strand, who serves as the Stampede's stick boy[25].

"They get to see the mental and physical commitment that these

14. eligibility /ˌelɪdʒɪˈbɪlɪtɪ/ n. 合格性
15. midget /ˈmɪdʒɪt/ a. 袖珍的; 少儿的

16. nix /nɪks/ v. 禁止; 拒绝
17. nab /næb/ v. 获得
18. billet housing 寄宿
    billet /ˈbɪlɪt/ n. 士兵临时营舍(这里指少年运动员们寄宿的地方)
19. time-honored /ˈtaɪmˌɒnəd/ a. 长期的

20. stipend /ˈstaɪpend/ n. 津贴
21. in return 作为回报
22. scrutinize /ˈskruːtɪnaɪz/ v. 细查

23. empty-nester 空巢者(一般指子女独立离家后留下的老人)

24. intensity /ɪnˈtensɪtɪ/ n. 强度

25. stick boy 为球队看管球棍的男孩

players have to make to get to the next level," Weckwerth said.

Players have to work hard on the ice, but they also have to be good citizens in their home and community and keep up their grades. For the high schoolers, that could mean showing up at class even after arriving home at 6 a.m. from an eight-hour bus trip.

"You'll look back on the bus on some of these long trips and the guys have their lights on doing their homework," Weckwerth said. "It's no fun."

And if that's not enough pressure, the players know that scouts[26] are watching every USHL game.

"There's always college and pro-scouts in the building," Weckwerth said. "Last year there were a lot more NHL guys here because they were on strike. And more upper-echelon[27] coaches within their organizations were here, versus just their regional scouts."

Some players will spend a year in the USHL before making the jump to the NCAA. For others, it could take up to three years to develop the skills and maturity to move on to the next level.

As a 17-year-old leaving his native Austria, Andreas Nodl had a tough time adjusting to the USHL last season. But Weckwerth said the 6-foot-1 Stampede forward[28] came into this season's training camp 13 pounds stronger, scored an opening-night hat trick and has been playing "like the handcuffs[29] were taken off."

Nodl is among the USHL leaders in goals and points this season, and has earned a full scholarship next year to St. Cloud State University in Minnesota. Earlier this week, he was selected for the Western Conference squad for the league's Feb. 7 All-Star game in Sioux City, Iowa.

"He could be another NHLer for us sometime," Weckwerth said. "He's got those skills."

In a developmental league such as the USHL, high turnover is a sign of success.

USHL players earned 131 Division I scholarships last year, and 26 from the league were selected in July's NHL Entry Draft—three in the first round, Gasparini said.

The Stampede's top alum[30], wing[31] Thomas Vanek, is excelling as a rookie this season for the Buffalo Sabres.

Redmond, who arrived in Sioux Falls just a month after turning 17, said he instantly noticed a difference in the talent level from Midget AAA. The Tier 1 players were more skilled and considerably

26. scout /skaʊt/ *n.* 球探

27. upper-echelon /ˈʌpəˈeʃəlɒn/ *a.* 高级别的

28. forward /ˈfɔːwəd/ *n.* 前锋

29. handcuff /ˈhændkʌf/ *n.* 手铐

30. alum /ˈæləm/ *n.* 校友
31. wing /wɪŋ/ *n.* 边锋

faster, and everybody worked hard.

"You get used to it as the games go on, but jumping right in is a change," he said.

Redmond will head back home to Michigan at the end of this season to graduate from his hometown high school. Until then, he said he'll continue to work hard on the ice and make his nightly calls to his parents, who've been following the Stampede's winning season over the Internet.

Redmond said the team's great chemistry[32] has made the experience enjoyable.

32. chemistry /'kemɪstrɪ/ n. 融洽的关系

"We don't really have anyone that doesn't want to be there, and everyone has fun," he said. "It just makes it easier to play and it's working for us."

Comprehension Questions

1. What is Zach Redmond and most of his United States Hockey League peers striving for?
2. Why did Zach choose South Dakota over his home state?
3. What is the practice of "billeting" that is mentioned in the article?
4. Apart from working hard on the ice what else is expected of the young hockey players?
5. In order to play professional hockey, players have to show a lot of commitment from a young age. Can you think of any other sports which require similar levels of commitment, starting from an early age?

Background Reading

The NCAA and How to Get a Scholarship

Athletic scholarships for undergraduate student athletes at Division I and Division II schools are partially funded through the NCAA membership revenue distribution. These scholarships are awarded directly by the NCAA colleges and not the NCAA. About $1 billion in athletic scholarships are awarded each year. Over 126,000 student-athletes receive either a partial or full athletic scholarship.

NCAA scholarships are offered in the following sports:

MEN. Baseball, Basketball, Cross Country, Fencing (击剑), Football, Golf, Gymnastics, Ice Hockey, Lacrosse (网棒球), Rifle (射击), Skiing, Soccer, Swimming, Tennis, Track and Field, Volleyball, Water Polo (水球) and Wrestling.

WOMEN. Archery (射箭), Badminton, Basketball, Bowling, Cross Country, Equestrian (马术), Fencing, Field Hockey, Golf, Gymnastics, Lacrosse, Rowing, Skiing, Soccer, Softball (垒球), Squash

(壁球), Swimming, Synchronized Swimming, Team Handball, Tennis, Volleyball and Water Polo.

The National Collegiate Athletic Association is a voluntary association of about 1,200 colleges and universities, athletic conferences and sports organizations devoted to the sound administration of intercollegiate (校际的) athletics.

Two of the purposes or aims of the NCAA are:

To initiate (发起), stimulate and improve intercollegiate athletics programs for student-athletes and to promote and develop educational leadership, physical fitness, athletics excellence and athletics participation as a recreational pursuit.

To uphold the principle of institutional control of, and responsibility for, all intercollegiate sports in conformity (一致) with the constitution and bylaws (规章制度) of the Association.

One of the stated "core values" of the NCAA is a commitment to protecting the best interests of student-athletes.

Whatever your standard or specialty, there are NCAA colleges that need you. There are over 600 colleges in the NCAA and NAIA system offering sports scholarships so there are 1000's of NCAA Scholarships out there in your sport, and many opportunities for young athletes.

Lesson 8

> 埃迪·库里(Eddy Curry)是芝加哥公牛队的中锋。由于几次感觉心脏不适而使主教练约翰·帕克森(John Paxson)怀疑他患有心脏病,担心上场会危及他的生命。而医院的检查结果却不能证实这一点。帕克森因而希望库里能做 DNA 检查以查明他是否有患心脏病的潜在危险,并承诺不论检查结果能否让库里继续打球,他都会得到优厚的待遇。然而库里却以身体状况属于个人隐私为由拒绝了这一要求。无奈之下,帕克森考虑是否要将库里这位非常具有潜力的中锋转会给纽约尼克斯队。

Troubling History
Bulls' Concern for Curry Based on Multiple Incidents

By Ian Thomsen
October 13, 2005
Sports Illustrated

A lot has been said and written about the Chicago Bulls' decision to trade[1] 22-year-old center Eddy Curry to the New York Knicks[2] amid medical concerns about Curry's heart. But here's something you didn't know: Curry had a second—and until now unreported— scare involving his heart during training camp a year ago, according to the Bulls.

"It was during a conditioning drill[3], and Eddy complained of chest pain and lightheadedness[4]," says Bulls GM[5] John Paxson. "We took him to the hospital."

Paxson says that a thorough examination at that time yielded[6] no explanation for Curry's symptoms. The 6-foot-11, 285-pound center went on to average[7] a career-high 16.1 points for the Bulls until March 30, when he complained of symptoms that were diagnosed[8] as heart arrhythmia[9]. "Eddy told our trainer that he had felt the same way two nights earlier during a game against Memphis," says Paxson.

No one realized it then, but Paxson viewed the heavily-publicized incident in March as strike two. He did not dare risk strike three.[10]

Based on the best medical advice the Bulls say they could find,

1. trade /treɪd/ v. 做买卖(这里指出售球员给其他俱乐部)
2. New York Knicks 纽约尼克斯队
3. conditioning drill 体能训练
4. lightheadedness /ˌlaɪtˈhedɪdnɪs/ n. 头晕眼花
5. GM (General Manager) 总经理
6. yield /jiːld/ v. 产生
7. average /ˈævərɪdʒ/ v. 达到平均水平
8. diagnose /ˈdaɪəgnəʊz/ v. 诊断
9. heart arrhythmia 心率失常
10. 在那个时候没有人意识到这一点,可是帕克森却把三月份发生的那次众所周知的事件看做是第二次错误。他不敢再冒第三次险了。"strike two" 和 "strike three" 均是棒球术语,指第二次和第三次击球,每个击球手有三次击球机会。

Paxson decided to bench[11] Curry for the remainder[12] of the season, even though Curry surely could have made a pivotal[13] impact on Chicago's six-game loss to Washington in the first round of the playoffs[14].

The Bulls spent the ensuing[15] three months investigating Curry's health. "Three years ago, Eddy told the Chicago newspapers that his mother had had a mild heart attack," Paxson says. "Later we asked him about it, and he said that no, it wasn't true. Of course, we were not able to [confirm] that kind of information."

Medical experts told Paxson that Curry needed to undergo a DNA test to show whether or not he was predisposed[16] to hypertrophic cardiomyopathy[17], the same heart disease that was linked to the tragic deaths of Reggie Lewis[18] and Hank Gathers[19] while they were playing basketball.

"In all likelihood Eddy doesn't have it (hypertrophic cardiomyopathy)," acknowledges Paxson.

But one can understand why Paxson was so cautious about letting Curry wear a Bulls uniform again. Based on last season's scares with Curry, as well as everything he was learning about heart disease, Paxson could not bear the responsibility of permitting Curry to play so long as there *was the slightest doubt* that playing the game could end his life. Paxson says that he and Bulls owner Jerry Reinsdorf were in full agreement on this issue: A DNA test showing that Curry was predisposed to a fatal[20] disease, in concert with[21] the two episodes[22] of last season, would have been enough to prohibit Curry from playing for the Bulls again.

It was probably the most important career decision Paxson will ever make. Not because it resulted in him trading a potential All-Star center. But because he saw it simply as a choice of life or death.

Curry's advisers told him that he was healthy and that he should avoid the DNA test for a host of[23] medical and ethical[24] reasons. The dispute between player and team touched on a larger debate about privacy and the value and reliability of DNA testing. "Everybody tried to make this an ethical employer-employee issue, which we never thought about," says Paxson. "We wanted to do everything we possibly could to safely put him back on the floor. We were never allowed to do that."

Paxson ultimately made two contract offers to Curry, a restricted free agent[25]. But both offers were contingent[26] on him taking the DNA

11. bench /bentʃ/ v. 使不参加比赛
12. remainder /rɪ'meɪndə/ n. 剩余的时间
13. pivotal /'pɪvətəl/ a. 关键的
14. playoff /'pleɪɔːf/ n. 季后赛
15. ensuing /ɪn'sjuːɪŋ/ a. 紧接着的
16. predisposed /ˌpriːdɪs'pəʊzd/ a. 易患某种疾病的
17. hypertrophic cardiomyopathy 肥厚型心肌病
18. Reggie Lewis 前波士顿凯尔特队前锋,1993 年因心脏病死于赛场上。
19. Hank Gathers 洛杉矶罗亚拉·马里蒙特大学(Loyola Marymount University)的天才球员,1988 年因心脏病死于赛场上。

20. fatal /'feɪtl/ a. 致命的
21. in concert with 与……相呼应
22. episode /'epɪsəʊd/ n. 事件

23. a host of 一系列的
24. ethical /'eθɪkəl/ a. 道德的;伦理的
25. free agent 自由球员,即不受合约束缚的职业队员。自由球员又分为两种:完全自由球员(unrestricted free agent)和受限自由球员(restricted free agent),自由球员制度称作 free agency system。
26. contingent /kən'tɪndʒənt/ a. 有条件的;视情况而定的

exam. If he passed the test, he would receive $32 million over four years. If the test indicated that Curry was predisposed to a potentially fatal heart condition, the Bulls promised him an annuity[27] that would pay Curry $400,000 annually for 50 years—a total of $20 million for someone who wouldn't be playing.

"It's hurting me that Eddy's now saying that we didn't care about him," says Paxson. "It's painful because Eddy's a good guy. We were trying to do the right thing for him, and for us, but more for him. As time went on, people were trying to get in the middle of it or trying to convince him we were trying not to do right by him. And reading his comments now I really do get the feeling that that he believes that we betrayed[28] him.

"We offered to give him $400,000 a year for 50 years if he took the genetic test[29] and failed it. That was not a basketball decision. That was a personal decision, and we made it because we care about him as a human being. To not have that seen as an important thing is very painful to me."

Paxson still doesn't understand why Curry, as a father of two with another baby on the way, would not want as much information as possible—whether the news was good or bad—about the condition of his heart. "Like I say, he probably doesn't have the disease," says Paxson. "But wouldn't you want to be sure for the sake of[30] your kids?"

Those concerns are now the province of the Knicks' front office after Isiah Thomas traded Tim Thomas, Mike Sweetney and draft picks for Curry and Antonio Davis and cleared Curry to resume his playing career, reportedly without taking the DNA exam.[31] Paxson neither questions their methods nor second-guesses[32] their decision and expresses hope that Curry enjoys an excellent career and a long, gratifying[33] life.

But if he never has another heart-related incident, don't take Curry's good fortune to mean that Paxson was wrong. The Bulls GM made the only decision that he could make responsibly, knowing everything he knew about Curry's previous health scares.

Medical ethicists[34] will debate the need and precise uses for DNA testing, but Paxson wasn't trying to break new ground[35] or set any kind of precedent[36]. He insists he was only trying to use all available resources to avoid putting a player into a situation that might literally kill him.

27. annuity /əˈnjuːɪti/ n. 年金

28. betray /bɪˈtreɪ/ v. 出卖；背叛
29. genetic test 基因测试
30. for the sake of 为了
31. 现在这一切都变成了尼克斯队前台办公室的忧虑。伊塞亚·托马斯(Isiah Thomas)用蒂姆·托马斯(Tim Thomas)、迈克·斯维特尼(Mike Sweetney)以及获选的新秀换取了库里和安东尼奥·戴维斯(Antonio Davis)。他批准库里继续他的球员生涯，据说并没有要求库里进行DNA测试。
Isiah Thomas 伊塞亚·托马斯，尼克斯队的篮球营运总裁。
draft pick 获选新秀
clear /klɪə/ v. 批准
resume /rɪˈzjuːm/ v. 恢复；继续
reportedly /rɪˈpɔːtɪdlɪ/ ad. 据说
32. second-guess /ˈsekəndɡes/ v. 做事后批评
33. gratifying /ˈɡrætɪfaɪɪŋ/ a. 悦人的；满意的
34. medical ethicist 医学伦理学家
35. to break new ground 开辟新天地
36. precedent /ˈpresɪdənt/ n. 先例

"This kind of thing will come up again and it needs to be addressed," says Paxson. "Had we played this out³⁷ and not traded Eddy, it would have raised some real questions that need to be answered. These are professional athletes who every day need to push their bodies to limits³⁸ that normal people don't need to reach. Common sense says that we—and they—need to find out as much as we can about their health. These genetic tests are going to save people."

37. to play sth. out 明知是假象，却故意接受
38. to push one's body to limits 使身体到达极限

Comprehension Questions

1. Which team did the Chicago Bulls trade their center Eddy Curry to?
2. Why did the Bulls GM, John Paxson, bench Eddy for the rest of the season?
3. Why did the medical experts tell Paxson that Eddy should undergo a DNA test? Did Eddy agree to the DNA tests?
4. What did Paxson offer Eddy Curry if he took the DNA test and failed it?
5. Do you think that it is fair for an employer to demand that one of its sports stars undertake a DNA test knowing that important decisions will rest upon its result?

Background Reading

Uncertainty Prevails (遍及) on Sports DNA Tests

Eddy Curry, a 22-year-old player in the National Basketball Association who missed 19 games last season because of an irregular heartbeat, refused the Chicago Bulls' request that he take a DNA test to determine whether he is susceptible (对……敏感的) to a potentially fatal heart condition. He was traded last week to the New York Knicks, and he passed his physical on Friday.

These are the facts. A great deal of uncertainty remains, however. Not just about Curry's health but about the increasingly sophisticated (复杂的) and perhaps intimidating (胁迫的) methods used to test and analyze the insides of athletes. What are the ethics of such testing? Does it work? Where might it lead? And how much information about a person is too much?

"I think there are valid points on both sides," said Peter Roby, director of Northeastern University's Center for the Study of Sport in Society. "A player must be careful about what source of information he allows people to get access to. Who the heck knows what's in your medical history or DNA?

"On the other hand, you have an organization that wants to make sure they can do all they can to protect their interests and investments before they commit upwards of $60 million to a player. So I can understand why they would want to use every possible means to investigate that."

Even those who do not have a stake (利害关系) in the matter have some concerns.

"What I'm nervous about is, I don't want to set a precedent where a boss or any third party—

military or the police—can force you to take a genetic test," said Art Caplan, director of the Center for Bioethics at the University of Pennsylvania. "It should be voluntary, and it should be between you and your doctor. The principle I'm trying to defend is, for that kind of test, a prediction (预言) about the future, you should be able to choose."

Mr. Milstein, Curry's attorney (代理律师), told the Chicago Tribune, "If employers could give employees DNA tests, then they could find out if there's a propensity (倾向) for illnesses like cancer, heart disease or alcoholism (酒精中毒). They will make personnel decisions based on DNA testing."

"I can argue both sides of the case very strongly," said Mrs. Salberg, founder and president of the Hypertrophic Cardiomyopathy Association. "In this particular situation, I don't think [testing] was an unreasonable request, just like I don't think it was unreasonable for Mr. Curry to deny it. He has his rights, and the team has their rights."

"I think it's a slippery slope (危险的处境)," Mr. Roby said. "With advances in technology and science, there are going to be situations where you will know just about anything and everything about someone in terms of what they put in their bodies and their history and what their future medical life will be ... It's important for people on both sides of the argument to work together."

Lesson 9

长跑爱好者 Lee Schneider 的父亲在 2000 年因血癌去世。从那以后他便以长跑的形式为血癌及淋巴癌协会募集资金。和 Lee 一样,还有很多人为了理想,为了其他的病人在长跑,在用自己的方式募捐。

Racing for a Cause

By Matthew Dale
May 2006
City Sports Magazine[1]

Lee Schneider's father, Jim, was dying of leukemia[2]. Outside of providing emotional support, there was little the son could do. Then Schneider read an article in a Bay Area newspaper about people running marathons and raising money to support the Leukemia & Lymphoma Society[3]. Schneider, at the time, was what you would call a recreational runner, putting in two miles a day to keep the weight down and to not feel guilty for indulging in[4] dessert.

Months later, on Leap Day[5] 2000, the elder Schneider died. He was 66 years old. But his legacy lives on because his son is fighting the good fight against cancer.

Schneider has run six marathons now. He has also mentored[6] runners, helping them cross off that lifetime 26.2-mile goal. Now the Leukemia & Lymphoma Society's board of trustees[7] president for[8] the Greater Bay Area/San Francisco Chapter, Schneider has helped raise hundreds of thousands of dollars to support leukemia and lymphoma research and support patient programs.

"This is something I can do to help," says Schneider, 44, who

1. *City Sports Magazine*《城市运动》,美国月刊,主要报道径赛与铁人三项,同时为体育爱好者提供有关训练、健康以及营养方面的信息,并介绍著名运动员与赛事。
2. leukemia /luːˈkiːmɪə/ *n.* 白血病
3. Leukemia & Lymphoma Society 白血病和淋巴瘤协会(1949 年成立于美国,是世界最大的自愿保健机构,致力于为血癌研究、教育和患者服务提供资金)
4. to indulge in 沉溺于
5. Leap Day 闰日(指 2 月 29 日)
6. mentor /ˈmentɔː/ *v.* 指导
7. board of trustees 托事会;董事会
8. president for 任……主席

lives in Walnut Creek, California.

Outpouring of Support

Be it the Challenged Athletes Foundation[9], Multiple Sclerosis Society[10], St. Jude's Children's Hospital, the Komen Breast Cancer Foundation or numerous other programs, hundreds of people like Schneider have been touched by a cause, then backed up those emotions with actions, raising funds so that others might live a better life.

It's one of the most common lines you'll hear from a Leukemia & Lymphoma Society runner:

"You think training for a marathon's hard? Try chemotherapy[11]."

Schneider, too, is moved by the cancer patient's plight[12]. He need only think of his father, who was diagnosed with cancer one day, then six months later died. But what moved Schneider even more was the outpouring[13] of support from friends and loved ones. He e-mailed family members and sent a mailer[14] to friends.

"I didn't do a follow-up call," he says. "I didn't want to be one of those annoying fundraisers." Then in came the donations ... $25, $40, $100, plus a $3,000 check from a labor union. In all, Schneider raised $9,000.

"The thing that really impressed me was how many people wrote $100 checks, people who $100 was a lot of money," he says. "It really made me think differently about giving to charities[15]."

An investment manager, Schneider used to routinely donate $25 and $50 to causes, and dropping $1 in the Salvation Army[16] kettle. Moved by those who supported him, Schneider donated $20,000 to charities last year.

Of his sizeable donations, Schneider says, "You make hay while the sun shines[17]. When things are bad, maybe I won't be able to donate as much."

At his father's funeral, Schneider delivered the eulogy[18]. Later, his father's wife gave him a ring that had been handed down by Schneider's grandfather. He wore the ring for his first marathons, using it for motivation when his legs and psyche[19] ached late in the run.

"I'd jokingly say (to his father late in the run), 'This whole leukemia thing is pissing me off. I'm pretty tired. Give me a hand here.' Then I'd look around and there were always leukemia survivors on the course, cheering you on. It put a lump in my throat[20]," says

9. Challenged Athletes Foundation 残疾运动员基金会
   challenged /ˈtʃælɪndʒd/ a. 残疾的
10. Multiple Sclerosis Society 多发性硬化症协会

11. chemotherapy /ˌkiːməʊˈθerəpɪ/ n. 化学疗法
12. plight /plaɪt/ n. 困境；苦境

13. outpour /aʊtˈpɔː/ v. 倾注；流出
14. mailer /ˈmeɪlə/ n. 附在信内的广告印刷品

15. charity /ˈtʃærətɪ/ n. 慈善团体
16. Salvation Army（基督教）救世军（一个慈善团体）
   salvation /sælˈveɪʃən/ n. 拯救，救助
17. to make hay while the sun shines 趁热打铁

18. eulogy /ˈjuːlədʒɪ/ n. 赞词；颂词

19. psyche /ˈsaɪkɪ/ n. 灵魂；精神

20. to put a lump in one's throat 使人哽咽欲泣

Schneider. Late in his first marathon, the Mayor's Midnight Sun Marathon in Anchorage, Alaska, a woman near a hill said to Schneider, as she did to so many runners, "God bless you for being here." To which Schneider replied, "No, God bless YOU."

Moved By the Challenged

Steve Diggs knew about the Leukemia & Lymphoma Society—running marathons, raising money and serving as a mentor to other runners. Then he dipped into triathlon, putting together runners to participate in the 1999 San Diego Triathlon Challenge (SDTC). The November event serves as the marquee[21] fundraiser for the Challenged Athletes Foundation (CAF).

At the SDTC, Diggs watched athletes like Willie Stewart, who lost his left arm in a work accident at 18 then recovered to run a 2:42 marathon and finish an Ironman triathlon in under 11 hours.

He watched Rudy Garcia-Tolson, then an 11-year-old who was born with webbing[22] behind the back of both legs that wouldn't allow them to be straightened. At 5, Garcia-Tolson elected to have his legs amputated[23]. Now 17, Garcia-Tolson won a gold medal at the 2004 Paralympic Games in Athens.

"You see Rudy, a kid running around with (prosthetic[24]) legs, and he's as happy as can be," says Diggs. "His legs were funded by CAF, and you say, 'I have to become involved.' You connect immediately when you see somebody with no legs running past you."

CAF is now Diggs' charity of choice. Started in 1993 to raise $25,000 for a fallen triathlete, CAF has now raised $7.5 million and stretches worldwide as far away as Ghana, gaining national exposure on ESPN[25] and The Oprah Winfrey Show[26]. In 2005, grants enabled CAF to purchase 41 basketball chairs, 35 handcycles[27], 17 road-racing chairs, eight tennis chairs, 12 quad-rugby[28] chairs, nine mono skis[29], 11 road bikes, three hockey sleds[30]—plus provided travel expenses for disabled athletes to attend more than 50 competitions.

Diggs leads a team of more than 30 athletes who collectively have raised more than $200,000 for CAF over the past three years. Athletes who participate in their training group raise a minimum of $2,000. They host events such as an offbeat[31] 'Teddies and Tennies' lingerie[32] run as well as too many auctions[33] to count.

Asked what keeps him committed to CAF, Diggs says, "It's the attitude of the (challenged) athletes. You see athletes who may have

21. marquee /mɑːˈkiː/ *a.* 吸引人的
22. webbing /ˈwebɪŋ/ *n.* 蹼；厚边
23. amputate /ˈæmpjuteɪt/ *v.* 截肢
24. prosthetic leg 义腿
    prosthetic /prɒsˈθetɪk/ *a.* 修复术的
25. ESPN (Entertainment And Sports Programming Network) 娱乐和体育节目网(1978年成立于美国，为体育广播有线网)
26. The Oprah Winfrey Show 欧普拉主持的谈话节目（欧普拉为美国著名"脱口秀"节目主持人）
27. handcycle /ˌhændˈsaɪkl/ *n.* 轮椅
28. quad-rugby 四人橄榄球
29. mono ski 单板雪橇
30. hockey sled 曲棍球棍
31. offbeat /ɒfˈbiːt/ *a.* 不平常的
32. lingerie /ˈlænʒəriː/ *n.* 妇女贴身内衣
33. auction /ˈɔːkʃən/ *n.* 拍卖

gone through a period of depression, recover and then wipe the floor with you[34] in an Ironman."

In Honor of a Loved One

Jean Logsdon was conceived[35] on the Indonesian island of Java, born in Australia and raised in Morocco and New York City. When she was 8, she crossed the Sahara desert with her mother, and as a young mother herself she passed her wanderlust[36] onto her two sons. When John and Mike Logsdon were barely out of diapers[37], the family crossed the United States from San Francisco in an old Ford van equipped to accommodate the rambunctious[38] boys.

"My father replaced the last row of seating with an old mattress[39] where John and I would wrestle and play until we'd worn ourselves out[40]," recalls Mike.

Adds John, "Those summers opened our eyes to the rich cultural and natural diversity that existed within our borders and fueled an insatiable[41] curiosity about the world at large[42]."

In 1996, Jean Logsdon was diagnosed with a malignant[43] brain tumor[44] that took her life later that year. Mike and John were 17 and 14 years old at the time. Nine years later, they embarked on a trip in honor of their mother. The brothers flew to Alaska last summer, and on July 26 embarked on a nine-month cycling adventure. Traveling about 70 miles a day and lugging[45] 100 pounds of equipment, they're riding 15,000 miles from Prudhoe Bay, Alaska, to Ushuaia, Argentina, the southernmost[46] city in the world.

Paired with[47] the National Brain Tumor Foundation's Racing Ahead program, the brothers aspire to raise $50,000 for brain tumor research in their mother's name.

If it were an adventure the brothers were looking for, they got it. They didn't come across a gas station or convenience store the first 500 miles of their journey, but did encounter some 40 bears, including a grizzly[48]. The brothers pedaled away[49] as fast as they could but the grizzly gained on[50] them quickly. Eventually, the bear stood on his hind legs[51], sniffed the air and stopped its pursuit.

"It must have realized we were people, not caribou[52]," says John. Of their zest[53] for adventure, he says: "My mother used to say, 'There's only so much you can learn in a classroom.' She said she'd never buy us a car, but if we wanted to travel, she'd help in any way she can."

---

34. wipe the floor with sb. 轻松击败某人
35. conceive /kən'siːv/ v. 怀孕
36. wanderlust /'wɒndəlʌst/ n. 旅行癖；流浪癖
37. diaper /'daɪəpə/ n. 尿布
38. rambunctious /ræm'bʌŋkʃəs/ n. 难控制的
39. mattress /'mætrɪs/ n. 床垫
40. to wear out 筋疲力尽
41. insatiable /ɪn'seɪʃəbl/ a. 不知足的
42. at large 普遍地
43. malignant /mə'lɪɡnənt/ a. 恶性的
44. tumor /'tjuːmə/ n. 肿瘤
45. lug /lʌɡ/ v. 使劲拉；用力拖
46. southernmost /'sʌðənməʊst/ a. 最南的
47. paired with sth. 和……一起
48. grizzly /'ɡrɪzlɪ/ n. 灰熊
49. to pedal away 蹬自行车逃走
   pedal /'pedl/ v. 蹬(自行车)踏板
50. to gain on 逼近；赶上
51. hind leg 后腿
52. caribou /'kærɪbuː/ n. 北美产驯鹿
53. zest /zest/ n. 热情；热心

Comprehension Questions

1. How is Lee Schneider fighting the good fight against cancer?
2. What is one of the most common lines you'll hear from a Leukemia and Lymphoma Society runner?
3. In 2005 what did the Challenged Athletes Foundation (CAF) purchase with the grants that had been raised?
4. What keeps Steve Diggs committed to the CAF?
5. Apart from long-distance running, are there any other ways to raise money for good causes?

Background Reading

Marathon: Key Points

- It's a long, long way. The modern marathon is run over 26.2 miles or 42.195 km.
- The marathon is the only discipline (项目) in athletics to have become a popular participation sport.
- After 20 miles many inexperienced runners 'hit the wall', an infamous experience suffered when their bodies have run out of fuel.
- Some people find it easier to "marathon" than others. This is partly due to their genes.

Born to marathon?

Some people are better adapted to marathon running than others. This might be by virtue of (由于) their build (体格), physiology (生理) or mental approach (意识). There is one crucial feature marathon runners must have to stand a chance of competing at the highest level. The right kind of muscles.
Marathon muscles

There are two different kinds of fibre (纤维) in muscle:

- 'Slow twitch' (抽动) fibres—these contract slowly but they can keep going for a long time.
- 'Fast twitch' fibres—these contract quickly but are rapidly worn out.

'Slow twitch' fibres are the key to successful marathon running. If a person has a preponderance (优势) of fast-twitch muscles there is no chance of him or her becoming a world-class marathoner. They might however make an ideal sprinter (短跑运动员). The marathon runner needs to have a large proportion of slow twitch fibres in their muscles. This characteristic is largely inherited but there is some evidence that training can make a small difference to the proportions of the different fibre types. Findings suggest that a marathon runner must avoid any sprint training at distances less than 100m. Likewise (同样的) sprinters must never engage in endurance exercise.

Genes for long-distance running?

The Kalenjin tribe (卡伦津人部落，主要分布在东非肯尼亚境内) lives in a province in the northwest of Kenya. Astonishingly, 12 of the world's top-20 distance runners are Kalenjin. Their seemingly effortless victories in some marathons have sparked off a passionate debate about genetic advantage in long-distance running.

Danish sports scientists have studied the Kalenjin runners and compared their style and physique (体格) with that of elite Danish runners. They noticed that their heart rate stayed remarkably low even when running as fast as 15 miles per hour over long distances. People from this region also have a good build for running with long, very thin legs. When the muscle fibres of Kalenjin runners were analysed they were found to be capable of converting oxygen into energy much more efficiently than the Danish runners.

Lesson 10

> 伦敦获得了2012年奥运会主办权,建筑师们优雅新颖的设计功不可没,特别是女建筑师扎哈·哈迪德(Zaha Hadid)设计的伦敦水上运动中心(Olympic Aquatic Centre)让人过目不忘,征服了国际奥委会的代表。然而本文作者却认为衡量一届奥运会是否成功的标准不应该仅仅是金牌、开幕式上燃放的烟花、电视转播权和赞助费,最重要的是应该看一届奥运会结束后能给世人留下些什么。他希望建筑师们能够从历史上各届奥运会的成败中汲取经验教训,让伦敦奥运会能够长留青史。

Building an Olympic Vision

By Dejan Sudjic
July 10, 2005
The Observer

It's not enough to put on a memorable Games: the structures left behind should look to the future too.

Nowhere was the news of the selection of London for the 2012 Olympics greeted with more enthusiasm than in the Clerkenwell[1] offices of Zaha Hadid[2]. Five months ago, when she had won the competition to design London's Olympic Aquatic Centre[3] in Newham, getting to build anything looked like a very long shot[4]. If the games went to Paris, the London Development Agency had promised that it would build some sort of swimming pool, even if on a much smaller scale. But nobody was being very specific about it.

With Wednesday's result, everything changed. Britain's first Pritzker Prizewinning[5] female architect finally has a major project to build in her home town. And, thanks to the spotlight that the games can concentrate on mainstream sports, it's a project that will make her a household name.

After questioning the quality of London's first plans for the Olympics—when cheesy computer renderings[6] for an athletic stadium from central casting, complete with fretwork[7] roof, and rivers of flag-waving cheery crowds were unveiled[8] last year—I was a little surprised to find myself asked to sit on the jury to help choose the

1. Clerkenwell /ˈklɑːkɪs/ n. 英国大伦敦伊斯林顿(Islington)自治市的毗邻地区,范围包括圣詹姆斯和圣约翰两教区。
2. Zaha Hadid 扎哈·哈迪德(英国顶尖的前卫建筑师、艺术家。她的作品引领了近来世界绘画、建筑、室内设计等领域的风潮。北京SOHO城的总体设计和广州歌剧院也是扎哈·哈蒂德的创作。)
3. Olympic Aquatic Centre 奥运会水上中心
4. long shot 成功希望很小的冒险
5. Pritzker Prizewinning 获得普利兹克建筑奖
6. cheesy computer renderings 粗劣的电脑绘图
7. fretwork /ˈfretwɜːk/ n. 带有三维回纹饰的装饰物;几何形浮雕细工
8. unveil /ʌnˈveɪl/ v. 揭开……的面纱;使公诸于众

architect to design the pool that will sit next to it. I was even more surprised when Zaha Hadid turned out to be our unanimous choice.

The bid organisation wanted something that was going to look eye-catching[9] enough to attract the attention of the Olympic Commission as it made its imperial progress around the world. But they were also desperate for a design that could be built as painlessly as possible, and which could be transformed into a regular municipal pool at the touch of a button[10] once the Games were over. Hadid produced a design that stood out even in an impressive field, but did not look like a safe choice. Despite having built nothing more relevant to the world of sport than a ski jump[11] in Austria, she did the bid proud. Her design, based on a sinuous[12], undulating[13] roof snaking[14] over the two pools it shelters, like a manta ray[15] floating over the sea bed, is strikingly beautiful. And, by all accounts[16], impressed the IOC's delegates too.

Unlike Olympic sports, the architecture of Olympic buildings is a borderless affair. Participants resemble mercenaries roaming the world, drafted in to shoot for gold for cities with the cash to buy their services before moving on.[17] Hadid was on the list to design New York's Olympic village, had the city ended up needing one.[18] Santiago Calatrava, whose crustacean-inspired[19] roofs for the Athens games caused so much trouble, is Spanish rather than Greek. His twin 300-metre elliptical[20] arches for the stadium, almost as tall as the Sydney Harbour Bridge, came within a whisker of[21] turning into a gigantic monument to ill-judged ambition. Its domed[22] glass roof, ostensibly[23] there to cool the arena in the punishing summer heat, was designed to provide the defining image for the games. Barcelona also used plenty of imported talent in 1992, including the Japanese architect Arata Isozaki to build its new stadium.

A successful Olympics is measured not just by the gold medal tallies[24], the firework displays that accompany the opening ceremonies or the receipts from the television rights and the sponsorship money, but most conspicuously[25] by what it leaves behind. With its soaring roof rising out of the Yoyogi park, Kenzo Tange's Olympic pool for the Tokyo Games[26] is still a landmark 40 years after it was built. It served to mark Japan's coming of age as a modern state after post-war reconstruction[27]. And Frei Otto's stadium in Munich[28]—despite the horror of the assassination[29] of the Israeli athletes at 1972 Olympics— is a magical structure. Its elegant tent-like roofs are so popular that

9. eye-catching /aɪˈkætʃɪŋ/ a. 引人注目的;耀眼的
10. at the touch of a button 毫不费力地
11. ski jump 滑雪跳台
12. sinuous /ˈsɪnjuəs/ a. 蜿蜒的;错综复杂的
13. undulating /ˈʌndjuleɪtɪŋ/ a. 波浪形的;起伏的
14. snake /sneɪk/ v. 迂回地取道,曲折地前进
15. manta ray 章鱼
16. by all accounts 据大家所说
17. 参与竞争的建筑师如同雇佣军一般游走在世界各地,应征为有钱购买他们服务的城市设计最好的作品,然后他们再继续奔走。
mercenary /ˈmɜːsənəri/ n. 雇佣兵
18. 哈迪德曾入选设计纽约的奥运村,倘若纽约当时能赢得奥运会主办权的话。
to end up 结果是
19. crustacean-inspired 从甲壳类动物身上得到启发。
crustacean /krʌˈsteɪʃən/ n. 甲壳类
20. elliptical /ɪˈlɪptɪkəl/ a. 椭圆的
21. to come within a whisker of (doing) sth. 差一点做了某事;某事差一点发生
22. domed /dəʊmd/ a. 有穹顶的;半球形的
23. ostensibly /ɒˈstensɪbli/ ad. 外表的,表面上的
24. gold medal tally 金牌榜
tally /ˈtæli/ n. 得分,标记牌
25. conspicuously /kənˈspɪkjuəsli/ ad. 突出地
26. the Tokyo Games 东京奥运会,(1964年在日本东京举行)
27. post-war reconstruction 战后重建
28. Munich /ˈmjuːnɪk/ n. 慕尼黑(德国城市,1972年奥运会举办地)
29. assassination /əˌsæsɪˈneɪʃən/ n. 暗杀,行刺

there was an outcry[30] when there was a move to demolish it.

But in the case of Montreal[31], and now sadly Athens too, the Olympic legacy is mainly seen in the form of debt. For Barcelona and Sydney, staging the Olympics was a rite of passage[32] that pushed each city to see itself as moving into the first division. For London, it is the legacy issues that are really what the Olympics are all about. They are certainly what has driven Ken Livingstone[33], a man with no previous discernible[34] interest in sport, to back the Games. Learning from Barcelona's experiences, he is planning to use the Games for the catalytic[35] effect that they will have on London's bleak[36] eastern fringes[37]. The Olympics will be focused on Newham[38] to help kickstart[39] London's eastward growth, in the attempt to find somewhere to put the extra 800,000 Londoners that Livingstone predicts will need to be housed in the next two decades.

In terms of sheer[40] spectacle[41], it's Beijing in 2008 rather than Barcelona in 1992 that London will have to beat. It will be a hard act to follow. The whole of Beijing is a construction site at the moment, much of it triggered[42] by the Olympics. In just four years, China will have designed, built and opened an airport larger than Heathrow[43]—rather less time than the lawyers spent arguing about Heathrow's own Terminal Five. More than 35,000 people are working three shifts night and day on the project. And the airport is just one of a dozen huge projects Beijing is building at furious speed[44] to transform the city in time for 2008. The Olympic park will have a 100,000-seat stadium, designed in the form of a giant bird's nest, by Herzog[45] and de Meuron[46], who were responsible for Tate Modern[47]. You can already see the stadium rising out of the ground: its circular shape has already emerged from the Beijing dust, giving it the look of a ruined colosseum[48].

Even China has been known to suffer occasional bouts of vertigo[49] in the course of its breakneck transformation[50] into an economic superpower. There was a pause last year while the leadership did its sums to see if it could afford everything it had planned for the Games. It decided that it couldn't and axed[51] the retractable[52] roof on the stadium, saving some money.

Architecture isn't an Olympic sport just yet, but it certainly has a lot to do with a successful Olympic bid. The architects newspaper, *Building Design*, goes so far as to claim that London beat Paris hands down, architecturally. Certainly London did infinitely more than

30. outcry /ˈaʊtkraɪ/ n. 大声疾呼
31. Montreal /ˌmɒntrɪˈɔːl/ n. 蒙特利尔（加拿大城市，1976年奥运会举办地）
32. rite of passage 通过仪式
33. Ken Livingstone 肯·利文斯通，（现任伦敦市长）
34. discernible /dɪˈsɜːnəbl/ a. 可辨别的；明显的
35. catalytic /ˌkætəˈlɪtɪk/ a. 催化的；起催化作用的
36. bleak /bliːk/ a. 萧条的
37. fringe /frɪndʒ/ n. 边缘
38. Newham /ˈnjuːəm/ n. 纽汉（英国英格兰东南部城市）
39. kickstart /ˈkɪkstɑːt/ n. 启动；发动
40. sheer /ʃɪə/ a. 真正的
41. spectacle /ˈspektəkəl/ n. 光景；情况
42. trigger /ˈtrɪɡə/ v. 引发，引起
43. Heathrow /ˈhiːθrəʊ/ n. （英国伦敦的）希思罗机场
44. at furious speed 以飞快的速度
45. Herzog 瑞士建筑师，北京奥运会主体育馆设计师之一
46. de Meuron 瑞士建筑师，北京奥运会主体育馆设计师之一
47. Tate Modern 全世界最著名的当代艺术博物馆之一，位于伦敦。因原在泰晤士河对面有一座名为Tate的博物馆，故这座新的博物馆被命名为Tate Modern。
48. colosseum /ˌkɒləˈsɪəm/ n. 罗马圆形大剧场
49. vertigo /ˈvɜːtɪɡəʊ/ n. 眩晕；晕头转向
50. breakneck transformation 极快的转变
51. axe /æks/ v. 大幅度消减（经费等）
52. retractable /rɪˈtræktəbəl/ a. 可缩进的；可缩回的

Manchester, which proposed putting the athletes into a village of mobile homes[53] for its Olympic bid.

But there is still room to do a lot more. The stadium design that the bid team showed the Olympic commission was an exercise in smoke and mirrors[54]. Longstanding stadium experts HOK worked with Allies and Morrison, and Foreign Office Architects, to produce a series of artists' impressions that are a long way from being a real building. That team is perfectly capable of producing a stadium that London can be proud of—a counterpart to Norman Foster's epic scaled triumphal arch[55] at Wembley. But there is still time to go back to the drawing board, and stage an architectural competition for the stadium.

The Olympic village could also be a chance for some genuinely new thinking about housing. The chance to do the Olympics again in London is unlikely to come in any of our lifetimes, so we should be ready do everything we can to make them really memorable.

53. mobile homes 移动房屋

54. smoke and mirrors 用来转移人们注意力的东西

55. epic scaled triumphal arch 规模巨大的凯旋门

Comprehension Questions

1. What competition did Zaha Hadid win five months ago?
2. What were the bid organisation looking for in the design of the Olympic swimming pool?
3. According to the article, apart from gold medal tallies, how is a successful Olympics measured?
4. What has driven the Mayor of London, Ken Livingstone, to back the games?
5. What would you say is the most important legacy that an Olympic Games should leave behind for the host country?

Background Reading

Greece Lays Out Post-Olympic Plan

Greece has finally announced how it plans to use dozens of sports venues built or restored for last summer's Olympic Games in Athens.

In its long-awaited announcement, the government confirmed on Wednesday that none of the venues would be sold off.

Instead the plan is to lease (出租) the majority of them to the private sector.

Having spent a record sum of at least $12bn (£6.4bn) on the games, Athens is under intense pressure to prove it was all worthwhile for Greek taxpayers (纳税人).

Most of the venues have remained closed since the games ended six months ago. According to documents given to the BBC, the basic construction work for more than 30 venues cost more than $3bn.

And now just maintaining them is costing the state more than $100m a year.

Yet until now the authorities have not had any serious plan for how such a large number of venues can be put to good use, as the Olympics themselves become little more than a distant memory.

It has now been announced that many will remain as sports facilities, with some extra commercial activity allowed, such as restaurants, cafes and theme parks (主题公园).

But others will be fully converted (转变，转换) into conference centres, museums and academies. The government insists plenty of Greek and foreign investors are interested in bidding for the leases, although officials admit some venues will be difficult to shift onto the private sector.

One Greek property developer told the BBC the government strategy was all wrong, and that it must sell some venues and use the money to subsidise (资助，付津贴) those likely to remain in state hands.

Otherwise, taxpayers will continue forking out (支付，交出) just to prevent once pristine (质朴的) Olympic venues from crumbling (崩溃), he says.

Lesson 11

> 位于伦敦的温布利体育场(Wembley Stadium)建于 1924 年,曾经在 1948 年举办奥运会,1966 年举办世界杯足球赛,由于年久失修被拆除重建。然而好事多磨,该体育场的竣工日期一拖再拖,眼看着要及时竣工举办 2006 年英国足总杯(FA Cup)的承诺化为泡影。文章轻松诙谐,读来令人忍俊不禁。

Wembley Stadium, can we fix it?
Er, well, sorry, no we can't, actually ...

Giles Smith
February 25, 2006
The Times

Paddy Power[1] closed its book[2] on Wembley after apparently noticing stadium construction workers placing big bets, writes Giles Smith

OUR thoughts this week go out to Martin Tidd, the UK director of Multiplex[3], who announced as long ago as May 2005 that he would be watching this year's FA Cup Final in the new Wembley Stadium. "I can absolutely guarantee that the FA Cup will be held at Wembley," Tidd said, "and I can absolutely confirm that my seat is there and I'll be sat there."

But that was before the FA anticipated, reasonably enough, that the cranes[4] might get in the way[5] and decided to stage the final in Cardiff[6]. A quiet afternoon lies ahead for Tidd on May 13, then—apart from the noise of drilling and banging, of course. On the plus side[7], though, I'm sure some of the builders will have the radio on, enabling him to keep up with the game. And parking should be a doddle[8].

In the months after Tidd made his bold declaration, optimism on the likelihood of a Wembley FA Cup Final in 2006 quickly evaporated. By this week, it was the construction industry's worst-kept secret. Paddy Power, the bookmaker[9], closed its book on the matter after only two days, having allegedly noticed (and this was surely the spot of the year) "men in hard hats placing big bets in the

---

1. Paddy Power 爱尔兰著名的博彩公司
2. book /bʊk/ n. 簿册;账目(这里指接受投注)
3. Multiplex 一家澳大利亚公司,承建温布利体育场的改建工程。
4. crane /kreɪn/ n. 起重机
5. to get in the way 阻碍;妨碍
6. Cardiff /'kɑːdɪf/ n. 卡的夫(英国威尔士主要海港城市)
7. on the plus side 从乐观的角度看
8. doddle /'dɒdl/ n. 轻而易举的事;不费吹灰之力的事
9. bookmaker /'bʊkˌmeɪkə/ n. 赌注登记经纪人

Wembley area". Superb stuff. Some of the people Multiplex were backing to get the job done were, apparently, backing themselves not to.

I'm looking forward to the episode of *Bob the Builder*[10] in which Bob, Scoop and Dizzy pop into Ladbrokes[11] to have a fiver[12] on themselves at 9–4[13] not to complete in time the underpass designed to spare[14] the local hedgehog[15] family. In the aim of disabusing[16] our children, once and for all[17], about what the world of contract building is really like, this episode must surely come.

Even so, the FA's announcement prompted[18] in the papers much tutting[19] and derision[20] and open accusations of bungling[21], most of it written by people whose experience of big construction projects is limited to putting up a shelf—or probably, to be more specific, to failing to get round to[22] it.

What is really surprising, surely, about the Wembley delays is that anybody is surprised. As anyone who has extended their kitchen knows only too well, all builders' estimates are, to an important extent, an act of creative writing and each of them is to be taken with a pinch of salt[23]—or, more specifically, with half a hundredweight[24] of salt, due for delivery on Thursday but delayed until Tuesday afternoon on account of a problem with the suppliers.

True, few of us see our kitchens, like Wembley, go over budget by more than £400 million, even if we end up going with a more expensive tile than we had intended to and have to get someone back to sort out the plumbing. But it's just a question of proportion and a builder's estimate doesn't suddenly start having a firm foundation in reality simply because he happens to be constructing a football ground. Where do you suppose the expression "a ballpark figure[25]" came from, if not from man's timeless experience of building sports stadiums? (I'm not sure this is true, actually. But it sounds good.)

Accordingly, I don't go with the people beating up[26] the FA for its part in "the Wembley fiasco[27]". On the contrary, the FA seems to me to have played a fairly tidy game. The staggering[28] £180 million lost by Multiplex on the Wembley project includes £14 million of penalties paid to the FA for delay. So this was a fixed-price contract with all liability for lateness and overspend passed on directly to the contractor. Go out now and propose a similar arrangement to the builder working on your kitchen extension and then stand back as the tea ejaculates[29], in a gale of[30] derisive[31] laughter, from his nose.

10. *Bob the Builder* 英国著名动画片《建筑师巴布》
11. Ladbrokes 英国最大的博彩公司，世界最大的零售赌注登记经纪公司。
12. fiver /ˈfaɪvə/ n. 面值五英镑的钞票
13. 9–4 四赔九的赔率，即下注的人如果赌赢，他下注的每4镑钱可以获得9镑的回报。
14. spare /speə/ v. 赦免；放一条生路
15. hedgehog /ˈhedʒhɒɡ/ n. 刺猬
16. disabuse /ˌdɪsəˈbjuːz/ v. 解惑；释疑
17. once and for all (= once and forever) 永远地，一劳永逸地
18. prompt /prɒmpt/ v. 激起；唤起
19. tut /tʌt/ v. 发出嘘声
20. derision /dɪˈrɪʒən/ n. 嘲笑
21. open accusations of bungling 把事情办糟而引来的公开责难 bungle /ˈbʌŋɡəl/ v. 把……办糟
22. to get round to sth. 做长久以来想做的事
23. to take sth. with a pinch of salt 对某事不太相信
24. hundredweight /ˈhʌndrədweɪt/ n. 英担，半公担(重量单位)
25. ballpark figure 经猜测认为是准确的数字
ballpark /ˈbɔːlpɑːk/ a. 差不多的；大约的
26. to beat up 打败；痛打
27. fiasco /fiˈæskəʊ/ n. 惨败
28. staggering /ˈstæɡərɪŋ/ a. 令人惊愕的
29. ejaculate /ɪˈdʒækjʊleɪt/ v. 射出，喷出
30. in a gale of 一阵
31. derisive /dɪˈraɪsɪv/ a. 嘲笑的，值得嘲笑的

Also, as great planning disasters of our time go, the new Wembley barely measures on the meter.[32] For truly award-winning budget-busting[33] and positively Olympian errors of time management, you've got to hand it to[34] the British Library—ten years late and costing £511 million, as opposed to the £32 million predicted. Alternatively, consider the Scottish Assembly building in Edinburgh, which, when it finally opened, three years off schedule, had cost £431 million, a more than tenfold increase on the original budget. By these standards, the new Wembley is cheap and on time.

In any case, I may not have been alone in finding the notion of "rushing to complete" a 90,000-seat sports stadium a faintly worrying one. Call me overcautious, but if I am going to be joining that quantity of people in a newly built football ground, I would like to be able to reassure myself that a suitable period has passed for "snagging"[35]. I would prefer to think that the seats, staircases and toilet facilities, among other things, have been bolted on[36] properly, rather than by some hyped-up screwdriver jockey[37] who managed to get 9-1 with William Hill[38] that he could finish the job by Wednesday.

Remember the Millennium Bridge in London? It swayed[39] because its designers had not adequately wondered about what would happen if people ever walked on it. Well, that's "rushing to complete" in a nutshell.[40]

I want to be as confident as possible that the stand I'm sitting in isn't going to start bouncing in sympathy the first time more than 50 people jump up and down inside it in unison[41]. And if that means a delayed opening and a few more million down the pan for Multiplex, then I'm with the FA in saying, "So be it.[42]"

So it's going to be another five weeks or so late. So the FA Cup Final can't be in London this year. So Jon Bon Jovi[43] is going to have to wait a bit before he gets to say "Hello, Wembley" in a pair of unfeasibly[44] tight trousers. So what? The new national stadium, by all accounts, will be a thing of wonder, an arena to match any in the world and a sports and rock'n'roll mecca[45] in which no unforeseen expense has been spared.

In the meantime, the Cup finalists and their followers must set up camp once again in the glorious Millennium Stadium, Cardiff, which cannot really be labelled a hardship[46]. Incidentally, it is normally the Millennium Stadium that gets a mention when noses are being thumbed[47] in the direction of the new Wembley. But let's not forget

32. 和当今的一些计划出了问题而引发的大漏子相比，新近的温布利体育场一事根本算不了什么。
33. budget-busting /ˈbʌdʒɪtˈbʌstɪŋ/ a. 经费超支
    bust /bʌst/ v. 使爆裂；使爆发
34. to have (got) to hand it to sb. 某人是最成功的（这里是反语，讽刺大英图书馆的修建工作居然比计划晚了十年才完工）
35. snag /snæg/ v. 清除困难
36. to bolt on 用螺栓固定住
37. hyped-up screwdriver jockey 兴奋的螺丝工
    hyped-up /haɪpˈtʌp/ a. 兴奋的
38. William Hill 全球最大的电话投注服务公司
39. sway /sweɪ/ v. 摇摆；摇动
40. 那就是"匆忙完工"的一个简单的例子。
    in a nutshell 简单地，简约地
41. in unison 一起地；一致地
42. So be it. 好吧。
43. Jon Bon Jovi 英国摇滚歌手
44. unfeasibly /ʌnˈfiːzɪblɪ/ ad. 不实际的；行不通的
45. mecca /ˈmekə/ n. 麦加；胜地；众人渴望去的地方
46. hardship /ˈhɑːdʃɪp/ n. 困苦；艰难
47. to thumb one's nose at sb./sth. 对……不屑一顾

that Laing, the contractor on the Millennium Stadium, lost £26 million on the project because of an overspend. That's building, folks.

Comprehension Questions

1. What did Martin Tidd, the UK director of Multiplex, announce as long ago as May 2005 and will his promise come to fruition?
2. What prompted the bookmaker Paddy Power to close its book on whether the new Wembley Stadium will be built to schedule?
3. What other big projects does the journalist mention as being completed late and over budget?
4. Where will the 2006 FA Cup final take place?
5. The FA Cup is the oldest football competition in the world and its reputation as the sport's premier domestic cup competition extends around the world. Can you think of any other domestic sports competitions that invokes such interest from an international audience?

Background Reading

Wembley Stadium

Wembley Stadium is a football stadium located in Wembley, London, England, which is currently being rebuilt, although it is well behind schedule.

Wembley Stadium is one of the world's most famous football stadiums, being the English national football ground since 1923.

Originally known as the Empire Stadium, it was built for the British Empire Exhibition of 1924, at a cost of £750,000, on the former site of Watkins' Tower. Sir John Simpson and Maxwell Ayrton were the architects and Sir Owen Williams was the Head Engineer. The stadium's distinctive Twin Towers became its trademark. Also well known were the thirty nine steps needed to be climbed to reach the Royal box and collect a trophy (and winners'/losers' medals).

The Stadium's first turf (草皮) was cut by King George V and it was first opened to the public on 28 April 1923.

The first event held at the stadium was the FA Cup final on 28 April 1923 between Bolton Wanderers (博尔顿队) and West Ham United (西汉姆联队). This is known as the White Horse Final. With an official maximum capacity of 127,000, the attendance was quoted as 126,947 but up to 200,000 people are thought to have squeezed in through the 104 turnstiles (十字转门) by the time the gates were closed, leaving tens of thousands still queuing outside.

It was thought that the match would not be played, that is until mounted police (骑警), including Police Constable George Scorey and his white horse, Billie, slowly pushed the masses back to the sides of the field of play for the FA Cup Final to start just 45 minutes late.

Because of that, when the stadium reopens the new footbridge (人行桥) will be known as the White Horse Bridge in honour of Billie.

The FA Cup final was played there every year in May (outside wartime) until 2000. It was also the venue for Finals of the FA Amateur Cup, League Cup, Associate Members' Cup and the Football League promotion play-offs.

As the home of the English national football team, in 1966 it was the leading venue of the World Cup. It hosted the final game, where the tournament hosts, England, emerged victorious from a 4-2 extra-time win over West Germany. Thirty years later, it was the principal venue of Euro 96, hosting all of England's matches, as well as the tournament's final, where reunited Germany won the cup by the first Golden Goal of football history.

Lesson 12

> 尼基·曼塞尔(Nigel Mansell)是英国著名的F1车手,他在一个赛季的16站比赛中独取9站冠军的记录一直是他傲视车坛的资本。历史上只有迈克尔·舒马赫于1995年和2001年刷新过这一记录。尽管战绩辉煌,老曼塞尔却深知赛车的危险性,因此他千方百计想要用高尔夫球分散两个儿子对赛车的兴趣,可是两个儿子偏偏要子从父业。无奈之下,Mansell也只好听之任之,必要的时候还伸出援手,助儿子们一臂之力。现在他的两个儿子在赛车场上也有了不俗的表现。真是俗话说得好,虎父无犬子。

Mansell Boys Happy to Drive Hard Bargain[1]

By Sarah Edworthy
February 17, 2006
Telegraph

"It was at the end of the straight and I thought I'll show him I can go around the outside of him..."

This is typical Nigel Mansell. Even at 52, he is combative, tenacious and still engaging his public by conjuring up overtaking manoeuvres of breathtaking audacity.[2]

But what's going on? Is he reminiscing[3] about wheel-to-wheel battles with Ayrton Senna[4]? Or is he re-enacting[5] that stunning round-the-outside pass[6] on Gerhard Berger[7], which he famously executed in 1990 on the Peraltada turn in Mexico, a 180-degree banked sweeper[8] taken in fifth gear?

No, he was talking about Mansell versus Greg Mansell, aged 18, and a recent incident at the end of the pit straight[9], going into Copse[10].

"He closed the door! Pushed me straight off the track. At 130 mph. I was shocked."

Even worse, Greg came back with a riposte[11]. "I think they call that squeezing, dad."

The Mansell family were calling it "a magical situation" yesterday, as brothers Leo, 21, and Greg unveiled the Unipart-sponsored[12] Formula BMW Championship cars in which they will make their racing debuts[13] on April 9, at Brands Hatch[14].

---

1. hard bargain 条件苛刻,没有让步的协议
2. 即使已经52岁了,可他还是好斗、固执,他惊险的超车手法仍然吸引着车迷的注意力。
   tenacious /tɪ'neɪʃəs/ a. 固执的、不屈不挠的
   to conjure up 用魔术变出;如用魔术般地做成
3. reminisce /ˌremɪ'nɪs/ v. 追忆往事
4. Ayrton Senna 艾尔顿·塞纳(著名一级方程式赛车手,效力于迈凯轮车队,在1994年圣马力诺大奖赛中因赛车事故丧生)
5. enact /ɪ'nækt/ v. 扮演(角色)
6. round-the-outside pass 跑道外圈超车
7. Gerhard Berger 格哈德·伯杰(前F1车手兼前BMW车厂竞技部门总监)
8. a 180-degree banked sweeper 一个180度的倾斜弯道
9. pit straight 赛车离开维修加油站后进入的直线跑道
10. Copse /kɒps/ n. 一段赛道的名称
11. riposte /rɪ'pəʊst/ n. 机敏的回答
12. Unipart-sponsored 由(英国)汽车零配件公司Unipart赞助的
13. debut /'debjuː/ n. 初次登场
14. Brands Hatch (英国)布兰兹·哈奇赛道

Pursued by their father around the Unipart HQ staff car park-smoking wheels here, a 'donut' spin[15] there—they prompted memories of Mansell mania[16].

The company first sponsored Nigel in Formula Three[17] in 1979; now they are launching the second generation. Will either be able to emerge from that bulldog-shaped shadow and forge a name of their own?[18]

Quite possibly, if looks and language are anything to go by[19]. Greg is the son who physically resembles his father, Leo offers familiar sound-bites[20]. "The Mansell name we've always had. People ask what's it like to have a famous dad. Well, what's it like not to have a famous dad?" he replied, when asked if his father's record was an intimidating one to follow.

Mansell senior conceded that for many years this scenario was his, and his wife Rosanne's, private nightmare. Nigel endured serious injuries in his career, including a broken neck. They had kept the boys away from speed, and steered them towards golf. Leo won a golf scholarship in the United States, both brothers play off a single-figure handicap[21].

"Golf is a wonderful way to make a living. You can pick your own calendar, play on the American Tour if you're good enough, play on the European Tour. If you don't feel well one week and need to pull out from[22] a tournament, you can do that, and then put another tournament in later," Mansell said.

"But motor racing is fixed. Your schedule is set in stone[23] from one year to another. It's very rigorous[24]."

Then the racing bug struck.[25] "It came like a whirlwind[26]. It hit us overnight. Greg was the one who initiated[27] it while his brother was in America. He said, 'Look, I would love to do karting[28]. That's all I want to do. Just give me the opportunity.'

"Our mistake was we gave him the opportunity and he loved it. Then Leo compounded[29] it. He came back and said, 'I'll have a bit of that.' So it took off[30] and here we are."

As brothers, Leo and Greg join an elite band with the Brabhams, Scheckters and Schumachers. As sons of a world champion, they are alongside Damon Hill, Jacques Villeneuve, Paul Stewart, Nico Rosberg, Nelson Angelo Piquet and so on. In the man the British public still refer to as "Our Nige", the boys have not only a fantastic measuring stick in a 1992 Formula One world champion[31] and 1993

15. 'donut' spin （使赛车）原地打转
    donut /ˈdəʊˌnʌt/ n. 甜面包圈
16. Mansell mania 对曼塞尔的狂热
17. Formula Three 三级方程式赛车（是高成本和高技术等级的单座位四轮赛车比赛，赛事等级仅次于一级方程式赛车。许多一级方程式车手在进入一级方程式赛车前都曾参加三级方程式赛车，所以三级方程式赛车一向被视为培育一级方程式车手的摇篮。）
18. 两兄弟能否从父亲成功的光环中崛起，塑造自己的声誉呢？
    forge /fɔːdʒ/ v. 打造
    bulldog-shaped 斗牛犬形状的，用以比喻好斗的老曼塞尔。
19. to go by 按照……判断；凭……判断
20. sound-bite /ˈsaʊndˌbaɪt/ n. 接受采访时言简意赅的回答
21. single-figure handicap 单差点（高尔夫球术语）
22. to pull out from 退出
23. to be set in stone 固定不变
24. rigorous /ˈrɪɡərəs/ a. 严格的
25. 后来，对赛车的狂热突袭而来。
26. whirlwind /ˈwɜːlwɪnd/ n. 旋风
27. initiate /ɪˈnɪʃieɪt/ v. 开始；发起
28. karting /ˈkɑːtɪŋ/ n. 卡丁车
29. compound /ˈkɒmpaʊnd/ v. 增加；使更复杂
30. to take off 起飞（这里指情况飞速地发展）
31. Formula One world champion 一级方程式世锦赛

IndyCar champion[32], but also an astute[33] judge.

He is a loving dad, but not an indulgent[34] one. "I had my personal tick-boxes,[35]" he maintains. "Are they committed? Are they passionate? Are they willing to learn? Do they have the turn[36] of speed? Do they want to live, breathe, eat and sleep motor sport? Unfortunately, we managed to tick every single box.[37] And then some."

"We've come out and supported them, albeit[38] a bit late, and what they've been able to do in this last eight months has been meteoric[39]. They both have the passion, and they both have the talent, which I never dared think they had."

Mansell's reputation was founded on an unquenchable[40] appetite to defy the odds[41]. At every level, obstacles were overcome. His grand prix record of 31 wins, 32 pole positions and 30 fastest laps came with attendant dramas.[42] "Expect fireworks" is the motif under which he is billed in the Grand Masters Series.[43] Does it concern him that his sons have not had to find that appetite for success, that it has come easily for them?

"I'd like to say 'yes', but, 'no', because we've been so tough with them. I said, 'I'm not putting a penny in. I'll take you karting, but if you want to go motor racing find yourself sponsors'. They said OK. I did make a few phone calls, and as things transpired[44], I received a few calls: 'Do your sons want to go motor racing? We'd like to sponsor them.' I was thinking, 'What? What? It wasn't as easy as this in my day.'

"Quite publicly Rosanne and I were dead[45] against it. They've had to persuade us, and they've done that on their own merit[46]. There's not much they won't do to achieve their goals. The thing I love is they're realistic. They're prepared to take one day, one month, a year at a time. As Leo said, 'It's like a dream' but they're keeping their feet on the ground[47], which I think is very creditable for ones of 18 and 21 years of age."

The brothers are close. What happens to family unity when, as team-mates competing for the same prize, one overshadows[48] the other? "What we'll do is play fairly and give them equal opportunity. What will be, will be," said the paterfamilias[49].

"We're a close-knit family and they care about and love one another. There might be some disappointment but I think they will genuinely be happy for the other to have any success at any time. If one has success, it will motivate the other." Ah yes, the next stage, sibling rivalry[50].

---

32. IndyCar champion 印第赛车锦标赛
33. astute /əˈstjuːt/ a. 机敏的;精明的
34. indulgent /ɪnˈdʌldʒənt/ a. 纵容的;溺爱的
35. 我有自己的一系列准则。tick-box 备选项前供人画√号的方格子 tick /tɪk/ n. 勾号
36. turn /tɜːn/ n. 才能
37. 不幸的是,我们在每个方格里都画了勾。(意思是他的儿子们符合了所有的这些准则。)
38. albeit /ɔːlˈbiːt/ conj. 虽然,即使
39. meteoric /ˌmiːtɪˈɒrɪk/ a. 使人眼花缭乱的
40. unquenchable /ʌnˈkwentʃəbəl/ a. 难抑制的;不能消灭的
41. ... defy the odds 藐视一切
42. 他的大奖赛记录为 31 个分站赛冠军,32 次杆位总数和 30 次最快圈数,而这一切都那么地富有戏剧性。
    attendant /əˈtendənt/ a. 相伴的;伴随的
43. "期待精彩"是大师系列赛中海报上宣传他的口号。
    motif /məʊˈtiːf/ n. 主题,主旨
    bill /bɪl/ v. 用海报宣传
    Grand Masters Series 大师系列赛
44. transpire /trænˈspaɪə/ v. (事情)发生
45. dead /ded/ ad. [口语] 完全地;绝对的
46. on one's (own) merit 凭借自身能力
47. to keep one's feet on the ground 脚踏实地
48. overshadow /ˌəʊvəˈʃædəʊ/ v. 遮蔽;使……失色
49. paterfamilias /ˌpeɪtəfəˈmiːlɪæs/ n. (男性)家长,户主
50. sibling rivalry 兄弟间的对抗

Comprehension Questions

1. What relation is Greg and Leo Mansell to Nigel?
2. What scenario has, for many years, been Nigel and his wife Rosanne's worst nightmare?
3. What alternative sporting career did Nigel and Rosanne try to steer their sons towards?
4. Which other sons of World Champions are mentioned in this article?
5. What would your reaction be if a close family member really wanted to pursue a career in a sport that is perceived to be dangerous?

Background Reading

Nigel Mansell

Born on 8 August, 1953, near Birmingham, Nigel Ernest Mansell first drove a car in a nearby field at the age of seven. Hugely determined, immensely aggressive and spectacularly daring, he was one of the most exciting drivers ever. With his win or bust (失败) approach—31 wins and 32 crashes—he became the most successful British driver and ranks third in the world in fastest laps, fourth in wins and fifth in poles (跑道内圈).

After considerable success in kart racing, he become the 1977 British Formula Ford champion, despite suffering a broken neck in a testing accident. Doctors told him he had come perilously close to quadriplegia, that he would be confined for six months and would never drive again. Mansell sneaked out of hospital (telling the nurses he was going to the toilet) and raced on. Three weeks before the accident he had resigned his job as an aerospace engineer, having previously sold most of his personal belongings to finance his foray into Formula Ford. Next, Mansell and his loyal wife Rosanne sold their house to finance a move into Formula Three. In 1979 a collision with another car resulted in a huge cartwheeling crash he was lucky to survive. Again he was hospitalised, this time with broken vertebrae in his back. Shortly after this, stuffed with painkillers and hiding the extent of his injury, Mansell performed well enough in a tryout with Lotus to become a test driver for the Formula One team. In his Formula One debut, at the 1980 Austrian Grand Prix, a fuel leak in the cockpit left him with painful first and second degree burns on his buttocks.

He stayed with Lotus for two more years, then moved to Williams in 1985. In his Formula One career he also drove for Ferrari before returning to Williams, winning the World Championship in 1992. In the following year he went to America to race in the IndyCar series where he immediately dominated, even on the unfamiliar high speed ovals, and became the 1993 IndyCar champion.

Part V Sporting Mosaic

In 1994, after 187 hard races in 15 tumultuous seasons, 41-year-old Nigel Mansell left Formula One racing for good. He retired a rich man, operating several business enterprises, including a Ferrari dealership and a golf and country club (he played golf to a professional standard) and lived the good life with his wife Rosanne and their three children.

"I had my fair share of heartaches and disappointments," he said of his career, "but I also got a lot of satisfaction. I only ever drove as hard as I knew how."

Lesson 13

> 为了 2012 的奥运会，英国政府需要大量征地，这其中就包括将位于伦敦东区的 Hackney Marshes 球场区中的很大一部分改造为供 2012 年奥运会期间使用的停车场。这块场地历史悠久，许多明星都在此踢过球，这块球场记载了他们的成长经历。这些人包括明星贝克汉姆，前英格兰队队长博比·摩尔等等。尽管奥组委的官员说征占用地将会在奥运会后归还，重新建成足球场，但是本文作者对此却并不持乐观态度。

Death by Tarmac[1]: the Sorry Fate of Hackney Marshes[2] in Pursuit of Our Olympic Dream

By Martin Samuel
September 28, 2005
The Times

The London Development Agency[3] (LDA) would like me to get its side of the story before writing about the dissonance[4] at the site of the London Olympics. It feels this column is not independent. Yet if I wanted to hear public servants dissemble[5] and divert[6], I could turn on the Labour Party[7] conference and learn from the professionals. "Olympic values are new Labour values," Tessa Jowell, Secretary of State for Culture, Media and Sport, said, and for a second we almost believed her.

Then the LDA let slip[8] that some of the most important and fertile[9] football pitches in the country are to be turned into an Olympic car park and the bubble burst once more.

A large chunk[10] of Hackney Marshes, where the heroes of English football from Bobby Moore[11] to David Beckham learnt to play, will be lost for at least 12 months as part of Britain's Olympic dream. Like Fish Island, where 170 businesses, some of them dating back to the 19th century, are to be sacrificed[12], the East Marsh will become a glorified[13] corporate[14] car park for 2012.

Once there were more than 120 pitches on the land, at least one third of which have disappeared. London can ill-afford[15] this latest death by tarmac and those occupying the Marshes are skeptical[16] that

1. tarmac /'tɑːmæk/ n. 铺沥青
2. Hackney Marshes 英国著名的足球公园，内有 87 个标准足球场。
3. London Development Agency 伦敦经济发展署
4. dissonance /'dɪsənəns/ n. 不协调，不一致
5. dissemble /dɪ'sembəl/ v. 假装不知道；掩盖真相
6. divert /daɪ'vɜːt/ v. 转移注意力
7. Labour Party 英国工党
8. to let slip 无意中说出
9. fertile /'fɜːtaɪl/ a. 肥沃的
10. chunk /tʃʌŋk/ n. 大块
11. Bobby Moore 博比·摩尔（英国著名足球运动员，曾任英格兰队队长）
12. sacrifice /'sækrɪfaɪs/ v. 牺牲
13. glorified /'glɔːrɪfaɪd/ a. 美其名曰的
14. corporate /'kɔːpərɪt/ a. 集体的；共同的
15. ill-afford /ɪl ə'fɔːd/ v. 很难支付；很难承受
16. sceptical /'skeptɪkəl/ a. 怀疑的

football will return post-Games. The LDA says it has a commitment to relocate the pitches for a year while construction takes place and then restore the land for recreational use, yet many think that faced with the potential for an exclusive, profitable real estate development by the river, the government may take the money and run. What gives them that idea? Well, of the 34,000 playing fields that have been lost since 1992–1945 per cent of the recreational space in Britain — how many do you notice being turned back into football pitches? There is another reason to distrust the government body that will make our Olympic dream a reality: it saves time. A continuing dispute[17] demonstrates how the LDA goes to work and it does not make pleasant reading.

ON MARCH 6, when this column first reported the plight[18] of the Marshgate Lane business community, trying to earn a living where Ken Livingstone thinks a sandpit[19] should be, I wrote: "Conspiracy[20] theorists say the LDA is marking time until after the International Olympic Committee select a host city on July 6. If London wins, the hoopla[21] will begin and the LDA will be able compulsorily[22] to purchase land without respect for local sensibilities[23]."

Fast forward to now, via one incredible night in Singapore, and compulsory purchase orders[24] (CPOs) are so much part of the future in East London that Downing Street feels comfortable mentioning them in official correspondence[25].

When the businesses occupying the Olympic site requested a meeting with the Prime Minister to voice[26] their concerns, a reply, written on behalf of Tony Blair by Geoffrey Norris, a senior policy adviser, dated September 16, 2005, stated: "It is not appropriate for the Government to comment on specific cases or issues whilst negotiations continue between the LDA and the businesses within the proposed Olympic zone, particularly given the Government's responsibility for considering any compulsory purchase order that may be made by the LDA."

This seems unfair until one factors in that, because the LDA is a government body, in reality the Government gets the final say on its own CPO: at which point it all makes perfect sense. This is independence, Government-style. If there is a playing field left in Hackney in the build-up to 2012, it will not be a level one.[27]

The 300 businesses that are to be the collateral[28] damage of our Olympic obsession[29] have long given up hope of an independent hearing[30]. On a Government-funded website they are depicted as

17. dispute /dɪ'spjuːt/ n. 争论

18. plight /plaɪt/ n. 困境

19. sandpit /'sænd,pɪt/ n. 沙坑
20. conspiracy /kən'spɪrəsɪ/ n. 阴谋

21. hoopla /'huːplɑː/ n. 喧闹
22. compulsorily /kəm'pʌlsərɪlɪ/ ad. 强制地
23. sensibility /,sensɪ'bɪlɪtɪ/ n. 感受
24. compulsory purchase orders 强制收买令
25. correspondence /,kɒrɪ'spɒndəns/ n. 函件
26. voice /vɔɪs/ v. 表达

27. 如果在准备2012年奥运会的过程中，能有一块球场留在Hackney的话，那么它也不会是平整的。(这是一句双关语，"a level playing field"的意思是"公平交易、竞争等"。这句的言下之意是，和政府打交道就没有公平可言。)
28. collateral /kə'lætərəl/ a. 附带损害的
29. obsession /əb'seʃən/ n. 困扰
30. hearing /'hɪərɪŋ/ n. 听证会

greedy and manipulative[31], unrealistic in their demands and malicious[32] in their use of the media. The truth is, they are ordinary people who smoke salmon, crush concrete, process waste and until recently had no public profile beyond names on a van.[33] They do not have the resources or platform of career politicians[34] or a platoon of[35] flunkeys[36] to keep the public on-message about[37] what will be done in the name of the London Games. Only when something occurs that is so obviously wrong—such as a football pitch turned parking space—does anyone ask whether our running track will not be laid over the broken bones of the little guys.

The advertisement for the role of chief executive for London 2012 specifies ruthlessness as a desirable trait. Yet in my dictionary a ruthless person is one showing no mercy, one who is thorough and forceful, regardless of effect. Do we need ruthless civil servants? When Jowell stood up to yoke[38] party politics to the Olympic spirit, she did not mention that Michael Corleone[39] better personified[40] the ideals of our Games than Pierre de Coubertin[41]. After all, what is a CPO other than a government offer you cannot refuse?

"We're not developers[42]," Liz Crawshaw, of the LDA, said, rather confusingly, when I asked her about post-Olympic gains, but this is not strictly true. The LDA is not a private developer, so the individuals involved in buying, selling and redistributing land in the capital do not become exorbitantly[43] wealthy, but, down the line, somebody will. For those on the right side of the CPO coin toss, London 2012 is a fantastic property deal with an Olympic Games attached. The Arup report[44], on which the Olympic bid is based, states that there are two areas of revenue[45] from the Games: staging/sponsorship and land disposals. It cites land disposal as the biggest net revenue earner.

The land on which the Olympic site is to be built is valued at about £1 million an acre as industrial property; with proper infrastructure and decontamination[46] it will rise to between £5 million and £6 million as residential land, according to Strettons[47] chartered surveyors.[48] A Government memorandum places revenue from land sales with the LDA. Even with the stadium legacy and if 50 per cent is turned over to low-income housing[49], there is good money to be made from seizing low and selling high; more so when those who are displaced foot the bill for eviction.[50]

A feature of the CPO plan is that a business cannot use public funds to better itself; the Government will pay only for like-for-like

31. manipulative /məˈnɪpjʊlətɪv/ a. 操纵的
32. malicious /məˈlɪʃəs/ a. 怀有恶意的
33. 事实上，他们只是很普通的人。他们或是烤鲑鱼的人，粉碎混凝土的人，或只是处理垃圾的人。直到最近，除了货车上的名字，他们不曾有过任何公众形象。
34. career politician 职业政治家
35. a platoon of 许多
36. flunkey /ˈflʌŋkɪ/ n. 奉承者
37. to keep sb. on-message about 使某人得知关于……的事

38. yoke /jəʊk/ v. 连接
39. Michael Corleone 影片《教父》中的黑手党头目
40. personify /pəˈsɒnɪfaɪ/ v. 体现
41. Pierre de Coubertin 皮埃尔·顾拜旦(现代奥林匹克之父)
42. developer /dɪˈveləpə/ n. 开发商

43. exorbitantly /ɪɡˈzɔːbɪtəntlɪ/ ad. 过度地
44. the Arup report: Arup 调查报告(是 Arup 公司受政府委托所撰写的一份报告。报告中评估了伦敦申办 2012 年奥运会的得失等等情况。)
45. revenue /ˈrevɪnjuː/ n. 财政收入
46. decontamination /ˌdiːkɒnˌtæmɪˈneɪʃən/ n. 净化；消除污染
47. Strettons 一家英国测量师公司
48. chartered surveyors 测量师
49. low-income housing 供低收入者居住的房屋
50. ...; more so when those who are displaced foot the bill for eviction. 当那些被迫搬迁的人支付搬迁费用时就更是如此了。
displace /dɪsˈpleɪs/ v. 被迫离开
foot /fʊt/ v. 支付
eviction /ɪˈvɪkʃən/ n. 被迫离开；被迫搬迁

repositioning[51]. By its nature, this cannot exist. No two properties are the same in size, feature and location. Any change will be for worse, or better; as the LDA is not legally allowed to fund a better move, it can offer only a worse one.

IF LAND is valued at £2 million and a decent new site costs £3 million, the business is £1 million out of pocket for the pleasure of being compulsorily purchased. The alternative is to accept an inferior site and compensation, a solution now being offered by the LDA. Yet compensation of how much and for how long? If inferior placement costs a business 25 per cent of its turnover[52], does the public take up that burden for one year or 20?

Some businesses operating from Marshgate Lane have been offered premises[53] farther from Central London on the wrong side of the Olympic building site, or in Beckton[54], next to a sewage works[55]. The offices of the LDA are in St Katharines Dock[56], a luxurious marina[57] near Tower Bridge[58] and arguably the finest slice of real estate in East London. No mugs, are they?[59]

The crux[60] of the matter is the affordability gap: the difference between the purchase price of the land and the cost of relocation for affected businesses. This is what the LDA has to say on its website: "Recent false claims made to the media include ... an inherent[61] affordability gap between existing sites and alternative sites. This is untrue. There is suitable land of comparable value nearby."

Yet in a letter dated February 9, 2005, Mary Reilly, the LDA chairman, tells a London Assembly member: "You make an important point about the affordability gap facing some businesses. We recognise this as a key issue." A letter from Gareth Blacker, director of development at the LDA, dated May 16, 2005, admits: "Businesses have also raised concerns should they wish to relocate to sites with greater value than their existing sites. The LDA recognises this is an issue." No more, apparently. Not since the bandwagon[62] got rolling.

"THE LDA process has been independently investigated and commended by the Royal Institute of Chartered Surveyors[63]," the LDA announces proudly. Yet what is this? On the Olympic bid website, under a list of supportive professional institutions, it prominently names the very independent RICS.

"We'll go to independent arbitration[64]," the LDA told me yesterday. Of course they will. With independents like that, who needs friends?

51. like-for-like repositioning 同类置换

52. turnover /ˈtɜːnˌəʊvə/ n. 营业额

53. premise /ˈpremɪs/ n. 房屋
54. Beckton 百客顿（城市名，位于伦敦东部）
55. sewage works 污水处理厂
56. St Katharines Dock 圣凯瑟琳码头
57. marina /məˈriːnə/ n. 码头
58. Tower Bridge 伦敦塔桥
59. 难道他们不是在抢劫吗？
60. crux /krʌks/ n. 关键
61. inherent /ɪnˈhɪərənt/ a. 固有的

62. bandwagon /ˈbændˌwæɡən/ n. 乐队花车
63. Royal Institute of Chartered Surveyors 英国皇家特许测量师协会

64. arbitration /ˌɑːbɪˈtreɪʃən/ n. 仲裁

Comprehension Questions

1. What does the LDA intend to do with Hackney Marshes and why?
2. What is the LDA committed to do with the football pitches located on Hackney Marshes during and after 2012?
3. According to the Arup report, what are the two areas of revenue for the Games and what is cited as the biggest net revenue earner?
4. "The Government will pay only for like-for-like repositioning" when carrying out compulsory purchase orders (CPOs). Why, by nature, can this not exist?
5. In your opinion, should the Government be allowed to profit from CPOs carried out for the purposes of hosting the Olympic Games?

Background Reading

Hackney Marshes

Hackney Marshes is an area of grassland on the bank of the River Lee in the London Borough of Hackney. It was originally marshland (沼泽地), but was reclaimed (翻造) using rubble (瓦砾) left over from air raids (空袭) during the Second World War.

Today the main use of Hackney Marshes is for Sunday league football, with 88 full-size football pitches marked out. On a typical Sunday, over 100 matches are played by amateur teams in several local leagues.

Hackney Marshes holds the world record for the highest number (88) of full-sized football pitches in one place.

Teams and individuals meet daily on the Marshes to indulge in (沉溺于) all kinds of sports from hockey to kite flying. Whether it's a serious game or just a knockabout (闹剧) there is always something going on and always someone showing off (炫耀) some serious skills. Run by the local council, Hackney Marshes is one of the most well known outdoor sporting facilities in London, if not the UK.

Over one hundred football matches are played here every Sunday during the season by both male and female teams. There are so many Sunday League teams, and indeed leagues to fit them all in to, that

anyone interested in getting muddy has the pick of the bunch (出类拔萃的人或事物) we're not even going to start naming all the teams that play here but five-a-side (五人制足球), under 21s, women and kids all play here as well as your twenty something lads letting off steam after a hard week at work. So whoever you are and whatever your level of skill get down there and ask around—you're bound to (一定要) get a game with someone!

  Hockey and rugby are also popular, and there are facilities for both. Again, many teams play matches and practice here for both sports, seriously and just for fun, so whatever level you are at the best thing you can do is go along and check out the competition. And if it all looks a bit rough and tumble (混乱), you may want to turn your attentions to the games of cricket going on in other parts of the ground.

  Finally, to some it may not be a sport, but to others, kite flying is as important as a match between England and France. Every year also sees the East London Kite Festival take over Hackney Marshes with demos (表演；演示), stalls (货摊) and competitions.

Lesson 14

> 什么样的运动员可以被称之为天才运动员?
>
> 天才运动员和伟大的运动员是不同的两个概念。史蒂夫·雷德格雷夫(Steve Redgrave)赢得了五枚奥运划艇赛金牌,书写了一段体育传奇,可就是他也没有被冠上天才运动员的头衔。
>
> 那么,天才运动员到底是什么样的呢?

Illusionists[1] Who Shade[2] the Rest with Nothing to Declare Except Their Genius

By Simon Barnes
September 30, 2005
The Times

It has been a week for contemplating the nature of genius. Like all others, I suppose, but Martin Scorsese's[3] documentary[4] on Bob Dylan[5], *No Direction Home*, broadcast on Monday and Tuesday, certainly brought the matter to mind. Dylan is the only genius that pop music has produced. He stands as far above the rest as Shakespeare towers above[6] everyone else that wrote a play.

It is not necessary to like Dylan, or for that matter, Shakespeare, to come to such a conclusion. You can, more or less objectively, state that these two created one masterpiece after another, in an immense[7] variety of forms and moods, on a scale that no one else has even thought of challenging.

And so, naturally enough, the mind strays from the love who speaks like silence and William Zanzinger and the night that plays tricks when you're trying to be so quiet, and turns to genius in other walks of life.[8] Like sport. Most people would agree that genius of a kind exists in sport — and most of us would be careful about the way we use the term.

After England had been scattered by Glenn McGrath[9] in the Lord's Test[10], I referred to him as "a genius". My friend and colleague Michael Henderson disagreed with the term, which got me thinking. I

---

1. illusionist /ɪˈluːʒənɪst/ n. 魔术师(这里指天才运动员)
2. shade /ʃeɪd/ v. 遮蔽
3. Martin Scorsese 马丁·斯科塞斯(美国著名导演,2003年因《纽约黑帮》获第60届金球奖最佳导演奖)
4. documentary /ˌdɒkjʊˈmentərɪ/ n. 记录片;文献片
5. Bob Dylan 鲍勃·迪伦(美国民谣歌手,在乡村音乐和摇滚乐中都有着很深的造诣)
6. to tower above 大大高出;远远胜过
7. immense /ɪˈmens/ a. 极大的;巨大的
8. 于是,很自然地,我的思绪从迪伦著名的歌词"无声的爱"跳跃到他的歌曲人物威廉·赞金泽以及歌词"那个吓得你不敢做声的黑夜",最后转到了其他领域内的天才。stray /streɪ/ v. 走离;偏离 walk of life 行业;阶层
9. Glenn McGrath 格兰·麦克格雷斯(澳大利亚著名板球运动员,任投手)
10. Lord's Test 在英国劳兹举行的板球比赛

had used it deliberately, and a touch[11] perversely, to make it quite clear that the collapse was as much a matter of McGrath's brilliance as England's errors.

But Hendo[12] disallowed genius for McGrath: but I don't think he—or anyone—would disallow the term for Shane Warne[13]. If you accept the concept of sporting genius at all, Warne is self-evidently a genius. But why, then, is McGrath, a man who has taken 500 Test wickets, not a genius? All at once, there is a hint that sporting genius is not quite the same thing as sporting excellence.

When Wisden carried out its search for the five cricketers of the 20th century, not a single fast bowler made the list: the best was Dennis Lillee[14] in sixth place. True, Wisden was not explicitly looking for genius, but the reluctance to give the supreme accolade[15] to a fast bowler—and fast bowlers win more Test matches than any other kind of cricketer—is significant.

Let us turn to football. Genius: well, we have to start with Pelé and Diego Maradona[16], and then get into beery[17] arguments about Zinedine Zidane[18] and Johan Cruyff[19] and George Best. What we won't do is talk about centre halves. John Terry[20], Terry Butcher[21], Tony Adams[22], forget it. A centre half is indispensable[23]: a great centre half is the team's rallying point of sanity[24] and safety and security. A team without a centre half is not a team. But no one looks at Sol Campbell[25] and says: "The man's a genius."

In England's World Cup-winning rugby union side, you might call Jason Robinson[26] a genius, for his thrilling, defence-scattering running[27]. You might even use the term for Jonny Wilkinson[28]. But England won the World Cup because of the driving force of Martin Johnson[29], and no one has suggested that Jonno[30] is a genius. You can complete the ultimate achievement in your sport and still be free of genius.

Everyone uses the term genius for Roger Federer. As with Warne, the term is self-evident, not a hint of controversy. The greatest tennis player that lived, in terms of grand-slam victories, is Pete Sampras, with 14, as compared with Federer's six and counting. No one considered Sampras a genius.

For that matter, the greatest achiever in the history of sport has never been called a genius. Sir Steve Redgrave[31] is everybody's idea of sporting greatness and if five Olympic gold medals do not make you a genius, it is crystal clear that genius is not the same thing as sporting

---

11. touch /tʌtʃ/ n. 一点；少量
12. Hendo 上文提到的 Michael Henderson 的昵称
13. Shane Warne 谢恩·沃恩（现澳大利亚板球运动员，任投手。他投出的球弧线怪异，很难接到）
14. Dennis Lillee 丹尼斯·利勒（前澳大利亚板球运动员，任投手）
15. accolade /ˈækəleɪd/ n. 赞美
16. Diego Maradona 迭戈·马拉多纳（阿根廷著名足球运动员）
17. beery /ˈbɪəri/ a. 带醉意的
18. Zinedine Zidane 齐内丁·齐达内（法国著名中场足球运动员）
19. Johan Cruyff 约翰·克鲁伊夫（荷兰著名足球运动员）
20. John Terry 约翰·特里（英格兰足球运动员）
21. Terry Butcher 特里·布彻（英国足球史上的最优秀的中后卫之一）
22. Tony Adams 托尼·亚当斯（前阿森纳和英格兰国家队的著名中卫）
23. indispensable /ˌɪndɪˈspensəbəl/ a. 不可或缺的
24. sanity /ˈsænɪti/ n. 神智健全；头脑清楚
25. Sol Campbell 索尔·坎贝尔（英国足球史上最优秀的后卫之一，控制空中球能力非常出色）
26. Jason Robinson 杰森·罗宾逊（橄榄球运动员，场上位置是边锋和后卫）
27. defence-scattering running 破坏对方防守的跑位
28. Jonny Wilkinson 约翰尼·维金森（橄榄球运动员，场上位置是外侧后卫）
29. Martin Johnson 马丁·约翰逊（橄榄球运动员，场上位置是前锋）
30. Jonno 马丁·约翰逊（Martin Johnson）的昵称。
31. Sir Steve Redgrave 史蒂夫·雷德格雷夫爵士（英国奥运划艇明星，是第一个获得五块奥运会耐力项目金牌的运动员）

excellence.

Let us go back to tennis. Sampras's game was based on naked[32] force of will. His chief weapon was usually considered to be his serve. In fact, it was his second serve: not only accurate and safe, but also brutally competitive. That reflected not his skill but his nerve. This is not a prosaic[33] quality. Sampras, like Redgrave, has the world's respect but from both, the word genius is withheld.

Federer's game is different. It is shockingly various. He is as myriad-minded[34] as ever Shakespeare was. He can play shots that no one else can, he can make the ball do things that you would think impossible. There is an aesthetic beauty to his game, as well as a sense of purpose. There is a kind of magic about it that we find deeply pleasing to watch.

In art, we use the term genius for the highest achievers: Homer[35], Dante[36], Shakespeare, Joyce[37]. In sport we frequently use the term for lesser achievers whose skills, for some reason, please us. In snooker[38], the serial winners Steve Davis[39] and Stephen Hendry[40] were admired all right but only Alex Higgins[41], Jimmy White[42] and Ronnie O'Sullivan[43] are called genius.

Sporting genius involves something of an illusion. Warne, Federer and Zidane offer the illusion of complicity[44], the stunning impression that the person who is doing everything possible to stop the genius is in fact co-operating with him. Thus competition assumes the air[45] of a dance, a ritual[46], something that is both spontaneous and immemorial[47]. There is a real beauty in this, for all that beauty is not the aim of the exercise. The beauty is incidental, and perhaps the more pleasing for that.

And all those who acquire the name of genius are able to supply another illusion, that they have some kind of immunity[48] from the laws that govern the rest of us. We think of a genius as a man apart, a man for whom the normal rules do not apply, Vincent van Gogh[49] being, if you like, the type specimen.

A sporting genius seems to have been let off the laws of physics. Gravity does not pull him down. A ball will behave not as Newton said, but according to some grander and more idiosyncratic[50] world view. Warne makes a cricket ball behave with a new and elusive[51] logic; Federer puts tennis ball and opponent on contrary strings; Zidane leaves defenders and goalkeepers lunging[52] at air.

Those who possess these talents often fall in love with them. All

32. naked /ˈneɪkɪd/ a. 明白的；毫无隐藏的
33. prosaic /prəʊˈzeɪ·ɪk/ a. 单调的；无趣的
34. myriad-minded /ˈmɪrɪəd'maɪndɪd/ a. 充满各种想法的
   myriad /ˈmɪrɪəd/ a. 无数的
35. Homer /ˈhəʊmə/ n. 荷马（希腊诗人，为古希腊两部著名史诗《伊利亚特》和《奥德赛》的作者）
36. Dante /ˈdænti/ n. 但丁（意大利文艺复兴的先驱，其代表作为《神曲》）
37. Joyce /dʒɔɪs/ n. 乔伊斯（爱尔兰作家，其代表作为意识流小说《尤里西斯》）
38. snooker /ˈsnuːkə/ n. 斯诺克（台球的一种）
39. Steve Davis 史蒂夫·戴维斯（斯诺克台球界的传奇人物，80年代曾在斯诺克世锦赛上六度夺冠）
40. Stephen Hendry 史蒂芬·亨得利（斯诺克台球界的传奇人物，90年代曾在斯诺克世锦赛上七次加冕）
41. Alex Higgins 亚历克斯·希金斯（英国著名斯诺克选手，在斯诺克台球界有"飓风"之称）
42. Jimmy White 吉米·怀特（英国著名斯诺克选手，斯诺克职业赛中最年轻的冠军）
43. Ronnie O'Sullivan 罗尼·奥沙利文（1993年获英国锦标赛冠军，目前最年轻的排位赛冠军得主）
44. complicity /kəmˈplɪsɪti/ n. 复杂性
45. air /eə/ n. 特征；特质
46. ritual /ˈrɪtʃuəl/ n. 仪式；程序
47. immemorial /ˌɪmɪˈmɔːrɪəl/ a. 不朽的；流芳百世的
48. immunity /ɪˈmjuːnɪti/ n. 免疫；免除
49. Vincent van Gogh 文森特·凡高（荷兰著名印象派画家）
50. idiosyncratic /ˌɪdɪəsɪŋˈkrætɪk/ a. 特质的；异质的；特殊的
51. elusive /ɪˈluːsɪv/ a. 难捉摸的
52. lunge /lʌndʒ/ v. 突然向前冲；扑等

athletes go out to win. Sampras set out to win by means of will, Federer by means of genius. All methods of winning have their drawbacks and a sporting genius can fall in love with his own gifts, and find himself seeking to create art and beauty above mere victory.

But to do so, even in the debased sporting use of the term, is to betray both sport and genius. If genius in sport is not used entirely for the purpose of seeking victory, it is an empty thing, a mere decoration: to be a Henri Leconte[53] or a Rodney Marsh[54]. If we accept that sport can bring out a kind of genius, we must also accept that in sport — even though on occasions they coincide gloriously — genius and greatness are not the same thing.

53. Henri Leconte 亨利·李康特（法国网球明星）
54. Rodney Marsh 朗尼·马殊（英国著名足球运动员）

Comprehension Questions

1. Why did the journalist, Simon Barnes, refer to Glenn McGrath as a genius?
2. In football, who does the journalist refer to as genius and who, despite their importance to the team, are not considered as genius?
3. According to the article, in terms of grand-slam victories, who is the greatest tennis player that has ever lived and is he considered to be a genius?
4. Who does the journalist refer to as not using genius for the purpose of seeking victory?
5. The article refers to Roger Federer as a genius because of the style in which he wins games and not simply because he wins a lot of games (like Pete Sampras does). Can you think of other sports players or teams who would be considered to be "genius" under the same logic?

Background Reading

Roger Federer

Born on August 8th 1981 in Basel, Switzerland, Federer began his tennis career at the age of 8, working his way up to make it to No. 1 in the world in the junior championships by 1998. That same year he turned pro, and by 2001 was ranked No. 1 in his home country.

As fate would have it, a groin (腹股沟) injury slowed his progress that year and into next. However, the tennis champ made a triumphant return in 2003 when he won against Mark Philippoussis at Wimbledon, his first Grand Slam title.

Since then, Federer has enjoyed astounding (惊人的) success as the No. 1 seeded player in the world, with more than $6 million in prize winnings, while becoming the first player since Swedish champ Mats Wilander to win three Grand Slam titles in a single season. Most recently, he came back from two sets down to take the Nasdaq-100 Open title with a thrilling 2–6, 6–7, 7–6, 6–3, 6–1 victory over Rafael Nadal.

In yet another stunning upset, Nadal later defeated Federer on the clay (粘土) courts of Roland Garros.

Firmly on grass at Wimbledon, however, Federer took another Grand Slam honor when he beat Andy Roddick for the 2005 men's title, and in another much-publicized match with Andre Agassi defeated the 35-year-old veteran player in an epic 6–3, 2–6, 7–6, 6–1 battle at the 2005 U.S. Open.

In 2006, Federer faced yet another showdown (摊牌，此处指一场鏖战) at the 2006 Australian Open against unseeded (非种子的) Marcos Baghdatis in the men's final winning 5–7, 7–5, 6–0, 6–2 for his seventh Grand Slam title.

Most recently, the Swiss champ fell once again to 20-year-old Rafael Nadal, at the 2006 French Open, but battled back against the Spaniard to win his 4th straight title at Wimbledon in July.

Lesson 15

> 2004年5月轻量级拳手喀什提洛(Jose Luis Castillo)和科雷勒斯(Diego Corrales)之间进行了一场堪称历史上最精彩的较量之一,最后科雷勒斯获胜。可是喀什提洛的支持者认为科雷勒斯在体力不支,行将溃败的关头故意将护齿掉在地上以获取喘息之机。科雷勒斯一方却坚称这纯属意外。
>
> 俩人约定2005年10月再战,重争高低。第二次较量会不会和第一次一样精彩?人们拭目以待。

Seconds Needn't Be Sloppy[1]

By Graham Houston
October 2005
Boxing Monthly[2]

The original brutal[3] war has been dubbed[4] one of the greatest fights ever. Now Jose Luis Castillo[5] and Diego Corrales[6] are set to do it all again. How can they smile at such a prospect? Because they love it. And Chico has already booked his hospital room for after the fight. Graham Houston previews.

Just about everyone agrees that the lightweight title fight between Diego "Chico" Corrales and Jose Luis Castillo last May was one of the greatest in history. So, can the rematch at the Thomas & Mack Center in Las Vegas on 8 October be anywhere near as good? We can but hope. Boxing history shows us that rematches are not always as good as the original, but it can happen. Carmen Basilio[7] and Tony De Marco[8] waged two violent conflicts for the welterweight title in the space of five months in 1955, both won in the 12th round by Basilio, and the second match might have been even more dramatic than the first. The second fight between Rocky Graziano[9] and Tony Zale[10] equalled the first for raw drama as they exchanged sixth-round change-of-fortune[11] KOs (although in a third meeting Zale won with a conclusive third-round blowout).

And I feel there is every chance Corrales and Castillo will serve up[12] another epic.

---

1. sloppy /ˈslɒpɪ/ *a.* 草率的(这里指不精彩的)
2. *Boxing Monthly*《拳击月刊》,英国著名拳击杂志,与美国《拳击台》齐名,是世界最具影响力的拳击刊物之一。
3. brutal /ˈbruːtl/ *a.* 残忍的
4. dub /dʌb/ *v.* 把……称作……
5. Jose Luis Castillo 琼斯·洛伊斯·喀什提洛(墨西哥轻量级拳击手)
6. Diego Corrales 迪尔古·科雷勒斯(美国轻量级拳击手)
7. Carmen Basilio 卡门·巴斯里奥(美国拳击手)
8. Tony De Marco 托尼·德·马可(美国拳击手)
9. Rocky Graziano 洛基·葛瑞加诺(美国拳击手)
10. Tony Zale 托尼·齐尔(美国拳击手)
11. change-of-fortune 改变命运的
12. to serve up 上菜(这里指上演一场精彩比赛供大家欣赏)

For one thing, we have the fighters' styles. Both like to press forward and take command, although Corrales deviated from his normal method with a classy[13] boxing exhibition when he gained his revenge over Joel Casamayor[14].

When the initial fight with Castillo was made, I thought that Corrales might try to keep it on the outside and use his height and reach[15]. As it turned out, trainer Joe Goossen's plan was for Corrales to stay on top of the durable Mexican and keep the fight at a fast pace, the reasoning being that Castillo builds up momentum and comes on strong late in a fight when allowed to be the one going forward.

Corrales's tactics[16] worked, but only just, because Chico looked on the very brink of[17] being stopped when he went down twice in the 10th, the much-debated "dropped mouthpiece[18]" incident giving him valuable seconds not only to gather himself but to rally and blast Castillo with a fight-ending series of power punches in that very same round.

Castillo and his promoter[19], Bob Arum, have made a lot of noise about the way referee Tony Weeks allowed Corrales to buy time by losing his gum shield[20] twice in what turned out to be the final round, although a point was deducted[21] on the second occasion, when Chico took out the protector[22] and dropped it while on the canvas[23].

Arum's position[24] is that Corrales should have been instructed to carry on boxing after the eight count without the gum shield being replaced, that a knockdown does not constitute what is called a "lull[25] in the action". But administrators I have spoken to support the referee, the feeling being that Weeks followed the rules.

Corrales's promoter, Gary Shaw, said in the immediate aftermath[26] that nothing should be allowed to detract[27] from his fighter's astonishing comeback[28], and many would agree, because the way Corrales turned what looked like certain defeat into sensational victory in mere moments was one of the most remarkable turnarounds[29] in ring history[30].

Still, the controversy hasn't hurt in making the rematch one of the most compelling fights of recent times. Because, let's face it, without the mouthpiece incident it is hard to imagine Corrales having won the fight, although as my ringside neighbour[31] in Las Vegas, broadcaster Max Kellerman, remarked, Corrales is perhaps at his most dangerous when hurt.[32]

Corrales will tell you that he had never given up on the belief that

13. classy /'klɑːsɪ/ *a.* 上等的
14. Joel Casamayor 卡萨马约尔（古巴拳击手）
15. reach /riːtʃ/ *n.* 臂长
16. tactic /'tæktɪk/ *n.* 战术；策略
17. on the brink of 濒于
18. mouthpiece /'maʊθpiːs/ *n.* （拳击手的）牙套
19. promoter /prə'məʊtə/ *n.* 赞助者
20. gum shield 护齿
21. deduct /dɪ'dʌkt/ *v.* 扣除
22. protector /prə'tektə/ *n.* 保护设备（这里指牙套）
23. canvas /'kænvəs/ *n.* 拳击场
24. position /pə'zɪʃən/ *n.* 立场
25. lull /lʌl/ *n.* 哄骗
26. aftermath /'ɑːftəmæθ/ *n.* 后果
27. detract /dɪ'trækt/ *v.* 减损
28. comeback /'kʌmbæk/ *n.* 复原
29. turnaround /'tɜːnəraʊnd/ *n.* 突然好转
30. ring history 拳击历史
31. ... my ringside neighbour 在拳击台边坐在我旁边的人 ringside /'rɪŋsaɪd/ *n.* （圆形表演场、拳击台等的）台边
32. ... Corrales is perhaps at his most dangerous when hurt. 科雷勒斯在受伤的情况下可能最危险。

he would nail[33] Castillo. He also says that although he removed the mouthpiece he never meant to drop it on the second occasion. I have supported his position in the matter but there is a more cynical[34] view, certainly held in the Mexican camp, that Chico knew very well what he was doing and used the so-called "mouthpiece rule" to his advantage. The Castillo faction[35] will not be swayed[36] from its belief that Corrales won by cheating.

All this means that there is a sense of unfinished business here, that the air needs to be cleared. The two simply had to meet again— "One More Time!" as the fight is billed[37].

In the last fight, Corrales looked the worse for wear[38] going into the unforgettable 10th round, both eyes bruised and swollen, left eye closing from below. But he had landed the bigger punches, wobbling Castillo at least twice, and two judges had Chico in front.

You would have to believe that each man took a lot out of the other physically[39] but they have had time to rest and restore themselves.

These are amazingly resilient[40] warriors. Both have been through the mill[41]. Corrales has had tough fights with the likes of Justin Juuko[42] and Roberto Garcia[43], both of whom he stopped. He was down five times in his loss to Floyd Mayweather Jr.[44] and three times in the two fights with Joel Casamayor when he boxed in the 130lbs (9st 4lbs) division. But at 135lbs (9st 9lbs) his chin seems to have improved: the 5ft 11ins Corrales says he was weakening himself getting down to 130lbs and is stronger as a lightweight and thus better able to absorb a punch[45].

Certainly Corrales stood up to[46] the best punches Acelino Freitas[47] could hit him with before outlasting and overpowering[48] the Brazilian in 10 rounds, and Freitas is considered a seriously hard hitter.

As for Castillo, he's 31, he's been a professional boxer for 15 years (they tend to turn pro young in Mexico) and he's had 60 fights, including four stoppage losses earlier in his career although I believe these were due to getting cut.[49] There were also his years as the chief sparring partner[50] for Julio Cesar Chavez[51], which must have put some wear and tear[52] on him.

Castillo fought two tough fights totalling 24 rounds with Stevie Johnston[53] when the Denver southpaw[54] was still a top-level fighter and there were another 24 rounds with Floyd Mayweather Jr. He defeated Juan Lazcano[55] and Joel Casamayor in 12-rounders.

33. nail /neɪl/ v. 打中
34. cynical /'sɪnɪkəl/ a. 讽刺的
35. faction /'fækʃən/ n. 派别（这里指支持者）
36. sway /sweɪ/ v. 动摇；清除
37. bill /bɪl/ v. 用海报宣传
38. the worse for wear 筋疲力尽；状态很差
39. took a lot out of the other physically 消耗了对方很多体力
40. resilient /rɪ'zɪliənt/ a. 有恢复能力的
41. to be through the mill 经历磨难
42. Justin Juuko 贾斯汀（乌干达拳击手）
43. Roberto Garcia 罗伯托·加西亚（美国拳击手）
44. Floyd Mayweather Jr. 梅威瑟（美国拳击手）
45. to absorb a punch 经受重击
46. to stand up to 勇敢地抵抗
47. Acelino Freitas 阿切里诺·弗瑞塔斯（巴西拳击手）
48. overpower /ˌəʊvə'paʊə/ v. 压倒；制服
49. ..., including four stoppage losses... 这包括他拳击生涯早期四次被击败出局，可是在我看来这四次都是因为他受伤出血而被裁判终止比赛。stoppage loss 击败出局，相当于 knockout。
50. sparring partner 拳击练习的对手
51. Julio Cesar Chavez 朱利奥·克萨尔·查维斯（墨西哥拳击手）
52. wear and tear 消耗
53. Stevie Johnston 史帝夫·约翰逊（美国拳击手）
54. southpaw /'saʊθpɔː/ n. 左撇子拳击手
55. Juan Lazcano 胡安·拉兹卡诺（美国拳击手）

So while Corrales has been in wars, Castillo has some mileage on him, too.[56]

Looking back at the first fight, there were times when Corrales was being backed up[57] by Castillo and once or twice he seemed to be weakening, but he always came back hard. In the 10th, though, it looked as if Corrales had finally come unhinged[58] when a left hook dropped him for the first time in the round: It seems he had been expecting the hook to the body that Castillo had been employing with success all night and the one on top surprised him.[59]

Castillo's mindset is probably uncomplicated: keep the pressure on Corrales, keep hitting him in the body, wear him down[60] and this time don't get caught unawares when the end is near.

And Corrales? He will probably be thinking that the tactics that worked last time can work this time. Just be more aware of Castillo's hook.

I can't see Corrales going to a "boxing" style, although he does have the option and it could work for him. But he was able to stay back and box against Casamayor with such success because the Cuban[61] is a counter puncher[62] and, with his height and reach, Corrales could pick up points in a set-piece[63] boxing match. But Castillo will be on his chest from the first bell.[64] Against this type of opponent, it makes more sense for Corrales—given his formidable[65] firepower—to make it an inside fight.

Each will have learned a lot about the other; each knows what will be in front of him. A long fight seems likely because last time each took the best shots of the other for round after round. Castillo knows he can knock Corrales down—but Chico knows he can dent[66] the Mexican fighter's Gibraltar-like chin.

I think that each man will be prepared to keep going through another grinding battle of attrition, neither wanting to back away, real never-give-an-inch[67] stuff. But there will be science, too: the shifting of positions up close so as to hit first and hardest in exchanges, the thought that goes into placement of punches, the subtle[68] nudges[69] with shoulders and shifting of feet to get better angles—"beautifully brutal" as Joe Goossen describes it.

Despite the disputed circumstances, the fact is that Castillo got stopped in the last fight and there might be a little doubt in his mind where none existed before. Corrales as ever will be prepared to go through whatever it takes for him to win the fight and I think that if

56. 所以当科雷勒斯历经恶战的时候，喀什提洛也参加了不少比赛。mileage /'maɪlɪdʒ/ n. 里程；英里数（这里指喀什提洛经历的拳赛）

57. to back sb. up 拳击术语，指一方将另一方打逼到拳台边缘，使其没有还击之力。

58. unhinged /ʌn'hɪndʒd/ a. 精神错乱的

59. 看起来科雷勒斯预料到会有这么一记勾拳打在他身上，而喀什提洛整晚也一直成功地运用着勾拳，只是最后的这一记让科雷勒斯防不胜防。
on top 另外的；附加的

60. to wear sb. down 使……疲劳

61. Cuban /'kju:bən/ n. 古巴人

62. counter puncher 打反击的拳击手，即受到对方攻击时才出拳的拳手。

63. set-piece 固定形式

64. 可是喀什提洛会从比赛一开始就逼近科雷勒斯打近身拳。（在这个句子中，his 指科雷勒斯）。

65. formidable /'fɔ:mɪdəbəl/ a. 强大的

66. dent /dent/ v. 使凹陷

67. never-give-an-inch 永不妥协

68. subtle /'sʌtl/ a. 微妙的

69. nudge /nʌdʒ/ n. 用肘轻推

and when the tide takes a decisive turn that the one more likely to give way mentally and physically will be Castillo. Corrales's heavy artillery[70] ultimately made the difference last time and I think it will probably do so again, at some point between the ninth and 12th rounds.

70. artillery /ɑːˈtɪlərɪ/ n. 攻击

Comprehension Questions

1. In the article which pair of fighters are set to have a rematch?
2. Which other famous rematches does the journalist refer to?
3. Which incident does the journalist refer to as "the most remarkable turnarounds in ring history"?
4. Who does the journalist think will win the rematch and how long does he think the fight will last?
5. Can you think of other famous rematches in sporting history that were just as compelling as the original match?

Background Reading

Lightweight

The lightweight division is the 130 pounds (59 kilograms) to 135 pounds (61 kilograms) weight class in the sport of boxing. Notable lightweight boxers included Bummy Davis, Ray "Boom Boom" Mancini, Roberto Duran, Hector Camacho, Julio Cesar Chavez, Benny Leonard, Joe Gans, Henry Armstrong, Tony Canzoneri, Carlos Ortiz, Ike Williams, Alexis Arguello, Floyd Mayweather Jr., and Diego Corrales. While not as popular as the heavier divisions among the mass of boxing fans, many find the often lightning-fast (快如闪电) action of the lightweight divisions more compelling than the relatively slower matches of the heavier fighters.

Roberto Duran is generally considered the best Lightweight of all time.

Other sports have lightweight divisions as well, such as kick boxing (搏击) and mixed martial arts (终极格斗;综合搏击). For men, these divisions typically include those who weigh around 60 kg (132 pounds). Women's divisions also use this weight class, but usually at a much lower weight than the men's divisions.